C000225303

POLICING THE NARROW GROUND

POLICING
THE
NARROW
GROUND

Lessons from the
transformation of policing
in Northern Ireland

edited by John Doyle

Policing the Narrow Ground: Lessons from the transformation of policing in Northern Ireland

First published 2010

by Royal Irish Academy
19 Dawson St
Dublin 2

www.ria.ie

This publication has been funded by the Department of Foreign Affairs in conjunction with the Northern Ireland Office. The ideas, opinions and comments contained herein are entirely the responsibility of the authors and do not necessarily represent or reflect the policies of the Department of Foreign Affairs or the Northern Ireland Office, or of the publisher.

ISBN 978-1-904890-66-9

British Library Cataloguing in Publication Data. A CIP catalogue record for this book is available from the British Library.

Printed in Ireland by Turner Print Group.

10 9 8 7 6 5 4 3 2 1

Contents

ACKNOWLEDGEMENTS

A work such as this inevitably involves securing the co-operation and commitment of a huge number of people, and my appreciation of them goes far beyond what any standard acknowledgement can encompass. First of all, I thank the authors. All of them responded positively and quickly to a request from me that they contribute to this book. All of them were already busy, some with enormous public commitments, yet they provided their contributions and graciously responded to queries, and indeed submitted updates, as the process of transformation in Northern Ireland was continuing through a very crucial debate on devolution as we all wrote.

The nature of a body such as the Independent Commission on Policing is that it leaves few archives behind for future researchers, and so I would like to thank in particular the members of the Commission who contributed to this book; they had to rethink their inputs of ten years earlier to write their chapters, therefore leaving some record of the process to complement their excellent *Report*.

I would also like to thank the Minister for Foreign Affairs Micheál Martin, TD, and the Secretary of State for Northern Ireland Owen Paterson, MP, for agreeing to write forewords for the book, and officials in both the DFA and NIO for all their assistance.

The genesis of this project lies in a conversation with Irish diplomat Eamonn McKee, then head of the Irish Department of Foreign Affairs Conflict Resolution Unit, and at time of writing Ambassador in Seoul. I am grateful for that conversation and for his support as the idea developed into a project and this book. Many politicians, diplomats and community activists agreed to be interviewed for this book. Most of them did not wish to be named, some from a sense of modesty, as they down-played their own contribution or insight, and some because they continue to be involved at a high level and did not wish to point publicly to previous disagreements with those with whom they now seek to work. I thank them all. I would like in particular to offer my thanks to the many officials in the Department of Foreign Affairs, where tradition dictates that they are not individually named. Conversations with officials there led to this project being developed and were invaluable in seeing it through to conclusion. Their role and contribution, on this and on other projects in my experience, always extend well beyond what is purely professionally required. Their knowledge, expertise, insight and analysis were always available to me during the production of this book and were always useful. I hope they will recognise their intellectual contributions, and I thank them all. As ever in these circumstances, they have no responsibility for the text as I have written it.

I would like to thank my university, Dublin City University. It provides a very supportive environment for research and the time and space to take on a project such as this. Academic colleagues and postgraduate students at the School of Law and Government and the Centre for International Studies in DCU have, over many years, also sharpened my own thinking on the Northern Ireland conflict and peace process. I would like to thank my colleague and partner Dr Eileen Connolly for, as ever, her insightful comments on my text. The errors and lack of clarity I add back in afterwards are my own fault.

I would like to acknowledge the publishers, the Royal Irish Academy. The Publications Office staff in the Academy are a delight to work with, and my thanks in particular to the managing editor on this project, Helena King, and her colleagues Maggie Armstrong and Fidelma Slattery, for editorial assistance and for design and typesetting, respectively. Thanks also to Martin Melaugh for allowing us to use his photograph of Maurice Harron's sculpture 'Hands Across the Divide' as part of the cover image. I would also like to acknowledge the staff in the offices of some of the authors for assisting with communications and logistics—in particular Keavy Sharkey, Yvonne Phillips, Lorraine Calvert and Olga Cordi.

Finally, I would like to thank my family: my parents Seamus and Marie for being supportive when they must have preferred that I stuck with my accountancy exams all those years ago; my colleague and partner Eileen and our children, Leah, Eamon, Seán and Orla, for putting up with the distractions caused by this book; and my granddaughters Beth and Anna, who (in Anna's case in some years' time) will like seeing their names in print. Finally, I would like to acknowledge and remember the matriarch of our extended family, Cornelia Doyle, who passed away, in her 95th year, in her beloved West Cork as the book was being planned.

John Doyle
Centre for International Studies, School of Law and Government,
Dublin City University, June 2010

FOREWORD
BY THE MINISTER FOR FOREIGN AFFAIRS

The publication a decade ago of the report of the Independent Commission on Policing for Northern Ireland, known of course as the *Patten Report*, was one of the milestones of the peace process. The Commission produced a blueprint for transforming policing in the North, a blueprint that it called 'A New Beginning'. In the year when David Ford has become the first Minister for Justice in the restored devolved institutions, we can say that the new beginning promised by *Patten* has been realised. This collection of essays by members of the Independent Commission, by those who were involved in implementing the Commission's recommendations and by distinguished academics brings together a series of important reflections on the journey from 1999 to now, reflections which I hope will inform policy-making, not just on this island of Ireland, but perhaps even further afield in the years ahead.

The Commission wrote that it had been encouraged to approach its task with 'imagination, common sense and generosity of spirit'. It did so successfully, using five tests as a matrix for its proposals—testing for effectiveness and efficiency; for fairness and impartiality; for accountability to the law and to the community; for a police more representative of society; and for the protection and vindication of the human rights of all. The Commission's report is a broad, strategic consideration of policing in the round, perhaps best described as a manifesto for transformation from 'force' to 'service'.

The implementation of *Patten*'s 175 recommendations has largely been achieved. This process has resulted in that transformation to service which lies at the heart of the Independent Commission's vision. Policing is being delivered for all the community by the community, with an acceptance of the police service unparalleled in the history of Northern Ireland. This reality facilitated the devolution of policing and justice powers back to locally elected representatives in the Assembly and Executive on 12 April 2010.

In moving the policing agenda forward in the decade ahead, I believe it is essential that what I call the spirit of *Patten*—that commitment to local accountability and transparency, by a police service representative of society as a whole—remains at the heart of our endeavour. The Policing Board, the District Policing Partnerships

(DPPs) and the Office of the Police Ombudsman allow all those with an interest in effective policing—from the grass roots, through political representatives to the very highest ranks of the PSNI—public spaces in which to discuss, agree and take forward objectives, but crucially also forums in which to review problems and failures. To these important institutions, we now add Assembly oversight and scrutiny.

That *Patten* spirit was all about changing the culture that surrounds policing. The accountability institutions are important elements of this: notwithstanding the at times bureaucratic imposition they may pose for individual police officers and local politicians, we should not lose sight of their purpose in bringing about that necessary cultural shift and associated perceptions of policing. These changes need to be further embedded in Northern Ireland society so that all police officers feel fully secure and welcome, living and socialising normally in those communities where they work.

Nonetheless, policing has been brought home to communities. It is more representative than ever before, with accelerated recruitment facilitating the development of a police service that looks ever more like the people it serves. Today, almost 30% of those in frontline policing are Catholic in background, while the number of female officers has doubled to nearly 26%. To complete this transformation, it is essential that men and women from all backgrounds and traditions are free and encouraged to apply to serve in the PSNI and that they have the support of their family, friends and local communities in so doing. The more the police service looks like the wider community, the more it is the community.

Bringing policing into communities, especially those perhaps traditionally perceived as 'hard to reach', has been part of the achievement of the last decade. Rights-based policing gives communities a sense of what they can demand and what they can expect; it also highlights that the resulting responsibilities go beyond police officers alone and that local communities themselves must play their part. Individual police officers, and the PSNI at an organisational level, have used cultural and sporting events to reach out into local communities. I look forward to the day when positive interaction between officers and communities becomes so regular and frequent an occurrence that it will no longer be seen as unusual or remarked upon. Although balances must be found between security considerations, including health and safety of police officers and civilians, and developing connections with a community, increasingly the sight of a police officer in even the most challenging arenas is unremarkable.

This is a transformation of which the people of Northern Ireland can be rightly proud. This is a transformation that needs to be cherished, for community confidence in a police service is a precious thing in any society.

There remains a small group of people who have over the past year attempted to undermine this community confidence. These criminals are without a mandate, without a vision; they act against the express will of the people of the island of Ireland, as expressed in referenda North and South.

While policing is never perfect, the *Patten* reforms—which have been described as 'goldplated'—have ensured that the PSNI operates world-class standards of accountability and transparency. The *Patten* process has delivered a police service that has the confidence of the community, confidence that is reinforced by the robustness with which community representatives can hold the police to account, underpinned by the guarantees provided by the operation of the Police Ombudsman and the Human Rights Act.

It has been particularly encouraging to note that many who were previously directly opposed to engagement with police are now actively involved in promoting the new policing arrangements. I am conscious that often this has not been an easy task for those concerned and, it must be said, neither for many within the policing family. The change from the RUC to the PSNI was difficult for many. I am grateful to all those men and women of the RUC and PSNI who worked so hard to deliver change. They continue to do so in fulfilment of their respective duties and oaths of office, but also, and more fundamentally, in the knowledge that change is a process rather than a destination.

High expressions of principle and ambition can sometimes fall hard against the reality of day-to-day policing work and the gritty step-by-step pursuit of local policing issues. At times, such police work and promotion of the new policing arrangements can be an actively dangerous undertaking. In particular, I recall the murder of Constable Stephen Carroll in March 2009 and the attempted murder of Constable Peadar Heffron last January. Such cases reinforce the value and importance of the excellent and ever deepening co-operation between the PSNI and the Garda Síochána. The co-operation between the two services and the solidarity between their members was well expressed by Garda

Commissioner Fachtna Murphy, when he said recently that 'an attack on one member of one force is an attack on both forces'.

I am also aware of challenges and threats to personal safety that have been received over the years by individuals working at Policing Board and DPP level and elsewhere in Northern Ireland. They and the family members and friends of those who have lost their lives or suffered injuries realise more than most how important their contributions have been. I thank all those concerned for having given of themselves so generously and courageously.

I also recall the tragic accidental deaths of Reserve Constables Declan Greene and Kenny Irvine and Constables Kevin Gorman and James Magee in south Down in November 2008. From the sad passing of these four officers, some small, symbolic but not insignificant, shreds of comfort and consolation can perhaps be drawn. Two were Protestant and two Catholic, and from amongst them one was a Gaelic footballer and soccer player and another was an active Orange Order member, bridging the range of traditions and interests across the community. All were from south Down, based at Kilkeel station in the county, and all had joined the PSNI during the three previous years. As they died in fulfilment of their duties, their legacies will endure and inspire all of us who seek a better future for the people of Northern Ireland and for relations between the peoples of Ireland and Britain.

The articles in this book focus on the work of the Patten Commission, on such themes as building cross-community support for policing, the human rights dimension and management and reform challenges. They include important perspectives on how the Commission's recommendations were implemented, including the important oversight process. The establishment and early functioning of the Police Ombudsman role is also covered, as are perceptions of change from the perspectives of human-rights organisations, and those of Policing Board and DPP members. They capture the valuable insights of those at the heart of the change process, insights that may resonate with those elsewhere who seek to draw on lessons from Northern Ireland as they address issues in an international context. I look forward to sharing these lessons internationally as part of our conflict resolution activities.

I would like to thank Chris Patten and his Independent Commission colleagues, and all those who contributed to the work that resulted in the publication of their report in September 1999. I also thank Dr John Doyle of Dublin City University and the Royal

Irish Academy for their agreement to compile and produce this collection. But most particularly, I would like to thank all those who helped in the process of policing transformation in Northern Ireland over the past decade.

As this is an initiative co-funded by the Irish and British governments, thanks are also due to my counterpart the Secretary of State for Northern Ireland and his officials. I trust that readers will enjoy and value the insights and analyses that this book contains.

Mr Micheál Martin, TD, Minister for Foreign Affairs
June 2010

FOREWORD BY THE SECRETARY OF STATE

In the decade since the publication of the *Patten Report* in September 1999, policing in Northern Ireland has undergone dramatic changes. Indeed, until earlier this year the UK government still had overall responsibility for policing in Northern Ireland. The transfer of policing and justice powers to a locally elected minister on 12 April 2010 put in place the final piece of the new policing structures envisaged in both the *Patten Report* and the Belfast Agreement of 1998. So this work is timely.

Policing was always going to be one of the most sensitive and difficult issues in the negotiations leading up to the 1998 Agreement. So it proved. The Agreement set out the ambition of providing a new beginning for policing in Northern Ireland, with a police service capable of attracting and sustaining support from the community as a whole. Responsibility for setting out the detail of how that might be achieved was handed to a Commission headed by Chris Patten.

It is important to recognise the highly charged political atmosphere in which the Commission operated. Since the foundation of Northern Ireland, nationalists and republicans had never accepted the legitimacy of the police. By contrast, most unionists had immense loyalty towards the Royal Ulster Constabulary, which suffered terribly at the hands of terrorists over a twenty year period. I believe that we continue to owe the RUC an immense debt of gratitude for the contribution it made to defending democracy and the rule of law. Over 300 officers were murdered and many thousands injured or maimed. Their courage and sacrifice was rightly recognised through the award to the RUC by Her Majesty The Queen of the George Cross, the highest civilian decoration in the United Kingdom.

Against this background the Commission set about carrying out its remit: 'to inquire into policing in Northern Ireland and, on the basis of its findings, bring forward proposals for future policing structures and arrangements, including means of encouraging widespread community support for those arrangements'. I would like to put on record my appreciation for the work of Chris Patten and his colleagues in going about their task in such difficult and sensitive circumstances.

They did not, of course, operate in a vacuum. Much work had already been done, following the first ceasefires in 1994, into how policing could be transformed in a more peaceful environment. I would like to pay tribute to Sir Ronnie Flanagan, much of whose 'Fundamental Review' in the mid-1990s is reflected in the final *Patten Report*. Ronnie made an immense contribution to the transition from RUC to PSNI, as have his successors Sir Hugh Orde and Matt Baggot.

Patten eventually made 175 recommendations. Of those, a small number—such as those relating to the name and symbols of the police service—were at the time highly controversial. They dominated the debate both in Northern Ireland and when the legislation to implement *Patten* was going through Parliament in Westminster in 2000. It is a matter of record that in opposition my party shared some of those concerns, though we were at all times supportive of the overall blueprint for policing that *Patten* set out.

Ten years on, Northern Ireland has probably the most accountable police service of any part of Western Europe. The Policing Board, made up of a majority of political representatives from all the main Northern Ireland parties, has been a great success story. At a local level District Policing Partnerships have worked well, sometimes in the face of intense provocation. We now have a locally elected Minister for Justice. At the same time, the operational independence of the Chief Constable—a fundamental doctrine of policing throughout the United Kingdom—has been preserved.

Crucially, for the first time in Northern Ireland's history, we have a police service that is broadly representative of the community it serves. Again, while the means of achieving this has been difficult for some, it has worked to the extent that the special recruitment provisions will finally cease next year. Policing is now a career choice for young men and women across Northern Ireland, irrespective of their community background. Moreover, public confidence in policing is today around the 80% mark—an exceptional achievement and one that would be hardly replicated in many other parts of the world.

We are all aware that significant challenges lie ahead. The nature of some of those was graphically brought home to us in 2009 by the shocking murder of Constable Stephen Carroll. While society has undoubtedly moved on in Northern Ireland, we still face a significant threat from criminal groups intent on dragging us back into the past. The PSNI will continue to bear down on these groups, who have absolutely no democratic mandate. They will do so with the full support of the British and Irish governments and with the full, and ever improving, co-operation of the Garda Síochána.

Policing is crucial to the future stability and therefore prosperity of Northern Ireland. The transfer of policing functions on 12 April was a hugely significant step, putting policing back in local hands for the first time since 1972. It is incumbent on everybody to work together to deliver effective law and order for all the people of Northern Ireland and to concentrate on the everyday issues that matter to them. It will help the PSNI deliver its overriding ambition to deliver the best policing and to put policing at the heart of the community.

I warmly welcome, therefore, the work of the Royal Irish Academy and Dr John Doyle of Dublin City University in producing this volume. In addition, I should like to thank the Minister for Foreign Affairs and his Department for their commitment to this project.

Rt Hon. Owen Paterson, MP, Secretary of State for Northern Ireland
June 2010

GLOSSARY

Anglo-Irish Agreement (Hillsborough Agreement, 1985)—An agreement signed on 15 November 1985 at Hillsborough Castle in Northern Ireland by the British and Irish governments. The agreement established the Anglo-Irish Intergovernmental Conference and gave the Irish government an advisory input into Northern Ireland's governance while also confirming the principle of consent, i.e. that the constitutional position of Northern Ireland would change only if a majority of its people agreed to join a united Ireland. The Anglo-Irish Agreement was strongly opposed by most unionists, and ultimately most of its inter-governmental provisions were absorbed into and superseded by the provisions of the 1998 Good Friday (Belfast) Agreement.[1]

Ard Fheis—The Irish language term, widely used in otherwise English language writing, for the annual conference of a political party.

Combined Loyalist Military Command (CLMC)—The umbrella organisation of the main Loyalist paramilitary groups.

Dáil Éireann—The popularly elected and most important chamber of the Oireachtas (Irish Parliament).

Democratic Unionist Party (DUP)—Since 2003, the largest unionist party in Northern Ireland. It was founded by the Reverend Ian Paisley in 1971, replacing a previous loose coalition called the Protestant Unionist Party, also led by Paisley. It is a more populist and generally more hard-line party than the more traditional Ulster Unionist Party. The DUP was led by Ian Paisley until 2008, when Peter Robinson was elected leader. See: http://www.dup.org.uk.

The Downing Street Declaration—A joint declaration issued on 15 December 1993 by the British Prime Minister John Major and the Taoiseach of Ireland Albert Reynolds.

Fianna Fáil—Generally the largest of the political parties in Ireland in most elections. The party was originally formed in 1926 from those who opposed the Anglo-Irish Treaty in 1921, and was led by Éamon de Valera until the late 1950s. It has been in government, as a single party or the dominant party in coalition, for most of its history (1932–48; 1951–54; 1959–73; 1977–81; March to December 1982; 1987–94; 1997 to date). See: http://www.fiannafail.ie/.

Fine Gael—Generally the second-largest party in Ireland. Its roots lie in an older party, Cumann na nGaedheal, which was formed from those who supported the 1921 Treaty with Britain in the 1922–23 post-independence Civil War. The title Fine Gael was adopted in 1933 when it merged with some other small parties. It the modern period, the party has sought to identify itself with the Christian Democratic tradition in European politics (Fine Gael has led governments in 1922–32; 1948–51; 1954–57; 1973–77 and 1995–97). See: http://www.finegael.org/.

First and Deputy First Minister of Northern Ireland—The First and Deputy First Minister occupy a joint office and lead the Northern Ireland Executive (the executive arm of the Northern Ireland Assembly). Under the power-sharing arrangements that exist for Northern Ireland, the First Minister and Deputy First Minister are drawn from the largest unionist and largest nationalist party.

Garda Síochána—(literally 'Guardians of the Peace'). The official name of the police force of Ireland, usually referred to simply as the Gardaí.

Good Friday Agreement (Belfast Agreement)—The normally used terms for the 'Agreement reached at multi-party talks' in Belfast on 10 April 1998 (which was Good Friday in that year in the Western Christian religious calendar). It was agreed by the British and Irish governments and the eight Northern Ireland-based political parties that participated in the talks. The DUP and the small (and now defunct) UK Unionist Party walked out of the talks when Sinn Féin was admitted. The principal provisions of the Agreement included the establishment of a Northern Ireland Assembly, led by a 'power-sharing' Executive (with ministerial posts shared in proportion to seats won in regional elections); the creation of a North–South Ministerial Council—to oversee harmonisation and co-operation between

Northern Ireland and Ireland; a British–Irish Intergovernmental Conference (replacing and superseding the former Anglo-Irish Intergovernmental Conference, established by the 1985 Anglo-Irish Agreement); and a British–Irish Council, which acts as a forum for discussion on building wider co-operation between the British and Irish governments, the devolved administrations of Northern Ireland, Scotland and Wales, and Jersey, Guernsey and the Isle of Man. The 1998 Agreement contained many other provisions, including a process for prisoner releases, decommissioning of weapons, 'normalisation' of security and the terms of reference for the Policing Commission.[2]

Irish Republican Army (IRA)—The term goes back to the Irish War of Independence (1919–21) and was adopted by the armed element of the national liberation movement. The term was used by successive incarnations of the IRA, who rejected the 1921 Treaty with Britain, which had introduced partition. In this book, unless explicitly referring to the earlier historic period, use of the term 'IRA' relates to the largest nationalist paramilitary group formed in 1969 (the so-called 'Provisional IRA'—see below) as a result of a split within the then small and clandestine IRA. While both the IRA and Sinn Féin deny any organic links—in part at least as the IRA is an illegal organisation in both Ireland and Britain—it is generally accepted that during the Northern Ireland conflict there was significant overlap at leadership level, even if the grassroots organisations were more separate. The IRA declared a ceasefire in 1994 and destroyed all its weapons under international supervision in 2005.

Labour Party—The Irish Labour Party, usually the third-largest of the political parties in Ireland, measured in terms of electoral support, has a social democratic focus to its political ideology. It has participated in governments with Fine Gael historically, and for one period with Fianna Fáil, but always as the significantly smaller party. See: http://www.labour.ie/.

Loyalist—The origin of the term in the Irish context is a person who is 'loyal' to the British monarchy. In modern Northern Irish politics it usually refers to supporters of the pro-union (with Britain) paramilitary groups—the UDA (which remained legal until 1992) and the UVF (which was illegal for most of the period of conflict in Northern Ireland). Occasionally, however, the term is used interchangeably with 'unionist' or simply to describe a more hard-line form of unionism. In this text we have restricted its use, unless explicitly defined otherwise, to supporters of the unionist paramilitaries

Nationalist—In the context of Northern Ireland, the term is used politically to describe those who support a united Ireland.

Progressive Unionist Party (PUP)—A loyalist political party linked to the Ulster Volunteer Force (UVF). The PUP was formed in 1979, and its main support base is the loyalist working-class communities of Belfast. See: http://www.pup-ni.org.uk.

Provisional IRA (PIRA or IRA)—The Provisional Irish Republican Army. Generally referred to simply as 'the IRA' or sometimes in journalistic short-hand as 'the Provos'. The PIRA was established in 1969 at the outset of the 'Troubles', following a split in the IRA at that time (see Irish Republican Army above).

Republican—In Northern Ireland usually used to describe a supporter of Sinn Féin. Its origin in this more specific usage is as a description of those who rejected the 1921 Treaty between the Irish nationalist movement and the British government—and who insisted on holding out for a 'Republic'. (The Treaty had offered 'Free State' status, with a British-appointed Governor General, and members of parliament were required to swear an oath of allegiance to the British Monarch.)

RTÉ—Raidio Teilifís Éireann is Ireland's national television and radio broadcaster.

Seanad Éireann—The Senate; the second chamber of the Oireachtas (Irish Parliament).

Sinn Féin—The name of the Irish political party led by Gerry Adams since 1983. The term (literally 'Ourselves Alone' in the Irish language) has been used by different organisations throughout the twentieth century, but was popularised by inaccurate descriptions in the press of the failed 1916 armed insurrection by nationalists as the 'Sinn Féin rebellion'. The name was used by the broadly based nationalist movement formed in 1917 that dominated the organisation of the proto-state until independence and which then split in the 1922–23 Civil War. The party was associated with the IRA during the conflict in Northern Ireland and had a socialist ideology in addition to its militant nationalism. It became the largest nationalist party in Northern Ireland in 2001. See: http://www.sinnfein.ie/.

Social Democratic and Labour Party (SDLP)—A nationalist political party founded in 1971 in Northern Ireland by a new generation of nationalists involved in the civil rights movement. It supports the aim of a united Ireland, but only through non-violent means. It was the largest nationalist party from its foundation until 2001, when it was over-taken by Sinn Féin. John Hume was leader of the SDLP from 1979 to 2001. See: http://www.sdlp.ie/.

Stormont—the geographical location of the Northern Ireland Assembly building. The term is often used as short-hand for the unionist government in Northern Ireland from 1922–72—as in the 'Stormont administration'.

Taoiseach—The official term used to describe the Irish prime minister.

Ulster Defence Association (UDA)—The largest of the loyalist paramilitary groups, formed in 1970. It was involved in attacks on nationalists from its foundation but claimed such attacks under a cover name: the Ulster Freedom Fighters (UFF). The UDA remained a legal organisation until 1992, which led to frequent protests from nationalists. It declared a ceasefire in October 1994, shortly after the IRA ceasefire.

Ulster Freedom Fighters (UFF)—The cover name of the Ulster Defence Association (UDA), used to claim responsibility for acts of violence.

Ulster Unionist Party (UUP)—Sometimes referred to as the Official Unionist Party or OUP or, simply, the Unionist Party. Founded in 1905, it formed every government in Northern Ireland from 1922 until the British government dissolved the parliament in 1972. It remained the largest unionist party in regional and Westminster elections (with the exception of EU parliament elections) until 2003. See: http://www.uup.org/.

Ulster Volunteer Force (UVF)—This name was originally used by unionist opponents of Home Rule for Ireland in 1912. The title was revived by a group opposed to the hints at reform by the Unionist Party government led by Terence O'Neill in the mid-1960s. Their attacks on nationalists began in 1966 in response to these suggestions of reform and long before the IRA launched its armed campaign. The UVF was declared illegal following the shooting of a Catholic civilian in June 1966. Generally perceived to be more disciplined and tightly organised than the rival loyalist paramilitary group the Ulster Defence Association, but it also included within its ranks one of the most sectarian loyalist leaders, Billy Wright. The UVF is associated with the small loyalist party the Progressive Unionist Party (PUP), which sought to organise a working-class loyalist base in a similar fashion to Sinn Féin's success in working-class nationalist areas. The PUP was never very successful in this attempt, however, and remained a marginal if at times high-profile party.

Unionist—In the context of Northern Ireland, the term is used politically to describe those who support the 'Union' with Britain.

Notes on terminology

In international writing on Northern Ireland, the terms Catholic and Protestant are widely used to define the political divisions in the region. Most nationalists are from a Roman Catholic background (even if not at all personally religious), and likewise most unionists are from a Protestant background. The proportion of each community that supports the dominant political ideology of the other, i.e Roman Catholic unionists and Protestant Irish nationalists, is difficult to estimate, but voting trends and problematic attitude surveys suggest it is in low single figures and similar for each community. However, Irish writing on the conflict usually uses the terms 'nationalist' and 'unionist' rather than Catholic and Protestant, as this more accurately reflects the nature of the conflict and the secular, if confessionally divided, nature of politics in Northern Ireland.

In this publication we have generally used the official geographical descriptor 'Northern Ireland'. Unionists usually use the term 'Ulster' to define the territory, but it is rarely used by nationalists, as they consider the province of Ulster to comprise all of its nine counties on both sides of the Irish border. Nationalists often use the term 'North of Ireland'—implying a more all-Ireland focus, and in the past Sinn Féin would use the even looser term 'Six Counties' (as Northern Ireland is divided into six local counties).

The official title of the Irish state is 'Ireland'. We use that term when referring to the state in official terms. The term 'Republic of Ireland' is often used in journalistic writing, but it is not used by the Irish state in official documents. Likewise, the official name of the British state is the United Kingdom of Great Britain and Northern Ireland, or UK. However, the term 'Britain' is widely used, and 'UK' is often used in public discourse to mean, in practice, the island comprised of England, Scotland and Wales.

NOTES

[1] The full text of the 1985 Anglo-Irish Agreement is available at: http://www.dfa.ie/uploads/documents/anglo-irish%20agreement%201985.pdf.

[2] For the full text of Belfast (Good Friday) Agreement, see: http://foreignaffairs.gov.ie/uploads/documents/Anglo-Irish/agreement.pdf. For further commentary, see John Doyle 'Governance and citizenship in contested states: the Northern Ireland peace agreement as internationalised governance', *Irish Studies in International Affairs* 10 (1999), 201–19; John Doyle 'Towards a lasting peace'?: the Northern Ireland multiparty agreement, referendum and Assembly elections of 1998', *Scottish Affairs* 25 (1998), 1–20.

INTRODUCTION

John Doyle

Security Sector Reform (SSR)—the transformation of military and policing institutions in post-conflict societies—is one of the most challenging issues in international conflict resolution. During the Cold War, when inter-state conflicts dominated international relations, ceasefires were usually followed by a withdrawal of forces. Therefore international involvement, if present at all, was generally limited to the interposition of peacekeepers along a ceasefire line. Civil wars, distorted by superpower interference, were also more likely to end militarily rather than by a negotiated settlement, as external support often exasperated and prolonged the local internal dynamics of conflicts. For as long as the Cold War lasted, in neither inter-state nor civil wars was the need for SSR seen as an important part of the post-conflict settlement. Since the mid 1990s, by contrast, most armed conflicts have been primarily internal or civil wars, even if they often have a strong international or regional context. These post-Cold War civil conflicts are more likely to be the subject of international mediation efforts and are statistically more likely than conflicts in earlier eras to end in a negotiated peace agreement.[1] Peace agreements at the end of civil wars, almost by definition, leave previously hostile political groups and armed forces sharing the same political and geographical space. In this context, new forms of government at the national level—usually involving power-sharing of some form—and security sector reform within the police and/or military, have emerged as some of the most crucial elements of the content of peace agreements signed over the past 20 years. The international community continues to struggle, however, with the planning and execution of SSR and, without a doubt, the development of best practice in this area is still evolving. In that respect, the Northern Ireland case has significance beyond those interested simply in that specific conflict.

Civil conflicts generally involve a highly polarised relationship between the official security forces of the state and those non-state actors challenging for state power or seeking to secede from the state.

There will often be a long history of poor and conflictual relationships between security forces and sections of the population before an armed conflict emerges. Even if the security forces were not a significant factor in the eruption of armed conflict, the nature and style of counter-insurgency operations in almost all conflicts has led to a sharp deterioration in relations between the police and army on the one hand, and the communities within which challenging non-state actors operate on the other. Northern Ireland was typical of many modern conflicts in this respect. By the time a peace agreement was negotiated, the community was highly polarised on policing and the future of the security forces. On the one hand, for the British government and unionists in Northern Ireland, the police were their defenders, who had bravely guarded them against a terrorist insurgency. For Irish nationalists, on the other hand, even those who had strongly opposed the IRA, the police were part of the problem; they were an unrepresentative force with a poor human-rights record, who had almost no support among the wider nationalist community and who could not provide a normal post-conflict policing service.

The Irish peace process was based on a transformation of politics, by means of a consociational power-sharing model,[2] with strong and institutionalised recognition of Irish nationalists' identity and desire for all-Ireland unity and formalised co-operation between the Irish and British governments. This is not the place to analyse in full the nature of the 1998 'Good Friday' Agreement, but in brief, the Agreement provided that executive and legislative power over most issues was to be devolved from London to a locally elected Assembly and Executive in Northern Ireland.[3] The Assembly's membership was decided by an electoral system of proportional representation, and ministerial offices in the power-sharing Executive were allocated between the political parties on the basis of their popular support. The IRA not only declared a ceasefire (in 1994) but ultimately destroyed its weapons (in 2005). Nationalists accepted that, notwithstanding their historical grievances over the partition of Ireland, Irish unity could only come about with the consent of a majority within Northern Ireland, where unionists (those who favour the link with Britain) still constitute a majority. On the other hand, nationalists were not required to abandon their goal of Irish unity, and the 1998 Agreement established a North South Ministerial Council and a number of cross-border executive agencies that would be tasked with developing policies on issues of mutual advantage, by agreement on both sides of the border. The nature of the internal governance arrangements in Northern Ireland also ensured that the posts of First and Deputy First Minister (in de facto terms joint and co-equal posts) would be shared between a unionist and a nationalist nominee, ensuring nationalist recognition and political power at the highest level. There were new arrangements for co-operation between the Irish and British governments; an advisory Council to bring together the two governments, the Northern Ireland Executive and the various devolved governments in the UK; and finally there was a range of measures on the release of prisoners, demilitarisation of society, new equality procedures, recognition of the Irish language, reform of the criminal justice system and a commission to examine the question of policing.

Given the nature of the political divisions within Northern Ireland, it was not possible during the intensive talks that led to the 1998 Agreement to reach consensus on the detail of post-conflict policing. There was agreement to establish an 'independent commission', which would be 'broadly representative' and have 'expert and international representation' to make recommendations on policing.[4] The terms of reference for this commission stated that:

> Its proposals on policing should be designed to ensure that policing arrangements, including composition, recruitment, training, culture, ethos and symbols, are such that in a new approach Northern Ireland has a police service that can enjoy widespread support from, and is seen as an integral part of, the community as a whole.[5]

By establishing such a commission, the negotiators in 1998 created space for a peace agreement to be reached without finalising the detail on policing. A similar procedure was used to make progress on the contentious issue of weapons held by illegal armed groups. The idea of a policing commission allowed the first hurdle to be crossed but it did not resolve the underlying problems. Even if a peace agreement could be signed, it would not be sustainable for very long without agreement on the substantive issues that the Independent Commission on Policing for Northern Ireland had been asked to address. The Commission therefore, once established, faced a hugely challenging task in drafting a report that would provide a basis for the transformation of policing in Northern Ireland and would meet the demands of its terms of reference, that a new police service 'can enjoy widespread support from, and is seen as an integral part of, the community as a whole'.

The difficulties, indeed the impossibility, of the parties agreeing a way forward on policing in 1998 was illustrated many times over the following ten to twelve years as the peace process faltered in its implementation. There were continuing and significant delays and disagreements about the sharing of power, cross-border co-operation, the issue of IRA-held armaments and the phased withdrawal of British troops, among other issues. In this context it is all the more remarkable that the Commission on Policing could complete the task it was set within a relatively short time frame and that its report, broadly speaking, laid the basis for the subsequent transformation of policing.

The publication of the report by the Policing Commission was, in many respects, as the title suggests a 'new beginning'; it was not a 'solution' or a 'settlement'.[6] It was to take another ten years for the institutional structure of accountability and control to be fully devolved from London to the local elected executive, but by that time many remarkable changes had already occurred—indeed were an essential part of the confidence building that was necessary to allow rival unionist and nationalists political parties reach agreement on sharing power in this contentious area. There are issues that remain to be resolved—not least that the new Police Service of Northern Ireland (PSNI) still does not fully reflect the demographic profile of Northern Ireland as between nationalists and unionists, and even less so as between men and women. However, the situation has been remarkably transformed. The political parties representing about 99 percent of nationalist opinion in Northern Ireland now both support the police service and encourage nationalists to join. This was most remarkably illustrated visually and metaphorically in March 2009 when the Sinn Féin MP and former IRA leader Martin McGuiness, now Deputy First Minister of Northern Ireland, stood side-by-side with the unionist First Minister Peter Robinson and the Chief Constable of the PSNI Hugh Orde in condemning the shooting of a PSNI police officer by a small IRA splinter group.[7]

There are some key issues that are worth highlighting in this introduction, which were fundamental to the Northern Ireland experience and which speak strongly to wider international practice. The first of these is the role of the Commission itself. Its terms of reference and composition were crucial factors; its independence, its representation of local views and its international character were essential components in laying a strong base on which the members of the Commission could establish their own *bone fides* and credibility. The manner by which they conducted their work was also crucial. Their decision to hold an extensive set of public hearings is highlighted by a number of authors in this book as being of immense value. On the other hand, they also made tremendous efforts, ultimately successfully, to persuade police officers of good faith that they had nothing to fear from the transformation of policing. Finally, in the actual content of their report they managed to produce a plan that ultimately did provide a blueprint. While it is always dangerous to highlight any one of the Commissioners' recommendations, they were particularly original and insightful in dealing with the question of what to do after the publication of the *Patten Report*. Had they functioned like a standard government commission and simply disbanded, leaving the government to make political choices on which bits, if any, of their *Report* to implement, they would have implemented the letter of their terms of reference but perhaps not the spirit. On the other hand it would have been impossible to appoint themselves as the overseers of the transformation. Thus, the proposal to establish an Oversight Commissioner from outside of Ireland and the UK was a very significant decision which provided an additional view, independent of government, on the degree to which the Commission's proposals were implemented. The Office of the Oversight Commissioner was to play a crucial role as an independent verification mechanism in later years.

Beyond the work of the Commission, the transformation of policing in Northern Ireland took place within the context of a developing peace process, which obviously shaped what happened. The 1998 Agreement is essentially consociational in character. It is based on an institutionalised model of power-sharing, which shares executive power between the political parties based on their electoral support and commits the state to greater equality and greater recognition of nationalists' political identity. Traditional models of consociationalism, as developed by Arend Lijphart, are, however, almost exclusively internally focused, and see external involvement in a conflict in largely negative terms. The Northern Ireland case extends or challenges Lijphart's original work, as external mediation and involvement is widely regarded as having played a very positive role in this case. This positive international dimension in Northern Ireland was visible at the level of process and in the substantive content of the 1998 Agreement. On process issues it was seen in the work of US President Bill Clinton, in the chairing of talks by US Senator George Mitchell and in the international involvement of various experts and diplomats from South Africa, Finland, Canada and the USA in relation to IRA arms and the monitoring of ceasefires, in addition to the Policing Commission. In the substance of the Agreement, a fundamentally important international dimension was enshrined in the North South Ministerial Council and the cross-border bodies and in the formalised co-operation between the Irish and British governments. Both of these dimensions—consociationalism and the international extension of that approach—were crucial to the transformation of politics and of policing in Northern Ireland. The power-sharing model at executive level created a model for power-sharing on the Policing Board and on local District Policing Partnerships. The logic of governmental level power-sharing also required some exceptional measures to deal with the unrepresentative nature of the police—ultimately leading to a period of 50:50 recruitment as between nationalists (strictly speaking, Catholics) and others. The international dimensions of the peace process were critical in building support for compromises between previously conflictual positions on policing and many other matters, and in creating a greater degree of power-balance between the unionist and nationalist communities and also to some extent between the Irish and British governments.

What is clear in the Northern Ireland case is that a significant transformation of politics and policing took place. During the conflict over 3,500 people were killed—in a region with a population of only 1.5 million. As the contributors to this book highlight again and again, there were intense community divisions on the role of the police in the conflict. Starting from this context, with the ceasefires of 1994 and the Agreement of 1998, the transformation of policing and the development of the wider peace process in Northern Ireland have been remarkable. This was no minor process of reform: nationalists and unionists were utterly divided on the issues at stake in policing and on wider governance, yet there are now new agreed structures of government and a police service and policing system that have widespread political and community support. To achieve this, both unionist and nationalist political parties and their supporters have made a journey towards agreement.

The following chapters, by a very diverse range of authors with many different perspectives on the overall political situation in Northern Ireland, are brought together with the purpose of allowing, just over ten years after the publication of the *Report of the Independent Commission on Policing for Northern Ireland*, those familiar with Northern Ireland an opportunity to reflect on the reasons for the Commission's success, and to allow others to draw their own lessons from this experience and make appropriate linkages that are relevant to their own context.

This book is organised into three sections. The first section consists of chapters authored by members of the Commission—setting out their perspectives on different aspects of its functioning and impact. The second section is comprised of chapters by some of those involved in implementing and overseeing the implementation of the *Report*. The final section includes the views of four academic analysts looking back at the Commission and its impact and placing it in an international context.

The Independent Commission on Policing for Northern Ireland was frequently referred to as 'the Patten Commission', after its chairperson Chris Patten. In his opening chapter, 'Personal reflections on chairing the Policing Commission', Patten discusses the possible motivations of a Labour government in inviting him to chair the Commission, and his own motivation in accepting, and provides an insightful account of the work he and his fellow Commissioners undertook. He writes at some length on the question of public accountability of policing and the challenge for the civil service, and indeed the then British Secretary of State, as they faced the prospect of losing their direct and exclusive control of policing. Professor Clifford Shearing, a leading academic criminologist now based in South Africa, discusses the shift from the considerable controversy over the recommendations of the *Patten Report* when it was published, to the now almost uniform praise for the *Report* and its recommendations. He discusses the 'design principles' that structured the recommendations and also highlights and explores the implications of the Commission's insistence that it was indeed a *policing* and not simply a *police* commission. Professor Gerald Lynch, from New York, one of the world's leading experts on criminal justice education, examines the question of human rights and policing and issues of police accountability. He also explores the often neglected issue of police training and the failure (to date) to provide a new police college in Northern Ireland—finishing with a question as to whether we should now consider a shift of police training into the mainstream higher education system. Kathleen O'Toole, a highly experienced senior US police officer, brings that perspective to this book as she did to the Commission, focusing in particular on issues of police management and community policing. Maurice Hayes, a former senior civil servant in Northern Ireland, explores the question of building cross-community support for policing, and also deals with the question of how the implementation of the *Report* would be monitored and over-seen. Peter Smith, a senior barrister and former member of the Ulster Unionist Party, discusses the reaction of that party, in particular its then leader David Trimble, to the Commission itself and the *Report*.

The second section of the book explores the implementation of the *Report*, through the reflections of some of the key people tasked with that role. Tom Constantine, an experienced US police officer and the first Oversight Commissioner, looks at the role of that innovative office and in particular how he and his colleagues within it created a system for evaluation of the *Report*'s implementation. Hugh Orde, Chief Constable of the PSNI from 2002 to 2009, reflects on his own leadership role over that period and especially the challenges of bring-ing the organisation through the process of change, of dealing with accountability, including the always controversial issue of intelligence, and the essential issue of 'policing with the community'. Nuala O'Loan, the first Police Ombudsman in Northern Ireland discusses her role in the creation of that office, the challenges of establishing its working relations with both police and public and some of the most high-profile cases that were investigated by her office during her seven-year term. Professor Desmond Rea, the first chairperson of the Northern Ireland Policing Board, along with the two vice-chairs who served with him, discuss the role of that body in providing a frame-work for public accountability and how the Policing Board interacted with the other actors involved in policing. Finally in this section, Maggie Beirne and Martin O'Brien, who both worked for the Committee on the Administration of Justice, Northern Ireland's leading civil-society organisation in this area, provide an insight into the perspectives of human-rights NGOs during the Northern Ireland conflict while the Commission was working, on the *Report* once launched and on its implementation.

The final section of the book includes the views of four academic researchers on the Commission and its impact. John Doyle, senior lecturer in international relations in Dublin City University, looks at the politics of policing reform, focusing on the views of the local po-litical parties, the very high level of division that existed during the conflict and how, and perhaps why, these views and divisions altered in the aftermath of the Commission's work. Mary O'Rawe, senior lecturer in law in the University of Ulster, discusses the importance of a gender perspective in the analysis of policing transformation, setting the Northern Ireland case in the international context and seeking to analyse why gender mainstreaming and the equal participation of women are so difficult in practice. Graham Ellison, senior lecturer in criminology in Queen's University Belfast, analyses police-community relations in the 'post-Patten' era. He offers a critical analysis of surveys on community attitudes and draws on his own research, conducted among working class communities in particular, to highlight the very real remaining challenges for the transformation of policing at community level in Northern Ireland. In the final chapter of the book, Mark Downes, Head of the International Security Sector Advisory Team at the Geneva Centre for the Democratic Control of Armed Forces, places the Commission's work and the Northern Ireland case in the wider international context of security sector reform in post-conflict countries.

The title of this book, *Policing the Narrow Ground*, is inspired by A.T.Q. Stewart's classic book on the history of Northern Ireland, *The Narrow Ground: Aspects of Ulster, 1609–1969*, in which he referred to the intensity of conflict historically in the small geographical space— the 'narrow ground'—that is Northern Ireland.[8] Those intense political differences remain. Nationalists have not abandoned their desire for Irish unity, indeed in many respects they are more confident now that they will achieve it. Unionists strongly retain their wish to remain part of the British state and, more than nationalists perhaps, are wary of the political future. Nonetheless, both political communities, through their mainstream political parties, have agreed a new form of government, an almost unique cross-border dimension to that governance and, as this book testifies, a new policing system—all within that narrow ground.

The Northern Ireland case clearly has its own unique character. The report of the Independent Commission on Policing for Northern Ireland is not a 'blueprint' for every other post-conflict situation, and the purpose of this book is not to suggest that it is. The Northern Ireland experience does, however, show that progress is possible, even in difficult circumstances, even where a community is almost totally polarised in its attitudes to the security forces and even where the implementation of a peace agreement has other challenges to face.

NOTES

[1] See, for example, Frank R. Pfetsch and Christopher Rohloff, *National and international conflicts, 1945–1995: new empirical and theoretical approaces* (London: Routledge, ECPR, 2000) and Peter Wallensteen, *Understanding conflict resolution* (London: Sage, 2007).

[2] Consociationalism is a model of power-sharing for divided societies associated with the work of academic Arend Lijphart. See, for example, Arend Lijphart, *Democracy in plural societies* (New Haven, CT: Yale University Press, 1977). For an analysis of consociationalism in Northern Ireland, see John McGarry and Brendan O'Leary, *The Northern Ireland conflict: consociational engagements* (Oxford: Oxford University Press, 2004) and John Doyle, 'Governance and citizenship in contested states: the Northern Ireland peace agreement as internationalised governance', *Irish Studies in International Affairs* 10 (1999), 201–19.

[3] The Agreement was signed in Belfast on 10 April 1998; the full text of the document is available at: http://foreignaffairs.gov.ie/uploads/documents/Anglo-Irish/agreement.pdf (hereafter cited as *Agreement*). For discussion of its content and the negotiating process, see John Doyle, 'Towards a lasting peace?: the Northern Ireland multi-party agreement, referendum and Assembly elections of 1998', *Scottish Affairs* 25 (1998), 1–20 and John Doyle, 'Re-examining the Northern Ireland conflict', in Vassilis Fouskas (ed.), *The politics of conflict: a survey* (Routledge: London, 2007), 132–46.

[4] *Agreement*, 27

[5] *Agreement*, Annex A.

[6] *A new beginning: policing in Northern Ireland* Report of the Independent Commission on Policing for Northern Ireland (Belfast: HMSO/Northern Ireland Office, 1999).

[7] See http://news.bbc.co.uk/2/hi/uk_news/northern_ireland/7934426.stm.

[8] A.T.Q. Stewart, *The narrow ground, aspects of Ulster, 1609–1969* (London: Faber and Faber, 1977), 130.

Part I

The Independent Commission
on Policing for Northern Ireland

CHAPTER 1

PERSONAL REFLECTIONS ON CHAIRING THE POLICING COMMISSION

Chris Patten

INTRODUCTION

I f asked to address whether the reform of policing in Northern Ireland (carried out to implement the report that bears my name[1]) has been a success, it is on the face of things unlikely that I will reply in the negative. I could allow myself to be provoked into a lengthy rebuttal of the views of those like London's *Daily Telegraph* and Ruth Dudley Edwards, who, when our report was first published, predicted that it would lead to disaster—in the latter's words to the surrender of Northern Ireland to local fascists.[2] But what is the point in cutting down trees to respond to such blatant and prejudiced stupidity? On balance, I think it is best to leave final judgement to others who may be capable of greater objectivity. All I would ask is that such a judgement should consider the tests for each recommendation that we set ourselves at the very start of our work and that we itemised in the report's first chapter:

• Does this proposal promote effective and efficient policing?
• Will it deliver fair and impartial policing, free from partisan control?
• Does it provide for accountability, both to the law and the community?
• Will it make the police more representative of the society they serve?
• Does it protect and vindicate the human rights and human dignity of all?[3]

Looking back over the decade and more since our report, has it provided in practice satisfactory answers to these questions? The best judges are the people of Northern Ireland, including the police service.

Two of my colleagues, who have contributed essays to this collection, deal with subjects that I might otherwise have written about. To do so would now be nugatory. Peter Smith covers the curious refusal of Ulster Unionist Party leader David Trimble to accept, even in private, and perhaps also to comprehend, the extent to which our report made it possible for him to achieve what he wished for, namely the establishment of a power-sharing executive with himself at its head. Maurice Hayes notes the extent to which many of our conclusions were the inevitable result of our terms of reference, so carefully negotiated as part of the Belfast Agreement by Mr Trimble among others. Senator Hayes wisely begins by drawing attention to the relationship between legitimacy and the use of force in a plural society. Readers of these (and other) essays by members of the Independent Commission on Policing for Northern Ireland will recognise how fortunate I was to be able to share responsibility for drawing up our report with so many wise and public-spirited individuals.

APPOINTMENT TO THE COMMISSION

So why did I agree to accept the chairmanship of the Commission in the first place? I hope that it will not seem too egotistical if I start with this question. I recall that at a public meeting—I think it was in Craigavon—a questioner provided the answer. 'I know why you're doing this, Mr Patten', he barked. 'You're doing it for the money'. Former Conservative Party chairman Norman Tebbit made a similar point, with an appropriate Biblical reference to Judas Iscariot's 'thirty pieces of silver'. The truth was rather more complicated than that, with no pecuniary footnotes.

I was telephoned shortly after Easter in 1998 by Secretary of State for Northern Ireland Mo Mowlam (while I was in New York). It was less than a year since I had left the post of governor of Hong Kong, shortly after which the Labour spin-doctors had leaked a story to the *Sunday Times* that I was about to be prosecuted under the Official Secrets Act for remarks, made in a book (largely about me) by Jonathan Dimbleby, concerning the UK's policy in the colony.[4] The reason for this smear was to distract attention from the news, which emerged on the same day, that the foreign secretary, the late Robin Cook, was leaving his wife. I was amused that not long after this, the alleged traitor was approached to chair the proposed commission on policing and security policy. Perhaps it was intended as rehabilitative therapy.

Anyway, the smear had served its purpose so we could all move on. Mo, whom I did not know at all well, said that she was speaking on the authority of the Prime Minister to offer me this assignment. The way she asked me reminded me of *num* questions in Latin—questions that expect the answer 'no' (a current example would be: 'Are you going white-water rafting and bungy jumping for your holiday, Lord Patten?'). She said that it was a very difficult assignment; that she thought my background made me an ideal candidate; and that her advisers had told her that I would not accept. However, she added that a mutual friend had told her that it was worth trying me because he knew how strongly I felt about Northern Ireland. I said 'yes' straightaway. Mo was surprised. 'Don't you want time to ask your wife?', she enquired. I told her that I would certainly speak to my wife about it but that she would say 'yes' too, as indeed she did. On returning to London, I went to see Mo Mowlam and Prime Minister Tony Blair and the wheels began to spin, with approaches being made to potential Commission members. My only condition for taking the job was that I should be able to have as the Commissioner's secretary Bob Peirce, my former diplomatic adviser in Hong Kong and a member of the Foreign Office whom I knew well and whose talents I greatly admired.

It was obviously useful for the Labour government to have a former Conservative minister in the job. This was not particularly because it enhanced the political claim that Mr Blair had a capacious and attractive tent to which he welcomed all-comers regardless of their party backgrounds. It seemed to me unlikely that anyone would think that this particular job qualified as a political perk. Plainly, however, appointing me had the advantage of looking like a reaffirmation that policy in Northern Ireland was bi-partisan. Support for the Commission remained bi-partisan, though from time to time it was a close-run thing. A former chairman of the Conservative back-benchers' committee, the so-called 1922 Committee, accused me of helping the government by doing such a tough job for them. He did not quite refer to their 'dirty work'. This seemed to me like a good description of exactly why I should do it, in order to sustain bi-partisanship. In professional party politics, we are all given an early lecture on how country comes before party. I am not sure that this disavowal of out-and-out tribalism is as widely accepted today as it once was. Whether or not someone is 'one of us' is an approach to appointments that has affected both the main political parties in Britain.

In any case, the main parties at Westminster had all endorsed the Belfast or Good Friday Agreement, without, in my view, the Labour government giving as much credit to former prime minister John Major as he deserved for starting the process that led to it.[5] In these circumstances, it seemed natural to me to accept a job that was so directly relevant to the successful implementation of the Agreement. I was to see in later years in other parts of the world the problems that could arise in dealing with internal conflict without bi-partisan consensus; that was, for example, what happened in Sri Lanka, where divisions between the main political parties made it very difficult for any government to agree a compromise with the Tamils without a constant fear of being attacked and undermined. In Northern Ireland, most of us shared the same analysis of what had divided the community, and even though we might differ about how many concessions could reasonably be offered by democratic politicians to end violence, there was little fundamental disagreement over policy, except on the extremes. For instance, there were still some in my own political party who shared the Enoch Powell view of the issue, arguing that all would be well in Northern Ireland if only we treated it like Wiltshire or Wolverhampton.

When our report was published in 1999, there were a few awkward moments when it seemed as though the agenda this faction espoused might win out. It was encouraged by the *Daily Telegraph* and animated, like that newspaper, by a sense of outrage that we had smeared and dishonoured police offices in Northern Ireland, especially the more than 300 who had lost their lives in terrorist attacks and the many thousands who had been injured. Ambivalence would have been a polite description of Conservative Party reactions to the report, though fortunately the idea that disabled Northern Ireland police officers should be paraded on the platform at a party conference was abandoned on grounds of taste. Conservative criticism of our proposals was probably mitigated both by the fact that I was a former party chairman with many friends still in senior positions in the party, and that I was not around to engage in controversy. I had by September 1999, immediately after the publication of the report, gone to Brussels to take up the post of EU Commissioner for External Relations. So bi-partisanship in relation to Northern Ireland more or less survived, helped in time by the successful bedding-down of our proposals and the cessation of violence.

IDENTITY POLITICS

One of the main reasons for my interest in Northern Ireland, and in the particular question of the role of the police, was a concern that had developed over the years about what Amartya Sen calls 'the politics of identity', or what the great French-Lebanese Arab Christian novelist Amin Maalouf calls 'the panthers of identity'.[6] Being sent as a junior minister to Northern Ireland in 1983 had started me thinking about my own identity. I was the descendant on my father's side of potato-famine Irish emigrants who had settled in Lancashire. My grand-parents were Catholic primary school teachers, employed in the slums of Manchester before the 1902 Balfour Education Act brought Catholic schools within the state system. I was a cradle Catholic, a Tory and a British passport-holder, whose forebears would presumably have been surprised to discover me closing down the British Empire. I was one of over five million people in Great Britain who had a trace-able link with Ireland—almost one in ten of the total population. There are a million more people living in Britain who were born in the Irish republic. I suppose that my own family background gave a gloss of veracity to the unionist politician John Taylor's allegation that the contents of our report could be explained by the fact that my family came from Donegal. As it happened they did not, though my long-dead step-father came from Co. Mayo. The geographical proximity was perhaps sufficient to give the slur legs. What John Taylor did not know was that my step-father's own father had been a member of the Royal Irish Constabulary until that force was disbanded.

The issue of my own identity—'Know thyself', Socrates instructed his pupils—had triggered my growing interest in the overall politics of identity, which has produced butchers and fanatics and has caused no end of bloodshed. I gave a lecture, partly about this subject, back in 1985 at the university in my parliamentary constituency, Bath. It was entitled 'Bath and Belfast—Two cities: one nation?' Much of the argument revolved at least implicitly around the question mark. In the lecture I drew attention to the complexity of Anglo-Irish relations, in terms of the inextricable intertwining of the people who have shared with such acrimony our archipelago off the European main-land coast. I argued that even our names—the Norman French 'Fitzgerald' and 'Molyneaux', the Scottish 'Paisley', the English 'Adams'—showed this; these names contrasting curiously from time to time with the views of those who bore them.

My principal argument was straightforward:

> We are not then the simple, single loyalty, pure-blooded people our tribal rhetoric or our political structures so often claim. It is possible…to feel affinity and loyalty to several places and concepts at once…We can, or should be able to do that without any psychological trauma or political inconsistency. The tragedy is that political and social pressures, sometimes from outside, have forced people into a mould in these islands that fails to reflect these simple truths and our complex inter-relationships. So the people and their politicians, in Northern Ireland particularly, risk tearing themselves apart. Motives are misunderstood. A clarity of objectives is cherished which no one could conceivably hold either in logic or reality. Political slogans are coined to mask private complexities and psychoses. 'Ulster is British'; 'Brits Out'; 'Ourselves Alone': they pull the wool over people's eyes. They all disguise, with sometimes fatal consequences, the unique reality of our relationship together.[7]

The police in Northern Ireland were caught at the heart of this identity trap: they were either custodians of nationhood or symbols of oppression. For the majority the police service was the 'we'; for the minority it was the 'other'. It is identity politics itself that does this, destroying any sense of community based on civic ideals. Our notion of community is narrowed to whatever set of affiliations we believe to be under threat or attack.

On a wider scale, such cramped and bitter tribalism has been glossed by some with the notion that it reflects a clash of civilisations, the most jarring example being the clash between the Christian and Islamic worlds. To arrive at this analysis, you have to dispense with much of the history of both religions. Moreover, as a Westerner you have to understand that you are being asked to sign up to a set of value judgements—allegedly tolerant Christianity on the one side, intolerant Islam on the other. As a proposition, this dichotomy does not stand up well in any analysis of much of the history of the twentieth century. Within Christianity itself we are offered a choice of 'tribes', none of which seems to allow room for the crucified or risen Christ; the option is a world where there is only original sin and no original virtue. The pope, archbishops and moderators could prostrate themselves for peace; but the tribes knew better. They believed, sure; they believed in ties of blood; so the blood flowed.

Within Northern Ireland, the police service was a victim of this identity politics, in part exemplified by its name, its flag, its badges, its emblem, its composition. The police were seen to serve one idea of the state, which gave comfort to some and caused unease to the others. When I was a European Commissioner dealing with the Western Balkans I came across a similar, though not exact, example of the un-acceptability of policing in a tribally divided community. The state of Bosnia and Herzegovina had been carved out of the dismembered and bloodily divided Yugoslavia at the end of a terrible war. It was made up of two entities, one mainly Serbian, the other overwhelm-ingly Bosnian with a Croatian minority. Members of the Orthodox church, Muslims and Catholics were required to live together in one state. They were reluctant to allow anything to work at a state-wide level, especially the police service. How could a Bosnian Muslim accept that his village could be policed by Serbian officers, or Serbs accept the opposite? Although these were people who had lived side by side, often amicably, in European empires (Austro-Hungarian and Ottoman) for centuries, they had then murdered and been murdered in the 1980s and 1990s and could not now accept the legitimacy of policing by a member of a different tribe. In West Belfast and the Creggan Estate in Derry, similar senses of suspicion and loyalty had held sway. So, policing became the community justice of the shotgun against the kneecap.

POLICING AND ACCOUNTABILITY

Tribalism as the received source of our identity as citizens has been a terrible evil. It has been destructive not only of civic idealism but of our safe-guarding of civil liberties. Dealing with issues like interroga-tion and public order in the course of our Commission's work, as well as the review we made of some past controversies, directly addressed the way in which democratic societies should best deal with organised violence that challenges their founding ideals. This is an issue that has arisen more generally, for example in both the US and the UK, in re-lation to the terrorist threat recognised so clearly ever since the al-Qaeda attacks in New York in 2001. In Britain there has been a tendency for Home Secretaries to react with a truncated regard for liberty in their efforts to contain the terrorist threat. The US went much further under the George W. Bush presidency, even espousing the torture of terrorist suspects and the abandonment of due process.

Our own consideration of the policing of violent criminality in Northern Ireland underlined for every member of my Commission the crucial importance for democratic governments to continue to act within the rule of law and with a regard for the rights of those accused of criminal acts. To abandon those principles appeared to all of us tantamount to blurring the distinction between the upholders of the law and those who sought to undermine it. Once a plural, law-based society abandoned those principles, we believed it had begun to change its own nature. What is more, we rather doubted the expediency of short-cutting a proper regard for civil liberties. Did abusive or aggressive treatment of suspects provide the sort of accurate information that could not be found through more humane methods? We rather doubted it.

We spent some time on visits to the US trying to ascertain American approaches to public-order policing. We were impressed by the array of technology that was available for this purpose. On the other hand, it appeared to us that a regard for the preservation of human life in policing was not as pronounced in American attitudes as it was back in Northern Ireland. Whatever the criticism of rubber bullets (plastic baton rounds to give them their proper name), they were clearly preferable to the lead variety. Police services in the US would plainly have had earlier recourse to ultimate deterrents—for example in coping with violent disorder—than was the case in Northern Ireland.

The custody and interrogation of suspects was a key subject of concern whenever we discussed our work with American lawyers and civil-liberty groups, and indeed when our report was published we made a special effort in the US to explain to these groups and to Congress what we were proposing. We felt under a strong requirement to gain support from these American interlocutors for what we were doing. If we had been producing our report during the Bush years I am not sure that I would have felt under a similar political obligation. Guantanamo, Abu Ghraib and the debate in America over waterboarding have rather reduced the world's regard for US organisations as arbiters of a proper regard for civil liberties. The way the world's only super-power behaves at home and abroad inevitably affects its credibility and public diplomacy.

We recognised our own accountability to international as well as domestic opinion. But what of the accountability of the police service that we wished to see emerge as a result of our report? We dwelt on this subject at some length in the opening chapter, since, as we pointed out, the ancient debate about accountability—*sed quis custodiet ipsos custodes?* 'who guards the guardians?' (Juvenal)—had a strong resonance in Northern Ireland. We strongly disagreed with the simplistic assertion of Lord Denning that the police officer is not a servant of anyone, save of the law itself. It is true that the police have the task of upholding the law. That puts them in a privileged position. However, they themselves have to act within the law and cannot do their job wholly effectively unless they have the support of the community that they serve. So the police are not independent any more than they are the servants of the state. They are independent in their operational judgement but accountable in how they use it. The constitutional arrangement of their accountability was particularly difficult to establish in Northern Ireland for two reasons.

First, during many years of coping with terrorist threats, the government in Belfast—in recent years the Northern Ireland Office—had been accustomed to exercise a tight grip over all aspects of policing. This was believed, perhaps understandably, to be essential to the maintenance of some degree of order in a disorderly community. It inevitably bred a nervousness about surrendering control, as well as a certain arrogance about the ability of any other set of arrangements to guarantee effective policing. When our report came out and the initial drafting of implementing legislation was put in hand, squeamishness about giving up control undoubtedly played a part in encouraging officials to dilute much of what we wanted to see happen in order to achieve broad accountability of the police service to the whole community. This sentiment was exacerbated by nervousness about some of those who would represent the community in ensuring accountability. They would inevitably include republicans as well as nationalists, and those on both sides of the Irish divide who had flirted with or been part of paramilitary activity. Was it really acceptable to give powers previously exercised by the state to those who had in the past wanted to overthrow it? Could those who had been on the other side of a riot from the flak-jacketed, baton-wielding police sit in judgement on how those police officers were doing their job?

Given the nature of the agreement struck to end the violence, the only answer to these questions had to be in the affirmative, though no one much liked to own up to it. It was ironic that once the legislation—much amended—to implement the recommendations of our report was in place, the concern turned in a different direction. How could republicans be induced to take up their share of the responsibility, on the Police Board and elsewhere, for holding the police to account? How could they be persuaded to encourage young Catholics—as the church authorities had now done—to join the police service? The Catholic bishops of Northern Ireland had told us, and it was plainly not an exaggeration whether or not you believed it to be fair, that there was a deep legacy of distrust between the nationalist community and the Royal Ulster Constabulary. They also pointed out, again, not over-egging the point, that the unionist community thought that it owned the police. In these circumstances how could you possibly deny the whole community a place in the constitutional arrangements for accountability—both those who had previously thought that the police belonged to them and those who had seen the police as at best unsympathetic and at worst the enemy? To have locked up key aspects of accountability for a reformed police service in the Police Department within the Northern Ireland Office would have aborted much of what we were required to do and wanted to do.

There was, moreover, a second philosophical issue about policing that reflects a serious debate among criminologists. It affected the accountability issues. It is difficult to think of many communities in any part of the world where this has been resolved in the sort of ways that we convinced ourselves were particularly necessary in Northern Ireland. If you believe that policing is not a matter in any community of 'us' against 'them', but a question of all of us being involved in the quest for stability and order under the rule of law, then the notion of accountability involves questions of police attitude and operational activity. It also requires a broad mesh of interventions between the police service and a wide array of community groups and individuals in every neighbourhood.

The reluctance of the civil service to countenance losing control of policing compounded the efforts made by the then Secretary of State for Northern Ireland, Peter Mandelson, to tinker with the legislation in order to find political accommodations with David Trimble and the unionists. They had noisily criticised the *Report*, especially the issues relating to the name and emblems of the police service. Lord Mandelson, as he has since become, clearly thought that he could circumnavigate or obfuscate the difficult issues of principle that we had believed to be unfudgeable, in a way that kept Trimble and the unionists on board the overall political project, without losing the support of the nationalists and republicans. Some of those efforts are chronicled in Jonathan Powell's book, *Great hatred, little room*.[8] Perhaps the politest thing to say is that Lord Mandelson proved to be less clever than he thought he was. A much weakened implementing bill had to be rewritten during its parliamentary passage in order to put back into it much of our report ('We want the whole of *Patten*', said the original bill's critics). Away in Brussels, I thought the best approach was to keep quiet and allow political reality to return the legislation to our original intentions. By and large that is what happened. Mr—now Lord—Trimble emerged weakened from the process, though able to take up the post of First Minister in the power-sharing executive. Lord Mandelson was soon out of Belfast for reasons unconnected to policing or policy, only to re-emerge much later as my successor in Brussels and then as the Pooh-Bah of Mr Brown's administration. Some people have subsequently suggested that we members of the Policing Commission should have remained involved politically with the issues in our *Report* after its publication in order to shepherd them through to the statute book. I think this would have been a bad idea. The *Report* spoke for itself. If we had hung around as its main protagonists, there is a danger that we ourselves, rather than what we had advocated, would have become the issue.

If we expected the police service to be accountable, then it was important for us to be as accountable as possible in the way we did our work. That persuaded us, without much internal discussion, to hold a series of public meetings around Northern Ireland. Some people argued that these meetings would be of little interest; no one, it was said, came to public meetings. This was wrong. We held, in all, 40 public meetings attended by over 10,000 people at which over 1,000 spoke. We were adamant on three issues. First, we could not hold the meetings under police guard and under government auspices. So far as security was concerned we would have to depend on the commitment to the whole process of those who controlled the paramilitary forces. Second, we should go everywhere that invited us, including places like Crossmaglen and Omagh not long after its terrible bombing. Third, local communities had to be responsible for the arrangements for and the chairing of the meetings. This placed us in the hands of worthy and respected local figures, who by definition usually lacked the experience of dealing with potentially embarrassing and awkward public confrontations that several Commission members had acquired during long public careers. But we were never let down. I recall in particular a meeting in Portadown on the Garvaghy Road estate, notorious because of the annual stand-off over the Orange Order march to Drumcree and because of its proximity to the site of the blatantly sectarian murder of Robert Hamill. The meeting was chaired superbly well by Rosemary Nelson, who had been the solicitor for several high-profile republican terror-ist suspects. She was assassinated by Protestant paramilitaries in March 1999.

The meetings were occasionally attended by pretty much our whole team, but more usually by a cross-section of the commission-ers. Everyone played their part; some, like Kathleen O'Toole, with the sort of empathetic engagement that was a tribute to character as much as experience. I can say without hesitation that these were the most difficult meetings I have had in my life. We had one particularly concentrated run of meetings in November and December 1998, after which I took my wife on a short pre-Christmas holiday to look at Italian paintings in order to try to regain my composure. The meetings had almost inevitably taken on some of the characteristics of truth and reconciliation sessions. While there was inevitably some propaganda and political posing, most of what we heard echoed the bloody record of hatred and division within a small community. It was an experience too emotionally draining and passionately felt to be summarised in a series of flash-back anecdotes. The stories we were told from both sides of the community divide were often so shocking as to be difficult for the speaker to narrate, but as Maurice Hayes recalled, often the very articulation of the grief and rage seemed to provide, for perhaps the first time, a cathartic outlet for the witnesses of atrocity.

I do not believe that the meetings helped to frame any particular recommendations, though they did underline the central importance of the subject of policing and gave us perhaps a better idea of what our priorities should be. They also confirmed our views about the rela-tionship between good policing and the community. Above all, if we had needed evidence that there were two legitimate Northern Ireland stories these meetings provided it. We could distinguish between good and evil, but how were we to adjudicate between two tribal stories of wrongs done and pain inflicted? Which cry of rage, reinforced by direct experience as well as imagination and myth, were we to take as the right one? In an emotional atmosphere, amidst charges and counter-charges, we had to be neutral assessors simply doing what we believed to be right, buoyed—certainly in my case—by a sense that often in politics the right course of action is also the expedient one. There is a clear path between sanctimoniousness and cynicism. Taking that path led to criticism that we had not paid tribute to sacrifices made and innocence outraged. To have done so would have been to betray our central understanding both of our terms of reference and of the situation that we had to address: namely that both of Northern Ireland's bitterly conflicted parties had their own witness to bear, their own story both imagined and true.

CONCLUSION

A decade on the story has started to change, despite the efforts of a few to turn back the pages. The Oversight Commissioner—one of our best ideas—has seen the reforms through. Dublin and Washington have been supportive, with former Taoiseach Bertie Ahern deserving a special tribute. Politicians in Northern Ireland squabble, but, even in their most partisan manifestations, they appear to support (even enthusiastically) the community's police service. Police officers have been removed from the very heart of the identity debate. The composition of the service is more balanced. Its present-day operations rarely excite controversy. There have been heroes in this process. Many of them are the leaders and members of the police service who have accepted and even embraced change. The Police Service of Northern Ireland has become the best working example of how to police a divided community. The story is not over; there may be more bloodshed. But the police service is a central part of Northern Ireland's new beginning, and that was not inevitable.

NOTES

[1] Independent Commission on Policing for Northern Ireland, *A new beginning: policing in Northern Ireland* Report of the Independent Commission on Policing for Northern Ireland (Belfast: HMSO Northern Ireland Office, 1999), generally referred to as the *Patten Report*.

[2] Ruth Dudley Edwards, 'Why inflict pointless wounds on Ulster's Protestants?; RUC officers face a future in which people they know to be terrorists become their colleagues', *Independent* (London), 10 September 1999.

[3] *Patten Report*, 6.

[4] Jonathan Dimbleby, *The last governor: Chris Patten and the handover of Hong Kong* (London: Time Warner Books, 1998).

[5] This Agreement was signed in Belfast on 10 April 1998; the full text of the document is available at: http://foreignaffairs.gov.ie/uploads/documents/Anglo-Irish/agreement.pdf.

[6] Amartya Sen, *Identity and violence: the illusion of destiny* (New York: W.W. Norton, 2006); Amin Maalouf, *In the name of identity: violence and the need to belong* (New York: Arcade Publishing, 2001); Maalouf, *On identity* (London: Harvill Panther, 2000).

[7] Chris Patten, 'Bath and Belfast—Two cities: one nation?', speech to the University of Bath, 1985.

[8] Jonathan Powell, *Great hatred, little room* (London: Bodley Head, 2008).

CHAPTER 2

THE CURIOUS CASE
OF THE *PATTEN REPORT**

Clifford D. Shearing

INTRODUCTION

The report of the Independent Commission on Policing for Northern Ireland, chaired by Christopher Patten, entitled *A new beginning: policing in Northern Ireland* (generally called the *Patten Report*) and published in September 1999,[1] has received a curiously uneven response over the past decade: Ellison describes its trajectory as 'torturous'.[2] Immediately upon its release it received a very warm reception from the government of the United Kingdom, which endorsed its approach and the thrust of its recommendations. The then Prime Minister, Tony Blair, welcomed the *Report* by saying that it 'charts the way forward in the interests of all the people of Northern Ireland'.[3] This support was soon eroded, however, once legislation began to be drafted to implement the *Report*'s recommendations. The bill brought before parliament in early 2000[4] to set up the framework for the implementation of the *Patten Report* proved to be a far cry from what the report had recommended. Thus, the government's initial rhetoric was not translated into action.

This was reversed to some degree by the time the bill was enacted; in effect, once this gap between rhetoric and action became the subject of rigorous political debate.[5] As a result of the very considerable public and political consternation about this gap, the proposed legislation was revised[6] and brought a little more in line with the *Report*'s recommendations. In commenting on this process Ellison writes:

> It was not until considerable pressure was brought to bear from the United States, the European Union, human rights organizations, and nationalist politicians within Northern Ireland that a revised implementation plan was

introduced in 2001 and amended legislation was introduced 2 years later. It was only at this point (in 2003) that
a number of the original ICP [International Policing
Commission] proposals came close to being approxi-
mated (e.g., enhanced powers for the Policing Board).[7]

At a local political level there were heated disagreements over the
Patten Report, with the unionists roundly condemning it. Indeed, the
leader of the Ulster Unionist Party at the time, David Trimble, described the *Report* as the 'shoddiest piece of work' he had seen in his
life.[8] The nationalists and the republicans were much more supportive
of the *Report* but condemned it for not going far enough. Many on
this side of the political divide, along with some academics, criticised
the Patten Commission for not acting as a commission of inquiry and
for not drawing conclusions about the rights and wrongs of the partisan conflict, and the role of the police in this conflict, which had
characterised Northern Ireland for so long.[9]

The police community, including the leadership of the Royal Ulster
Constabulary (with the possible exception of Chief Constable Sir
Ronnie Flanagan), did not care much for the *Report*, and many roundly
condemned it, seeing it as an unwarranted attack on what had been a
courageous and effective police force that had held the line in the face
of terrorist attacks.[10] Surprisingly, given this view, it was also argued
by many within the police community that the *Report* had done little
more than take up recommendations from an earlier internal police
report, which had recommended very similar changes, but without
properly acknowledging the work of that earlier internal report.

There were also differences within the academic and NGO community in Northern Ireland about the *Report*, with many seeing its
strengths, but also its fundamental weaknesses. These sectors of society
were often as critical about what the *Patten Report* had not done as what
it had done. For example, one criticism levelled at the *Report* was that
it had not grounded itself carefully in the written and oral (through
hearings) submissions made to the Commission by indicating more
clearly how its recommendations were related to these submissions.
The argument here was that the *Report* had not clearly indicated which
voices the Patten Commission had heeded and which it had not.[11]

There is nothing surprising about this level of debate and disagreement from so many quarters, given that the *Patten Report* was
launched into the middle of an ongoing political conflict. It soon
became the proverbial political football.[12] What is curious, given this

fraught beginning, is that the *Patten Report* has, after a decade, emerged remarkably untarnished. Indeed even the police—the Police Service of Northern Ireland (PSNI)—have now embraced the *Report* and the changes it brought about. The PSNI has positioned itself internationally as an exemplary police organisation, largely because it has become a Patten-compliant organisation. This claimed compliance has enabled the development of something of a PSNI 'brand' that is used—along with, interestingly, the history of the service—to market the PSNI internationally as a force that understands and can respond effectively to terrorism and inter-group violence. The Royal Ulster Constabulary of old has become what might be thought of as the Patten Police, and is internationally recognised as such.[13]

Under a section heading 'Selling "Patten": the creation of a global brand', Ellison and O'Reilly cite Shaun Woodward, MP, then Secretary of State for Northern Ireland—speaking in 2007—as follows:

> The policing arrangements here [Northern Ireland] are fast becoming a model for many other countries: the PSNI is the equal to any other police force in the world and can be proud of the standard set and the success achieved.[14]

Much the same is true of what might be thought of as the 'Patten Institutions'—the Policing Board, the Office of the Police Ombudsman and the Oversight Committee.[15] These institutions, like the PSNI, have received considerable international attention and praise.

Today, there is widespread support for the view that the *Patten Report*, and its vision of policing, provides an example of the very best thinking about contemporary policing, and that it constitutes a benchmark that policing around the world can and should look to for guidance. The *Report* is now widely recognised as providing an exemplary set of recommendations that has relevance far beyond Northern Ireland's shores.[16] This view of the *Patten Report* and its recommendations is nicely expressed by Graham Ellison in the title of his 2007 paper on the Patten Commission and its proposals, 'A blueprint for democratic policing anywhere in the world?'[17]

THEMES OF THE *REPORT*

How is this to be explained? How is it that a report that was so contentious when it was released has become so widely supported and endorsed by what were many of its fiercest critics? The answer, I want to suggest, lies in the way the report was structured. It has three themes, and on each of the themes the *Report* took a principled stance rather than one that sought to play to the political gallery. The Commission took the long view and very deliberately sought to enunciate design principles and to link these to specific recommendations. What is apparent in retrospect is that these principles have proved to be sound. It is the soundness of these principles rather than the specific recommendations that has served to elevate the *Patten Report* internationally.

Taking a principled stand took considerable courage, as some of the members of the Commission were regarded by many in the wider community as being aligned to particular political positions, and there was an expectation that they would advance these political interests within the Commission. The fact that this did not happen and that arguments were engaged and settled, not on a partisan basis but on a principled basis, has proved, in hindsight, to have served both the interests of Northern Ireland and the international policing community very well indeed. It is this wisdom and soundness that has allowed the *Patten Report*, and the institutions that arose from it, to emerge as an internationally recognised Patten brand that is today serving these institutions very well. It is this principled approach that elevated what was initially a decidedly controversial report to one with an exemplary international status, despite the fact that not all of its design principles have been realised through the implementation process. More than its specifics, what have elevated the *Report* to its present status are its design principles.

What were the three themes or streams and what debates did they engage? And what were their design principles? The first theme had very much to do with the Northern Ireland context, the conflict over policing and the peace process. This theme engaged the symbolically charged issues that the Commission had to consider—issues such as the name of the police, the uniform, the badge and so on. These issues were at the heart of the debate that was raging within Northern Ireland at the time the Commission was sitting, and they consumed much of the discussion about the *Report* once it was released. In adopting a principled stance towards these issues the Commission sought to remain aloof from the specifics of this debate and to address questions about what would be the best symbols to embrace as policing moved forward into a new, peaceful dispensation. The Commission considered what symbols and associated meanings would be most likely to serve the police and the province in the future—in simple terms, what symbols and meanings would most likely contribute towards a peaceful tomorrow in Northern Ireland.

The position adopted by the Commission was to move towards more inclusive symbols that were focused on the future rather than on the past. It was agreed that these ought to be neutral and free from association with the contested Irish versus British sovereignties of Northern Ireland, but ultimately negotiated and decided by the new institutions created by the *Report* itself. This created much acrimony at the time the *Report* was released, and indeed, as I have already suggested, much of the debate in the popular media was focused on symbols. What time has shown is that the symbols ultimately chosen have indeed been unifying, so that today there is considerable agreement that the decisions made by the Commission were the right ones. These symbols are very much part of the brand that the Patten institutions market internationally.

Associated with this theme are the Commission's recommendations relating to the composition of the PSNI—quota issues relating to the need to balance the ethnic and political composition of the police. Here the focus was on the symbolism of the composition of the police as well as on the effect that a different composition would have on policing sensibilities. The recommendations in relation to the composition of the police service, and the changes they have fostered, have proved to be vitally important for the way the police and policing are conceived in Northern Ireland today.

The second theme that emerges from the *Report* is that of conventional 'good policing'.[18] This theme or stream is expressed in the recommendations that the *Report* makes with respect to the everyday, sensible things that any police organisation should focus its attention on and do well. A good example in this regard is training. Good training is obviously important and the *Report* insists on this. Another important feature of this stream was the emphasis that the *Report* gave to a standard feature of good thinking within policing: namely, the importance of communities as resources that foster good policing. In picking up this theme the *Report*, however, did more than simply talk in conventional terms about 'community policing'. Instead, it called for a rethinking of this concept, proposing the idea of 'policing with the community'. In this regard, the *Report* argues that 'policing with the community' is more than seeking community support for the police, and conceives of the community as an essential feature of effective policing. Communities, for *Patten*, are seen very much as a resource that the police should seek actively to engage with as a partner; such resources are used to create policing networks, of which the police service is only one part.

It is this second, more conventional stream—albeit with radical elements, such as the *Patten* conception of the relationship between police and communities—that, along with the first theme, provided the agenda for police reform in Northern Ireland. To this must be added the idea promoted by *Patten* that human rights and policing should not be regarded as being at odds, but as consistent and as encompassing each other. It was on these two themes of recommendations and their associated principles that the police have focused their attention in transforming themselves and their policing practices. It is these two themes that provided the basis for the establishment of the PSNI as 'Patten's police', and it has been the service's ability to realise this agenda that has established it as an exemplary police organisation internationally. *Patten* is the brand that the PSNI now markets internationally.

The third theme, and the most radical within *Patten*,[19] is to be found in the report's recommendations regarding the governance of policing, rather than with policing itself. One of the most significant proposals within this governance theme has to do with the *Report's* critique of what for many years had been a key building block of accountability arrangements for police. While acknowledging the vital importance of ensuring that police are not subjected to undue political interference in operational matters, the Commission argued that the notion of 'operational independence' for police had effectively swung the governance pendulum too far towards the police and their leadership. This, the Commission argued, had created a situation whereby chief constables had become less accountable to the public, and to their political representatives, than was appropriate.

The reason for this, the Commission argued, was that the notion of operational independence, while appropriately protecting police from political interference to ensure the freedom to exercise their professional judgement within a framework of the law and general ministerial direction, had gone too far in insulating police in Northern Ireland from post-factum political and public accountability. As an alternative to operational independence, the Commission argued for the notion of 'operational responsibility'. The principle developed here was that, while police and police leaders were responsible for the way in which police operational matters were conducted, their decisions and their actions should not be immune from scrutiny after the fact. This rethinking of the nature and scope of police independence has received considerable support, not only within Northern Ireland but within the United Kingdom more generally.[20] This principle and the thinking it embraces may well constitute one of the most fundamental and far-reaching impacts of the Patten Commission, both in Northern Ireland and elsewhere.

THE FOCUS ON POLICING

Another crucial way in which the Patten Commission has shaped not only policing in Northern Ireland but policing generally, can be found in its insistence that it was indeed a *policing* and not simply a *police* commission—an insistence that was fully consistent with the wording of its terms of reference. The distinction between policing, as a set of arrangements that involved both police and others, and the activities carried out by police, enabled the Commission to take two important conceptual steps in its analysis and recommendations that have extended the public debate around policing in several significant ways.

The first of these, as I have already noted, was the Commission's use of the term 'policing with the community' in preference to 'community policing' to draw attention to, and to emphasise, the necessity of acknowledging that communities could, and should, be actively engaged in policing in partnership with the police service. This constituted what might be thought of as a 'whole of society' approach to policing, which has significantly influenced debate around how police can, and should, relate to policing undertaken by others. Within Northern Ireland, where much policing within communities had often been brutal and illegitimate,[21] a clear distinction needed to be made between legitimate and illegitimate forms of community engagement in policing. To make this distinction, the *Report* both condemned the illegitimate forms of popular policing that had come to characterise much community involvement in policing, while at the same time keeping open the space to enable legitimate forms of policing with the community. This was done by insisting that not only should police engage in policing with the community, but that communities should engage in policing *with the police*.

Another way in which the Commission took advantage of the conceptual space opened up by distinguishing between police and policing was through the twin notions of a 'policing budget' and a 'policing board'. These were both decidedly radical innovations introduced by the *Report*. Associated with both these notions was the *Report*'s proposal for the establishment of District Policing Partnership Boards. The *Report* recommended that these partnership boards be able to raise taxes outside of the provincial policing budget to fund local initiatives for policing with the community. These key sets of recommendations were either not implemented (for example, a policing budget and the local taxes) or were implemented in name only (the 'policing' board that was established was very much a 'police' board). A clear sign that the government did not intend to take on these radical policing innovations is found in the name of the legislation from 2000 mentioned above—it is a 'Police Act' and not a 'Policing Act'. Topping, in commenting on these departures from the *Report*'s recommendations, comments that 'Patten's broad vision was effectively dismissed'.[22] He goes on to argue that:

> While the PSNI have been radically transformed in line with Patten's first 'stream' of reforms [reform of the systems of policing], the changes to policing on the ground through the second stream [setting out a broader vision for policing] have been largely negligible.[23]

Nonetheless, in a comment on the *Patten Report*'s recommendations for 'robust oversight and accountability mechanisms', Ellison notes:

> In a relatively short period, the Policing Board has demonstrated a level of commitment in relation to police oversight and accountability never before seen in Northern Ireland and, in the words of the Committee on the Administration of Justice has 'established itself as a more effective and powerful body than the previous Police Authority for Northern Ireland'.[24]

Some movement has taken place with respect to the idea of a local policing fund with the establishment of Community Safety Committees. These bodies have access to a 'policing budget' made available by the Northern Ireland Office as part of arrangements that took place in response to recommendations of the Justice Review Panel that reported soon after the Patten Commission.[25] While these more radical proposals have not been implemented in the way envisaged by *Patten*, they, along with the recommendations for 'operational responsibility', have had an important and lasting impact on thinking about policing internationally. This set of radical recommendations has served to promote an increasing awareness of wider possibilities that should be explored in governing policing. Today, these notions and their associated recommendation have come to define what policing governance arrangements are or should be moving to embrace.

Two other important governance institutions associated with the *Patten Report* have been implemented. The first is the Office of the Police Ombudsman. While the recommendation for the creation of this office did not originate with *Patten*—it came from an earlier set of recommendations from one of the Patten Commissioners, Maurice Hayes—the report fully endorsed this governance mechanism. This office has come to be well regarded internationally as an instance of exemplary police oversight.[26] Second, a significant institution recommended by *Patten* that proved to be of central importance to the reshaping of the PSNI was the Office of the Oversight Commissioner, which provided for an extraordinarily detailed level of public accountability with respect to the implementation of the *Patten* reforms. The Oversight Commissioner issued informative and regular reports that audited progress, particularly progress by the PSNI, in implementing those recommendations of the *Patten Report* that had received endorsement by the UK government. Like other Patten institutions, the Oversight Commissioner has come to be regarded as 'an example of international best practice'.[27] Recently, the government of Jamaica has created a similar body—an Oversight Committee—to monitor and report on the implementation of recommendations of a panel, endorsed by the government, that had reviewed policing within Jamaica.

CONCLUSION

To return, by way of conclusion, to the question raised at the outset of this paper: what accounts for the shift from considerable controversy over the recommendations of the Patten Commission a decade ago to the now almost uniform praise for its *Report* and those recommendations? The answer, as I have argued, lies in the fact that the Commission, in drafting its *Report*, did not play to the local political sensibilities and debates, but sought instead to identify and address generic issues and debates within policing, and to develop a principled response to them. These issues covered three crucial areas: the symbolic and associated changes required to enable the Royal Ulster Constabulary to move beyond its past; the enunciation of principles of good, ordinary policing; and finally, the development of principles of policing rather than simply of police, and a discussion of the governance implications of this trajectory.

The *Patten Report* is not unlike a good children's story—it carries within it several different but closely woven strands that speak to different issues and different audiences in both a unified and unifying manner. It is this that accounts for the curious tale of the history of the *Patten Report* and the way in which it moved from being a report surrounded by acrimony and fierce debate to one that sets out a model for policing and policing governance that is widely acclaimed—an acclaim that today comes from many of the constituencies that were initially among its most vocal critics.

Whatever *Patten* did for policing in Northern Ireland,[28] perhaps its most important contribution was the shift in thinking about policing that it introduced into the public domain. *Patten* broadened the pool of ideas with respect both to the nature of policing and its governance, and in doing so has contributed to an ongoing 'rethinking' and 're-designing' of the institutions and practices of policing.[29]

NOTES

* The role of the members of the Patten Commission in crafting the analysis and recommendations set out in the *Patten Report* has of course been recognised and acknowledged. What has perhaps not been sufficiently acknowledged is the contribution of Bob Peirce, the secretary to the Commission, who was seconded from the Foreign and Commonwealth Office. Bob was exceptionally talented in overseeing the research staff of the Commission and, even more importantly, in assisting the Commissioners in turning their arguments and conclusions into the text of the *Patten Report*.

Thanks to Elaine Atkins, Michael Kempa and Ricky Rontsch for their kind assistance in the preparation of this chapter.

[1] Independent Commission on Policing for Northern Ireland, *A new beginning: policing in Northern Ireland* Report of the Independent Commission on Policing for Northern Ireland (Belfast: HMSO Northern Ireland Office, 1999).
[2] Graham Ellison, 'A blueprint for democratic policing anywhere in the world?: Police reform, political transition, and conflict resolution in Northern Ireland', *Police Quarterly* 10 (3) (2007), 243–69: 243.

3 Tony Blair, quoted in 'RUC report "the way forward"', BBC news report, 9 September 2009, available at:
http://news.bbc.co.uk/2/hi/uk_news/northern_ireland/442844.stm.
4 The text of this legislation is available at: http://www.parliament.the-stationery-office.co.uk/pa/cm199900/cmbills/125/2000125.htm.
5 Aogán Mulcahy, *Policing Northern Ireland: conflict, legitimacy and reform* (Cullompton, Devon: Willan, 2006), 169–70.
6 See Police (Northern Ireland) Act 2000; the text of this legislation is available at: http://www.opsi.gov.uk/acts/acts2000/ukpga_20000032_en_1.
7 Ellison, 'A blueprint for democratic policing anywhere in the world?', 253.
8 See BBC news report, available at: http://news.bbc.co.uk/2/hi/uk_news/northern_ireland/765174.stm.
9 Mary O'Rawe, 'Transitional policing arrangements in Northern Ireland: the can't and the won't of the change dialectic', *Fordham International Law Journal* 26 (2002–03), 1015–73.
10 Aogán Mulcahy and Graham Ellison, 'The language of policing and the struggle for legitimacy in Northern Ireland', *Policing and Society* 11 (3–4) (2001), 383–404.
11 O'Rawe, 'Transitional policing arrangements in Northern Ireland', 1041.
12 For a review, see Mulcahy, *Policing Northern Ireland*, 169–72.
13 Graham Ellison and Conor O'Reilly, 'From empire to Iraq and the "war on terror"': the transplantation and commodification of the (Northern) Irish policing experience', *Police Quarterly* 11 (4) (2008), 395–426.
14 Ellison and O'Reilly, 'From empire to Iraq and the "war on terror"', 408.
15 For a discussion of these, including the District Policing Partnership, see Mulcahy, *Policing Northern Ireland*, 172–8.
16 Mary O'Rawe, 'Human rights, transitional societies and police training: legitimating strategies and delegitimating legacies', *St. John's Journal of Legal Commentary* 22 (1) (2007), 199–259; John R. Topping, 'Diversifying from within: community policing and the governance of security in Northern Ireland', *British Journal of Criminology* 48 (2008), 778–97.
17 Ellison, 'A blueprint for democratic policing anywhere in the world?', 243.
18 For a review, see Mulcahy, *Policing Northern Ireland*, 179–86.
19 See Michael Kempa, 'Tracing the diffusion of policing governance models from the British Isles and back again: some directions for democratic reform in troubled times', *Police Practice and Research* 8 (2) (2007), 107–23, 116–17; Topping, 'Diversifying from within', 778–97; Paddy Hillyard and Michael Tomlinson, 'Patterns of policing and policing Patten', *Journal of Law and Society* 27 (2000), 394–415.
20 Stephen P. Savage, 'Give and take: the bifurcation of police reform in Britain', *Australian and New Zealand Journal of Criminology* 40 (3) (2007), 313–34: 318.
21 Hillyard and Tomlinson, 'Patterns of policing and policing Patten', 395.
22 Topping, 'Diversifying from within', 783.
23 Topping, 'Diversifying from within', 792.
24 Ellison, 'A blueprint for democratic policing anywhere in the world?', 254.
25 O'Rawe, 'Human rights, transitional societies and police training', 238.
26 See Ellison and O'Reilly, 'From empire to Iraq and the "war on terror"'.
27 David H. Bayley, *Changing the guard: developing democratic policing abroad* (Oxford: Oxford University Press, 2006), cited in Ellison, 'A blueprint for democratic policing anywhere in the world?', 263.

[28] See Oversight Commissioner, Office of the Oversight Commissioner, *Final Report* (19 May 2007), available at: http://www.oversightcommissioner.org/reports/pdfs/may2007.pdf. For a comprehensive assessment, see also Ellison, 'Blueprint for democratic policing anywhere in the world?', '[n]otwithstanding the earlier difficulties, the process thus far has been a broadly successful one, albeit perhaps more so in an organizational and institutional sense', 253.

[29] Philip Stenning, 'Governance and accountability in a plural policing environment—the story so far', *Policing 3* (1) (2009), 22–33: 31.

CHAPTER 3

HUMAN RIGHTS
AND POLICE REFORM*

Gerald W. Lynch

Quis custodiet ipsos custodes?
'Who will guard the guards?'
'Who polices the police? Who has custody over the custodians?'

INTRODUCTION

This age-old question was first asked by the Roman poet, Juvenal. He tells the story of a young prince who is going off to war. He puts the safety of his new, young wife in the hands of the palace guards. The guards will guard his wife, but he wonders who will guard the guards? Who will police the police?

Who will police the police? The answers to this question are at the core of human rights and police reform. Throughout the deliberations of the Independent Commission on Policing for Northern Ireland, we struggled mightily as to what importance should be allocated to the issues of human rights and human dignity. We finally concluded that these issues should be front and centre. The first three substantive chapters in the Commission's *Report* deal with Human Rights (Chapter 4) and Accountability (Chapters 5 and 6).[1] There are 175 recommendations in the *Report*. The very first recommendation states that 'There should be a comprehensive program of action to focus policing in Northern Ireland on a human rights-based approach'.[2] The *Report* unequivocally asserts that 'Upholding human rights and upholding the law is one and the same thing'.[3]

APPOINTMENT TO THE COMMISSION

The late Senator Edward Kennedy initially recommended former FBI agent William Barry to the Commission. Mr Barry did not accept the nomination for health reasons. Upon Mr. Barry's recommendation, Senator Kennedy then nominated me. In June 1996 I spoke to the Irish Ambassador to the United States, Seán O Huiginn, whom I had known since he was the Irish Consul General in New York, and I also spoke to the US Ambassador to Ireland, Jean Kennedy Smith.

In June 1998 I had had several meetings with Ambassador Smith with regard to a conference on 'Crime, Justice and Public Order' that had been held in Dublin in June 1996. Ambassador Smith had agreed to be the plenary speaker at that Conference and to host a reception for all the delegates in her residence in Phoenix Park.

In the first week of June 1996 the nation of Ireland was shocked and convulsed by the murder of a member of An Garda Síochána (the Irish police service), Detective Jerry McCabe, in Adare, Co. Limerick, in an attempted bank robbery by the IRA. Amidst the mourning and recriminations the then Taoiseach (prime minister), John Bruton, addressed the conference on 'Crime, Justice and Public Order' at Dublin Castle. He apologised to the nation of Ireland for its inability to protect the police in carrying out their daily duties. The blatant, broad-daylight murder of Jerry McCabe was viewed as a severe attack on public order. It was the first police fatality in eleven years.

Ambassador Jean Kennedy Smith took a leadership role in calling the Garda Commissioner Patrick Culligan; Mrs Anne McCabe, Jerry's widow; Detective Ben Sullivan, Jerry's partner; and myself to an early Saturday morning meeting at her residence. The Ambassador proposed a Fellowship between the Garda Síochána and John Jay College of Criminal Justice in New York. She proposed that the Fellowship would bring together Irish and American police officers in exchange of personnel, exploring 'best practices', technological advances, ethical issues, training and police–community relations. I was flabbergasted and delighted at the ambassador's Fellowship proposal. I asked the Ambassador why she had chosen a Fellowship Exchange. She said, 'My family has learned that in the face of tragedy it is important to develop a positive, forward-looking, life-affirming course of action which people can rally around'. Garda Commissioner Culligan gave his full support. Mrs McCabe indicated her enthusiastic support for the Fellowship. I asked Ben Sullivan what he thought. With tears rolling down his cheeks, said, 'Jerry would have loved it'.

The Fellowship Exchange began in September 1996, with private funding. Funds were solicited in Ireland and in the United States. In one evening in New York at the home of Brehan and Bettina Murray, over $75,000 were raised. The first Fellow from the Garda Síochána was Guard John McCabe, Jerry's son. Since 1996 over 60 exchanges have taken place, with great enthusiasm and energetic ideas for new and improved policing. An annual lecture takes place at John Jay College on the Friday before St Patrick's Day. Each year the lecture is give by an Irish-American author or journalist. The Irish government has continued to support the Exchange over the past fifteen years.

With all this as background, the then Taoiseach, Bertie Ahern, asked Ambassador Smith for some nominations for the Policing Commission. She said she would only submit one nomination—my own. The official notification came from Ambassador Seán O Huiginn and from Prime Minister Tony Blair's office. Prime Minister Blair's office asked whether, if I were to be nominated the next morning, I would accept the appointment. I said I would accept.

BEGINNING THE *REPORT*

It is not an exaggeration to say that there was nearly total scepticism that the Patten Commission would get anywhere. The old suspicions and fears of clashing cultures, not just religious differences, would swamp any chances of success. The hatred of the RUC (Royal Ulster Constabulary) on the nationalist side and the reverence for the RUC on the unionist side were implacably ingrained and buttressed regularly by new tales of horror and heroism. It was widely believed that a mutually agreed-upon policing in a divided society in a democracy was unobtainable.

To begin with, the Commission did not get off to a good start. The Secretary of State for Northern Ireland, Mo Mowlam, announced the composition of the Commission at a meeting of the Fraternal Order of Police. None of the announced names had been reviewed by the Irish government. Upon learning of the names put forward, Taoiseach Bertie Ahern flew to London to meet with Prime Minister Tony Blair. The Taoiseach presented three names, and after much discussion my nomination alone was agreed upon.

There were many versions of that meeting at 10 Downing Street. All versions agreed upon the intensity of the exchange. It seemed to boil down to the Taoiseach taking either one name or no name at all. Secretary of State Mo Mowlam had already announced the names of the Independent Commission, and to add three more names was considered unacceptable. My nomination alone was thus presented and approved by both the British and the Irish governments.

THE WORK OF THE COMMISSION

What were the factors that led to the work of the Commission and its ultimate achievements? There were so many pieces that must be acknowledged then and now. In no order of importance, but in an attempt to touch on the salient factors, I suggest the following:

- Was the population finally ready for normalcy? After 800 years of battling, should peace not be tried?
- What impact did the 40 public hearings held by the Commission have? This was a daring, never-done-before idea of going to the people to express their concerns and comments, and to hear their criticisms and recommendations. Over 1,000 people spoke to the Commission. Over 2,500 written comments, recommendations and criticisms were submitted and were read by the Commissioners. There were many other meetings with police organisations, police veterans, police widows and people blinded or maimed by police baton rounds (rubber and plastic bullets). The Commission met in church basements, municipal buildings, school gymnasiums, and with civic, fraternal and religious organisations.
- The Commissioners visited every police subdivision, some several times. (I asked Chris Patten why we were going out over and over again to the police subdivisions and police meetings. He said that, 'If we don't get the police on our side we will get nowhere'.)
- The Commission presented human-dignity policing as the best type of policing.
- There was confidentiality throughout the fifteen months of hearings, reports and meetings and there was no leak or cover-up.
- At the next-to-last meeting of the Commission, the final report was read out loud, every fact was checked, every figure questioned, every hypothesis summarised.
- At the final meeting the report was read aloud again, with the same exhaustive scrutiny. Chris Patten said, 'If we get one fact wrong it will be used as indicative of supposed errors throughout the *Report*'. No incorrect facts were identified, therefore buttressing the credibility of the Commission's recommendations.

At this remove of ten years, it is not now entirely clear what were the most determining factors in the broad acceptance of the 175 recommendations of the Patten Commission's *Report*.

POLICE REFORM

Human rights and police reform are inextricably joined. Martin Luther called for the Church to be *semper reformata*, always reforming. Unless the police subscribe to that principle, corruption, brutality and racism will flow like a tsunami. An example from my city, New York, is illustrative. This is an example of the inability of American law enforcement to police itself, in this case the New York City Police Department. With regularity, every 20 to 25 years for the last century, an independent civic commission has had to be set up to deal with the police corruption scandals in New York: 1894, the Lexow Commission; 1913, the Curran Commission; 1932, the Seabury Commission; 1949, the Dewey Commission; 1970, the Knapp Commission; 1993, the Mollen Commission.

After every scandal, there has been a wave of reform—for a time. Theodore Roosevelt became Police Commissioner after the revelations of the Lexow Commission and swept the New York City police clean of corruption. Patrick Murphy arrived in 1970, in the wake of the Knapp Commission and revelations by detectives Frank Serpico and David Durk that massive bribe-taking had infested the Police Department. Murphy proceeded to institute the most far-reaching, innovative reforms since Roosevelt's time. Periodic independent commissions are a good step forward, but a much more holistic and systematic, 'root and branches' approach must be instituted—namely, universal, higher education for all police officers.

THE POLICE COLLEGE

The most difficult of the *Patten Report* recommendations to get implemented was the Police College (Recommendation 131): 'The Northern Ireland police should have a new purpose built police college and the funding for it should be found in the next public spending round'.[4] Obviously, the 'next public spending round' came and went.

There was, of course, the issue of new money, but the delay may well be better explained by the multitude of philosophical differences of opinion on what the Police College should be and do. The big question is how should police be educated? I believe the answer is simple and unequivocal: 'like everybody else'. It would save great expense if, like every other profession, police officers received their education, their job training and their badge in that order, instead of the other way around. Separate, insulated police academies not only are not equal to the institutions of their collegiate colleagues, but maintaining the separate system is actually what prevents policing from becoming a true profession.

The still prevalent model of the police as separate and distinct from the rest of society in the way they are trained and educated can be traced back to the assumptions of Sir Robert Peel, who founded the 'Police of the Metropolis' in London in 1829. Sir Robert, whose officers came to be nicknamed 'Bobbies' after him, basically sought to hire night watchmen who could sound the hue and cry for help if crooks were at work. It was their brawn and alertness that were of value, and not much more. They were not supposed to be gentlemen; therefore, they needed no education.

Contrast this with the approach of J. Edgar Hoover, almost 100 years later (1927). Upon taking over the Federal Bureau of Investigation, Hoover required that his agents not only graduate from college but also be either lawyers or certified public accountants. Whatever else may be said about Mr Hoover and what occurred during his five-decade reign as director of the FBI, he was dead right in demanding that his agents be fully and rigorously educated in liberal arts institutions before they could even begin their FBI training. Unfortunately, the model chosen by Sir Robert Peel is still much more the norm than the standard set by Hoover and the FBI: the failure of policing to fulfil its potential is precisely because higher education is not a prerequisite for police officers.

In the 1960s President Lyndon Johnson made a great contribution to American policing by championing the Law Enforcement Education Program (LEEP), which provided the fund for more than 500,000 police officers to begin their college education. Today, throughout the US, colleges similar to John Jay College of Criminal Justice provide higher education for the thousands of young men and women who wish to further their law enforcement careers. (John Jay alone has over 14,000 students pursuing baccalaureat, masters and PhD degrees.)

How, then, will these new standards affect the future behaviour of American police? What impact will they have on historically entrenched patterns and practices of corruption, brutalising, misuse of force and other abuses of authority? I believe we can envisage the day when the mentality of professional policing will replace the rote obedience to the 'blue wall of silence', and when professional conduct and integrity will be a more powerful motivation for police officers than will the negative subculture of any particular department. This will never come about, however, if police agencies add more in-house courses targeted to emerging local problems; nor will mandating more well-intentioned but ineffective 'community relations' sessions for newly promoted officers lead to the desired result.

If that course of action actually worked, it surely would have succeeded by now. When the vast majority of the police 'profession' perform in accordance with a code of conduct and ethics such as the United Nations Universal Code of Ethics for Law Enforcement,[5] or many of the codes developed by individual police agencies and organisations, there will be a standard to supersede the 'customs', mores or accumulated bad habits of any particular jurisdiction. A reporter from the *San Juan Star* in Puerto Rico follows the same journalistic code as a reporter on the *San Jose Mercury-News* in California. A psychologist from Portland, Oregon, follows the same guidelines of ethical behaviour in the practice of therapy as does the psychologist in Portland, Maine.

Are there violations of ethical codes committed regularly by members of any profession that has such codes? Certainly there are; but they are clearly seen as such. Violations of a profession's code of ethics are viewed as a fundamental betrayal of what the profession stands for. Those who are guilty of betrayals are punished for their transgressions. The ultimate test of a profession's validity and credibility is whether it can police itself. This is one answer to 'Who polices the police?' Another answer is civilian oversight of the police. Like the military, the police report to civilian oversight of their activities.

The criteria for passing a self-policing test are: whether the profession's standards are acceptable to the public; whether those standards are the norm for conduct locally; whether, via the process of peer review, meaningful penalties, warnings, censure and dismissal occur on a regular basis, without favouritism or bias. None of these criteria can be met, and thus the test cannot be passed, without a national, and indeed international, core of similarly educated police officers who, in the course of their educational experience, have grappled with the moral and ethical issues involved in policing.

There should be two fundamental and overriding goals in the profession of policing. The first is to police the community. The second is to police the police. Unless the second goal is pursued with as much intensity and commitment as the first, the police will inevitably find that their ability to meet that first goal has been fatally undermined.

CONCLUSION: HIGHER EDUCATION FOR POLICE

Looking at the American experience, as one model, we see the original requirement for education was for the fields of divinity, medicine and law. In 1862 the so-called 'Land Grant Act' was passed by the US Congress, to assist farmers to team up with colleges and universities to create agricultural and technical (ag. and tech.) colleges. This team-work brought about great improvements in American agriculture, giving the country the moniker of the 'breadbasket of the world'. The dry-goods salesman, the banker and the auto-maker joined forces with higher education to create the great business schools. The builder, the mason and the carpenter combined with the power of the academic community to develop the leading schools of architecture and engi-neering. In the twentieth century the separate schools of education, social work and nursing became full partners in degree-granting liberal arts education within the university setting.

In contrast to these developments toward university settings for higher education, law enforcement remains one of the last major pro-fessional callings relying on insular, non-degree-granting academies that have little or no affiliation with higher education. Police educa-tion has stayed not only separate, but narrowly focused. There is no liberal arts in police academies, nor does the curriculum routinely discuss most historical, philosophical, moral and public policy issues of the day.

Given the delay in developing a new police college for Northern Ireland due to the difficult situation in regard to public funding, might this not be an appropriate time to revisit the whole issue of police education and training in Northern Ireland? This is an oppor-tunity for the police to join the rest of the professions in the enterprise of higher education.

NOTES

* Excepts from this chapter were first published in Gerald W. Lynch, 'Impact and importance of human dignity training for emerging democracies in the newly inde-pendent nations of Eastern and Central Europe', in Gerald W. Lynch (ed.), *Human dignity and the police: ethics and integrity in police work* (Springfield, Illinois: Charles C. Thomas, 1999), 98–103.

[1] Independent Commission on Policing for Northern Ireland, *A new beginning: policing in Northern Ireland* Report of the Independent Commission on Policing for Northern Ireland (Belfast: HMSO/Northern Ireland Office, 1999) (hereafter referred to as *Patten Report*). The text of the report is available at: http://cain.ulst.ac.uk/issues/police/patten/patten99.pdf.

[2] *Patten Report*, Summary of Recommendations, 107.

[3] *Patten Report*, 18.

[4] *Patten Report*, 119.

[5] This code of ethics was adopted by the General Assembly of the UN at its 106th plenary meeting on 17 December 1979. See the text available at: http://www.un.org/documents/ga/res/34/a34res169.pdf.

CHAPTER 4

THE PERSPECTIVE OF A CAREER POLICE OFFICER

Kathleen M. O'Toole

INTRODUCTION

I was surprised to receive the call from the Director of Policing and Security in the Northern Ireland Office in May of 1998, offering me the opportunity to serve on the Independent Commission on Policing for Northern Ireland (the Patten Commission). My initial thought was, 'Only those living through The Troubles could comprehend the political complexities and deep human suffering there'. I disclosed to him that I had limited understanding of the region's history and politics. He replied, 'I would consider that an advantage. We are interested in your perspective as a police practitioner'.

I brought the practical perspective of a career police officer to the Patten Commission. It is the same perspective I present in writing this chapter. The overarching theme of my paper is the importance of sound leadership and management in bringing about change in policing, particularly in Northern Ireland. I recount my first introduction to 'community policing' in Belfast. I provide an overview of the recent evolution in democratic policing on a more global scale. I highlight aspects of the Patten Commission's work and note the role that police executives have played throughout the transformation to the Police Service of Northern Ireland and since its creation. I conclude by offering observations on the current state of policing in Northern Ireland; one that differs dramatically from my first impression.

COMMUNITY POLICING—NORTH BELFAST: 1996

In early 1996, more than two years prior to the establishment of the Patten Commission, I was invited to Belfast to attend meetings and present lectures on the subject of community policing. It was my first trip there. My initial meeting was scheduled at the North Queen Street RUC Station. As a career police officer who has always preferred the beat to the boardroom, I was pleased to learn I would have an opportunity to patrol with one of the station's newly established 'community policing' teams.

Superintendent Stephen White greeted me on arrival at the station yard, which to me looked more like a maximum security prison than a neighbourhood police station (blast walls, barbed wire, bomb-proof ramps, security cameras, heavily armed personnel). He introduced me to the supervisors of his community policing team who were ready to commence their patrols. I was naïve, to say the least. I expected to venture off on a walking beat to engage cordially with residents and local business people. Instead, I was led to an awaiting armoured Land Rover. I climbed into the cramped rear compartment, where I was surrounded by police officers in full tactical gear—helmets, body armour, machine guns and semi-automatic side-arms.

As we exited the secure confines of the police car park, I peered through the narrow windows of the Land Rover and realised we were not alone. We were travelling in a convoy with military vehicles. Each time we stopped briefly at a traffic intersection, an armed soldier emerged from the roof hatch of one of the military vehicles to conduct a 360-degree security assessment. So began my introduction to 'community policing' in Northern Ireland.

On two occasions during our 90-minute tour, the convoy stopped in the heart of a housing estate and those of us in the rear of the Land Rover exited. I was told this was a new strategy devised by Superintendent White, as he recognised the need to get the police out of vehicles, on walking patrols, engaging with the communities in the New Lodge and Tiger's Bay. Given the security situation at the time, this was very risky business. The police officers divided into two groups. The first group walked cautiously down one side of the street while the other did the same on the opposite side. The vehicles stayed in close proximity to those on foot. A military helicopter flew in circles overhead, providing a watchful eye from the air. At the end of the block, the team reunited and quickly filed back into the awaiting Land Rover. But for the symbols, it was difficult for me to distinguish between loyalist and republican areas. People we encountered kept their distance. The exception was a gang of young children in a loyalist estate who suddenly appeared from behind parked cars to throw rocks at the passing Land Rover.

George Bernard Shaw's aphorism about two countries separated by a common language came to mind.[1] At that time, the term 'community policing' had very different connotations in North Belfast and Boston.

A NEW PARADIGM OF DEMOCRATIC POLICING

Later, when returning to Belfast to begin work with the Patten Commission, I recalled my 'Land Rover experience'. It became my personal reference point for the unique challenges in Northern Ireland policing that the Commission needed to address. At the same time, I knew that the Patten Commission could not confine its deliberations solely to local policing issues. To come up with a sustainable model for future policing in Northern Ireland, the Commission also had to take into account major advances in democratic policing around the world.

The Patten Commission's remit to create a 'new beginning' for policing in Northern Ireland coincided with a dramatic shift in thinking about democratic policing. As someone who began her police career two decades prior to my Patten Commission experience, I felt I was already witnessing a new policing paradigm first hand. I was passionately committed to the emerging model: a more strategic, transparent, accountable and collaborative form of community policing. It was a model that differed significantly from the policing we practised when I was a young officer patrolling the streets in downtown Boston.

When I attended the Boston Police Academy in 1979, I was taught to fight the 'war on crime' in America. We referred to ourselves as members of the 'police force' and it never occurred to us that we were actually a 'police service'. Police leaders dictated the agenda without the benefit of community consultation. We raced from one '911' radio call to the next. Our performance was measured primarily in terms of response times and the number of arrests we made. Enforcement was the priority and our vocabulary did not include the words prevention, intervention or collaboration. Unfortunately, our 'war on crime' failed. Children were dying in our streets. Violent crime statistics sky-rocketed across the United States and the quality of life in many of our city neighbourhoods seriously deteriorated.

In the mid 1980s I was introduced to a highly respected American academic, George L. Kelling. He was conducting research in Boston and actually patrolled with me in my police car from time to time. I always respected the quality of Kelling's research, as he gathered most of his data at the most valuable source—in the field, at the front line of policing. We had some spirited conversations and I learned a great deal from him. Together with James Q. Wilson, Kelling had published a thought-provoking article entitled, 'Broken windows'.[2] The piece acknowledged the breakdown of the relationship between the police and the community and the failure of reactive, rapid-response policing in the United States. It proposed a new framework that emphasised the importance of engaging in community partnerships to address low-level crime and quality of life issues. The authors theorised that such practice would prevent the emergence of more serious crime and disorder in neighbourhoods and also build community trust and confidence in the police.

The authors further developed their 'broken windows' theory in 'Thinking about crime'[3] and 'Making neighborhoods safe'.[4] Shortly thereafter, criminologist Herman Goldstein emphasised the need for more strategic, community-based policing in his book, *Problem-oriented policing*.[5] The new theories prompted much debate among academics and practitioners alike. There was growing recognition that modern police services must operate more strategically, and that success was dependent on closer engagement and trust between the police and those they serve. However, reaching definitive views on the new theories required testing in the real world.

My early mentor, William J. Bratton, appointed Commissioner of the New York Police Department in 1992, provided the most notable testing laboratory—New York City. He put his professional reputation on the line in doing so. In spite of some vocal sceptics, he embraced these new ideas and worked with his command team to develop practical strategies that would translate the theory into practice. They developed 'Compstat',[6] a system that combined technology and management tools to produce timely and reliable information on the variety of crimes and disorder that plagued the various neighbourhoods of New York City. Using real-time information, Commissioner Bratton and his team were able to provide valuable data to local police commanders who were held accountable for tackling both major crime and nuisances, such as low-level drug dealing, aggressive panhandling or begging and graffiti. As a result, the commanders were able to deploy resources strategically to intervene and prevent crime, rather than simply respond as had been the case previously. Underpinning the entire strategy was a passionate commitment to police professionalism and community involvement.

Bill Bratton won the hearts and minds of career cops and diverse New Yorkers. He transformed the NYPD in just two years. The strong theory-based management approach to policing, coupled with Bratton's charismatic and collaborative leadership style, led to a dramatic decrease in crime and an improved quality of life throughout the five boroughs of New York City. Putting like-theory into practice, many other thoughtful and dynamic police leaders began to cultivate similar successful approaches in their agencies.

A NEW MODEL FOR POLICING IN NORTHERN IRELAND

Explicit provision was made in the Belfast/Good Friday Agreement for the establishment of the Independent Commission on Policing for Northern Ireland.[7] This was recognition that the complexities of the policing issue were not amenable to resolution within the Agreement itself and that further study was required. Defined simply, the Commission's remit was to create a 'new beginning' for policing in Northern Ireland.[8]

On his appointment as chairman of the Commission, Chris Patten lost no time in launching a rigorous process of public consultation and international benchmarking in regard to policing. For me personally, the Commission's public meetings throughout Northern Ireland were immensely informative and inspiring. I was deeply moved by the countless stories of courage and loss expressed by ordinary people representing very different perspectives. People openly discussed their experiences of policing in the past, and many of them articulated their visions for future policing in a more peaceful environment.

At the same time, the Commission was eager to learn of the new developments and trends in democratic policing beyond Northern Ireland. Members visited police services and related organisations in Europe, South Africa and North America that had faced significant challenges and undergone substantial change. Hundreds of international police executives and reputable academics contributed to the process by sharing their personal knowledge and experiences. In formulating its recommendations, the Patten Commission carefully considered both the diverse community input and international expert consultation. The combined inputs laid a strong foundation for a robust framework for democratic policing. Looking back, it is striking to note that only a limited number of the Commission's recommendations related to the unique culture and challenges of

Northern Ireland. The majority of them set out precepts for democratic policing that could apply anywhere in the world.

THE ROLE OF POLICE MANAGEMENT
IN POLICE REFORM

Whether in New York, London, Dublin or Belfast, policing is a messy, complicated business. Driving reform and achieving excellence require capable leadership and strategic management. Innate talent and strong personal values are essential, but the importance of professional development of police managers cannot be understated. Many people rise through the ranks as highly competent uniformed officers and detectives, but have difficulty making the transition from supervising police operations to more strategic police management. In an ever-changing world, being the head of a major police organisation is a demanding role. The most effective police leaders are those who can effectively articulate the need for change and innovation in policing, demonstrate the ability and determination needed to bring about change and succeed in bringing on board their police officers and the community.

In recent years, more governments have recognised the need to attract and develop capable police leaders and managers. It is desirable to appoint highly talented individuals with natural leadership ability and notable police management credentials, but much more needs to be done to cultivate leadership potential in police organisations so that there is a strong pool of candidates from which to choose. I am impressed by the substantial investment by the United Kingdom in continuing professional development for police leaders. Unlike the United States, where police leadership training and development remain uneven and haphazard, the UK has instituted rigorous promotion criteria and developed structured leadership programmes for aspiring police bosses. There are also excellent learning opportunities for police managers by way of professional secondments and educational programmes outside the police environment.

In my experience, the UK approach to leadership development scores best in enabling participants to put into practice what they learn. In recent times, the Police Service of Northern Ireland has reaped the benefits of this strong commitment to professional development at the highest level. No one group or individual can be credited with the remarkable transformation that policing in Northern Ireland is experiencing. However, the successes to date would not have been achieved without the capable and determined leadership of Chief Constable Sir Ronnie Flanagan and his successor, Sir Hugh Orde. Both men are intellectually bright and possess natural leadership qualities. They each acknowledge that they benefited greatly from the variety of professional development opportunities they accepted before and during their service as Chief Constable.

Long before the Patten Commission was established, Sir Ronnie Flanagan was developing and leading a change agenda for the RUC. In 1995 it was announced that the RUC and the Police Authority would partner on a 'Fundamental Review of Policing' in light of the changing times and emerging peace. Sir Ronnie became the project's champion.[9] The Patten Commission was briefed on that review during the early weeks of its work and incorporated several aspects of it into the Commission's findings and recommendations.

In addition to developing a vision and plan for change, Sir Ronnie Flanagan demonstrated courageous leadership when the Commission's findings were published in September 1999.[10] As Chris Patten noted during the news conference that day, 'There is pain in what we are saying, but I would also argue that there is a gain which more than makes up for that'.[11] I knew for a fact there would be significant pain for the police community; not only for serving members of the RUC, but for retirees, disabled police officers and the families of those who had been killed or injured in the line of duty. I knew, too, that there would be sharp divisions in the wider community on the Commission's recommendations. The Commission had provided a roadmap for future policing in Northern Ireland, but it would require capable, visible leadership on several fronts to enable all concerned to commit to it as the way forward. For his part, as head of the RUC at this critical juncture, Sir Ronnie calmly and thoughtfully recalled the sacrifices of his members but, at the same time, acknowledged the need to move policing forward. He accepted the Commission's report in its entirety and committed to a rigorous implementation programme.

Sir Ronnie Flanagan and his team commenced work immediately on reforms that did not require changes in the law, and, in anticipation of legislation, developed a longer-term framework for dealing with the balance of the Commission's recommendations. They rightly gave priority to broadening their recruitment process to attract increased numbers from the minority community. Sir Ronnie never wavered, publicly or privately. He stuck to the *Patten Report* roadmap and was determined to transform the RUC and, subsequently, PSNI into a police service that would attract the widespread support of diverse communities in Northern Ireland. Most important, he convinced members of his service that they were on the right path and succeeded in bringing them with him. In March 2002 Sir Ronnie Flanagan retired from the PSNI to serve as Her Majesty's Inspector of Constabulary. At the time of his departure implementation of the *Patten* recommendations was well underway, but there was still much work to be done. I recall thinking: 'I do not envy Hugh Orde. Ronnie Flanagan will be a very difficult act to follow'.

Sir Ronnie Flanagan and Sir Hugh Orde are two very different personalities. Sir Ronnie is engaging and diplomatic. As a native of Northern Ireland, he has a keen understanding of the cultural and historical complexities there. Sir Hugh is a no-nonsense, blunt-talking Englishman. He enjoyed a stellar reputation as he rose through the ranks of the London Metropolitan Police. He had been exposed to policing in Northern Ireland as a senior staff member of the Stevens Inquiry team.[12] At the time of Sir Hugh's appointment as Chief Constable in Northern Ireland, many casual observers focused on the differences between the two personalities. However, Sir Hugh and Sir Ronnie share many attributes and experiences that were essential to transforming the police service in Northern Ireland. They are both smart, energetic leaders. They are strategic managers who clearly articulated their vision and constructed pragmatic action plans. They nurtured credible and committed individuals throughout the PSNI and delegated appropriate authority to them. They recognised the importance of accountability and transparency in policing. They understood that policing would never succeed without widespread community trust and worked tirelessly to build stronger community ties.

From a police management perspective, Sir Ronnie Flanagan and Sir Hugh Orde have always worked hard in maintaining strong links with the most important people in a police service—those on the front lines. They did not micro-manage front-line delivery of police service, but always kept in touch with their front-line personnel, particularly at times of tragedy and greatest challenge. Both were highly visible and readily accessible to members of the police service and the community they served. When they made mistakes, personally or professionally, they held themselves to account publicly and accepted responsibility. As with all police leaders, decisions and positions taken by Sir Ronnie and Sir Hugh on individual aspects of police business are open to scrutiny, and undoubtedly there are people who dispute lines they took, or failed to take, on various matters of policing. However, I expect that most fair-minded people would not dispute the broader leadership contributions of Ronnie Flanagan and Hugh Orde in regard to the transformation of policing in Northern Ireland. I anticipate that will also be the judgement of historians.

When acknowledged for their contributions to policing in Northern Ireland, both Sir Ronnie Flanagan and Sir Hugh Orde consistently deflect the compliments and praise the team efforts of all concerned. Certainly, it has been and continues to be a successful team effort in which the police and the community can take great pride. That said, those who have closely followed post-*Patten* developments generally agree that the ongoing change within the police service would not have progressed so effectively to date without the right leaders at the right time. Sir Ronnie Flanagan and Sir Hugh Orde: two very different personalities, but two very effective leaders and managers.

REALITY CHECK—ANTRIM ROAD: 2007

The scene at the Waterfront Hall, Belfast in February 2007 was remarkable. A capacity attendance had gathered for 'Policing the Future', a two-day conference hosted by Sir Hugh and the PSNI, with assistance from the Police Executive Research Forum (PERF). There were dozens of highly regarded police chiefs from Europe and North America. There were academics and media. Most important, there were politicians and other community leaders representing very diverse perspectives in Northern Ireland.

I was honoured to be a conference presenter, but more so welcomed the opportunity to acquaint myself, first hand, with the latest changes in policing in Northern Ireland. While I had followed the progress of implementation of the *Patten* recommendations through the reports of the Oversight Commissioner and feedback from friends on the ground, I was not expecting the consistent positive message I heard over the course of those two days: 'The Police Service of Northern Ireland is an emerging model for policing in a democratic society'. Certainly, the Patten Commission aimed to create such a model, but to hear diverse representatives of the community reiterate the positive message was remarkable. As I listened, I had flashbacks to contentious community meetings during the Patten process at which I had heard very different messages about policing in Northern

Ireland. Was it possible that cross-community public sentiment had shifted that radically in less than eight years?

In my mind, I could not satisfactorily answer that question in the confines of the Waterfront Hall. I opted to have lunch that day at Intercomm on the Antrim Road. Intercomm is a grass-roots conflict resolution and community development organisation. Its members include ex-combatants, republican and loyalist. I had met some of them during the course of my Patten Commission work and knew that I could count on them for straight answers. I suspected their message might differ from what I heard at the Waterfront Hall but, to my surprise, this was not the case. Those in attendance unanimously confirmed that there was increasing confidence in the emerging police service and cited specific examples of constructive relationships they had developed with the police in their neighbourhoods.

CONCLUSION

First-time visitors to Northern Ireland today are unlikely to appreciate the extent of change that has enabled police officers to patrol without armoured vehicles and military escorts. Each time I see PSNI personnel on horseback in Belfast City Centre or on walking/cycling beats elsewhere in Northern Ireland, I am amazed that normalised policing has progressed to such an extent in less than a decade. I will never claim to be an expert on the history of or recent developments in Northern Ireland. Only someone who has lived through The Troubles can claim that title; but I am certainly a more informed commentator now than I was during my first 'community policing' patrol in North Belfast. As I see it, professional police leaders—Sir Ronnie Flanagan and Sir Hugh Orde—have faithfully implemented the *Patten* recommendations and left a strong policing legacy to the recently appointed Chief Constable, Matt Baggott.

Stern policing challenges still remain in Northern Ireland, most notably in the form of the dissident threat and the senseless tragedies that continue to occur from time to time. There is also pressure on the PSNI to continue with the reform agenda, with an expanded commitment to community policing. As someone who came to know policing in Northern Ireland in different times, however, it is hugely significant for me that these challenges are being faced in a new policing environment. Policing in Northern Ireland has turned a very significant corner. There is no going back. With the consent and support of the overwhelming majority, Northern Ireland has realised its 'new beginning' for policing.

NOTES

[1] Quote attributed to George Bernard Shaw, *Reader's Digest* (November 1942).

[2] George L. Kelling and James Q. Wilson, 'Broken windows', *Atlantic Monthly* (Washington: Atlantic Monthly Group, March 1982).

[3] James Q. Wilson, 'Thinking about crime', *Atlantic Monthly* (Washington: Atlantic Monthly Group, September 1983).

[4] George L. Kelling and James Q. Wilson, 'Making neighborhoods safe', *Atlantic Monthly* (Washington: Atlantic Monthly Group, February 2002).

[5] Herman Goldstein, *Problem-oriented policing* (New York: McGraw-Hill, 1990).

[6] 'Compstat', first introduced by NYPD, is now the term widely used in the US for this approach to using crime statistics. For a discussion of the concept, see William F. Walsh and Gennaro F. Vito, 'Meaning of Compstat: analysis and response', *Journal of Contemporary Criminal Justice* 20 (1) (2004), 51–69.

[7] See Belfast/Good Friday Agreement, available at: http://foreignaffairs.gov.ie/u-ploads/documents/Anglo-Irish/agreement.pdf.

[8] Northern Ireland Office, *Agreement*, available at: http://www.nio.gov.uk/agree-ment.pdf (13 November 2009), see Paragraph 1 of Section 9, 'Police and justice'.

[9] See RUC/Police Authority, *Summary and key findings from the fundamental review of policing* (Belfast: RUC, 1996).

[10] Independent Commission on Policing for Northern Ireland, *A new beginning: policing in Northern Ireland* Report of the Independent Commission on Policing for Northern Ireland (usually referred to as *Patten Report*) (Belfast: HMSO/Northern Ireland Office, 1999).

[11] *Independent*, 'Patten accused of "ghastly blunder" over RUC report', available at: http://www.independent.co.uk/news/uk/home-news/patten-accused-of-ghastly-blunder-over-ruc-report-739822.html.

[12] The Stevens Enquiry was established initially in 1989 to investigate collusion in Northern Ireland between loyalist paramilitaries and the state security forces. For further information, see *Stevens Enquiry: overview and recommendations*, which was published in April 2003 and is available at: http://cain.ulst.ac.uk/issues/collusion/stevens3/stevens3summary.htm.

CHAPTER 5

BUILDING CROSS-COMMUNITY SUPPORT FOR POLICING

Maurice Hayes

INTRODUCTION

T he terms of reference for the Independent Commission on Policing for Northern Ireland contained in the Belfast/Good Friday Agreement required the members of the Commission to 'bring forward proposals for new policing structures and arrangements, including means of encouraging widespread community support for those arrangements'.[1] It might therefore be seen as something of an omission that the Commission did not respond formally in its final report to the second (admittedly subsidiary) element of the task.[2] It might be assumed that the commissioners did so, not through oversight, but in the belief that the structures proposed in response to the main element of the terms of reference would themselves produce a police service capable of winning widespread support in the community.

It has always seemed to me that the main agency for securing public support for and backing of the police in any society must be the police themselves. How they perform their functions, how—individually and as a group—police relate to the society they serve, is the main determinant of how they are regarded. This is particularly the case in a divided society. If the mark of good governance in such a society is how it treats its minority, the way in which minority groups perceive the police must be of particular significance. This is certainly the case in circumstances where to oppose the government or to seek changes in the status quo, however peacefully, is seen by those in power to be subversive, and where the police, as instruments of state power, become enforcers not only of the law, but of government policy. Seen by the majority as defenders of their rights and privileges, of order and good government, they may appear to the minority as oppressors, charged to keep them in their place and their opponents in power.

If, as Weber has it, the force needed by a state to impose its will is inversely proportionate to its legitimacy,[3] then police reform in Northern Ireland depended crucially on finding an agreed basis on which to found legitimacy. In the prolonged and often tortuous process that led to the Agreement, it soon became evident that two issues were inextricably linked in the search for a resolution of the conflict—how the area was to be governed and how it was to be policed.

THE POLICING COMMISSION

It became increasingly clear that there could not be a settlement that did not deal with policing, and that the participating parties could not deal with policing until the political structures had been settled, if at all. To escape from this Catch-22 dilemma, and in order to get an agreement within the time-frame they had set themselves, the politicians therefore set the issue of policing to one side and delegated resolution of this matter to an independent commission. It may be that they wished to depoliticise the issue by turning it into a technical problem, to be dealt with by a panel of international experts. However, policing was, and remains, a deeply political matter in any society—although the Commission, in the event, was resolutely non-partisan and non-political in its consideration of the issues.

The politicians did, however, very helpfully, define the problem and lay down the limits within which it might be solved. The Patten Commission did not start with a clean sheet, much less import or dream up solutions. The terms of reference, both in the body of the Agreement and in the Annex dealing with policing, were clear and specific. As members of the Commission were asked to bring forward proposals for a police service that could enjoy widespread support from, and be seen as an integral part of, the community as a whole; delivered in constructive and inclusive partnership with the community at all levels, and with the maximum delegation of authority and responsibility. We were exhorted to consult widely and to consider means of encouraging widespread community support for the arrangements proposed.

The Agreement itself had located the debate on policing within a new political dispensation, which would 'recognise the full and equal legitimacy and worth of the identities, senses of allegiance and ethos of all sections of the community in Northern Ireland'.[4] Within that context, the police service should be professional, effective and efficient, fair and impartial, free from partisan political control; accountable both under the law for its actions and to the community it serves; representative of the society it polices and operating within human rights norms; in constructive and inclusive partnership with the community at all levels; and with the maximum delegation of authority and responsibility. In particular, the Annex required us to consider composition, recruitment, training, culture, ethos and symbols.

The Commission felt entitled to rely on these texts, and to assume that the parties that had made the historic agreement on the future of Northern Ireland had done so in full knowledge of what they expressed. It came as something of a surprise afterwards to discover that David Trimble had intended the reference to an independent policing commission as a means of 'long-fingering' policing as an intractable issue that would torpedo the process, putting off the evil day when it would have to be confronted, hoping that this might provide time to reach a resolution more amenable to his unionist electorate.[5] Even now, it seems odd that he should appear at the same time to accept the salience of policing as an impediment to securing agreement, and deny the need to deal with it.

The reference to 'the whole community' may be regarded as more than a little utopian, as expressing a unity of purpose, a cohesion and a shared identity that society in Northern Ireland had rarely, if ever, exhibited. It is better interpreted as a euphemism for satisfying the separate parts of a divided society in a way that did not cause them to come into conflict unduly with each other. In this context, the concept of acceptance is better defined as a settlement that could be broadly regarded as tolerable by the two main groupings on either side of the fundamental line of cleavage, and identified as unionist/Protestant and Catholic/nationalist/republican. This is not to disregard other minorities, especially young people on both sides, women and the small ethnic minorities present in Northern Ireland, but it did mean that as well as the substance of policing, symbols, badges, uniforms, oaths and practices that asserted the identity of one side and were seen to be oppressive or patronising by the other had to be taken into account. Having been specifically directed to consider these issues, it is hard to accept that some of those who were party to the Agreement should regard the injunction in the terms of reference as an invitation to preserve the status quo.

There was, it transpired, an even more fundamental divergence in the interpretation of the Agreement itself. The text of the Agreement and the public utterances of the parties at the time were persuasive of the concept of a new beginning (specifically, indeed, for policing) and for (in the cliché of the time) parity of esteem for both traditions. Indeed we took some time, in discussion with the contracting parties, including the two governments, to establish that this was in fact the case. It came as some surprise, after the event, to discover that Mr Trimble's view was that nationalists had, by their acknowledgement of the constitutional position of Northern Ireland as an integral part of the United Kingdom as long as a majority so willed, accepted the legitimacy and the propriety of all the outward signs, symbols and cultural expressions of that connection.[6] This view was very far from recognising 'the full and equal legitimacy and worth of the identities, senses of allegiance and ethos of all sections of the community'. Had it been expressed in the brief to the Commission it would have torpedoed the Agreement and ended all hope of arriving at a form of policing that had any hope of being accepted, even by moderate nationalists.

It is significant that the report produced by the Commission should have invoked Bishop MacNeice and Sir Robert Peel—the one to underline the importance of a new beginning, a forward looking vision, putting aside the things that divide, the other to return to the fundamental values of British and Irish policing: protection of the citizen and the prevention of crime.[7] A police service likely to meet the requirements of the Agreement would have to meet the tests of effectiveness, impartiality, accountability, a culture of human rights and an organisational structure conducive to consultation, co-operation, delegation and subsidiarity. We also saw policing as a matter not only for the police, but as a collective responsibility, a partnership for community safety avoiding the traditional 'them' and 'us' concept of policing. A police service founded on these values would in itself be the means of securing community support of and backing for the police.

The approach of the Commission to its task may also have contributed to eventual acceptance of the recommendations in the *Patten Report* and of the policing arrangements based on them. While primarily intended as a process of public consultation and as a listening exercise for the Commissioners, rather than proselytism, the open nature of the discussions provided an element of transparency, allowed the public to contribute and express their views on past policing and their requirements for the future. It did promote a debate on policing; it engaged people in the process at all levels; and, in identifying the issues, generally prepared people for the outcome.

In addition to receiving submissions from political parties and others in response to public advertisement, the Commission held open public meetings in every District Council area—sometimes three in a day, at which more than 10,000 people attended and more than 1,000 spoke. There were 2,500 written submissions (including those made at meetings), and petitions bearing several thousand signatures. As well as that, the members of the Commission visited every police station in Northern Ireland and held discussions with rank and file officers, and from time to time with a reference group of experienced middle-rank officers. There were extensive consultations too with youth groups and NGOs and local councillors and community groups. Individual Commissioners conducted their own private canvasses and informal contacts with academics and others to supplement the focus groups, the opinion polls and the cultural audits that had been commissioned.

As a result, the Commission felt confident that the proposals had been tested for practicality and acceptability across a wide spectrum. Interestingly enough, the least helpful discussions turned out to be with criminologists. If economics is the dismal science, criminology is the hopeless one. 'Nothing works', we were told.

THE NEW POLICE SERVICE

To meet the requirement of accountability, the Commission had recommended the involvement of locally elected politicians at every level—on the District Policing Partnerships, on the Policing Board and, ultimately, after the transfer of responsibility for policing, in the Northern Ireland Assembly.

Acceptability of the new police service was to be achieved, among other things, by a progressive increase in the number of Catholic/nationalist members, from under 8% to something nearer proportionality. To achieve a critical mass, a temporary expedient of 50:50 recruitment was recommended. This was not as radical as it appeared. At school-leaving age (the target age for recruitment) there was near parity between the communities; the method had been used in the Canadian public service; and it had, incidentally, been suggested by one senior unionist spokesman.

It had become clear in our discussions with young people that young Catholics in the target age-range, particularly in those areas where relations with the police had been most abrasive, would not join a body called the Royal Ulster Constabulary (or indeed Royal anything) or one carrying the badges and symbols associated with that organisation. It was this more than anything that dictated the change of name and symbols. Without the participation of Catholics, a new policing body could not be representative, and as such would fail the test of acceptability. Interestingly, too, young people in both communities, especially in working-class areas, and especially young women, were found to have had the same experience of policing and similar attitudes to the police—and these were generally negative.

The invocation of the principle of subsidiarity in the terms of reference of the Commission found expression in the *Report* in the espousal of community policing and a structure designed to devolve budgets and authority and to empower the local community police officer. A hierarchical organisation was to be turned on its head to recognise the crucial importance of the interface between the individual police officer and the citizen and the local community

IMPLEMENTING THE *REPORT*

It is an anomaly in the role of a Commission such as ours that it ceases to exist once its report has been signed. In the language of the trade it is *functus officii*—a dead duck, in other words, with no part to play in explaining or implementing the proposals suggested in its report, or even in advocacy for its adoption. Individual members of the Policing Commission could, of course, speak as such, but we had agreed, in view of the political sensitivity of our report, and having reached consensus on each and every recommendation, to refrain from comment or debate. Sometimes, in these cases, the commission chairman remains as a symbolic authority figure, able to speak out; but Chris Patten was to leave for a post on the European Commission shortly after our *Report* was published, which largely precluded him from comment. So the *Report* was left in the hands of the Secretary of State for Northern Ireland, and without a champion from among those who knew best what had been intended, to speak on its behalf. Indeed it was for this reason that the report contained the strategically important recommendation for the appointment of an Oversight Commissioner, to ensure full and timely implementation of the recommendations.

Another Catch-22, however, was that the Oversight Commissioner could not be appointed until the legislation giving effect to the recommendation contained within the *Report* had been passed. This meant that during the consultation period and the passage of such legislation, the *Report* had no champion at all. To protect it from cherry-picking by the government or emasculation by politicians or police there was only the weight of public opinion and the political parties in Northern Ireland, three of which were opposed to the report—the Ulster Unionists and DUP because they thought it went too far, and Sinn Féin because it felt it did not go far enough.

Given the terms of reference and the context of the Agreement, we found it surprising that David Trimble should regard the *Report* as little more than a basis for discussion. It was not Holy Writ, but once published it became, for most people, the acceptable compromise on policing. If Sinn Féin rejected it as inadequate, they were certainly not going to settle for less. Thus, Trimble's efforts to turn the tide could only raise false hopes, and Secretary of State Peter Mandelson's attempts to throw him a political life-line were bound to fail.

Critical to acceptance of the *Report*'s recommendations was the attitude of RUC members, who, despite the sacrifices they were being asked to make (and indeed had made), accepted *Patten* as the way forward for policing in a peaceful society, as preserving a unitary force, as providing for accountability while avoiding political interference in operational matters and as a chance to make a new beginning. In this process, the espousal of the thrust of the *Report* by the Chief Constable, Sir Ronnie Flanagan, was critical. Without his rapport with his officers and their respect for him, and his formidable communication skills, it is highly unlikely that an orderly transition to a new order could have been effected.

As it was, the bill to implement the recommendations, when published, fell far short of the ideals of the *Report*—to the extent that it required some 150 amendments to get it back on the rails.[8] With unionist parties opposing and Sinn Féin abstaining in the parliamentary debate, it was left to the SDLP to carry the fight for the *Report*. In this context, the efforts of Seamus Mallon and Eddie McGrady should not be underestimated, any more than the courage of many of their party colleagues in later taking up places on the Policing Board and District Policing Partnerships (DPPs) in the face of intimidation, abuse, attacks on property and threats to life and limb.

Most of the public debate about the *Report*'s recommendations centred on the more political issues, such as the name of the proposed police service, the symbols and the aim of 50:50 recruitment. Of equal importance, and fundamentally destructive of the *Report*, were the attempts in the legislation to reduce the influence of the Policing Board, to shift the balance of power back towards the Secretary of State and to emasculate the DPPs. This largely reflected the culture of the Northern Ireland Office (NIO) and those who had had charge of policing under one label or another over the years. Having looked at policing through one set of lenses, they were not likely to embrace change of this order. There was also a desire to keep policing in 'safe hands', and a deep distrust of elected representatives. The proposal that councils could raise money to support local policing priorities was dismissed out of hand; and the subsequent establishment of parallel Community Safety Partnerships was clearly designed by the NIO to nobble the emerging DPPs.

Once the Policing Act became law, enshrining most of the recommendations from the *Patten Report*, the role of the Oversight Commissioner became increasingly important in setting objectives and timeframes and securing compliance. The Policing Board showed its independence and the ability to call for explanations from the Chief Constable and to hold him to account. The Police Ombudsman (an office set up following an earlier report, but endorsed by *Patten*) was an essential component of the structure of accountability.

As the structures bedded in and were seen to work, as young Catholics joined in numbers and as the PSNI showed an even-handed competence under the leadership of Chief Constable Hugh Orde, Sinn Féin was ultimately forced by community and political pressure to come on board. The final proof of acceptability was the ability of the Policing Board to agree unanimously on the selection of a new Chief Constable in succession to Sir Hugh Orde and for Sinn Féin leaders to welcome his appointment.

CONCLUSION

There is still much to be done. Peace has been achieved, but the threat from dissident republicans remains a nagging reality. Community policing has not been achieved, nor the devolution of budgets. Indeed, the rush by the PSNI to abandon the 27-district-command structure for one based on 6 or 7 district commands, in anticipation of local government reorganisation, reflects a rather old-fashioned appetite for centralised control that runs counter to the *Patten* vision. Much has been achieved. Further progress will depend, as in the past, on the police themselves and their willingness and ability to establish constructive relationships with the communities they serve and with the other social agencies.

The Commissioners believed that, ultimately, the test of acceptability of the police service in Northern Ireland could be met not by public-relations campaigns, marketing exercises or re-branding initiatives, but by the performance of the police themselves and the judgement of society. 'By their deeds ye shall know them'. As Michael Staines, first Commissioner of An Garda Síochána put it in more troubled times in 1922, in relation to the unarmed police service he was setting up in the middle of a civil war, (the police) '…will succeed, not by force of arms or numbers, but on their moral authority as servants of the people'.[9]

This must remain the ultimate test of acceptability.

NOTES

[1] The agreement was signed in Belfast on 10 April 1998; the full text of the document (hereafter cited as *Agreement*) is available at: http://foreignaffairs.gov.ie/uploads/documents/Anglo-Irish/agreement.pdf. For the terms of reference of the policing commission quoted here, see Annex A, paragraph 1.

[2] See *A new beginning: policing in Northern Ireland* Report of the Independent Commission on Policing for Northern Ireland (Belfast: HMSO/Northern Ireland Office, 1999) (hereafter cited as *Patten Report*). The full text of the report is available at: http://cain.ulst.ac.uk/issues/police/patten/patten99.pdf.

[3] Max Weber, *Economie et société* [*Economy and society*], (Paris: Tome 1, Plon, 1971).

[4] See *Agreement*, §9 'Policing and justice', paragraph 1.

[5] Dean Godson, *Himself alone: David Trimble and the ordeal of Unionism* (London: HarperCollins, 2004), 474.

[6] Godson, *Himself alone*, 472.

[7] See *Patten Report*, 3–4.

[8] Police (Northern Ireland) Act (2000); the text of this legislation is available at: http://www.opsi.gov.uk/acts/acts2000/ukpga_20000032_en_1.

[9] Garda Síochána Historical Society, engraving on entrance stone at the Garda Museum, Dublin Castle, see: http://www.esatclear.ie/~garda/garda.html.

CHAPTER 6

POLICING AND POLITICS

Peter Smith

INTRODUCTION

Shortly after the press conference at which Chris Patten had made public the report of the Independent Commission on Policing for Northern Ireland,[1] David Trimble, then 'shadow' First Minister, launched a scathing attack on the report, describing it as 'flawed and shoddy'.[2] In fact, it was to turn out that these epithets were directed at only 3 of the 175 recommendations made by the Commission: those relating to the renaming and rebadging of the Royal Ulster Constabulary to remove references to the British state, and to positive discrimination in the recruitment of Catholics in order to redress the existing religious imbalance of the RUC in favour of Protestants.

I was the only member of the Commission from a unionist background. I had joined the Ulster Unionist Party in the late 1960s, when I was a member of the staff of the Law Faculty at Queen's University, Belfast (another faculty member was David Trimble). A staunch supporter of Terence O'Neill and his reformist policies, I worked for the O'Neillite faction of the deeply divided UUP in the 1969 general election in Northern Ireland, in which O'Neill failed to attract sufficient support to sustain him in office. That year I left the Law Faculty to practice at the Bar, and not long afterwards I dropped out of politics. I became involved again in the early 1980s and rose to become an office bearer of my local Ulster Unionist branch, of the constituency association and of the Ulster Unionist Council (UUC). On election as an honorary secretary of the UUC (for some reason that I was never able to discover, there were four of them) I became entitled to a seat on the Ulster Unionist Executive and, as an office bearer, was involved in the running of the party.

Against the background of a looming deal between the British and
Irish governments that eventually became the Anglo-Irish Agreement
of 1985,[3] I and a number of others, including Frank Millar—then
general secretary of the party and later to become London editor of
the *Irish Times*, devised a scheme that would return devolved government to Northern Ireland. Our objective was a voluntary coalition
led by the Ulster Unionists and the SDLP, designed to isolate Sinn
Féin, undermine Ian Paisley's DUP and bolster the political centre.

Persuading the UUP leadership to support our scheme would
have been a very difficult achievement. Jim Molyneaux was wedded
to the Powellite integrationist doctrine that the position of Northern
Ireland in the United Kingdom could only be maintained by the
unionist MPs at Westminster insisting that Northern Ireland must be
treated in all respects in precisely the same way as the other parts of
the UK. As we later learned, it would also have been impossible to sell
our devolution plan to the SDLP. Besides his enthusiasm for what
became the Anglo-Irish Agreement, that party's leader, John Hume,
saw the future not in terms of isolating Sinn Féin but in drawing it
into the political sphere; an objective that he, with the help of others,
eventually managed to achieve.

By this time, the mid 1980s, David Trimble had also become a
member of the UUP. He was deeply distrusted by the leadership
because of his active participation in an unofficial body, the Devolution
Group, which, as its name implies, took a fundamentally different view
of what Northern Ireland's constitutional position should be from that
of the party leadership. I regarded the Anglo-Irish Agreement as a ca-
tastrophe for Unionism. It seemed to me to present an insuperable
obstacle to any kind of internal political deal in Northern Ireland,
something that I and those who thought like me considered to be an
essential prelude to the ending of violence. Further participation in
politics seemed pointless and so I left the party and turned, once again,
to concentrate on my law practice and my family.

THE POLICING COMMISSION AND
UNIONIST INTERACTIONS WITH IT

I was proved wrong by the Belfast Agreement, which emerged on Good
Friday 1998.[4] Shortly after it was reached, I and a number of colleagues
at the Bar sought to support the Ulster Unionist referendum campaign
in favour of the Agreement, particularly by raising funds. As a result,

although I had not rejoined the party, I was asked to attend daily early morning meetings at headquarters (colloquially called 'prayers'). At one of these meetings I was taken aside by Ken Maginnis, then UUP MP for Fermanagh and South Tyrone and the party spokesman on policing. I had got to know Ken well during my time as a party officer. He asked if I would be interested in serving on the Independent Commission on Policing for Northern Ireland, one of the elements in the Belfast Agreement, which the Ulster Unionists had, of course, endorsed. Not long afterwards I was asked to meet a senior civil servant who repeated the invitation. I re-read the portion of the Belfast Agreement dealing with policing, including the terms of reference for the Independent Commission, and discussed the risks with my wife. I decided to accept. Whilst personal security was a consideration, I felt that the resolution of the policing problem was essential to securing peace and that it was incumbent on me to play my part.

Throughout the period between the appointment of the Commission and the publication of its report fifteen months later I assumed that, because the RUC and policing generally were very important and sensitive issues for unionists, I would be approached by unionist politicians who would seek to impress on me the vital interests of their community. Surely they would have a view as to how the Commissioners' terms of reference might be interpreted in a way that, if not protecting them, at least catered for those interests? It became apparent at an early stage, however, that, for reasons I could not discern, unionist politicians were not interested in talking to me. Not long after my appointment, a colleague at the Bar arranged for me to meet a number of senior Ulster Unionist politicians (not including Ken Maginnis or David Trimble) over dinner. The intention was to provide them with an informal opportunity to brief me about their concerns. To my surprise, they spent the entire evening talking about everything but policing. Every time I or my colleague tried to bring the conversation round to policing, our fellow diners moved to other topics as swiftly as they could.

This pattern persisted throughout the remainder of the period it took us to produce our report. Unionist politicians made submissions to the Commission that, for the most part, did not deal with the Commissioners' terms of reference (an honourable exception was that furnished by Ken Maginnis) but with what they perceived were their constituents' concerns—particularly that the symbolic aspects of the RUC be left untouched and that there should be no discrimination in future recruitment. David Trimble's submission was a very per-functory list of 'dos' and 'don'ts'. Apart from a couple of coincidental meetings with Ken Maginnis and a request from a representative of the Orange Order to meet a delegation from that body (which I accepted but which was not pursued), no one on the unionist side, including David Trimble, sought to discuss any aspect of the Commission's work with me.

REACTION TO THE *PATTEN REPORT*

It was against this background that, initially, I was shocked and puzzled by Trimble's 'flawed and shoddy' outburst. It seemed to me to be inevitable that if the objectives set out in the Commission's terms of reference were to be achieved, the British connotations of the name and badge of the RUC would have to go—if not, how could people from the nationalist/republican tradition, making up approximately 40 percent of the population of Northern Ireland, be expected to join, or even support, the police service? To my mind the logic of the terms of reference was inescapable. What else was meant by the requirement that:

> ...[the Commission's proposals] should be designed to ensure that policing arrangements, including composi-tion, recruitment, training, culture, ethos and symbols, are such that in a new approach Northern Ireland has a police service that can enjoy widespread support from, and is seen as an integral part of, the community as a whole?[5]

I also imagined that Trimble, and many if not all of his party col-leagues, must have understood this too. Surely they must have read the words they had signed up to on Good Friday in 1998? Significantly, none of the submissions to the Policing Commission made by union-ists contained any indication as to how the objectives inherent in the terms of reference could have been met without these crucial changes.

Initially there was a firestorm of unionist protest, directed more at Trimble and the Ulster Unionists than at the Commission. When he became Secretary of State, Peter Mandelson made a ham-fisted attempt to 'save Trimble' by attempting to water down the *Patten Report* recommendations that were causing embarrassment to Trimble and his party. This served only to threaten the vitally important support of the SDLP for the new policing arrangements, and eventually Mandelson's efforts had to be abandoned. It turned out, however, that the firestorm was not quite what it seemed. It did not signal that unionist politicians or the unionist community were prepared to boycott the re-named police service or the accountability structures (we had proposed that the new Policing Board and what became the District Policing Partnerships should all include elected politicians). When the Policing Board was finally constituted, two years after we had reported, not only Trimble's Ulster Unionists but also the DUP took their seats, together with the SDLP. And not long afterwards the Board, with the support of the representatives of all three parties, reached unanimous agreement on the new badge for the Police Service of Northern Ireland. In spite of the rhetoric, what had to be done in order to resolve the policing problem was done.

WHY DID TRIMBLE REACT AS HE DID?

So, what of Trimble's assertion that the report was 'flawed and shoddy'? In his book Dean Godson asserts that Trimble's

> failure to find out anything about Peter Smith's views on policing when he approved the former UUC Honorary Secretary's appointment to the Patten Commission turned out to be disastrous for him.[6]

I believe this assertion to be profoundly mistaken. In order to secure the position of First Minister of Northern Ireland, sitting voluntarily in an Executive with Sinn Féin, Trimble had to achieve two things: the Provisional IRA had to decommission its weapons and Sinn Féin had to support the police. Without the latter, the achievement of the former, important though it would be, would not be enough. Trimble could not collaborate in government with a party that did not support the police: his electorate simply would not have worn it.

So, how was republican support for policing to be achieved? Trimble and his Ulster Unionists could not be seen to make the necessary concessions to Republicanism. The task of changing the RUC was therefore to be handed over to an independent commission, and this was duly provided for in the Belfast Agreement. For Trimble, the terms of reference of the Policing Commission had to require that the changes necessary to enable Sinn Féin to back the police would be made. These had to include changing the name and the badge of the police service: no one could seriously believe that Sinn Féin could ever be induced to support the 'Royal Ulster Constabulary' with its harp and crown badge symbolising, even to unionists, the British presence in Ireland. The terms of reference for the Commission did require that these changes be made. However, Trimble had one further problem. The Commission had to include someone from a unionist background. If that person, once appointed, balked at endorsing the necessary recommendations on changing the name and badge of the police by producing a minority report or, even worse, by resigning, then neither Trimble nor his party could ever accept the necessary changes.

So, Trimble needed a unionist who would do what had to be done. As he accepted, when interviewed by Frank Millar: 'I knew Peter, I had known him for a long time, knew of his somewhat liberal disposition'.[7] He also knew that I was a lawyer and, being a lawyer himself, must have known that I would interpret the terms of reference in the same way that he interpreted them; that if I accepted appointment to the Policing Commission I would deliver on those terms of reference.

That Trimble needed the policing issue sorted tends to be confirmed by other passages in Millar's book. Millar himself comments that:

> ...for all his public fury...over Patten, his answers reinforce my suspicion that he actually never felt about the RUC issue in quite the same way as the unionist rank and file; that, though he was undoubtedly conscious of the political difficulty it spelt for him, he was looking to what Tony Blair likes to call 'the big picture' and reasoning that this was pain necessary to the process of political change.[8]

I think that this explains why Trimble never made any contact with me. Had he done so and acknowledged to me that he understood what I had to do, he risked this becoming public knowledge after the Commission report had been published, and consequently risked being vilified by his unionist political opponents for selling the pass. On the other hand, of course, he could not risk attempting, even for form's sake and in the mildest possible terms, to persuade me somehow to induce the Commission to fudge the name and badge issue in case our recommendations failed to meet Sinn Féin's minimum requirements. If we had done so, Trimble would have eventually fallen at the policing hurdle even if he did get Provisional IRA decommissioning.

Whether the silence of Trimble's colleagues can be explained in the same way I find difficult to judge. Some must have made the same analysis. Others may have believed that with my past involvement with the Ulster Unionist Party I would naturally resist the name and badge changes. Yet others may have had concerns but either thought that they had done enough in their submissions or felt inhibited when it came to bearding someone in my position.

Millar's book also throws light on why Ken Maginnis did not attempt to make contact with me. Millar responds to a suggestion from Trimble that Maginnis would concede that he should have been in close contact with me by pointing out that it was his understanding that Maginnis would not concede anything of the sort: that Maginnis did not attempt to speak to me as he felt that it might not have been appropriate to approach someone who was an independent and explicitly non-party member of an international commission.[9] At this point in the narrative Trimble, perhaps significantly, switches his attack to Chris Patten. If I am right, the last thing that Trimble would have wanted would have been someone I respected like Maginnis trying to persuade me not to do what Trimble believed had to be done.

I am now convinced that Trimble's angry outburst on 9 September 1999 was a smokescreen. It may be that he subsequently wavered in the face of the ferocity of unionist resentment at the name and badge proposals, but I believe that he was immensely relieved that the controversy eventually died down after the establishment of the Policing Board. At that stage it would have been apparent to him that the report of the Commission had succeeded in clearing the way for the endorsement of policing by Sinn Féin, something that eventually happened when that party joined the Policing Board in 2007 without one word of the *Patten Report* or its recommendations having been altered.

By that stage, however, Trimble was already politically dead; his career as First Minister having foundered not on the issue of policing, but on the failure of the Provisional IRA to decommission its weapons in time to save him. That gift it eventually bestowed on Ian Paisley and the DUP.

TRIMBLE'S LEGACY

It would be wrong for me to conclude without paying tribute to David Trimble's role in the achievement of agreed policing in Northern Ireland. Irrespective of precisely why Trimble was prepared to take the political risks involved, the Patten Commission would never have come into existence had Trimble not been prepared to endorse its creation. More importantly, the Commission would never have been in a position to make the crucial recommendations it did had Trimble not persuaded his party to support the Belfast Agreement which, of course, included the terms of reference for the creation of the Commission.

POSTSCRIPT

A matter of days after our *Report* was published I received a letter from my local Ulster Unionist branch, of which I had once been chairman. In spite of the fact that I had not been a member of the party for over ten years, the letter announced my expulsion on the grounds of my involvement in insulting the RUC. I replied to the letter, saying that I was surprised that I had been condemned without an opportunity to defend myself, describing this as 'a travesty of British justice'. The response was a summons to the next branch meeting, which I refused to attend on the grounds that the members had already made up their minds. I did, however, invite the branch to send two office bearers to meet me at my home.

This invitation was accepted, and one evening two men came to my house. I explained why I had joined with my colleagues on the Commission in making the recommendations on policing that unionists found so hurtful. The older of the two, after some initial challenges, lapsed into the frequent repetition of the observation that 'We should have hanged the lot of them long ago'. The younger, a research student at Queen's University who turned out to be the son of Michael McGimpsey, who later became an Ulster Unionist minister in the Northern Ireland Executive, listened intently and asked a number of very perceptive questions.

We parted on cordial terms. I never heard from the branch again.

NOTES

[1] See Independent Commission on Policing for Northern Ireland, *A new beginning: policing in Northern Ireland* Report of the Independent Commission on Policing for Northern Ireland (Belfast: HMSO/Northern Ireland Office, 1999) (hereafter cited as *Patten Report*).

[2] *Irish Times*, 10 September 1999; repeated in the House of Commons, see Hansard debates, col. 1210, 6 April 2000.

[3] Information on this agreement can be found on the CAIN website at: http://cain.ulst.ac.uk/events/aia/index.html; and the text of the agreement is available at: http://www.dfa.ie/uploads/documents/anglo-irish%20agreement%201985.pdf.

[4] Belfast/Good Friday Agreement; the text of the agreement is available at: http://foreignaffairs.gov.ie/uploads/documents/Anglo-Irish/agreement.pdf (hereafter cited as *Agreement*).

[5] *Agreement*, 32.

[6] Dean Godson, *Himself alone—David Trimble and the ordeal of Unionism* (London: HarperCollins, 2004), 823.

[7] Frank Millar, *David Trimble: the price of peace* (Dublin: Liffey Press, 2004), 91.

[8] Millar, *David Trimble*, 97.

[9] Millar, *David Trimble*, 92.

Part II

Implementing the transformation of policing

CHAPTER 7

THE ROLE OF THE
OVERSIGHT COMMISSIONER

Tom Constantine

INTRODUCTION

There is always a temptation, when explaining or writing about one's own performance in public office, to be a little too complimentary. I am proud, justifiably I hope, of the accomplishments of the Oversight Commissioner's team in Northern Ireland. However, in all reality, there have been others who made even more significant contributions to the overall success of the police reform programs in Northern Ireland.

In my opinion, first among the equals are the citizens of Northern Ireland. It was their courage, wisdom and foresight that created the environment that led to the Good Friday Agreement and, as a result, to the report of the Independent Commission on Policing for Northern Ireland.[1] These same citizens turned out by the tens of thousands to what we in the United States refer to as 'Town Hall' meetings throughout Northern Ireland. Perhaps more impressive than this turnout, was the demonstration of the courage of those who attended the meetings. Many of these participants were the surviving families of police officers killed in the line of duty, or the children of people who died in conflict with the police or the army. Amazingly and commendably, despite sorrows and sometimes bitterness, they were willing to work together toward a safer place for their children or grandchildren. In my opinion, the real heroes underlying police reform are the citizens of Northern Ireland.

The second most important ingredient that made police reform possible has been the work of Christopher Patten and the talented individuals who were willing to serve on the Independent Commission. They dedicated their time and expertise in an extraordinarily demanding schedule of meetings, interviews and the *Report* review. This commitment by the Commission is evidenced by the outstanding product widely referred to as the *Patten Report*. In the course of a 45-year career in police work, I have seen hundreds of commissions and subsequent reports. However, only two such reports stand out: the *Patten Report* and the 1967 President's Commission report in the United States, on crime in a free society. That report, titled 'The Challenge of Crime in a Free Society', was issued by the President's Commission on Law Enforcement and Administration of Justice.[2] This study was prepared at a time when violent crime in the United States was increasing dramatically, and violent riots were occurring in many of the major urban areas and college campuses. The study encompassed every facet of the criminal justice system, from policing to corrections, and the Commission responsible for it was made up of leading individuals from academia, government and the community. I always believed it was the Gold Standard of such reports, and the *Patten Report* was of equivalent quality.

Throughout our efforts in Northern Ireland, the Oversight Commissioner's team relied on the *Patten Report* to ensure we were being true to the objectives on policing reform that were agreed upon. When I assumed the responsibility of Oversight Commissioner, Christopher Patten and many of the members of his Independent Commission gave freely of their time to explain in detail the reasoning behind their decisions. Furthermore, two members of the Commission, Dr Maurice Hayes and Mr Peter Smith, continually assisted me during my many visits to Northern Ireland, and I am forever grateful.

At times when we discuss the success of police reform in Northern Ireland, the efforts of the former Royal Ulster Constabulary and the present Police Service of Northern Ireland are overlooked. Nowhere in the modern history of policing in a democratic society has a reform program of such magnitude and scope been attempted. When all of the reports had been written and all the oversight implemented, it was always the police that were required to carry out the recommendations. The changes would have been difficult enough in any environment, but the emotional impact of changing names, symbols and uniforms can never be underestimated. The Oversight Commissioner's team found the senior leadership team, mid-level supervisors and front-line officers to be very intelligent, tactically skilled and, despite the emotional impact, committed to moving forward in the hope of securing a safer society for all of Northern Ireland.

SELECTION OF AN OVERSIGHT COMMISSIONER

The selection of the appropriate person to lead any office such as that of the Oversight Commissioner is critical to the eventual success of the oversight process. It is possible that individuals from other professions who possess the appropriate values of integrity, impartiality and fairness could be candidates. Often in the United States we look to the judiciary to hold such posts. However, it is my firmly held belief that the candidate for the oversight responsibilities in Northern Ireland required policing experience, preferably at the chief executive level. The reason for this is that the person appointed needed to have the confidence of the public and, simultaneously, credibility with the policing community. I believe it was my background in this regard that caused the government to select me as the first Oversight Commissioner in Northern Ireland. My life experience, which was set out in the first of our office's reports, can be summarised briefly.

I was a career law enforcement official with 40 years of public service, starting as a uniform trooper with the New York State Police; this is the largest state police agency in the United States, with a total complement of 5,000 sworn officers. In 1986, after serving in every available uniform and plain-clothes rank, I was chosen by Governor of New York Mario Cuomo as the Superintendent of the New York State Police, the first person in 30 years to rise from the ranks to that position. In 1994 I was appointed by President Bill Clinton to direct the 9,000-member U.S. Drug Enforcement Administration. I served in that post for five years. Much of my police career involved the investigation of organised crime and narcotics enforcement, but also managerial issues of police training, accreditation and internal affairs. In addition, I have served on the boards of the International Association of Chiefs of Police (IACP), the Division of State and Provincial Police of the IACP, and have been recognised as an international expert on law enforcement issues.

In March 2000 representatives of the British Embassy in Washington, D.C. made contact to inquire if I would be interested in the position of overseeing police reform in Northern Ireland. Prior to agreeing, it was important that I be allowed to review the *Patten Report* in depth. Although I, like many, followed the events leading to the signing of the Good Friday Agreement[3] with a sense of admiration, it was essential to understand exactly what this new concept of the Oversight Commissioner entailed.

As the process of my selection progressed through various stages, the idea that I could be some part of the peace process in Northern Ireland was an important motivator. The only precondition that I had for acceptance was a commitment from the government that it was philosophically and financially committed to implementing the *Patten* recommendations and that the Oversight Commissioner would have full independence from political influence. The government representatives reassured me on both counts. On 29 May 2000 the then Secretary of State for Northern Ireland, Peter Mandelson, announced my appointment as Oversight Commissioner for Policing Reform in Northern Ireland. This new position as envisioned by the Patten Commission and the announcement of the individual selected for the position attracted significant attention from media outlets in Ireland, Northern Ireland, the rest of the United Kingdom and the United States.

In the initial stages of assuming the post of Oversight Commissioner, it was extremely important to establish standards of integrity, fairness and professionalism for the office. The public and media attention directed at this new position of overseeing the *Patten* recommendations was far beyond anything that I had ever witnessed in a lengthy career in law enforcement. It was obvious from the very beginning that the efforts of the Oversight Commissioner and the subsequent Oversight Reports would be held to intense scrutiny and high standards by a public with a history of divided opinion on policing.

Unfortunately, immediately following the announcement by Mr Mandelson of the appointment of the new Oversight Commissioner, a major controversy arose. It had been understood prior to my accepting the appointment that the government was firmly committed to implementing the recommendations of the *Patten Report* and that the Oversight Commissioner would have full independence. However, subsequent to accepting the offer and virtually concurrent with the announcement of the appointment, the Northern Ireland Office released the May 2000 Implementation Plan.[4] On an initial reading, this 93-page plan appeared to fulfil the *Patten* recommendations. However, a closer reading and analysis by the interested parties in Northern Ireland led to claims that a number of the recommendations had been altered or diluted in such a way that the original objectives of the recommendations were not being fulfilled.

If the Office of the Oversight Commissioner were to gain the confidence of the citizens of Northern Ireland, this issue had to be addressed. As this oversight position was such a new and different concept, there was no historical reservoir of public confidence. The critics of the May 2000 Implementation Plan immediately focused, for example, on the lack of statutory independence of the Oversight Commissioner. The problem was exacerbated by the fact that I, as the first Oversight Commissioner, was from the United States and largely unknown to the citizens of Northern Ireland. Thankfully, major international law enforcement organisations and elected representatives such as U.S. Congressman Ben Gilman, who had been a major supporter of the peace process in Northern Ireland, rallied to my side and attested to my qualifications. However, more was needed if the reputation and values of this newly created institution were to survive. Due to the Implementation Plan issue, the question often presented to me was had I been appointed to oversee the Patten Plan or the Mandelson Plan? My response to this question was that I had accepted the position of Oversight Commissioner in order to evaluate the recommendations as they were formulated by the Independent Commission on Policing for Northern Ireland.

This issue of independence, which should form the very foundation of the credibility of the Office of the Oversight Commissioner, could have had a seriously negative impact on the entire process if not resolved: it would not have been feasible to await a lengthy statutory resolution, therefore it was necessary to articulate a personal philosophy of independence. The media and numerous interest groups were advised that it was my policy that the independence of the office was to be based on a belief that if influence, political or otherwise, were directed at the Office of the Oversight Commissioner, I would with regret resign from the position and publicly explain the reason for my resignation. This policy was reported in a number of venues and the issue of independence never had to be raised again. It is important to note that at no time during my tenure as Oversight Commissioner did anyone attempt to in any way influence the independence of the Office.

The remainder of my first visit to Northern Ireland was less eventful but interesting. The long days and nights were filled with detailed briefings by key government officials. It was important to learn as much as possible about the culture that I would be working in for the next three to four years. The government presenters were obviously very intelligent and provided information in an objective and professional manner without any sense of bias. The key government contact during this initial stage of establishing the Office of Oversight Commissioner was Ronnie Armour, a most impressive career civil servant. Additional meetings were conducted with the leaders of the political parties in Northern Ireland. Understandably, political leadership was courteous but reserved, as judgement was to be made based on the parties' observation of the efforts and results of the Office of Oversight Commissioner. However, it was important to meet with these individuals on a face-to-face basis so the principles and values of the Oversight Commissioner could be delivered without filters.

A much more relaxed but equally important relationship was initiated with the leading clerics from the major religious denominations (Catholic, Church of Ireland, Methodist and Presbyterian). These clergy were a source of great strength during this initial period of establishing the Office of Oversight Commissioner. These relationships continued throughout my tenure. I have many fond memories of the wisdom, guidance and strength that were gained from them. Based on this experience, it is my opinion that anyone embarking on an oversight process where there is a history of conflict incorporate the sincere and thoughtful wisdom that the clergy can provide.

RECRUITING A TEAM

Ordinarily when a new institution like the Office of Oversight Commissioner is created, the most important management task is developing the necessary support staff. The scope and magnitude of the *Patten* recommendations were such that the existing government institutions either had assigned or were planning to assign large numbers of personnel to manage this major change project. To monitor the efforts of the hundreds of people working on implementation, it was my belief that my office would require commensurate support staff. In the initial stage the entire complement of staff consisted of one Oversight Commissioner and only one young civil servant, Mr Dean Coates, who, although very competent, was not sufficient by himself to fulfil our responsibility.

There was some initial reluctance on the part of the Northern Ireland Office to commit the financial support to staffing. However, because the failure of the Office of Oversight Commissioner to perform as was envisioned by the Patten Commission would incur such high costs, it was essential to convince the Northern Ireland Office of the need for proper staffing. I argued that it was imperative that the oversight process had the credibility necessary for the citizens of Northern Ireland to believe change was actually taking place. This could not be done on the cheap. Even though I had, in my lengthy policing career, faced many difficult issues, I had never been in a position where a failure on my part could cause damage to a long-sought peace process. To its credit, the Northern Ireland Office understood the reasoning for adequate staffing and was supportive throughout the process.

The second stage of establishing the Office of Oversight Commissioner was to recruit individuals who had the essential background and values to serve on the oversight team. The most important of these qualities was a demonstrated history of integrity, fairness and professionalism. Because the attention to the oversight process was so intense, the background of each of us serving would be subject to close examination, and any hint of impropriety would seriously damage the confidence in this new office. Noah Webster, one of the founders of the United States, may have put it best when he said, 'the virtue of men is of much more consequence to society than their abilities'. The following are the individuals selected to serve on the Oversight team, and their backgrounds at the time of appointment:

• DAVID BAYLEY, PHD

A distinguished professor in the School of Criminal Justice, University at Albany, State University of New York, Bayley is a specialist in international criminal justice and has a particular interest in policing. He has conducted extensive research in India, Japan, Australia, Canada, Britain, Singapore and the United States. His work is focused on strategies of policing, the evaluation of police organisations, organisational reform, accountability and the tactics of patrol officers in discretionary law enforcement situations. Professor Bayley is an internationally recognised expert in police accountability and human rights.

• ROY J. BERLINQUETTE

A 36-year veteran of the Royal Canadian Mounted Police (RCMP), Mr Berlinquette retired as the Deputy Commissioner of the 6,000 member force for the RCMP responsible for policing the north-west region of Canada. He also served as Commanding Officer of 'J' Division (New Brunswick) and Officer in Charge of RCMP

Protective Operations in Ontario. He was a key participant in the change strategy of the RCMP and has specific expertise in the area of police training.

• AL HUTCHINSON, CHIEF OF STAFF TO THE OVERSIGHT COMMISSIONER

Mr Hutchinson served for 34 years with the RCMP, retiring as an Assistant Commissioner. He began his career as a constable, and after a succession of promotions to increasingly responsible positions, he was appointed as the Commanding Officer of 'O' Division (Ontario). In this command, he supervised the 1,200 members of the RCMP responsible for activities in Canada's largest province. Mr Hutchinson has extensive experience in general duty policing, economic crime, drug enforcement, human resources and change management.

• G.H. (GIL) KLEINKNECHT

Mr Kleinknecht is a career law enforcement official, who for the past 35 years served in a number of executive positions at the municipal, county and federal level. From 1973 to 1990 he was the Chief of the St Louis County, Missouri, Police Department. He then went on to become the Associate Commissioner for Enforcement of the United States Immigration and Naturalization Service, responsible for the activities of over 9,000 agents and officers. From 1997 to 2000 he served as the Assistant Director of the United States Marshal Service in Washington, D.C. He was a key member of the Board of Officers of the IACP from 1988 to 1995. He also directed the first accreditation of a federal law enforcement agency (US Marshals Service) by the Commission on Accreditation for Law Enforcement Agencies (CALEA) and continues as a professional assessor for that organisation.

• ROBERT LUNNEY

Mr Lunney is a career law enforcement official who has been a consultant on public safety and policing, most lately associated with the Police Executive Research Forum in Washington, D.C. He served with the RCMP, Chief of Police in Edmonton and Chief of the Peel Regional Police in Ontario. He is a Past President of the Canadian Association of Chiefs of Police and a former member of the Executive Committee of the IACP. Mr Lunney was involved in the accreditation of seven Canadian police agencies for the CALEA and has extensive experience as an innovator and practitioner of Community Oriented Policing.

• CHARLES D. REYNOLDS

Chief Reynolds is a 40-year career veteran in law enforcement who is currently a police management consultant. He served as a police chief in several communities in New England. He was chosen by the 18,000 law enforcement executives of the IACP to be their President. He is former Commissioner of the CALEA. In addition, Chief Reynolds currently serves as an independent auditor for the United Sates Department of Justice, reviewing, assessing and critiquing police performance in states or municipalities that have been found to have a pattern or practice of civil rights problems.

• ROBERT WARSHAW

Mr Warshaw is the former chief of police in Rochester, New York, and Statesville, North Carolina. He has also held senior executive positions in DeKalb County, Georgia and Maine, Florida. He has served on several assignments, monitoring court-ordered reviews of police organisations in the United States.

• MARK REBER

Mr Reber was employed by the RCMP in 1993 in the Internal Affairs Branch working on police discipline, public complaints and conflict of interest issues. He managed comprehensive organisational change, strategic planning and police labour relations. He was responsible for policy planning and the administrative responsibilities of the Office of Oversight Commissioner.

Each of these experts was designated as having primary responsibility for a segment of the proposed reforms, congruent with their specialised expertise and also in handling additional secondary responsibilities for other areas.

Although the members of the oversight team were selected solely on the basis of their experience and values, the fact that the team was divided almost equally between representatives of Canada and the United States proved to be an asset. It was my concern that if the oversight team was composed solely of experts from the United States, our efforts and reporting might have been viewed as limited in scope. Our experience in incorporating the talents of policing experts from Canada added significantly to the value of our reports.

From the very beginning, it was impressed on the team that this project would be like no other on which they had ever served. We were fully aware of the sacrifices and courage on the part of the citizens of Northern Ireland in reaching a peace agreement. It was also our collective belief that the Independent Commission on Policing had produced an outstanding blueprint for policing in Northern Ireland. As a result, we viewed it as our responsibility to ensure that all aspects of the *Patten Report* were implemented, and were seen to be implemented.

The members of the oversight team took this charge very seriously and made rigorous evaluations of all of the institutions within Northern Ireland that had the responsibility for implementing change in the policing system. As the oversight process continued, the team gained great respect for the efforts of the police and other affected agencies. At the same time, we took great pains to maintain an official and objective relationship with those who we were evaluating, to ensure that our efforts were seen to be independent and credible.

DEVELOPING STANDARDS

After the oversight team was recruited and vetted, the next stage was establishing a process to measure the implementation of the *Patten* recommendations. As previously mentioned, the report of the Independent Commission was recognised for the outstanding quality of its research and its excellent analysis of the issues. However, as a policy report, it had certain limitations for the oversight process. The *Patten Report* did not include any specific measures to monitor progress in relation to its 175 recommendations.

Because the Implementation Plan of May 2000 had been called into question, the entire evaluation process had been stalled for months as the issues were being resolved in a lengthy legislative process. It was impossible to establish a monitoring process until the issues were resolved by statute. As Oversight Commissioner I felt that it was important for all the institutions involved in the massive and dramatic change in policing strategy in Northern Ireland to understand fully what standards would be used in the oversight process. It was equally important that the community be made aware of the rigorous method that would be utilised to ensure that the *Patten* recommendations would be implemented comprehensively and faithfully.

The newly created oversight team conducted extensive research, beginning with a detailed review of all of the literature pertaining to policing in Northern Ireland. In addition, the team reviewed the latest information about trends on best policing practices being utilised throughout the world, with a special emphasis on programs in Canada, Europe and the United States. In developing a system to measure the implementation of the *Patten* recommendations, I relied on the talent and experience of the individuals selected to serve on our team: because they had served in police departments at every level, they were keenly aware of best practices. Furthermore, they had experiences acting as monitors for police accreditation programs in Canada and the United States.

Each of the team members was assigned a specific subject area of the *Patten Report*. It was the responsibility of that individual to develop a set of performance indicators for the recommendation in his area of responsibility. The team member originally assigned to develop the performance indicators for a specific recommendation was then required to forward his product to a second member of the team for a peer review. This resulted in a number of additions and deletions, further refining the indicators. The team of consultants then met in the United States for a peer-group analysis of each of the recommendations and a detailed review of the related performance indicators. As a result of this meeting, each of the team members made a number of adjustments to his list of performance indicators. At the conclusion of this peer-group review, a revised list of measures of performance was established.[5]

In February 2001 the team and I conducted an 11-day site visit to Northern Ireland. The purpose of this trip was to discuss in detail the nature of the performance indicators with those individuals, agencies and institutions that were to be subject to the monitoring process by the Oversight Commissioner. In developing the list of performance indicators, the Oversight Commissioner incorporated, where appropriate, the comments and suggestions from all interested parties. Based on the results of this February 2001 visit, a comprehensive report identifying 772 performance indicators was finalised. This report was held in abeyance until September 2001, pending the outcome of the multi-party negotiation process and the issuance of an official and current Implementation Plan.

In the process of discussing the draft performance indicators with affected parties, we stressed three points about their application. First, performance indicators should not be used by agencies as the final measure of progress in achieving the reforms proposed in the *Patten* recommendations and subsequent legislation. The indicators were only an instrument to commence the evaluation of progress and provide an outline of the 'best practices' that were expected to be adopted. Responsibility and accountability for complete and comprehensive fulfilment of the reform proposals was vested with the affected institutions. Second, I took the position, as Oversight Commissioner, that it would be inappropriate to speculate on just how much financial support would be required for the change process to be implemented. However, I also stated unequivocally that lack of appropriate financial support could adversely affect policing reform as much as lack of political will or bureaucratic resistance to change. The Oversight Commissioner would therefore examine any contributing impact on policing reform where financial support was an issue. Third, because we based our performance indicators on current best policing practices, we constantly monitored changes and trends in this area and made adjustments as necessary.

In its second report, in September 2001, the Office of the Oversight Commissioner disseminated the 772 performance indicators developed for *Patten*'s 175 recommendations.[6] We now had an effective method of base-lining each of the *Patten* recommendations that had been vetted and discussed publicly. This demonstrated to everyone in Northern Ireland that an international team of policing experts had developed a model of best policing practices to measure reform progress over time. We hoped that through media disclosure, the public would have confidence that the Oversight Commissioner and his team took their responsibility seriously and that the oversight process would be rigorous and demanding. The table was now set for the actual on-site evaluations.

THE PROCESS OF EVALUATION

The process of evaluation consisted of three stages. All of these stages were predicated on the performance indicators having already been provided to the various agencies that were required to implement the changes and report on their progress. The consulting team also established the reporting protocols and time frames for reporting.

The first stage was to determine whether the appropriate administrative steps had been taken to implement the *Patten* recommendations.
In other words, the team determined whether the police or others were
in administrative compliance with what they were required to do. The
oversight team requested that the agencies involved in the change
process provide all available documents (reports, policy changes, annual
revisions and orders) that were specific to the implementation of the
Patten recommendation in question. The requests for this information
were presented directly to the designated senior representative of each
agency. Any misunderstanding or concern over the requests was to be
addressed by having the chief executive of the agency communicating
those concerns directly to the Oversight Commissioner.

Second, members of the Oversight Commission conducted personal interviews with the senior officers or teams involved in the
respective change issue. If required, meetings were conducted with the
principals implementing the change. This step was intended to follow
up on the results developed in the document review stage. Third, the
members of the Oversight Team conducted site visits to policing facilities throughout Northern Ireland. Although this level of review was
labour intensive, it was essential to ensure that change was actually
taking place. This element of the review process included observations
of performance indicators and interviews of line employees.

At the conclusion of each stage of the evaluation process, the
results were analysed by the entire oversight team. We prepared pre-
liminary reports evaluating the progress of the respective agencies on
each recommendation, as demonstrated by the attainment of the performance indicators. As one would expect, few recommendations were
implemented immediately. Progress was incremental, beginning with
the issuance of policies and directives, followed by management initiatives in the field and culminating in observable changes in activity.
The evaluations were conducted approximately 3 to 4 times per year
and included an in-country deployment of the expert consultants of
10 to 12 days for each on-site visit. In the event that an additional
evaluation of an area deemed to be critical was needed, arrangements
were made for an extra deployment and evaluation.

The value of having experienced police executives with such vast
knowledge of best police practices was again evidenced when the oversight team engaged in its on-site evaluations in Northern Ireland. The
members of the team could review the policies and planning documents that the policing institutions were utilising in the initial stages

of the implementation process in the context of the *Patten* objectives. In essence, these policy directives were to serve as a road map both for those responsible for implementation and for the oversight evaluations. If it was determined that proposed policy directives did not appear to fulfil the *Patten* recommendations, the oversight team could intervene early enough in the process for the appropriate adjustment to be made. The experience of the oversight team allowed for the interviewing of key members of the policing institution to be much more effective and productive. They were aware of the key issues that needed to be focused on and what were the appropriate lines of inquiry. Over time, the representatives of policing institutions also gained a sense of confidence that the evaluation process would be objective and, although demanding, fair to all concerned.

Perhaps the most interesting aspect of the evaluation strategy was the on-site visit to virtually every police facility throughout Northern Ireland. Due to the time limitations, the oversight team utilised most evenings and every weekend to conduct these visits. The middle-level supervisors and front-line patrol officers within the police service were very open to the visits and fully co-operative. As a result of these visits and discussions, the oversight team came to the conclusion early on that the police in Northern Ireland, whatever their historical complications, were a talented and intelligent group of people who cared deeply about Northern Ireland and the people who lived there. Several members of the command staff were world-class leaders who compared positively to any police executives we had met during our careers. The willingness of the leadership along with the rank and file of the RUC, and subsequently the PSNI, to accept such a massive change project was probably without parallel in any similarly sized police organisations in Western society.

Subsequent to each of the on-site evaluations in Northern Ireland, the entire oversight team would meet off-site in Canada or the United States. It was at this stage that each member of the team would present his findings, which would be subjected to analysis by the other members of the team. The two most important reference documents at this off-site evaluation meeting were the *Patten Report* and the approved Implementation Plan. Whenever we had a question about our observations, we would always go back to *Patten* to ensure that we were being faithful to those objectives and not interjecting our own opinions. The end result of the meetings was a consensus on the official oversight evaluation that was to be presented to the government and made public.

Although we were fortunate always to reach consensus, it was the stated internal policy of the office that the report and its opinions would be the sole responsibility of the Oversight Commissioner.

In an effort to further validate the results of the evaluation, the Oversight Commissioner gained the support of the IACP. This association of over 18,000 police chiefs is the pre-eminent group of law enforcement executives in the world. With the support of the executive committee, the then president of the IACP, Michael Robinson, agreed to establish a 'Blue Ribbon' panel of incumbent police chiefs to assist in a peer review for specific decisions. This peer group was to be brought together annually to provide input on the best police practices as they might apply to the Northern Ireland oversight process and decisions.

The final step in each of the evaluations was the presentation of the official report to the British government. Simultaneously the Oversight Commissioner scheduled personal meetings with the Secretary of State for Northern Ireland, Chief Constables of the RUC and later the PSNI, leaders of the political parties, leaders of the major religious denominations, the Policing Board, the Police Ombudsman, the Police Federation and a number of interested groups. The purpose of these personal meetings was to explain in detail the Oversight Report and the basis for our conclusions. This schedule of meetings was prepared in advance of the public release of each official report.

At the time of the public release of the official report of the Oversight Commissioner, an entire day was set aside for meeting with various representatives of the print, radio and television media. Public interest in Northern Ireland in policing and in the oversight reports was, in my experience, extraordinary. A number of individuals and groups would review our reports virtually line by line. In fact, the public and media interest in the oversight reports was a major asset in continuing progress on implementing the *Patten* recommendations. In reality, the authorities of the Oversight Commissioner are limited. The commissioner cannot promote, demote or provide financial incentives; all he can do is publish a report outlining the progress or lack of progress that occurs on implementing the *Patten* recommendations. However, I originally seriously underestimated the impact of the public release of the oversight reports and the subsequent media analysis of the results. It became apparent almost immediately that individuals and agencies saw the findings of the Oversight Commissioner as a professional report card, and they expended a great deal of effort to try to have a positive review from the Oversight Commissioner. In essence, they wanted a good grade on their report card.[7]

LESSON LEARNED

The change programme envisioned by the Patten Commission was massive in its complexity. Coupled with the emotional impact associated with the changes to policing in Northern Ireland proposed by the *Patten Report*, the change program was unlike any other ever attempted in modern history, with the exception of the restructuring and reform undertaken by the occupation forces after World War II. Because the Patten Commission was concerned that its report would either gather dust on bureaucratic shelves or be 'cherry picked' for selective implementation, the Patten Commission developed the concept of the Oversight Commissioner.

This was novel and untested. The eventual role, strategy and product were left to the first Oversight Commissioner to develop. There were no operational guidelines other than several brief paragraphs calling for the creation of the office and the publication of the reports.[8] One thing was sure, the people of Northern Ireland had risked an incredible amount on policing reform as part of the peace process. As the first Oversight Commissioner, I knew that the work to be undertaken through my office had to be a well thought out and professional oversight process. A famous general in the United States, Gordon Sullivan, wrote, 'Hope is not a method', and from my belief, failure was not an option.[9]

The eventual success of any peace process in a divided society depends greatly on a shared belief that the policing institutions have the confidence of all citizens. However, achieving that objective is a difficult and challenging task. The program of police reform in Northern Ireland was extraordinary in its scope and complexity. As a result, the existing policing institutions were asked to make many difficult changes. Not least of these changes were those to the official name, uniforms and symbols of those institutions. It is important not to underestimate the emotional impact of these symbolic changes on a proud organisation that became so deeply involved in a violent civil conflict that had cost it so many lives. The role of the Oversight Commissioner was to ensure that the agreed upon changes were fully implemented despite the bitter history in Northern Ireland. We tried at all times to be sensitive to that history and respectful of those who served as police officers there. One of the other caveats for evaluators such as the Oversight Commissioner and his team was not to go beyond their designated role. Far too often we have all experienced so-called outside experts who begin to lecture or try to dictate to the institutions they are evaluating. It was for this reason that the Oversight Commissioner's team adhered strictly to the objectives of the *Patten* recommendations and the agreed upon Implementation Plan. At times, outside interest groups will try to influence and extend an oversight process into other issues. These requests should be avoided and politely declined.

A major issue to consider when establishing an oversight post is the appropriate length of tenure for the position. Sufficient time should be allowed to establish an oversight process and for the policing institutions being evaluated to initiate the change process. It is also important that the oversight commissioner have enough time to ensure that the priority recommendations are being implemented in full and be able to demonstrate to the public that progress is actually occurring. If the length of tenure is too brief, there is a tendency for large bureaucracies to believe they can avoid change by just delaying the process. Conversely, there is potential for difficulties if the tenure is too long or has no sunset date. Agencies and politicians can become dependent on the outside oversight commissioner to make the difficult decisions. These decisions are more correctly the responsibility of elected and appointed public officials. When new institutions have been developed, they should be encouraged to accept responsibility for performance and not depend upon the oversight or prodding of external examiners. Furthermore, monitoring is an exciting, high-status undertaking, and in most cases it pays well. There is a temptation, therefore, for outside auditors to overstay their usefulness.

When the Patten Commission recommended the position of Oversight Commissioner it was for a term appointment of five years with a possible extension. When I accepted the appointment, the legislation and implementation plan set the term at three years. In my personal experience the most important impact of an external monitoring office occurs in the first three to four years. As my appointment began to reach the outer limits of my term, the incumbent Secretary of State for Northern Ireland requested that I consider remaining in the post for an additional two years. As the experience of being the

Oversight Commissioner was so interesting and rewarding, and my admiration for the people of Northern Ireland so great, this was a tempting offer. However, it was my belief that my success in Northern Ireland had a shelf life. Although it was a difficult decision, I believed it would not be appropriate to continue in the position for many more years. I agreed to extend my original three year term for an additional six months, to allow for an orderly transition. Eventually, the Office of Oversight Commissioner was to continue until 2007.[10] Based on my observation, the optimum tenure for the office would have been between four and five years. Extending the term for seven years was probably not in the best interests of the policing institutions in Northern Ireland. The Policing Board, Ombudsman's Office, Her Majesty's Inspectorate of Constabulary and a myriad of other agencies were fully able to continue appropriate governance of the police at the four- or five-year-term of the Oversight Commissioner.

When the tenure of any external evaluation such as the Oversight Commissioner is extended, it is important to guard against complacency. The evaluations must always be the result of rigorous and objective analysis of actual results. It is not sufficient to consider intended progress on recommendations as actual results. Each time that I conducted a meeting of the oversight team, it was emphasised that it was our role to make our judgements on real fulfilment of the *Patten* objectives. In fact, we appropriated a motto used by the late president of the United States, Ronald Reagan, in disarmament talks with leaders of the former Soviet Union. That motto, 'Trust but Verify', accurately describes the philosophy of the Office of the Oversight Commissioner as we carried out our responsibility in Northern Ireland.

CONCLUSIONS

As the peace process in Northern Ireland and the resulting police reform were such an overall success, there has been significant interest in them from other nations. The model for Northern Ireland, with an independent commission and oversight process, does provide a template for consideration. However, Northern Ireland possessed certain unique assets that became important keys to success. First, the peace process emerged from a decision by the vast majority of the affected parties and governments that there was a need to end the violence. Despite decades of violence and a terrible loss of life on all sides of the dispute, courageous people stepped forward to negotiate a peaceful solution. I often wondered as I met with people who had lost so many loved ones whether I, if I had lived through similar trauma, would have been able to overcome the bitterness. This negotiated and agreed upon peace process is the fundamental reason that the peace has continued and police reform has been successful in Northern Ireland. Without a consensus for peace and reform, it is doubtful that the Northern Ireland model could be successful in other divided societies.

The other asset in the Northern Ireland experience was that of the policing institutions. Although over time the violence had transformed the Royal Ulster Constabulary into a paramilitary force, it had the talent and structure to implement the required changes. To be sure, these changes were difficult and at times we encountered delay and some resistance. However, as it became clear that the Office of the Oversight Commissioner was made up of talented and dedicated police professionals who were committed to ensuring that the recommendations of the policing commission were implemented, we observed the full co-operation of the policing institutions.

One of the disappointments in the oversight process was the unwillingness on the part of government to provide financial support for the recommended capital improvements. It is important to remember the charge of the Patten Commission that its recommendations were a consensus agreement and should not be 'cherry-picked'. When accepting the appointment to become Oversight Commissioner, I was assured that there was a commitment by the government to fund fully the required changes. Unfortunately, that has not proved to be the case. The most graphic example is the failure to fund the building of a new police training facility to replace the antiquated Garnerville police college. Although I made numerous statements in my reports to point out the deplorable conditions at Garnerville, ten years on the promise of a new facility remains unfulfilled. Because the citizens and the police made difficult decisions to implement changes, I always thought it unfair for government to not fulfil its share of the bargain.

On a personal note, I would like to thank the government and the citizens of Northern Ireland for trusting me to become the Oversight Commissioner. I have had many positions and titles in the course of a 45-year career in law enforcement. The experience of overseeing police reform in Northern Ireland is one that I will treasure forever. Although my great-grandparents came from Ennis in Co. Clare, I grew up in a racially and ethnically mixed neighbourhood in the city of Buffalo, New York. As a result, I had little knowledge of Irish history or culture. As a career law enforcement official, I watched from a distance and with a sense of sadness the reports of violence in Northern Ireland. That somehow I would be afforded an opportunity to play some small part in the peace process was very special. In many ways, my experience in Northern Ireland may have been the most important stage of a long career in policing. It is with a great sense of pride that I can tell my six children and fourteen grandchildren that I played a role in the Northern Ireland peace process.

NOTES

[1] Independent Commission on Policing for Northern Ireland, *A new beginning: policing in Northern Ireland* Report of the Independent Commission on Policing for Northern Ireland (Belfast: HMSO, 1998). Hereafter cited as *Patten Report*.

[2] The President's Commission on Law Enforcement and Administration of Justice, *The challenge of crime in a free society* (Washington, D.C: Government Printing Office, February 1967), available at: http://www.ncjrs.gov/pdffiles1/nij/42.pdf.

[3] This Agreement was signed in Belfast on 10 April 1998; the full text of the document is available at: http://foreignaffairs.gov.ie/uploads/documents/Anglo-Irish/agreement.pdf (11 March 2010).

[4] This plan, released by the British Secretary of State for Northern Ireland Peter Mandelson, purported to set out how the how the report's recommendations would be implemented by the British government; see the text available at: http://cain.ulst.ac.uk/issues/police/patten/nio190102.pdf . After much controversy a revised plan was issued in August 2001, see http://cain.ulst.ac.uk/issues/police/patten/patten2001.pdf.

[5] Office of the Oversight Commissioner, 'Overseeing the proposed revisions for the policing services of Northern Ireland—Report 1 (16 October 2000)', (Belfast: Office of the Oversight Commissioner, 2000). The text of the report is available at: http://cain.ulst.ac.uk/issues/police/oversight/oversight-rep1-161000.pdf.

[6] Office of the Oversight Commissioner, 'Overseeing the proposed revisions for the policing services of Northern Ireland—Report 2 (12 September 2001)', (Belfast: Office of the Oversight Commissioner, 2000). The text of the report is available at: http://www.oversightcommissioner.org/reports/pdfs/sept2001.pdf.

[7] During my term as Oversight Commissioner (2000–03), the Office published nine reports. They can be accessed on: http://cain.ulst.ac.uk/issues/police/source.htm.

[8] *Patten Report*, Recommendations 172–5.

[9] Gordon R. Sullivan, *Hope is not a method: what business leaders can learn from America's Army* (New York: Broadway Books, 1997).

[10] The final report (the nineteenth) from the Office of the Oversight Commissioner was published on 31 May 2007; the text is available at: http://cain.ulst.ac.uk/issues/police/oversight/oversight-rep19-310507.pdf.

CHAPTER 8

LEADING THE PROCESS OF REFORM

Sir Hugh Orde

IN THE BEGINNING

When I arrived to begin work as Chief Constable in Northern Ireland, the *Patten* agenda was underway; my task was to turn all the dialogue into action. I inherited a service that had already got a new uniform and a new name—the Royal Ulster Constabulary changed, literally overnight on 4 November 2001, into the Police Service of Northern Ireland. Such a change should not be underestimated, and, for some, the immense pain and hurt associated with it remains to this day.

The change in name was significant and emotional in equal measure, but it was only the beginning of colossal organisational change. Despite the fine start that had been made, when I took up the post there were still some 170 *Patten Report* recommendations (that had been accepted) yet to be implemented.[1] These included: the recruitment of an Oversight Commissioner with 772 performance indicators; the introduction of new, independent accountability mechanisms; a severance scheme that would mean the loss of valued skills; the reorganisation of special branch; the biggest IT roll-out in Europe; and the delivery of 'Policing with the Community'. All of these aspects of the new police service had to be delivered against a challenging backdrop that included a substantial dissident republican threat; a loyalist paramilitary feud; ongoing political instability; the legacy of the past; and intense international, national and local interest.

Over the last number of years the Police Service of Northern Ireland has not just accepted change. It has embraced change. In fact, it has frequently been the initiator of change against a very difficult political and policing backdrop. Looking back on my seven years in command at the PSNI, I think that the key learning for me was the critical importance of listening, of teamwork and of empowerment.

LISTENING, LEARNING AND EMPOWERING

As with any programme of change, understanding the history and listening to players who wanted to talk was a critical first step in the process of transformation undertaken by the police service. Whilst those in official or elected positions were clearly important, equally informative were the quiet conversations I had with those behind the scenes who had interacted (both positively and negatively) with the police over many years. The complexity of the problem was compounded by the disengagement of Sinn Féin. It was clear that the party needed to be convinced that the new world was going to be different, before risking its credibility with the electorate and signing up to support the new policing process.

History has, on occasions, a short memory. The three parties that did engage on policing matters from the beginning were sufficient to start the process. I remain very clear in my mind that without the SDLP my task would have been almost impossible. Whilst the relationship was hugely challenging (and rightly so), members of the SDLP were on the Policing Board, and sufficient legitimacy was enshrined in that institution for the accountability framework to be seen as meaningful.

In terms of organisational leadership, I had to have the support of my entire senior management team and an overwhelming majority of officers and staff. To gauge this, I used a remarkably straightforward and unscientific approach called 'getting out and about'. I spent valuable time with my senior commanders working as a team, in a safe environment, which allowed everyone the space to speak openly, and to understand and respect each other's views on how we should manage the huge challenge of reform. District commanders and heads of departments were equally important, as they would be the drivers and deliverers of reform. Undoubtedly, in the beginning many people would find this new world uncomfortable. I looked to all my leaders to support and inform their officers and staff as we moved forward, and to reassure them continually that the changes we were implementing were about making us more, not less, effective. The quality of these men and women and their willingness to move forward was a vital asset in implementing and maintaining a process of reform that continues to this day.

Every single officer and staff member also undertook a two-day change familiarisation course. I and my senior team attended to show solidarity and to reinforce the fact that we were all going through the same emotional journey. Whilst this was a *Patten* recommendation, it had to be more than just window dressing. The raw emotion was clear to see, but so too was the enthusiasm for change. There is a limit on what can be achieved in sixteen hours of training, but the process itself sent a clear message that changes were going to take place. It also allowed a new code of ethics (unique at that time) to be formally introduced to the organisation.

As the reform agenda progressed it was important to get a first-hand read-out of how it was working and the impact it was having. Talking to my officers and staff in person was the best way of achieving this, and so we embarked on a programme of 'Briefings'. The structure was simple: a two-hour opportunity for all members of the service to interact with myself and the senior team. During my tenure 27 briefings were held, bringing together up to 300 colleagues at a time. First and foremost the briefing was an opportunity to thank the officers and staff for stepping up to the mark; but it also allowed those at the front end of the reform process to challenge and discuss what wasn't working, as well as what was.

I was nervous before each event, but always reassured afterwards. I believe such occasions should never be comfortable for a chief—if they are, it is highly likely that you are not learning from the experience. Through the briefings I learnt a lot about the organisation I commanded. The officers and staff I met at all levels continually reflected a deep desire to improve the service, balanced with a frustration that they felt unable or even powerless to achieve the necessary changes within the 'rules'. I, and my senior colleagues, took the feedback very seriously and used it to shape our decisions as we moved forward.

THE CHALLENGES OF REFORM

I was not surprised by the appetite for reform that existed within the police service, but it was very reassuring to know first-hand. Of course, those who wanted no part of the new world had a dignified opportunity to leave the service through the severance programme. Whereas this programme was very expensive, it created the headroom that allowed us to recruit 440 new officers a year. The severance scheme, together with the *Patten* recruitment recommendation of 50% new officers from the Catholic community and 50% from all other communities, facilitated a shift in the organisational mix of the service: from 8.23% Catholic in November 2001 to 27% Catholic officers in August 2009. The Service is well on target to achieve the *Patten* target of 30% by 2011. The same radical shift in personnel also allowed for an increase in the number of female officers from 13% to 24% over the same period.

Fifty:fifty recruitment was a sensible but highly controversial recommendation. Whilst it ensured a shift in the balance of the membership of the police service, there was hurt and anger that non-Catholics, including the next generation from police families with long histories of service in Northern Ireland, could be denied the opportunity to join. The balance of recruitment was a regular question at meetings I attended with sixth-form school pupils, and the subject of many conversations as I travelled throughout Northern Ireland. There was immense pressure to step back from this recommendation. Resilience, however, is a key requirement in leading change. I came under sustained pressure from many who thought they could overturn this recommendation. Legal challenges were mounted, defended and won. The fact that over 8,000 people would apply for 400 places in the regular recruitment programmes and that 37% of applicants have always been from the Catholic community spoke loud and clear— the majority of the community in Northern Ireland understood the need for this challenging legislation and would not be deterred by it.

The radical shift in personnel brought with it other issues, namely the departure of many highly skilled, professional colleagues. In particular, I lost detectives with substantial service and found myself creating a new Criminal Investigation Department (CID) structure without some of the key players. Instead of worrying, we took decisive action and appointed young and enthusiastic officers to the department, and provided them with the relevant training. These officers are now gaining the experience they need, and given that we reduced crime and increased our clear-up rate, the strategy clearly worked. In fact, the PSNI is one of the lead services in the UK national CID training programme.

Operationalising reform

With such a huge programme for change, and little time to achieve a noticeably different approach, I had a very clear vision in my head. The critical shift to be achieved was one of empowering the front line to deliver local policing, whilst professionalising the central structure to deliver against serious and organised crime.

Critically, at the frontline was the shift to 29 District Command Units. In my opinion, far too many to facilitate efficient service delivery, but necessary as a first step. *Patten* clearly recognised that accountability at the local level was the critical success factor. Small commands to start with, coupled with investment to soften the fortresses masquerading as police stations, maximised the chance for success. The consequence was substantial cost, which was borne by the Treasury. Indeed, the provision of a separate income stream was also essential. The cost of *Patten* has, conservatively, been estimated at £647 million. Substantial investment to facilitate reform allowed us to develop more efficient and effective methods of service delivery. The PSNI consistently exceeded targets for efficiency savings and reported sustainable efficiency gains in excess of £100 million in recent years.

Empowering the frontline was only successful because officers were ready for the challenge. Commanders showed a clear willingness to take on additional responsibility to drive the business of policing forward. Centralised budgets were devolved, with 83% managed locally. Crucially, devolved budgets allowed district commanders a flexibility to use some cash to fund effective community projects and initiatives—allowing us to bring more than just good-will to the table. Centrally, my deputy chief constable created a 'Policing with the Community Fund', which facilitated the funding of vitally important local partnership initiatives. Such initiatives included sports programmes for young people vulnerable to interface violence, or the funding of a domestic abuse worker within the community to liaise directly with police. As local police were empowered to work with local community leaders to develop and implement such projects, confidence and relationships built at a local level continued to drive the partnership agenda at a strategic level.

A substantial element of human resource management was also devolved to local commanders. As a result, sickness levels, which were appalling in 2002, began to tumble. The number of working days lost through sickness decreased from 229,407 in 2001/02 to 90,984 in 2007/08. In simple terms, 138,423 more days of policing were achieved at no additional cost. This dramatic change was clear evidence of the impact of empowering front-line staff—sickness was now everyone's responsibility and not just an issue that was managed centrally. Professionals in the area of human resources added value and expertise at the local level, while effective strategies to look after injured or ill staff, and a harder line where necessary, all contributed to the substantial decrease in the number of days lost through sickness.

While the frontline was empowered to deliver local policing, efforts were ongoing to improve the professionalism of the central structure to deliver against serious and organised crime. This was where the creation of the Crime Operations Department came to the fore. Establishing such a department was not a *Patten* recommendation, but I believed it was a key objective to effectively facilitate the reform process. The department was a significant and important achievement that delivered an effective and consistent professional approach to the management of intelligence and the investigation of serious organised and terrorist crime whilst maximising resources. Intelligence is a difficult but important aspect of policing. Like any other police service in England, Scotland, Wales or the Irish Republic, the PSNI could not operate effectively, or fulfil its primary function—to prevent and detect crime—unless it used intelligence. But, in Northern Ireland, perceptions around intelligence were, and continue to be, weighted with the experiences of the past. The establishment of the Crime Operations Department allowed significant re-organisation in relation to intelligence operations. It enabled new systems and processes to be put in place to deal with this difficult area of policing, and thereby to ensure that mistakes of the past would not be repeated. The PSNI has an absolute commitment that the gathering and use of intelligence must be for the protection of the human rights of all citizens. This commitment is underpinned by legislation and substantial regulation, including the European Convention on Human Rights and the Regulation of Investigatory Powers Act (2000).[2]

As time progressed we also managed to transfer national security intelligence from my command to that of the Security Service—bringing us into line with the rest of the United Kingdom. From a professional perspective this made sense, though the transition had to be managed very carefully. While the decision to transfer national security was made by parliament in London, I needed to ensure that all of the concerns raised by individuals and organisations were fully considered in the new arrangements, in order to give the highest degree of confidence possible in the new approach to all interested parties.

I set out five principles, which included that the PSNI would be informed of all counter-terrorist investigations and that all Security Services intelligence relating to terrorism in Northern Ireland would be visible to the PSNI. I was clear that these five principles would have to be agreed to by the Security Service if I was to have confidence in the new arrangements. The matter became such a sensitive issue that the principles were included in the St Andrews Agreement.[3] Keir Starmer, then human-rights adviser to the Northern Ireland Policing Board, and now director of public prosecutions for England and Wales, recognised in his 2007 human rights annual report that the significance of the five principles could not be overstated.[4] With these arrangements in place, national security responsibility was transferred to the Security Services in October 2007.

Reform, performance and the delivery of
'Policing with the Community'

Many of the texts on managing change suggest that as an organisation redefines itself, performance can drop. This was a major concern for the PSNI bearing in mind the scale of what we were being asked to do. To judge how successful implementation of the *Patten* recommendations has been, it is legitimate to look at performance. Between 2002/03 and 2008/09 incidences of crime in Northern Ireland dropped from a high of 142,496 to 110,094—a decrease of 23%. This massive change was in no uncertain terms due to the style of policing that my officers were determined to deliver to the community.

Patten's chapter on 'Policing with the Community' set out the style of policing it hoped that Northern Ireland would achieve.[5] This chapter laid out the ideals to which police officers truly aspire. Indeed, the ideals go back to 1829 and the principles established by Sir Robert Peel. As I have frequently said, they are not 'rocket science' but they have stood the test of time. 'The general principles of an efficient police'[6] were the first reports new officers were obliged to learn word perfect when I began my career in 1977. They can be summarised as: the protection of life; the prevention of crime; and the detection and prosecution of offenders once a crime has been committed. These principles are underpinned by the notion of policing by consent and the police being very much part of the community. 'The police are the public and the public are the police'[7] accurately sums up the ideal structure for policing.

In my view, it still holds that the decision to become a police officer is motivated by a sense of vocation. When I arrived in Northern Ireland it was clear that the officers I met were motivated by the same desire to serve as I had been when I became a police officer.

There was, in my judgement, no cultural block to the implementation of the *Patten* recommendations in this area. Yet, Northern Ireland presented a very challenging policing environment. Many within the community had a distrust or hatred of the police, and quite often a police officer's desire to deliver a service to the community was obstructed by a serious threat to his or her life. This situation meant that the style of policing that developed to allow officers to respond to calls for help had relied on military support. The backdrop in Northern Ireland was some way from the notion of policing by consent, as many were not prepared to give their consent to police delivering a service within their community. Indeed, the stark realisation of that dissent is brought home to anyone who has visited the RUC Memorial Garden at Police Headquarters in Belfast. *Patten* clearly recognised the opportunity the historic Good Friday Agreement had created to change and work towards a more traditional model of policing. It would have failed at the first hurdle if officers were not prepared to adapt their style and approach. In doing so, we were asking them to take a different approach to risk.

It was the absolute desire among the officers of the PSNI to 'police with the community' that ensured *Patten*'s concept became a reality—despite the challenging environment. Countless brave decisions made by so many within the service at every level meant that officers began to walk where they previously drove, drive where they previously flew—proving through action that they were prepared to engage, to protect and to serve. It was, in my judgement, the brave decisions of the front-line officers to do things differently, coupled with an equal willingness by some in the community to meet us half way, that set the standard.

As the years passed, these early decisions and opportunities that were successfully exploited by police and communities alike laid the ground for momentous developments. As confidence was built the circumstances were created that allowed an end to military support for routine policing. Operation Banner[8] was the largest and longest running military campaign in the history of the British Army. It finally drew to a close in April 2007. Today—like any other police service—the PSNI uses only specialist military support. This includes the knowledge and experience of Army Technical Officers to deal with bomb disposal. While several momentous developments such as the ending of Operation Banner were widely publicised, there were many, many others that took place in quiet rooms between community representatives and neighbourhood sergeants and constables. I remain convinced that without the 'quiet conversations' and effective local policing arrangements, the feedback to those in community leadership positions would not have been sufficient to give them the confidence to engage publicly with policing.

Today, the principles of 'Policing with the Community' apply to all police officers and staff in the PSNI because they all have a role to play in delivering the service. What the community sees on a daily basis is the visible delivery of policing, but front-line policing is dependent upon services provided by a network of police officers and police staff who provide administrative support, training, logistics and other specialist skills. In addition, the backroom includes all the intelligence gathering capability now shared between the Security Services and the PSNI to ensure that officers are fully informed of the current threat bespoke to their area. Without this support policing simply would not work.

The change in style and delivery of policing has been so fundamentally important to the advancement of peace in Northern Ireland that it has become a target for the very small minority of people who wish to perpetuate the past. Dissident republicans continue to target the delivery of policing with the community. Throughout 2008 there were numerous attacks on police officers both on and off duty. In March 2009 dissident republicans murdered Constable Stephen Carroll as he responded to a call for help from a member of the community in Craigavon. Days earlier they had murdered two young Sappers, Mark Quinsey and Patrick Azimkar, at Massereene Army barracks hours before the two soldiers were to fly to Afghanistan. Since then, there have been many more attempts to take the lives of police officers, and in an even more sinister development, the lives of officers' families.

While dissident republicans may be targeting police officers and those with links to the Security Services, they have shown total disregard for anyone whom they may kill or injure in the process. Those involved in planting bombs in farmers' fields; setting devices under family cars; launching rockets at police officers on a community beat in a small town have shown a complete lack of respect for human life—not just the lives of those they seek to murder, but the lives of those in the local community. In terms of how the *Patten Report* dealt with this, it ensured that several scenarios would need to be considered as the end game drew near, in particular the definition of 'normality' for society in Northern Ireland. It is right to say that the current environment is still by no means 'normal', which has substantial implications for policing for 2011 and beyond.

Despite the significant threat to their lives, however, the officers of the PSNI remain committed to the delivery of 'Policing with the Community'. They continue to push boundaries and break down barriers. They want to serve. They want to deliver a style of policing that is visible and community based. It is to their huge credit that they have achieved so much and are determined to continue to thwart the dissident republican objective of a return to the streets of the army and all that went with policing the Troubles.

Policing reform and the role of accountability

Whilst community policing created opportunities to build confidence, a number of additional developments were vital to facilitate and embed confidence in policing. If the PSNI is to retain its privileged position as an operationally responsible service, then it must be subject to robust challenge. *Patten* made recommendations on democratic accountability, transparency, legal accountability and financial accountability. While all were uniquely important, the formation of the Northern Ireland Policing Board and the District Policing Partnerships (DPPs) were perhaps the most fundamental in the process of change in policing in Northern Ireland.

From a personal perspective, the public meetings of the Policing Board were very important. I ensured that as many of my senior team as necessary attended these meetings, to deal properly with the wide variety of questions ranging across all policing disciplines. I missed only 2 of the 65 meetings held during my time in office, and only then with the permission of Policing Board. The debates were always challenging, but the ability to have such debates in an open and transparent arena could only be beneficial to policing. As senior police officers, we had to hold our nerve and do the right thing operationally and professionally whilst ensuring all stakeholders—elected and non-elected, statutory or voluntary, national or international—were given the opportunity to inform, advise and shape decisions in a real and meaningful way. One consequence of such a substantial and inclusive approach is time, and many decisions were delayed as parties demanded more time or information or sought judicial review. Reflecting on the process, I still think it was the right way to go. I believe that it allowed everyone some space to debate and challenge very sensitive areas of policing reform whilst allowing us to continue to drive the process forward. Our determined, incremental approach over time has stood the test of time.

The DPPs provided another unique and important part of the process of bringing policing into the community. Through the Northern Ireland Policing Board and DPPs, *Patten* put in place not just accountability mechanisms, but also structures that facilitated conversations between police and communities and allowed effective working relationships to develop. That the Policing Board and the DPPs are now fully representative of the community is one of the greatest achievements of the last ten years and is testament to the strength and benefits of the structures and the members—both political and independent—who made the choice to be facilitators of progress in policing. In particular, those individuals that stepped forward to join the first Policing Board and District Policing Partnerships must be credited for recognising that while *Patten* had set out a blueprint for policing, only by joining the new policing structures could the blueprint be managed, shaped and implemented in a way that everyone believed in.

Whilst not part of the *Patten* recommendations, the provision of an independent and impartial complaints system through the Police Ombudsman for Northern Ireland was also important in building confidence in policing. Over the years the Ombudsman's office has proved its independence, and although at times its reports have made difficult and challenging reading, the role of the Ombudsman is recognised as a vital structure by both the community and police officers in Northern Ireland.

Policing reform and the political context

During the process of reform, a key reason for taking immense care without being tentative was that policing was critical to political progress. The post-Belfast Agreement advances would not have taken place without a clearly communicated determination from policing leaders to deliver and implement the *Patten Report* that became the operating reality for those who engaged in policing for the first time.

Between 2002 and 2006/7, the changing political climate in Northern Ireland went hand-in-hand with the normalisation of policing. Confidence increased and crime fell. Undoubtedly, a police service is at its most effective in tackling all crime when it has the support of the community and the community has the confidence to engage. Repeated independent public opinion surveys conducted on behalf of the Policing Board continue to reveal increasing levels of support for policing in Northern Ireland. The increasing community support that has become more and more routine allows for a better concentration of resources on priority and emerging problems, and crime figures are less likely to be over-inflated by the one-off events.

It was not always the case. Sinn Féin's refusal to join the structures or encourage people from their community to join or engage with policing slowed the rate of progress of policing with the community. Full political representation on the Policing Board was critical to ensuring that progress could continue. As is so often the case, communities were always moving ahead of the politicians in their acceptance of policing and their desire to move on. In a general sense, quiet conversations at every level of the organisation with many people from local communities were making a difference—slowly, convincing people that proper accountability of policing was best achieved through membership of the institutions created by *Patten* for that purpose. So, while symbolically the police service's first public meeting with Sinn Féin was important in breaking down barriers, my officers had been talking over many years to any member of the community who had a desire to move things forward and resolve local issues.

CHANGE AS A CONSTANT—UNFINISHED BUSINESS

Ten years on, whilst there is still some distance to go, a profound shift in both police and community thinking has occurred. Policing with the community is now a reality in many areas of Northern Ireland where previously it would have been regarded as unobtainable. The world has moved on, and Northern Ireland no longer fills the pages of the national or international press every day for all the wrong reasons. Huge steps have been taken by those in leadership to create a Northern Ireland that is looking forward and seeks to build a future where every child lives without fear and enjoys the experiences and opportunities offered in a peaceful community, in which diversity is embraced.

But the end game is still to be played out. The future is not without its challenges—some of them very serious. Financially, the world is a very different place, with cuts across the public sector as a reality. The only debate is scale. As police (and all policing partners') budgets come under increasing pressure, many projects that have been so critical to building relationships and understanding could reduce or fold. It will require brave leadership from the politicians and resolve from all in civic leadership roles to finally bring the prize of a sustainable peace to Northern Ireland. The reality is that for policing on the ground, a failure to achieve political progress creates a vacuum for those wishing to perpetuate the divisions of the past. With the devolution of policing and justice, Northern Ireland has taken another important step towards a brighter and more stable future. As long as there is a public will and a political will to go forward—there is hope. As long as there is hope—those who oppose the peace process will be deprived of the community support that they need to survive.

The progress to date would not have been achieved without the hard work and engagement behind the scenes as people got to know each other better. It was those meetings, where risks were taken and relationships built, that have been absolutely critical to the success of the changing policing environment in Northern Ireland. This work continues to take place every day, and as long as it does Northern Ireland will continue to develop and progress will be unstoppable.

NOTES

[1] Independent Commission on Policing for Northern Ireland, *A new beginning: policing in Northern Ireland* Report of the Independent Commission on Policing for Northern Ireland (Belfast: HMSO/Northern Ireland Office, 1999) (hereafter cited as *Patten Report*).

[2] Council of Europe, 'Convention for the Protection of Human Rights and Fundamental Freedoms'; the text of the convention and its amending protocols is available at: http://www.echr.coe.int/nr/rdonlyres/d5cc24a7-dc13-4318-b457-5c9014916d7a/0/englishanglais.pdf. The text of the Regulation of Investigatory Powers Act (2000) can be accessed at http://www.opsi.gov.uk/acts/acts2000/ukpga_20000023_en_1.

[3] An agreement reached between the British and Irish governments and the main political parties in Northern Ireland in October 2006, designed to allow the restoration of the Northern Ireland Executive, which had been in suspension, and including an agenda of other items, such as: Sinn Féin supporting the PSNI and all parties supporting the devolution of authority for policing to the new Northern Ireland Assembly and Executive. For the full text of this agreement, see: http://www.nio.gov.uk/st_andrews_agreeement-2.pdf.

[4] Northern Ireland Policing Board, 'Monitoring the compliance of the Police Service of Northern Ireland with the Human Rights Act 1998', Human Rights Annual Report 2007. The text of this report is available at: http://www.nipolicingboard.org.uk/nipb_hr_ar-2.pdf.

[5] *Patten Report*, Chapter 7, 40–5.

[6] See 'Brief definition and history of policing', on the history pages of the website of the Metropolitan Police Service, available: http://www.met.police.uk/history/definition.htm.

[7] Robert Peel, speech in the House of Commons, 15 March 1839.

[8] Operation Banner was the official name given to military operations in Northern Ireland from 1969 to 2007, see http://www.mod.uk/DefenceInternet/FactSheets/OperationBannerNotableDates.htm.

CHAPTER 9

THE POLICE OMBUDSMAN FOR NORTHERN IRELAND— SOME REFLECTIONS

Baroness Nuala O'Loan, DBE

INTRODUCTION

In October 1999 I was appointed Police Ombudsman-designate, to establish the Office of the Police Ombudsman for Northern Ireland.[1] From 6 November 2000 I held office by royal warrant for a non-renewable term of seven years,[2] and was charged to provide a system of independent, impartial investigation of the police in Northern Ireland. I was to exercise my powers 'in the way best calculated to secure the confidence of the people and of the police in the [police complaints] system'.[3] It was a significant challenge. At this stage, Northern Ireland was still not wholly at peace. The work of the Police Ombudsman's Office had to be done in the context of what had happened during the 30 years of what we euphemistically called 'the Troubles' and of what was continuing to happen.

During the Troubles, 303 police officers, 711 military personnel and some 2,100 civilians died. In their excellent publication *Lost Lives*, David McKittrick *et al.*[4] state that between 1969 and 2001, 394 republican paramilitaries and 159 loyalist paramilitaries died. Between 1969 and 2009, 50,329 people were injured. In the eleven years since the Good Friday Agreement of 1998, which was negotiated following an IRA ceasefire on 20 July 1997, 89 people have died and over 1,000 have been injured as a result of paramilitary-style attacks.[5] The toll of the Troubles on the population of 1.7 million people was huge. Very few people in Northern Ireland who lived through the Troubles were not, in some way, touched by violence.

It is important to place the creation of the Office of the Police Ombudsman in the context that led to it. As the Troubles developed there were wide-ranging consequences for policing and security in Northern Ireland, which affected the whole community. These consequences, which are common to many conflict situations, included:

- the internment, beginning on 9 August 1971, of hundreds of republican men aged from 17 years old—neither awaiting trial nor convicted of an offence—for up to three years. The injustice of internment, and its economic and social consequences, caused massive resentment and generated huge resistance to the law;
- the use of unlawful interrogation techniques, during both internment and investigation, which led to proceedings by Ireland against the United Kingdom in the European Court of Human Rights and resulted in a finding that the United Kingdom had used techniques that amounted to inhuman and degrading treatment in breach of Article 3 of the European Convention on Human Rights;[6]
- the use of certain policing techniques—such as rubber and plastic bullets (which led to the deaths of 17 people), 'stop and search', and methods of public order policing—led to further disconnection between the police and the people;
- serious levels of post-traumatic stress disorder across the whole community, especially among police officers who had to deal on a daily basis with the consequences of bombings and shootings and with the constant knowledge of the risk attaching to policing;
- the breakdown of normal policing activity, which became secondary to the policing of the conflict. In some areas police could not answer a call for help for many hours, if at all;
- the routine murder of informants to deter others from assisting the police and security forces;
- a declaration by the IRA that police officers, prison officers and anybody who worked for or with the police were 'legitimate targets' for murder. Catholics joining the police service were specially targeted for assassination by the IRA. The number of Catholic police officers dropped from 11% to 7% during the Troubles;
- the murder of lawyers and members of the judiciary by paramilitaries from both sides;
- repeated bomb explosions that destroyed police stations and many investigation files and evidential exhibits, which were critical in the prosecution of those who were engaged in murder and other serious crimes;

- the destruction of the Forensic Science Laboratory by an estimated 2,000-pound IRA bomb on 23 September 1992; 20 people were injured, the laboratories destroyed and approximately 700 houses were damaged in the blast. This led not only to extensive loss of evidence, but also to the temporary loss of the forensic facility and function, which had a significant impact;
- the further separation of the anti-terrorist arm of the Royal Ulster Constabulary—the Special Branch—from the rest of the service. Normal flows of intelligence to crime investigators became hampered, leading to frustration among CID[7] officers. The Special Branch was described to the Patten Commission by police officers as 'a force within a force';
- the development, in the absence of laws or effective internal controls regulating the handling, control and management of informants, of serious problems that led to a situation in which some informants were able to commit serious crimes without being made amenable for those crimes;[8] and
- allegations during the Troubles that police and the security forces operated a 'shoot to kill' policy—using lethal force where lesser force would have sufficed to bring terrorists under control. Recommendations for prosecutions of police officers for perverting the course of justice were rejected by the then government.

The impact on the people and police of Northern Ireland

All this led to growing distrust and disconnectedness of many people from policing and constitutional processes. By the end of the Troubles this had happened in both loyalist and republican communities. In some areas there was a growing reliance on paramilitaries for policing. In some communities, such as the UVF[9]-dominated area of North Belfast, there was a growing awareness that certain individuals were not made amenable for crimes even when members of the public gave evidence against them. This led to greater distrust of the policing and justice system.

As the police were criticised and the calls for reform became more strident, police morale began to suffer. When peace began gradually to emerge and as a constitutional process began to develop, police officers came to the realisation that they had to deal with working with many of those who had sought to kill them previously. In this context, Dr Maurice Hayes, at the request of the British government, conducted research into the possible options for the delivery of a police complaints service. His report, *A Police Ombudsman for Northern Ireland*, produced in 1997, led to the passing of the Police Act of 1998, which created the Office of the Police Ombudsman.[10]

ESTABLISHING THE OFFICE OF THE POLICE OMBUDSMAN

I was determined that the Office of the Police Ombudsman would be of service to all our people, and that it would be impartial and evidence-driven. Stakeholders such as the police, the police associations and the Northern Ireland Office were invited onto the Project Broad, so that the procedures and relationships would, from the very beginning, be the product of consultation and discussion. I spent months just talking to anyone who would talk to me about what this new service should look like, in order to make it accessible and to enable people to have faith in it and to avail of it. It was felt that the key characteristics for the Office should be integrity, service, impartiality, fairness and accountability.

As we acquired premises and recruited staff during the summer months of 2000, the general situation in Northern Ireland remained tense. I was temporarily located in a former biscuit factory in East Belfast. With rioting and other disruption, the situation was so volatile that I repeatedly had to send staff home early; but with bus services being cancelled people could not get home, and there was a sense of danger. Loyalist tensions then spiralled out of control and the Shankill area[11] erupted into terrible violence. Hundreds of families were displaced and homes were burned as loyalists attacked each other. The police struggled simply to contain the violence. At that point I had recruited several experienced investigators from across the world. They were due to come to Belfast a week after the trouble flared in the Shankill, but most of them decided not to come—thinking now that Northern Ireland was not the peaceful, post-conflict place they had believed it to be.

The Office of the Police Ombudsman for Northern Ireland opened on 6 November 2000 with an initial 57 members of staff, of a complement of 103. That complement grew over the years to 151. We operated across Northern Ireland and provided a service 24-hours-a-day, every day. The staff were representative of the community we served, as were our complainants.[12] We were charged to investigate complaints and other matters involving all police officers in Northern Ireland.[13] As the years passed we were also asked to assume responsibility for complaints against the Serious Organised Crime Agency and Her Majesty's Revenue and Customs operating in Northern Ireland, and finally against specified non-police personnel employed by the Police Service of Northern Ireland. We were also required to gather statistical data about complaints, and to research—and later to investigate—police policy and practice. This led to the publication of many reports on matters such as police use of batons, police searches of homes and the treatment by police in Northern Ireland of solicitors and barristers.

In addition to public complaints, we received cases from the Chief Constable, from the Secretary of State, from the Policing Board and, in the event that there was evidence, for example, that a police officer had perjured himself in court, or that there was fabrication of evidence for a trial, from the Director of Public Prosecutions. The requirement for an investigation by the Police Ombudsman's Office was also identified by a judge hearing a case against a man charged in connection with the August 1998 Omagh bombing: the judge was concerned about some of the evidence given in his court by police officers. The Criminal Cases Review Commission (CCRC), which looks at the safety of convictions and which also has power to refer to appeal cases in which it suspects that a conviction is unsafe, also referred cases to us. The CCRC referred, for example, the case of a young man who was convicted of murder on confession evidence presented in a Diplock Court.[14] It was alleged that police officers had fabricated the confession evidence. The conviction was overturned by the Court of Appeal. We investigated this case and made the necessary recommendations to the Prosecution Service. Finally, I had the power to investigate in specified circumstances without any complaint or referral, if I thought that an investigation was desirable in the public interest.[15] We inherited over 2,000 complaints from our predecessor organisation, and in the first few years of operation multiple legislative changes increased the responsibilities and duties of the Police Ombudsman.[16]

We had full police powers—including powers of arrest, entry, search and seizure—and access to all police materials and information, which was essential for the Office to be able to carry out its duties fully. We could, and did when necessary, arrest police officers. We seized, as evidence, police vehicles, batons, guns, etc., as well as police officers' mobile phones, computers, papers and other material. The exercise of those powers brought their own challenges, some unintentionally humorous. In one early case a police officer was alleged to have kicked and injured an individual. My investigator sought to take possession of the officer's boots. Initially the officer refused to co-operate, but in the end the sergeant handed the boots over, with a memo for me which read: 'Dear Police Ombudsman, herewith Constable X's boots. Please return same within 24 hours or provide a new pair'. In other cases the resistance was more serious. Some Scenes of Crimes Officers refused, briefly, to work at cases in which we were investigating police officers, despite the fact that they had a duty so to do. Information which should have been made available to us was withheld. All this had to be dealt with swiftly and robustly.

Relationships with the people

The general public in Northern Ireland had to be aware of the new system for dealing with complaints and had to believe that it was there to serve them if they were to have confidence in it. The service had to be accessible. For reasons of security and cost we could not operate from more than one site. We did not use police premises to meet complainants. We made arrangements with organisations like the Northern Ireland Citizens Advice Bureaux, Northern Ireland Women's Aid and the Chinese Welfare Association to use and pay for private rooms in their premises. This dealt with one of the big fears that people had—of being seen to complain about the police. It also meant that we could meet people at locations that were convenient and in which they felt comfortable. Finally, we arranged that the Office[17] would be open to complainants during normal working hours, and that we would be available by appointment after those hours. No forms had to be filled in by complainants, unless they wished so to do. Complaints made directly to the police had to be faxed to us immediately. We had a policy whereby we would meet any group who wished to meet us, and consequently my staff and I met thousands of people over the seven years I served as Police Ombudsman. Very often these people wanted to see us, to ask us questions and to assess for themselves whether we really were going to provide a service that was independent and impartial. We printed literature that informed the public about what we could and could not do. We published all our research and public investigative reports on the Office's website.[18]

Relationships with the police

A strategy to develop the relationship between the Office and police officers was created very early on. It was aimed at achieving the maximum involvement possible at all levels and on all occasions between members of staff of the Office and police officers, to encourage confidence. Policing in its widest sense was involved in the process of creating the Office of the Police Ombudsman.[19] Chief officers assured us of their commitment to the Police Ombudsman's office, and we established a pattern of high-level meetings to facilitate the work. Over the years we met police officers at all levels regularly; had six-weekly meetings with the Discipline and Legislation Committee of the Police Federation;[20] and had extensive involvement in police training for new probationers, final probationers, Senior Investigation Officers, and for use of firearms and CS spray. This enabled us to meet and speak to almost all new officers. It also ensured that police officers knew what was expected of them at all times, and how the Police Ombudsman's office would respond if we became involved in an incident. On occasion we had to work in incidents in which the PSNI was investigating possible civilian crime, whilst we were simultaneously investigating.

COMPLAINTS AND INVESTIGATIONS

During my years in office as the Police Ombudsman we received on average 3,000 complaints a year, containing 5,000 allegations (a complainant might allege wrongful arrest and assault, for example). Many of our investigations were relatively uncomplicated. For example, a young man was arrested for a crime. He was taken to a police station and was being fingerprinted. On a video recorded in the police station the young man could be seen saying something to the policeman taking his fingerprints, then the policeman pushed him violently and he crashed over a chair, banging his head against the door. That police officer was convicted of assault and dismissed.

Another case came to us from an American observer at a parade. She filmed a convoy of police Land Rovers leaving the scene of some public disorder. All was quiet again. Nine Land Rovers left the area peacefully. The tenth, however, veered suddenly and at speed onto wasteground, where a group of people were watching the police leave. The police driver was convicted of dangerous driving and is no longer a police officer.

Over the years I spent in office we investigated many matters that were referred to us by the Chief Constable, including every use of CS spray for a six-month period following the introduction of the equipment, and every police shooting. Any death that may have resulted from the conduct of a police officer had to be referred to us by the Chief Constable. We investigated many such deaths: two deaths by police shooting, deaths in custody, deaths from road traffic accidents involving the police, deaths from police car pursuits, deaths where the last person to see the deceased was a police officer.[21] In each case we had to establish and report on whether there was any police culpability, and also to prepare the papers for the coroner's inquest that had to be held into such deaths.

One such case involved investigation into the circumstances in which Mr Neill McConville was shot three times by a police officer on 29 April 2003. Police had begun monitoring the movements of a red Vauxhall Cavalier car, after they learned that 'man A' was in the car, and that he was planning to collect a firearm that was subsequently to be used in an attack on a named individual. Two police vehicles were ordered to pursue the Cavalier and stop it from behind. The crew commander of the lead police pursuit vehicle twice asked for, and received, confirmation of the order. By this stage Mr McConville was driving the Cavalier. The two police cars caught up with the Cavalier on a relatively straight section of the road. Officers shouted a warning that they were armed and ordered the men in the Cavalier to stop. When they failed to do so the police cars brought the Cavalier to a standstill. It came to rest sitting across the road, but continued to 'rev' loudly as the driver tried to put it into gear. Officers believed that he was about to drive over a police officer who had been knocked down and was lying injured directly in the path of the Cavalier. The gun used by one of the officers slipped into automatic mode, and as a consequence three shots were fired when only one shot was intended. Mr McConville died as a consequence of his injuries.

This police operation, which resulted in the first fatal shooting by the PSNI, was poorly managed by senior officers. The order to stop the car 'from behind' was a high-risk strategy, and I criticised senior officers for failing properly to consider alternative options. The officer who fired the fatal shots was justified in using his firearm to protect the life of a colleague.[22]

Initially I had a duty only to investigate contemporaneous cases; that, however, changed in May 2001 when I was required to investigate historic cases without any time limit. Many of these cases derived from our troubled past in Northern Ireland. The allegations in these older cases came from across the community: from Protestant families, Catholic families, people of other faiths and none, people from military and policing backgrounds, people from Prison Officer families. They all complained of police misconduct, alleging either that the police allowed a murder to happen, participated in the murder, or did not investigate it properly in order to protect the murderers.

Older cases were more difficult to investigate. Often papers could not be found, had not been completed properly, or had been taken home by officers who had nowhere to store them at work. When I dealt with the case of Mr Sam Devenney in Derry, who died some time after he and his children were savagely attacked by police officers in their home in 1969, I was told by police that the investigation file could not be found. We tracked down a copy of the original in the Metropolitan Police archives in London.[23] The family could not understand why there had been no prosecution. We found that the Northern Ireland government had declared an amnesty in respect of all crimes committed at the critical time. The amnesty lasted six months. There could be no prosecution, even if the actual officers who attacked Sam Devenney and his family had been identified. People had forgotten the amnesty in the maelstrom that followed. In 2003 a chief officer publicly apologised to the Devenneys for what had happened.

When we were investigating the case of Mr Sean Brown,[24] who was abducted and murdered by loyalist paramilitaries at the GAA[25] ground in Bellaghy in 1997, the police investigation files could not be found. A lengthy hunt ensued, and they were finally located in the roof space of a police station. An enterprising officer, faced with having to work in a very cold police station, and there being too many files and no storage space for them, had decided to put the files in the roof space as insulation. The alleged collusion by police in the murder of Mr Brown was not found when my office conducted its investigation in this case, but we did determine that there was a failed police investigation. When we sought to investigate a complaint about the police response to the murder by republicans of mother of ten Mrs Jean McConville,[26] there were very few investigation papers available. Despite the fact that her children had told the police about their mother's abduction in 1972, nothing had been done for over twenty years. Mrs McConville was said to have been murdered as an informant. However, I was able to establish conclusively that she had not been an informant.

Investigating cases involving incidents that had occurred during the Troubles was always challenging. In December 2001 I reported the findings of my inquiry into the Omagh Bomb, in which 29 people and two unborn children died and hundreds were injured.[27] I was very critical of the way in which the police Special Branch operated. I found that there had been intelligence available before the bombing but that it had not been handled properly. A limited trawl of intelligence available after the bombing identified over 300 pieces of intelligence that should have been provided to the Omagh Bomb police investigation. Only 22 percent of that information was made available to the investigators. Information that should have been made available to me was not disclosed. Many police officers responded to the investigation magnificently. However, some police witnesses inexplicably varied their accounts, while others sought to avoid the investigators, refused to make statements, or made only limited statements and refused to expand on them. The police investigation of the Omagh bomb was found by an RUC review to be very flawed, and to have been seriously under-resourced. The emergent findings had been reported in May 2000, but eighteen months later effective action had still not been taken. At senior management level the response to my investigation was defensive and at times unco-operative. Overall, I found that

> the judgment and leadership of the Chief Constable and
> ACC Crime have been seriously flawed. As a result of
> that, the chances of detaining and convicting the
> Omagh bombers have been significantly reduced.[28]

It was a profoundly difficult moment, but the evidence had to be presented faithfully.

In 2002 a man called Raymond McCord made very serious allegations that his son had been murdered by a police informant, (whom we called 'informant 1') and that that informant and others had been protected from prosecution for serious crimes for years.[29] 'Operation Ballast', as we called our enquiries into Mr McCord's complaint, involved an investigation lasting over four years, as a consequence of which we confirmed most of Mr McCord's allegations, and found that a group of police informants who were members of the UVF had been engaged in the most serious of crimes between 1991 and 2003.

We examined not only matters relating to the investigation of Mr McCord's son's murder, but also the police handling and management of identified informants, and information received by and about them over a period of twelve years. We identified links between named individuals and fifteen murders, ten attempted murders and seventy-six other crimes. It was a huge investigation. Police computer systems were examined, and more than 10,000 police documents were recovered, including material held within intelligence systems, personal records, police journals and crime files and from other sources. Corroborating material was also recovered from a number of other agencies and organisations.

More than 100 serving and retired police officers were interviewed, 24 of them under caution. Three retired officers were arrested because they would not attend voluntarily for an interview under criminal caution, while a fourth officer who was to be arrested agreed to attend for interview. Despite assurances that witness details would be anonymised in any public statement, some retired officers—including two former assistant chief constables, seven former detective chief superintendents and two former detective superintendents—refused to assist the investigation. We were particularly concerned that retired officers, who had had significant responsibilities within the Special Branch and who undoubtedly could have assisted the inquiry, refused to do so. In the absence of any justifiable reason why these officers behaved as they did, we identified, from police documentation, records and interviews, collusion in many situations, including the following:

• the failure to arrest informants for crimes to which those informants had allegedly confessed, or to treat such informants as suspects for crime;
• the arrest of informants suspected of murder, their subjection to lengthy sham interviews by their own handlers, at which they were not challenged, and their release on the authorisation of the handler;
• the giving of instructions to junior officers that records should not be completed and that there should be no record of a bombing incident;
• the withholding of information about the location to which a group of murder suspects had allegedly fled after a murder: the consequence of this was that Criminal Investigation Department (CID) officers were searching in Belfast for people whom they thought to

be the murderers, whilst the Special Branch had information about
the actual location to which these suspects had gone;
• the cancelling of the 'wanted' status of murder suspects 'because of
lack of resources', and doing nothing further about these suspects.

Decisions which had been made by the RUC not to adopt proper
rules relating to the handling, supervision and management of informants meant that it was not possible to attribute responsibility to
individual officers for actual breach of rules. I found that the effect of
the dysfunction which we identified was that,

> whilst undoubtedly Special Branch officers were effec-
> tive in preventing some bombings and shootings and
> other attacks, some informants were able to engage in
> terrorist activities including murders without the
> Criminal Investigation Department having the ability
> to deal with them for some of those offences…Whilst
> acting as [informants] and with the knowledge of some
> Special Branch and some CID officers, informants
> moved through the ranks of the UVF to senior posi-
> tions…Informant 1's [activities were] not challenged
> by Special Branch and the activities of those who
> sought to bring him to justice were blocked repeatedly.
> Records were minimized, exaggerated, fabricated and
> must also have been destroyed. Informant 1 would have
> been well aware of the level of protection which he was
> afforded.[30]

As the investigation progressed I brought necessary matters to the
attention of the Chief Constable, the Secretary of State and the
Surveillance Commissioner. In response to this, from 2003 there was
a massive programme of change within the PSNI. Further necessary
changes were identified in the 'McCord Report'.[31] The response by the
then Chief Constable, Sir Hugh Orde, to those recommendations is
recorded in the Report: 'We have detailed below our acceptance of
the recommendations and the actions which have been or will be
taken in respect of each one'.[32] The 'McCord Report' was accepted
not only by the Chief Constable but also by the Prime Minister, the
Taoiseach, the Secretary of State for Northern Ireland and the Policing
Board. Following the publication of my Report, the PSNI Historical
Enquiries Team launched its investigation into the crimes committed

by civilians and identified in Operation Ballast. A number of men now stand charged with very serious offences.

CONCLUSION

Any conclusion about the effectiveness of the Office of the Police Ombudsman must lie with those whom it served and who were investigated by it. In that regard, 86% of people surveyed believed that we were independent; 78% believe that we were impartial; 84% thought we were fair.[33] Police officers who had been investigated and were anonymously surveyed reported high levels of confidence in the Office—90% of officers who had been investigated believed their investigator was impartial, 84% believed the investigator was fair and 90% believed he or she was professional.[34] It was a demanding job. We made evidence-based recommendations for the prosecution of police officers when they had to be made, and we moved to ensure that officers were subject to disciplinary action where necessary. In cases where what went wrong was not the fault of a junior officer, but rather a failure of management or supervision, we dealt with that failure. When policing had been properly conducted, we said so. When officers acted bravely, we said so.

Over the years we engaged with many agencies, organisations, groups and individuals in Northern Ireland and across the world to enhance our work, and to share what we had learned with those who sought to develop similar systems of independent, impartial police accountability. It was a great privilege to hold office as the first Police Ombudsman for Northern Ireland, and to work with so many committed and professional people both within and without the Office.

NOTES

[1] See http://www.policeombudsman.org.
[2] See Police (NI) Act (1998), Section 51 and Schedule 3; the text of this legislation is available at: http://www.opsi.gov.uk/acts/acts1998/ukpga_19980032_en_1.
[3] See Police (NI) Act (1998), 51(4).
[4] David McKittrick, Seamus Kelters, Brian Feeney and Chris Thornton, *Lost lives: the stories of the men, women and children who died as a result of the Northern Ireland Troubles* (Edinburgh and London: Mainstream Publishing: 1999), 1494.
[5] Police Service of Northern Ireland Statistics; available at: http://www.psni.police.uk.
[6] Ireland vs UK (1978) (Application no. 5310/71) European Court of Human Rights. The interrogation techniques that had been used were wall-standing; hooding; sub-

jection to noise; deprivation of sleep; deprivation of food and drink. The British government gave a commitment that such techniques would never be used again.

[7] Criminal Investigation Department—focused on 'ordinary' crime.

[8] See 'Statement by the Police Ombudsman on her investigation into the circumstances surrounding the death of Raymond McCord Junior and related matters', January 2007; available at: http://www.policeombudsman.org/Publicationsuploads/ BALLAST%20PUBLIC%20STATEMENT%2022-01-07%20FINAL% 20VERSION.pdf. (Herafter cited as 'McCord Report'.)

[9] Ulster Volunteer Force—one of the two major loyalist paramilitary organisations.

[10] Maurice Hayes, *A police ombudsman for Northern Ireland: a review of the police complaints system in Northern Ireland* (Belfast: Northern Ireland Office, 1996); the text of the Police (Northern Ireland) Act (1998) is available at: http://www.opsi.gov.uk/ acts/acts1998/ukpga_19980032_en_1.

[11] A working-class district of Belfast, where loyalist paramilitaries were relatively active.

[12] See *Developments in police complaints—7 years on, overview of trends and patterns in police complaints*, November 2007; available at: http://www.policeombudsman.org/ Publicationsuploads/5018S%20PONI%20Trends%20&%20Patterns%20web2.pdf, pp 55–61.

[13] The RUC (from 4 November 2001 the PSNI), Larne Harbour Police, Belfast Harbour Police, Belfast International Airport Police and the Ministry of Defence Police.

[14] The 'non-jury' trials used for most serious criminal cases in Northern Ireland from the mid-1970s onwards.

[15] See Police (NI) Act (1998), 55(6), 'any matter in respect of which there was no complaint and which appeared to indicate that a police officer may have committed a criminal offence or behaved in a manner which would justify disciplinary proceedings'.

[16] See all legislation affecting the work of the Police Ombudsman on the website of the Office: http://www.policeombudsman.org/modules/pages/legislation.cfm.

[17] The Office of the Police Ombudsman is located at 11 Church Street, Belfast BT1 1PG.

[18] See http://www.policeombudsman.org for the text of the various reports published.

[19] The Project Broad, comprised of inter alias representatives of the RUC, the Northern Ireland Office and the three police associations—the Police Federation of Northern Ireland, the Superintendents' Association and the Chief Police Officers' Staff Association.

[20] During my time as Police Ombudsman I was never granted a meeting with the Police Federation Central Council. My successor, a former police officer, was invited to meet them before taking office.

[21] Statements under Section 62 of the Police (NI) Act (1998) and associated press reports can be found on http://www.policeombudsman.org.

[22] 'Report into the circumstances of the death of Mr Neil McConville on 29 April 2003', available at: http://www.policeombudsman.org/Publicationsuploads/McCONVILLE.pdf.

[23] 'Report into the circumstances of the death of Mr Samuel Devenny', available at: http://www.policeombudsman.org/Publicationsuploads/devenny.pdf.

[24] 'Report on the investigation into the murder of Mr Sean Brown', available at: http://www.policeombudsman.org/Publicationsuploads/Sean%20Brown%20report.pdf.

[25] Gaelic Athletic Association—a very large amateur sporting organisation, involved in running 'Gaelic' sports—the most popular sports in terms of both participation and attendance in the nationalist community in Northern Ireland (and in Ireland).

[26] 'Report on the complaint by James and Michael McConville regarding the police investigation of the abduction and murder of their mother Mrs Jean McConville', available at: http://www.policeombudsman.org/Publicationsuploads/JEAN%20 McCONVILLE%20Final%20report%20August%202006.doc.

[27] The bomb exploded in Omagh on 15 August 1998.

[28] The 'ACC' is the Assistant Chief Constable. See 'Statement by the Police Ombudsman for Northern Ireland on her investigation of matters relating to the Omagh Bombing on August 15 1998', Section 7.4, 12; available at: http://www.policeombudsman.org/ Publicationsuploads/omaghreport.pdf.

[29] See 'McCord Report', available at: http://www.policeombudsman.org/ Publicationsuploads/BALLAST%20PUBLIC%20STATEMENT%2022-01- 07%20FINAL%20VERSION.pdf.

[30] 'McCord Report', §8, Conclusions and recommendations, paragraphs 33.11 and 33.14.

[31] See 'McCord Report', Appendix A, 154–60.

[32] See 'McCord Report', Recommendations, 147

[33] See *Developments in police complaints*, 52–3.

[34] See *Developments in police complaints*, 23.

CHAPTER 10

PUBLIC ACCOUNTABILITY: THE POLICING BOARD AND THE DISTRICT POLICING PARTNERSHIPS

Desmond Rea, Denis Bradley and Barry Gilligan

INTRODUCTION

T he policing change process in Northern Ireland has been described as one of the most complex and dramatic ever attempted in modern policing history. A tanker truly had to be turned, and now is the right time to provide perspectives on that process from the Policing Board, an organisation that was established to play a central role in delivering the vision for policing contained in the independent policing commission's *A new beginning: policing in Northern Ireland* (generally referred to as the *Patten Report*).[1] It is hard to comprehend the speed with which the last ten years have passed, and in considering *Patten* over the last decade it is important to remember where Northern Ireland was before. Two processes running side by side have brought Northern Ireland out of the 'Troubles'. First, the political process based on the Good Friday Agreement of 10 April 1998; and second, the (more difficult) peace process. Out of the former came the emphasis on policing and *Patten*.

Policing forms an integral part of our society and a central part of any democratic society; however, in Northern Ireland no issue has been more difficult or divisive. Historically, policing in Northern Ireland has not received the support of the whole community it served, as it was not considered to be representative of, or accountable to, the community. Given the history, it was recognised that for the peace process to succeed, policing would play a pivotal part.

There is no doubt the *Patten Report* generated intensive political and public interest in the 175 recommendations it produced. Many focused on the more controversial aspects of the *Report*, such as the proposed changes to the name and emblem of the police service or the positive discrimination provisions for police recruitment (50% Catholic–50% non-Catholic). However, the fact is, in its totality, the *Report* provided a blueprint for modern policing worldwide. A blueprint that represented professionalism and excellence in policing and police accountability that put policing with the community at the heart of its work. A blueprint that provided for restructuring and review that would allow the service to meet community needs and ensure a joined-up approach. Reforms that were designed to ensure that the whole community could have confidence in the delivery of the policing service, and a policing service that has human rights embedded in all aspects of its work.

THE ESTABLISHMENT OF THE POLICING BOARD

The Policing Commission's proposal for a new structure of accountability was designed to ensure effective and democratically based oversight of policing and the creation of a close partnership between the police and local communities. Central to this was the establishment of a Policing Board to replace the Police Authority, which did not have any democratic basis. This new board would have a new, clear statutory primary function to hold the Chief Constable and Police Service to account.

The creation of the new board was a signal of a new beginning for police accountability, as for so many aspects of policing in Northern Ireland; and to succeed as the new policing accountability body it was recognised that it must command respect and credibility and have real power and responsibility. The enabling legislation to support the creation of the new policing architecture had generated political controversy. So, perhaps the first challenge for the new policing oversight body was to get the *Patten Report* onto the discussion table at the Policing Board. The then Chief Constable of the Royal Ulster Constabulary (RUC), Sir Ronnie Flanagan, had endorsed the *Report*, which sent a clear signal to the policing family that the time was right for change. (Sir Ronnie had been author of an earlier *Fundamental review of policing* that had recognised the need for policing change).[2]

On 4 November 2001 the then RUC evolved into the Police Service of Northern Ireland (PSNI), and the new Northern Ireland

Policing Board (the Board) was created with 19 members in total, including a chairman and vice-chairman. Ten of these are elected members of the Northern Ireland Assembly appointed under D'Hondt principles.[3] Back in 2001, members of the Social Democratic and Labour Party (SDLP) endorsed the new policing arrangements and took their seats on the Board. Sinn Féin (SF) took its seats on the Board in May 2007, delivering full political support for the policing arrangements in Northern Ireland.

The work of the Board is wide-ranging in respect of its statutory duties, which include measures to ensure effective oversight and monitoring of the work of the police, and encouraging the engagement of the community with the police. It is the role of the Board to secure the delivery of an effective, efficient and impartial policing service for Northern Ireland and to hold the Chief Constable to account for that. The Board also has a supporting role for policing in terms of ensuring that the police have the resources necessary to do the job. Its work is delivered through meetings and through the work of its committees. The Board's meetings normally comprise three sessions: a private session for Board members and officials only; a private session where the Board is joined by the Chief Constable and his chief officers; and a public session that members of the public and media are invited to attend. Injecting openness and transparency into policing oversight has formed a key part of the new accountability arrangements in Northern Ireland, and during the lifetime of the Board its work has generated significant local, national and international interest.

ACHIEVEMENTS OF THE POLICING BOARD

The Board has achieved much since its establishment in 2001, particularly in its early life when many of its tasks were undertaken during a period of elongated political uncertainty, and not without controversy. During this time the Board has put in place mechanisms to monitor and assess the performance of the Chief Constable and the PSNI, including a human-rights monitoring framework and a code of ethics for police officers. The Board has set objectives for the Police Service to meet in order to shape policing across Northern Ireland. It has also taken the lead on securing the resources necessary to deliver effective and efficient policing, while holding the Police Service to account for the way in which it has managed and used the resources it has been given. It has overseen and monitored the reform of the

PSNI's Crime Operations Department and made difficult decisions successfully in a complex political environment.

In its early life, the Board also had to manage and deal with the fall-out from events that had serious ramifications for policing and indeed politics. The Castlereagh break-in, the Stormont investigation that precipitated the collapse of the Assembly and the Northern Bank robbery are events that required the Board to exercise its accountability role.[4] These events, combined with issues such as the ongoing threat from dissident groupings and incidents of serious civic disorder, illustrate the unique environment in which policing has had to operate in Northern Ireland. Despite real progress in the programme of normalisation, policing is not yet normal, because Northern Ireland is not yet normal; but policing is now accountable. With Northern Ireland's political institutions suspended for a large part of the Board's life, many commentators viewed the Board as the 'only show in town', and it delivered on the promise of real police oversight through the reform programme.

The change programme has moved at a rapid pace. Tom Constantine, the first Oversight Commissioner for policing reform Northern Ireland, described the process as 'complex and of a magnitude that is virtually unparalleled in…scope'.[5] That change has delivered a blueprint for modern policing. The Board steadily moved forward the recommendations in its remit, and in a business-like manner dealt with, and delivered on, a major programme of work. This work has not gone unnoticed, and senior police officers, politicians and policing experts from around the world have come to learn about the work of the PSNI and the Board.

With that interest also came support. Current and previous British and Irish prime ministers (Taoisigh) and presidents of the United States have taken a close interest in the progress taking place in policing in Northern Ireland. The most important people during the last ten years, however, have been the people of Northern Ireland. All of the Board's work has been undertaken on their behalf, and the Board is ultimately accountable to them. In the opening remarks at the first meeting in public of the Policing Board it was said that: '…as the Board begins its work, it has the ability to shape the future of policing in Northern Ireland'.[6] The public and historians will judge how well it has done and continues to do this. The following sections of this chapter examine some of the key areas of the Board's oversight and accountability work over the last ten years.

New PSNI emblem

In the first few months of its existence the Board agreed a new emblem for the Police Service. *Patten* had recommended that 'the Police Service adopt a new badge and symbols which are entirely free from any association with either British or Irish states'.[7] Symbols are important in Northern Ireland and there is no doubt that many were surprised that consensus was achieved on the badge and emblem issue. The emblem, as agreed by the Board, encapsulates the promise of the Good Friday Agreement that the majority of people in Northern Ireland were working to achieve. It explores the notion of inclusiveness and parity through the simple stylistic representation of a variety of symbols that reflect diversity, hope and the desire mutually to respect and protect difference through policing. The sunburst surrounding the roundel represents a new beginning or new dawn for the new PSNI. The shape is echoed in the central star, and the six spaces between its rays are set with a series of symbols—all of equal prominence. These symbols include: scales of justice, a harp, a torch, an olive branch, a shamrock and a crown.[8] The centre-piece houses the Cross of Saint Patrick,[9] which places all six symbols in the context of Northern Ireland.

PSNI composition

Central to the *Patten Report* was, of course, the size, structure and composition of the service. The *Report* recognised that 'the consent required right across the community…for effective policing has been absent', and asked in respect of police services in democratic societies, 'how can the police be properly accountable to the community they serve if their composition in terms of ethnicity, religion and gender is vastly dissimilar to that of their society?'[10] For policing to earn the trust and the support of the community, it needed to be representative of it. This was clearly not the case as at 31 December 1998: there were 8,457 full-time officers in the RUC, of which 704 (8.3%) were Catholic, against a Catholic population of 40%; at the same time just 11% of RUC officers were women.

Patten opted for a recruitment profile of 50% non-Catholic and 50% Catholic over a 10-year period. The 50:50 recruitment provision in the *Report* has proved highly controversial and caused much public debate, but in reality has delivered real compositional change in a short space of time. The service is on course to meet the compositional target of 30% Catholics by 2011, and in the recruitment competitions held, there has been a steady applicant rate of 37% from the Catholic community.

With almost 100,000 applications received in the first 15 recruitment competitions, it is very clear that policing now represents an attractive career choice. Another welcome change has been the increase in female representation in the service. The Board developed and published a gender action plan to monitor the number of women employed in the PSNI, which includes support staff and staff within the Board. Since 2001 the percentage of female police officers in the service has increased from 11% to the current level of 25%, which is a very positive result. On a less positive note, it is disappointing that more progress has not been made in the representation of civilian staff. The 50:50 recruitment provisions apply to appointments of 6 or more staff, but there is a lot more to do in effecting compositional change to civilian staffing levels.

Omagh report and Special Branch reform

On 15 August 1998, within four months of the signing of the Good Friday Agreement, the Omagh bomb exploded.[11] The juxtaposition was stark: 29 people and 2 unborn children died as a result of the attack, and 220 people were injured. It was the largest single loss of life in 30 years of what is euphemistically referred to as the 'Troubles'.

Not long after the Board was established the Police Ombudsman for Northern Ireland, Nuala O'Loan, published a highly critical report on the police investigation of the Omagh bombing.[12] The Ombudsman's report, which was the subject of intense media scrutiny, was presented to the Board in December 2001, and in January 2002 the Chief Constable delivered to the Board the PSNI's rebuttal to the report. At such an early stage in its existence, this controversial and emotive event presented a major challenge for the Board, and the action it took was constructive and pragmatic, and provided a basis for progressing the reform of policing at a critical time.

The Board did not shirk its responsibilities in dealing with the response to this critical report. After meeting with the Police Ombudsman and unanimously accepting the findings and recommendations of her report, the Board put in place and implemented its own actions to deal with issues flowing from the report. The Board outlined four key actions as follows:

- the Board would appoint a deputy chief constable to act as an independent scrutineer of the investigation;
- the Chief Constable would request HMIC[13] to conduct a full review of the policy, practices and procedures in relation to murder enquiries in Northern Ireland (this became known as the *Blakey Report*);[14]
- the Board would request HMIC to conduct a focused review of Special Branch (this became known as the *Crompton Report*);[15] and
- the Board would establish a monitoring system for the implementation of any recommendations arising from the above reviews.

Prior to this, the former commissioner for the London Metropolitan Police, Sir John Stevens, undertook a number of inquiries in Northern Ireland, which broadly centred on allegations of collusion between security forces and loyalist paramilitaries[16] in Northern Ireland. His third report (*Stevens 3*) made some recommendations about, inter alia, major investigations, the sharing of intelligence and exhibit management, which corresponded with the findings of *Blakey* and *Crompton*.[17]

The Board's review of the dissemination of intelligence between Special Branch and other parts of the Police Service has formed the basis for major change in how the police shares intelligence. The Board's *Crompton Report* recommendations, combined with the findings from the *Blakey* and *Stevens 3* reports, formed the basis for the establishment and structuring of the Police Service's new Crime Operations Department. All of which was closely scrutinised by the Board, with information presented in the Board's public sessions. The area of intelligence, the reform of Special Branch and the handling of informants are issues on which legitimate questions have been raised, but the oversight of reforms in these areas has led to significant changes. The dedicated structure and staffing put in place for the Crime Operations Department ensures that the policies, processes and practices for the management of intelligence now meet national professional standards and provide for public confidence and a better public service.

As part of the oversight of the reform to this area of work, the Board instigated meetings with the local head of MI5, who meets with the Board bi-annually to discuss issues of mutual interest. Indeed, in the transfer of National Security in 2007, as part of the St Andrews Agreement,[18] the Board's human-rights advisors were given responsibility for human-rights proofing the intelligence sharing protocols between PSNI and MI5. Another Police Ombudsman Report, 'Operation Ballast', was published in January 2007 and documented the findings of an investigation into matters surrounding the death of Raymond McCord Junior.[19] This critical report officially exposed the extent of collusion between police officers and illegal loyalist paramilitaries. As suggested by the Ombudsman, the Board agreed to monitor the implementation of her recommendations, which fall within the remit of the PSNI. The Board also tasked its human-rights advisors to examine, validate and report on the implementation of the 17 recommendations in the Ombudsman's report that dealt with the PSNI, in order to provide assurance to the Board. In the interests of openness and transparency copies of these reports have been published, so that the wider community could also have confidence that the new processes and practice were now subject to the highest scrutiny and oversight.

Human rights and policing

Chapter 4 of the *Patten Report* stressed 'the importance of human rights as the very purpose of policing' and recommended:

- a new oath to be taken individually by all new and existing police officers, expressing an explicit commitment to upholding human rights;
- a new code of ethics, to replace the existing, largely procedural code, integrating the European Convention on Human Rights into police practice;
- that all police officers, and police civilians, should be trained (and updated as required) in the fundamental principles and standards of human rights and the practical implications for policing; and
- that the performance of the police service as a whole in respect of human rights, as in other respects, should be monitored closely by the Policing Board.

The introduction of the code of ethics for the Police Service in February 2003 marked a milestone for human rights and policing in Northern Ireland and further afield. For the first time, a code laid down the standards of conduct and practice for police officers, and set out their rights and their obligations under the Human Rights Act (1998). Human rights are a fundamental element in policing, and achieving and maintaining standards such as those outlined in the code of ethics is a critical factor for sustaining community confidence in the delivery of policing. The code of ethics now in place sets out the standards of behaviour that are acceptable and those that are not.

The Board also has a statutory responsibility to monitor police compliance with the Human Rights Act. To meet this important oversight role, the Board, with the assistance of expert advisors, developed and published a robust monitoring framework to scrutinise how the police meet their human-rights responsibilities across key areas of the PSNI's work, such as use of force; public order; policy; training; victim's rights; operations; and treatment of suspects. In March 2005 the Board published its *Human Rights Annual Report*, the first of its kind in European and international policing. In this first report, the authors concluded that in their view the PSNI had done more than any other service to achieve human-rights compliance.[20] Each year since, detailed reports with recommendations have been produced to guide the PSNI. Since that time, the Board has continued to assess human-rights performance and report on progress against implementation of recommendations made. The Board has also published two major reports on how the police have met their human-rights responsibilities in policing contentious Belfast parades.

The human rights accountability mechanisms that are in place provide for a model of best practice. Indeed, the express statutory duty to monitor compliance with human-rights legislation that was placed on the Board was extended to other police authorities across the UK in 2008; and the model framework adopted in the UK mirrors the Northern Ireland approach. Work in this area does not stand still, however, and in 2009 the Board progressed the first human rights thematic report on the subject of domestic abuse. This gave the Board's Human Rights Monitoring Framework a new dimension and has received positive feedback from police and those working with the victims of domestic abuse. Without doubt, all aspects of the Board's work in human-rights oversight has been groundbreaking and has played a key part in confidence building.

Policing with the community / Establishment of District Policing Partnerships (DPPs)

The *Patten Report* used the phrase 'Policing with the Community' to describe the policing style that the Commission wanted to see develop in Northern Ireland: the police working in partnership with the community; the community thereby participating in its own policing; and the two working together, using resources to solve problems affecting public safety over the longer term, rather than the police, alone, reacting short-term to incidents as they occur. *Patten* recognised the need for this engagement to take place in a structured way, and to facilitate this recommended that District Policing Partnerships (DPPs) be set up in each Council area.

The 26 DPPs were set up by the Board in 2003 and, overall, are a genuine success story, with around 500 local people now shaping local policing issues. The partnerships have become an integral and accepted part of local policing and have provided the forum for grassroots engagement in a way that has never happened before. Each DPP covers the same area as the local Council and PSNI Area Command Unit, and the partnerships consult with the public to find out what policing and crime issues are of concern within their Council district. These consultations take place in many different ways, from surveys to focus groups, to meetings with local community forums and residents.

Membership of DPPs comprises of Councillors and independent members; Councillors are in the majority by one. The Board appoints the independent members and in doing so seeks to ensure that the membership of each DPP is representative of the community it serves. This is a statutory duty for the Board, and in making the original appointments the Board took into account the community background, gender, age, race, sexual orientation and disability of those seeking appointment to ensure representativeness. This was not an easy task and for some it proved controversial; where all the elected members were men, for example, the Board appointed all women independents. The initial appointment process represented one of the largest simultaneous public appointment processes ever undertaken in Northern Ireland. Since that time, DPPs have been reconstituted on two occasions and, like the Board, since 2007 now have the benefit of full political support. DPPs ensure that local people have a voice on police service delivery, and thus have contributed in a unique way to building community confidence in policing. Through their outreach and engagement work, DPPs have worked to make communities safer and to provide assurance on issues of concern. During their first term, which was completed on 31 March 2006, DPPs held over 400 meetings in public. Since that time the public has continued to use the democratic platform of the DPPs to have a say on local policing issues.

Policing in Northern Ireland has unique challenges, and that very definitely has an impact on how policing is delivered on the ground; however, real progress has been made. The PSNI has undoubtedly sought innovative ways to deliver a twenty-first century policing service, and this work continues to evolve. Policing with the Community is a top priority for the Board members, and in particular for those in the Community Engagement Committee, who have been working closely and building relationships with key groups and individuals to make sure that, in line with its statutory duty, the Board encourages co-operation with the police to prevent crime; and that the needs of the public are identified when setting targets and developing policing policy.

The groups with which the Community Engagement Committee works represent minority ethnic and language groups, older people, the LGBT community, people with disability, women and young people. The Board believes it is important that local people have a voice on policing and encourages them to become involved in decisions that affect them, their community and their neighbourhood. In consultations with a range of groups and organisations, the Board has strived to ensure that the community has a platform to inform the policing agenda. This has allowed it to strengthen the relationship between the community and the police and assist the Board in holding the Chief Constable to account. Part of the consultations undertaken resulted in the Board launching its Community Engagement Strategy in September 2008, outlining how it engages with the public on policing. There is, of course, still work to be done, particularly within the loyalist and republican communities; however, the commitment from policing to do this exists, as does the commitment from the Board to ensure that everyone has access to a good service.

Public satisfaction with and confidence in policing

One of the statutory duties of the Board is to assess the level of public satisfaction with police performance. The Board also carries out this function in relation to DPPs, in assessing the level of public satisfaction with the performance of the police in an area and with the DPPs themselves. This also includes assessing the effectiveness of the DPPs in obtaining the views of the public about matters concerning policing and the co-operation of the public and the police in preventing crime.

In order to fulfil this duty, the Board has set 'confidence in policing' as one of the main objectives in the Policing Plan 2009–2012. To measure the targets associated with this objective, the Board, on a twice yearly basis, commissions two independent surveys.[21] The survey published in December 2008, comprised 1,956 randomly selected households across Northern Ireland, and a total of 1,213 people aged 16 or over were interviewed. The findings from this survey show that the vast majority of people (93%) feel very/fairly safe in their local community; and 86% of respondents have, 'some', 'a lot' or 'total' confidence in the PSNI's ability to provide a day-to-day policing service for everyone in Northern Ireland.

It is also interesting to compare responses to questions asked soon after the Board was established in November 2001 with those published more recently. In April 2002, 79% of respondents stated that they had 'some', 'a lot' or 'total' confidence in the PSNI's ability to provide an ordinary day-to-day policing service for all the people of Northern Ireland. This had increased to 86% in September 2008. Also in the April 2002 survey, 69% of Catholic respondents stated that they had 'some', 'a lot' or 'total' confidence in the PSNI's ability to provide an ordinary, day-to-day policing service for all the people of Northern Ireland. This had increased significantly to 84% in September 2008.

In relation to the work of the Board, in the April 2002 survey findings, 70% of respondents who had heard of the Board stated that the Board is working at least adequately. This figure increased by 8 percentage points to 78% in September 2008. Also, 72% correctly identified that the organisation was independent of the police in September 2002, the same as the September 2008 finding. Northern Ireland is a relatively safe place to live; however, in terms of confidence levels, the Board and the PSNI realise that surveys often do not reflect the views of the local community and questionnaires can be too simplistic to have any real meaning. There is a need to drill down to a local level to find out how confident people really are in the service provided by the police, and what additional measures the Board can take to raise confidence in these local communities.

Appointment of senior police officers

Another key role of the Board is the appointment of senior police officers, and to date it has appointed two chief constables, two deputy chief constables and six assistant chief constables (ACCs) to the PSNI. These processes have been rigorous and, aside from an incident in 2002 that required an apology to be issued, the Board's processes have incorporated best practice. The appointment panels comprise representation from the political parties, and since 2007 all panels have had the benefit of input from all the parties represented on the Board. The PSNI Chief Constable was the first senior police officer in the UK to undergo a formal appraisal. The Policing Board introduced the 'Performance and Development Review' and 'Performance Related Pay' systems in 2004/05, with the willing co-operation of the then Chief Constable, Sir Hugh Orde, in advance of the national agreement on 'Chief Officer Bonus Schemes'.

THE CHALLENGES AHEAD

Finalising the ten-year programme of change in the policing process in Northern Ireland is firmly on course. There are areas where attention needs to be more clearly focused; however, the vast majority of issues are off the table. In May 2007 the Board, as part of its governance role, took on responsibility for overseeing the implementation of the majority of the *Patten Report* recommendations identified by the Oversight Commission as still outstanding. The Board commissioned a report in June 2008, which concluded that 17 of the 32 outstanding recommendations could be considered to have been implemented or closed at that stage, leaving 15 to be dealt with.

Some of the remaining recommendations, such as the 'appearance of police stations' and the 'new police college', will remain a challenge from a fiscal perspective; others, such as 'community policing as a core function', remain a challenge from an organisational and strategic perspective. The Board will continue to monitor the outstanding recommendations and, looking to the future, realises that policing must continue to grow and evolve if it is to survive and meet the changing needs of the people of Northern Ireland. Indeed, the recent appointment of Matt Baggott as Chief Constable[22] marks a new chapter in policing history, and in leading the PSNI forward his experiences will bring a new perspective, focus and dynamic to the delivery of the police service in Northern Ireland.

Looking back on what has been achieved, tribute must be paid to the former Chief Constable of the PSNI Sir Hugh Orde, who has made a significant contribution to policing in Northern Ireland. His style and approach brought an energy to policing that was right for that part of the period of change. His understanding of the issues, his openness with the Board and his willingness to push the boundaries brought an important momentum to the job in hand. Thanks to his leadership, Northern Ireland now has a police service that has been subject to a reform process that means it now represents what is best in modern policing practice, oversight and accountability.

As the Board has moved forward, lessons have been learned; and in that respect policing and the work of the Board is no different from the work of any other organisation. The Board itself recognised the need for inspection of its own work, and in May 2005 established an Independent Assessment Panel to assess its performance and effectiveness over its first four years of operation. The ethos of continuous improvement is one that the Board has integrated into its governance arrangements.

Although the Board has delivered on many aspects of its work, there are issues that in hindsight might have been handled better. Without doubt, however, the willingness of the Board to reach consensus on difficult issues and to take decisions based on what is right for policing sends a positive message to the wider community. All of the Board's decision-making was firmly grounded in providing the best possible policing service for the people of Northern Ireland. The Board and PSNI now face a number of challenges in ensuring that we live in safer communities. Managing the impact of a reducing police budget on the delivery of front-line policing is one of them, as is building public confidence in policing where there has traditionally been a lack of community support.

From the Board's perspective the challenges focus on the delivery of a high-quality policing service to everyone through the better use of resources. Central to this is getting more police officers out from behind desks and on the ground, to further improve the service to the community and continue to build partnerships to reduce crime and make communities safer. Of course, the issue of funding and resources has also formed a major part of the discussions around the devolution of policing and justice. The Board supports the concept of devolution as set out in Recommendation 20 of the *Patten Report*, which states: 'Responsibility for policing should be devolved to the Northern Ireland Executive as soon as possible, except for matters of national security'.[23]

However, the Board believes its role and powers should not be diminished under the proposed devolution arrangements, and contends that the Chief Constable should remain accountable solely to the Board for the delivery of a policing service in Northern Ireland; and it further believes that the Chief Constable's operational responsibility should not be undermined when policing and justice powers are devolved. These principles represent the unanimous view of the Board, and these fundamental principles must be embedded in the framework for devolution, with appropriate arrangements and protocols put in place to ensure that they are given full effect.

Of course, whilst the majority of people in Northern Ireland are looking forward, sadly there remains a minority of people in our community who wish to return to the past. The murders of Constable Stephen Carroll and the two soldiers at Massereene Barracks, Sappers Mark Quinsey and Patrick Azimkar, in March 2009, marked a tragic milestone and provided a stark reminder that Northern Ireland is not yet a normal society. The attacks sent shockwaves across the wider community, bringing an unwelcome reminder of the troubled past. However, the condemnations of these murders from right across the community and political spectrum demonstrated unity and resolve that those who carried out these acts will not be allowed to undermine the peace process; or the policing progress. Without doubt, the image of the First Minister and Deputy First Minister standing shoulder to shoulder with the Chief Constable to condemn the murders could not have sent a stronger message that those trying to drag us backwards will not succeed.

Threats such as these murders will not deter the Board from moving forward on policing, and while much has been achieved, now is the time to look beyond that and lay a path for the future that embeds and builds on the values enshrined in the *Patten Report*. Neighbourhood policing must now be taken a stage further and be truly responsive to the needs of local communities. Both the Board and the PSNI are committed to this and will be working in partnership to ensure the delivery of the best possible policing service to all the people of Northern Ireland.

There is still a long way to go in building a shared future. Policing will continue to play a key role in that but cannot carry the full burden of resolving deeper societal issues, including our troubled past. This is difficult and sensitive work, but it is work that must now be grasped by political leaders. Reflecting on the past ten years has, without doubt, reinforced the enormity of what was asked of, and delivered by, policing. No other police service in the UK or in any other country has in modern times had to manage and implement such fundamental change while continuing to police a changing society. Ten years on it is testimony to all those involved that so much has been achieved, and that should not be forgotten.

NOTES

[1] Independent Commission on Policing for Northern Ireland, *A new beginning: policing in Northern Ireland* Report of the Independent Commission on Policing for Northern Ireland (hereafter referred to as *Patten Report*) (Belfast: HMSO/Northern Ireland Office, 1999).

[2] See 'Summary and key findings from the fundamental review of policing' (Belfast: RUC, 1996).

[3] The Ministerial posts in the Northern Ireland executive are also allocated proportionally, based on seats won at the previous Assembly election—using a mathematical model called the d'Hondt formula. See the following link for details: http://education.niassembly.gov.uk/a_level/activities/dHondt.pdf

[4] These were three controversial, high-profile issues. In each case the event itself was highly political and therefore the police operations and responses would potentially have significant political impacts.

'Castlereagh': There was a breach of security and a break in at the Special Branch office in Castlereagh that is involved in dealing with police informants; see http://news.bbc.co.uk/1/hi/northern_ireland/2298675.stm.

'Stormont': Sinn Féin's offices at Stormont were raided on 4 October 2002 as part of a major police investigation into intelligence gathering. The police subsequently apologised for the 'style' of the policing operation.

The Northern Bank robbery—the largest cash robbery ever in Northern Ireland—was allegedly carried out by the IRA, and led to intense political difficulties.

[5] Office of the Oversight Commissioner, 'Overseeing the proposed revisions for the policing services of Northern Ireland—Report 1 (16 October 2000)', (Belfast: Office of the Oversight Commissioner, 2000), 28. The text of the report is available at: http://cain.ulst.ac.uk/issues/police/oversight/oversight-rep1-161000.pdf.

[6] See the minutes of first Board meeting, available at: http://www.nipolicingboard.org.uk/7_november_2001_.pdf.

[7] *Patten Report*, Chapter 17, paragraph 17.6

[8] Traditional symbols of justice, peace, and British and Irish identity.

[9] An uncontroversial symbol in Northern Ireland.

[10] *Patten Report*, Chapter 1, paragraph 1.5.

[11] This bomb was detonated in Omagh town centre by an IRA splinter group, labelled the Real IRA, that opposed the peace process and had left the mainstream IRA. The term 'dissident group' was generally used in Ireland to describe such groups, none of which had any significant public support.

[12] See the Police Ombudsman's statement on her investigation into the Omagh bombing, available at: http://cain.ulst.ac.uk/issues/police/ombudsman/po121201 omagh1.pdf.

[13] Her Majesty's Inspectorate of Constabulary—an official body overseeing the efficiency and effectiveness of the police forces in England, Wales and Northern Ireland.

[14] A Report on 'Murder Investigation in Northern Ireland', was commissioned by the PSNI and completed by then Her Majesty's Inspector of Constabulary, David Blakey. The terms of reference agreed for the review were: The HMIC will undertake a review of current structures, resources, strategies and processes in relation to the investigation of murder in the particular circumstances of Northern Ireland. The report is not in the public domain.

[15] The Northern Ireland Policing Board requested a focused review into the handling of information between Special Branch and other parts of the Police Service following its consideration of the Police Ombudsman's 'Report on matters relating to the Omagh Bombing on August 15 1998' (which was published in December 2001 and is available at: http://www.policeombudsman.org/publicationsuploads/omaghreport.pdf). The report for the Policing Board was prepared by then Her Majesty's Inspector of Constabulary Sir Dan Crompton. Sir Dan's report was presented to the Board in November 2002 and made eleven recommendations. The *Crompton Report* is not in the public domain.

[16] In Northern Ireland the term 'paramilitaries' is reserved for illegal armed groups.

[17] Sir John Stevens was commissioned in 1999 by the former Chief Constable, Sir Ronnie Flanagan, to conduct an independent investigation into the murder of Belfast solicitor Mr Pat Finucane and associated matters raised by the British Irish Rights Watch Organisation and by the Report of the UN Rapporteur, Mr Param Cumwaraswamy. The report as published contained 21 recommendations, and a copy can be found at: http://news.bbc.co.uk/1/shared/spl/hi/northern_ireland/03/stephens_inquiry/pdf

[18] This agreement, on the devolution of power to Northern Ireland, was reached between the British and Irish governments and the political parties in Northern Ireland following discussions in October 2006. Further details on the agreement and its outcome are available at: http://www.taoiseach.gov.ie/eng/Government_Press_Office/Government_Press_Releases_2008/Government_Press_Releases_2006/Documents_released_after_talks_at_St_Andrews.html.

[19] This report is available at: http://www.policeombudsman.org/publicationsuploads/BALLAST%20PUBLIC%20STATEMENT%2022-01-07%20FINAL%20VERSION.pdf

[20] For all reports, see http://www.nipolicingboard.org.uk.

[21] See Policing Board website for details: http://www.nipolicingboard.org.uk/index/publications/omnibus-surveys.html.

[22] He was appointed as Chief Constable of the PSNI on 11 August 2009, and his was the first appointment for which Sinn Féin was represented on the interview board.

[23] *Patten Report*, Chapter 6, paragraph 6.15.

CHAPTER 11

THE PERCEPTION OF POLICING CHANGE FROM THE PERSPECTIVE OF HUMAN-RIGHTS NON-GOVERNMENTAL ORGANISATIONS (NGOs)

Maggie Beirne and Martin O'Brien

INTRODUCTION

This chapter will focus on the perception of policing change in Northern Ireland from the perspective of an independent human-rights group, both in the wake of the publication of *A new beginning: policing in Northern Ireland*, the Report of the Independent Commission on Policing for Northern Ireland[1] in September 1999, and in the early years of implementation of its recommendations. However, to understand fully the significance of the *Patten Report* itself, and the difficulties faced in implementing its recommendations, it is important to situate the *Report* in some historical context.

POLICING PRE-*PATTEN*

Policing had long been a contentious issue in Northern Ireland. In essence, before the changes initiated by the *Patten Report*, the police were seen by many as composed of members of the one (majority) community, with responsibility for policing the other (minority) community. As the state came under increasing criticism, and eventually violent attack, the Royal Ulster Constabulary (RUC) was seen (by many in both communities) as a force for maintaining order, and therefore as defending the status quo.

This 'political' role for policing put the RUC centre-stage when the most recent phase of 'the Troubles' started. An official government

inquiry into the causes and nature of the street disturbances and violence in Derry in October 1968—the Cameron Commission[2]—
determined that one of the major factors in the sense of grievance that
led to the street disturbances was the

> resentment, particularly among Catholics, as to the ex-
> istence of the Ulster Special Constabulary (the 'B-
> Specials') as a partisan and paramilitary force recruited
> exclusively from Protestants.[3]

The report also cited a number of problems with the policing of the
violent disturbances, and concluded that the conduct of the police
'was an immediate and contributing cause of the disorders which subsequently occurred'.[4] Interestingly, an important recommendation of
the *Cameron Report* was the establishment of an independent system
for investigating allegations of police misconduct—a reform that took
almost 40 years to be substantively implemented.[5]

One is left wondering, 'what if' this basic safeguard had been introduced in the 1960s? Would an early and effective response to genuine
complaints have prevented grievances about policing from festering?
Instead, in the absence of an independent complaints system, the
police were excoriated over the death of people like Samuel Devenney
(father of nine and one of the first casualties of the conflict);[6] TV pic-
tures of civil-rights marchers being brutally attacked; allegations of
involvement in shoot-to-kill operations; excessive and abusive use of
emergency powers; ill-treatment in interrogations; harassment of
defence lawyers; collusion; and sectarian policing.[7] Both the reality and
the perception of police wrong-doing contributed to feeding and fu-
elling the conflict.

The 30 years from 1968 to the signing of the Belfast or Good
Friday Agreement in 1998 was a tragic period in terms of the loss of
life.[8] Police officers bore severe losses because they were considered 'legitimate targets' by republican paramilitaries and were thus deliberately
targeted for assassination: 303 police officers were killed during those
years and thousands injured. Yet the terrible extent of the fatalities
among police officers was mis-used by some segments of society to
obscure the reality that policing was a cause as well as a consequence
of increasing political polarisation in Northern Ireland. Those raising
legitimate policing concerns were ignored (where possible) or, when
they could no longer be ignored, were demonised and characterised as
'fellow-travellers' of those responsible for the killing of police officers.

POLICING PRE-*PATTEN* FROM THE
PERSPECTIVE OF NGOs

At the very heart of the practice of policing in any democratic society is the principle of 'policing by consent'. This principle is, however, unattainable in situations where the police are seen to be defending a status quo that, in the eyes of a sufficient number of people, is unacceptable. In Northern Ireland, the police were required to perform a highly militarised function, and police weaponry, transport and buildings all deterred, rather than facilitated, interaction with civilians.

Whilst the police were becoming more militarised, civil society organisations were in retreat. Peaceful protest was irretrievably damaged by the events of Bloody Sunday in 1972,[9] which led also to the demise of the Northern Ireland Civil Rights Association (NICRA).[10] An organisation committed to change by way of peaceful protest and civil disobedience was rendered manifestly incapable of securing change, and genuine grievances remained unaddressed. The 1970s saw the highest level of violent deaths in Northern Ireland, and it was not until the 1980s that a concerted and sustained effort was made to develop a broad range of cross-community, non-governmental efforts on policing and justice issues. The Committee on the Administration of Justice (CAJ) came into being in 1981, after a conference at Queen's University Belfast recommended the creation of a permanent, independent watchdog body to review and monitor the administration of justice.[11]

From the outset, many of CAJ's publications and interventions related to the powers of the police—an examination of emergency law, stop-and-search practices and interrogation techniques. A consistent concern from 1982 onwards was the need for an effective complaints system, and CAJ issued regular publications on this topic.[12] Police accountability was also an ongoing topic on CAJ's agenda,[13] as were concerns around public-order policing.[14] Yet, despite consistent campaigning, it would be fair to say that NGOs like CAJ were 'fire-fighting' much of the time. CAJ reported on police abuses, proposed structural and legislative changes and tried to secure domestic support for its proposals. Over time, however, it became apparent that sufficient domestic pressure was either not forthcoming or, more often, inadequate to the task. Indeed, the very fact that groups like CAJ criticised bad police practices from an impartial human-rights perspective left it occasionally isolated. In a divided society where the 'us and them' dynamic reigns and everyone is expected to be loyal to one side or the other, independent criticism can often be portrayed as misguided or even deliberately dangerous.[15]

In part to counter any such isolation, CAJ increasingly sought external support for, and endorsement of, its efforts. Human-rights NGOs hoped that, since the UK government was unresponsive to domestic pressure, it might be more amenable to international pressure and criticism. This proved to be the case, in part because the early 1990s was a time when the UN treaty bodies were beginning to flex their muscles.[16] So, by way of interventions at the United Nations,[17] with the US president, at hearings in the US Congress[18] and at the European Court of Human Rights,[19] CAJ sought to embarrass domestic authorities into tackling serious human-rights abuses in Northern Ireland. The 'naming and shaming' efforts were invaluable,[20] but progress was extremely slow; there was still little constructive engagement on the part of the authorities and change appeared frequently to be grudgingly secured.

The first ceasefires in 1994 changed this. At the local level, communities prepared the ground for change and started to hold small-scale conferences and debates to explore, with some excitement, the concept of policing a peaceful society.[21] On the official side, the winds of change were also blowing and in 1996 the then assistant and subsequently Chief Constable, Ronnie Flanagan published the 'Fundamental review of policing'.[22] Though it presented a largely technocratic, rather than fundamental, reform agenda for policing, Flanagan's initiative suggested that a window of opportunity was opening up for constructive dialogue. NGOs like CAJ started to think beyond documenting immediate policing problems, and began to develop a more comprehensive picture of how human-rights compliant policing should look in future. Joint statements with international human rights groups, 'Chatham House rule' events and a large cross-community conference, all contributed to a more forward-looking policing and justice agenda.[23]

Even with the breakdown of the ceasefire, when policing change seemed again to become a far-distant aspiration, CAJ pursued its work on a major piece of international comparative policing research. The eventual report (*Human rights on duty*)[24] looked at best practice in terms of training, composition, organisational structures, legal and democratic accountability and transitional arrangements. Drawing on experiences of policing change from Australia, Belgium, Canada, El Salvador, the Netherlands, South Africa and Spain, the report developed a detailed blueprint of good policing. The timing of its publication could hardly have been more fortuitous; it was completed in November 1997, thus placing CAJ and others in Northern Ireland in an ideal position to inform the thinking of all the political parties engaged in the peace negotiations of early 1998, and thereafter.

THE PATTEN COMMISSION STARTS WORK

Having looked at experiences around the world, one of the conclusions reached in *Human rights on duty* was that political will is a major factor in preventing or facilitating successful change in policing. In particular, the report noted with regard to Northern Ireland that

> some aspects of policing change are dependent on reaching a political settlement. However, it will be difficult if not impossible to reach such a settlement where policing remains unaddressed.[25]

The signing of the Belfast/Good Friday Agreement only a few months later confirmed the truth of the above analysis.[26] Policing was a major building block of the Agreement and, despite the fact that the issue had always previously sharply divided nationalists and unionists, the right language, and the right process for further negotiations, were eventually agreed.

The Agreement set out clearly the terms of reference for what was to become the Patten Commission, and—due in part to lobbying by CAJ and others[27]—listed various benchmarks against which the Commission's work would eventually be measured. The text, negotiated very carefully by all parties to the Agreement, required that the Commission be independent, broadly representative with expert and international representation amongst its membership, and consult widely, including with non-governmental expert organisations. In particular, the text set out in some detail the policing issues to be addressed, and the importance of future policing arrangements being human-rights compliant.

Having long argued that an international independent commission into policing in Northern Ireland was required, NGOs were eager to co-operate with the Patten Commission once it was established. CAJ secured an early meeting and also sent observers to many of the Commission's public evidence-gathering sessions, and to the hearings held across Northern Ireland. The Commission was quickly made aware of the wide international consensus about what constituted good policing;[28] its real challenge, however, was to determine how to apply that learning in the political cauldron of Northern Ireland. In effect, the Commission had been asked to provide an expert report that would 'depoliticise' the policing debate as far as possible. Such a mission required not merely technical competence, but political acuity and courage.

The Commission was brave in many regards. It tackled head-on the question of under-representation of Catholics in the police and proposed a radical quota system for recruitment. It argued that the Agreement's promised 'new beginning' to policing necessitated the creation of different cultural symbols and a new sense of identity, and it addressed the difficult issues of downsizing whilst diversifying its membership. The Commission also insisted that human rights should be central to all future policing arrangements. Some of the other proposed reforms were merely those that any professional, modern police service would embrace: improved IT systems, greater internal delegation of authority and budgets, etc.

In other regards, however, NGOs believed that the Commission had inadequately met its challenge. On occasion, the inadequacies seemed to be largely a problem of 'gaps' or silences. For example, why did the Commission pay so little attention to the issue of gender? There was also very limited discussion of socio-economic factors and the experience of policing in working class areas (a problem in many societies, not just Northern Ireland). Why did the Commission focus on religious identifiers rather than political ones: was the challenge not to recruit nationalists and republicans, rather than Catholics per se?

One particularly glaring oversight was the fact that in a 130 page report, the Commission devoted only two paragraphs to emergency legislation. The Commission was not blind to the importance of the issue—quoting others (apparently with approval) to the effect that, 'much of the dissatisfaction with policing, in both loyalist and republican areas, stems from the use of emergency powers'.[29] The longevity and extent of Northern Ireland's emergency laws had facilitated the abuse of police powers; and the operation of the Special Powers Act was cited as one of the grievances that triggered the disturbances examined by the Cameron Commission in 1968.[30] Groups like CAJ thought that the Patten Commission was misguided to have ignored or downplayed the legal framework within which most policing—and policing abuses—had occurred in Northern Ireland.

Another NGO criticism of the Commission was its decision to focus on the future of policing and largely disregard its past. Although it was tactically understandable (the Commission needed to secure as much consensus as possible for its final recommendations), this approach was problematic and also led to internal contradictions in the report. For example, the report notes explicitly that 'bad apples' must be dealt with,[31] but—with one minimal exception, discussed later (see discussion of the oath on page 154 below) —chose not to deal with them. CAJ and others thought that past policing problems could not be reduced to the actions of a few 'bad apples'. Moreover, it seemed particularly unacceptable that the Commission, having explicitly recognised that, at the very least, some individual officers had abused their position, still did not propose any action to deal with those officers.

A third failure was inexplicable, particularly in tactical terms. In hearings across Northern Ireland, it was clear that people had very varied experiences of policing. Men and women, young and old, nationalists and unionists, the police and those they policed, middle-class and working-class people, urban and rural dwellers, had all experienced policing quite differently. The scars of residential segregation in Northern Ireland meant that few of these experiences were shared across different communities. A fuller recording of these realities on the ground would have provided a more incontrovertible basis for the Commission's eventual proposals. The Commission would have done a great service to Northern Ireland by providing society with a deeper analysis of the policing problems (both real and perceived) that the Agreement, and subsequently the Commission itself, sought to address.

PASSING THE BATON?

It is a sine qua non of any change process that those most involved must own the process, and take responsibility for its implementation. From an NGO perspective, the experience of the Patten Commission left something to be desired in this regard—though at least one innovative recommendation certainly bears replication elsewhere.

The first problem was the vacuum created immediately upon launching the Commission's *Report*. Once the *Report* had been issued, the Commission no longer existed. In abstraction, this is entirely proper: expert committees must pass the baton onto those responsible for implementation and should not remain like a ghost at the banquet, second-guessing everyone else. In reality, however, the vacuum created by the Commission's departure from the debate was to prove problematic. One difficulty lay in the fact that not everything in the *Report* was self-explanatory, so contradictory interpretations were often placed on the findings. With the exception of press conferences to launch the report, and the attendance of the two local members of the Commission at a CAJ conference in October 1999,[32] no member of the Commission was available to explain publically what had been intended by their findings. Still less were they present to defend and push for effective implementation of their package of recommendations. This allowed people not merely to dispute the findings (which they were likely to do anyway), but also to interpret or mis-interpret the *Patten Report* in justification of their own strongly held views, normally without fear of contradiction.[33]

It quickly became apparent, however, that an even larger problem than that of how the baton was passed was to whom would it be passed? The establishment of a Commission, and fairly detailed terms of reference, had been set out in the Good Friday/Belfast Agreement, and as such had been supported by all parties to the Agreement (and those endorsing it by way of referenda). That configuration of forces was not, however, in place by the time of the final report, and the UK government became the 'default' recipient of the recommendations. Indeed, it is interesting to note that the Agreement merely states that 'The implementation of the recommendations arising from both reviews (those of policing and criminal justice) will be discussed with the political parties and with the Irish government'. The UK government's role in initiating the discussions, and presumably in implementing the results of those discussions, is unstated, but evident nonetheless.

The UK government, in the person of the then Secretary of State for Northern Ireland, Peter Mandelson, immediately 'welcomed' the Patten Commission *Report*. Subject to a consultation period, the implication was that the government would in good faith proceed to implementation of the 175 recommendations. No-one doubted that implementation would be a challenging task; but the Commission had clearly assumed it to be a feasible one. However, the experience of NGOs like CAJ was that government was not willing to accept the spirit, and in some cases not even the letter, of the Patten Commission *Report*. After extensive lobbying and campaigning by CAJ and others, Secretary of State Mandelson duly noted that the government had taken on board more than 150 amendments to its initial legislative proposals to implement the *Patten* recommendations. Since these amendments were substantive rather than technical in nature, it was difficult to square the government's initial rhetoric (supposedly welcoming the report) with the reality (its unwillingness to implement it). Speaking in December 2009, Maurice Hayes, one of the members of the Commission said of this period:

> As it was, the Bill when published fell far short of the ideals of the *Report*—to the extent that it required some 150 amendments to get it back on the rails…fundamentally destructive of the *Report* were attempts in the Bill to reduce the influence of the Policing Board, to shift the balance of power back to the Secretary of State and to emasculate the DPPs. This largely reflected the culture of the NIO and those who had had charge of policing under one label or another over the years. Having looked at policing through one set of lenses, they were not likely to embrace change of this order. There was also a desire to keep policing in 'safe hands' and a deep distrust of elected representatives…[34]

It is not necessary years later to re-hash all of the disagreements between Her Majesty's Government and NGOs like the CAJ around the Patten Commission *Report*.[35] Suffice it now to cite briefly a few examples. One problem lay in the apparent unwillingness of the government to implement those recommendations that were anathema to the police. Secretary of State Peter Mandelson, in introducing the parliamentary debate on the *Patten Report*, said

> I should like to take this opportunity to refer to the Royal Ulster Constabulary. I honour those in Northern Ireland who have taken so much and have sacrificed so much in the course of their duties to protect all the people of Northern Ireland. They deserve our gratitude and from me they will get it unstintingly. Our job is to develop a police service in Northern Ireland that builds on the best traditions of the RUC…[36]

When the government asserts that the police in Northern Ireland have always done a good job, it is far from clear why there is any need to embrace the radical change programme proposed by *Patten*. This contradiction is well exemplified in the discussion about a new police oath.

Patten had, in the view of groups like CAJ, failed to tackle the past adequately, except in one small regard. One of the recommendations urged that all new and serving police officers would swear a new oath, which, amongst other things, promised to uphold the human rights of all.[37] Note that this oath did not state, or even imply, that human rights had not previously been upheld by the police (though they had not). The oath merely required that all police officers in future would be bound by their oath to uphold human rights. This recommendation—intended, albeit in a minimal way, to reassure those critical of policing in the past—proved unacceptable to the police,[38] and to government. Instead, whereas the new legislation required all new officers to swear to uphold the oath, serving officers were not so required.[39]

Elsewhere, government chose to disregard entirely, or interpret very narrowly, a number of the *Patten* recommendations. For example, *Patten* endorsed earlier findings about the importance of an entirely independent police complaints system.[40] Forty years on from the *Cameron Report*, such a system was at last being established. However, the Commission went further and recommended that this independent complaints system should look at policing policies and practices, so as to ensure that the learning from individual cases of wrong-doing could be drawn upon to improve policing overall. A legislative proposal to this end was consistently opposed by government; only after extensive lobbying was the measure introduced in 2003.[41]

Passing on the baton in a transitional change process to the very government that had responsibility for policing in the past is bound to be problematic. The dilemma is well highlighted by the plastic bullet (officially called Plastic Baton Rounds (PBRs)) controversy.[42] In its *Report*, the Patten Commission spoke disparagingly of the official handling of this debate in the past:

> In view of the fatalities and serious injuries resulting from PBRs, and the controversy caused by their extensive use, we are surprised and concerned that the government, the Police Authority and the RUC have collectively failed to invest more time and money in a search for an acceptable alternative. We were able to discover very little research work being done in the United Kingdom (except in the development of more accurate PBRs). By contrast, we were impressed by the efforts being made [elsewhere]…[43]

The UK government responded to the *Patten* call for more research into public order weaponry by establishing yet another internal review, with no independent medical or human-rights expertise. Not surprisingly, the committee determined that plastic bullets, albeit 'better' (presumably, in the words of *Patten* 'more accurate') ones, should be retained. In response to interventions by many NGOs about the particular risk posed by this weapon to children, new guidelines were issued. Unfortunately, instead of recognising the risks, the new guidelines merely clarified for plastic baton gunners that children and young people could be targeted in exactly the same circumstances as adults.

In particularly intense parliamentary exchanges around the draft legislation, the government withstood most attempts to strengthen the role of the Policing Board, which was a new civilian oversight body proposed by *Patten*. The first drafts of legislation did indeed make provision for a board, but included few of the safeguards that the Patten Commission had argued were necessary to ensure that the body would command the necessary community-wide confidence. Again, government's strong resistance to real change was only resolved over time, and as a result of several legislative attempts.[44]

These examples indicate some of the implementation problems experienced in the immediate aftermath of the launch of the Patten Commission's *Report*. It is worth noting here, however, before proceeding to subsequent implementation phases, that the Patten Commission did recommend one innovative measure that proved very useful: a measure that may be worth considering elsewhere when policing change is underway. *Patten* proposed that an oversight commissioner be established to monitor implementation of the *Report*'s recommendations.[45] To command confidence in Northern Ireland, it was further proposed that this person be neither British nor Irish, and that when appointed, he or she should put regular reports on implementation, or difficulties in implementation, in the public domain. Though groups like CAJ were somewhat critical of how this proposal was dealt with in practice, the principle was excellent. At the very least, the effort towards the transformation of policing was being made visible by way of independent public reports. CAJ criticised the fact that the post of oversight commissioner came into being when the legislation (with all its inadequacies) on implementing *Patten* was already in place, and argued that sometimes the oversight commissioner was taking a minimalist tick-box approach, rather than actively embedding the spirit of *Patten*'s work.[46] Nevertheless, the oversight reports provided groups like CAJ with excellent and reliable data, allowing them to continue their public and private debates with those interested in policing change.

POLICING TRANSFORMATION: PERCEPTION
OF HUMAN-RIGHTS NGOs

There is no doubt that policing in Northern Ireland is unrecognisable now when compared to the situation described at the start of this chapter. There has been an important, and necessary, transformation of policing, and much can be learned from it.

The changes introduced by the Patten Commission are bearing fruit. Figures show that the under-represented Catholic population, which constituted 8.3% of the police at the time of the *Patten Report*, constituted 26.14% of the service in March 2009.[47] The determination to attract under-represented groups has also led (without the use of quotas) to an important increase in the number of women officers.[48] There is a completely independent complaints system, which has increased community confidence in policing. There is an extensive range of new and revised police policies that have been actively proofed for their human-rights and equality implications. Training has been overhauled, and gradually NGOs working on domestic violence, with migrant workers, and the gay community, are being encouraged to assist the police in the design, as well as the delivery, of that training. The police are accountable under the law, and by the implication of the Human Rights Act as it relates to arrests, interrogation, house searches, parades, protests, etc. They are routinely examined in both theoretical and operational contexts. The police are also more accountable to the communities served, and the Policing Board now incorporates all of Northern Ireland's major political traditions.[49]

One of the most telling images symbolising how far policing has come in the last decade was that of the First and Deputy First Ministers (Peter Robinson of the DUP, and Martin McGuinness of Sinn Féin, respectively) standing on either side of the Chief Constable of the Police Service of Northern Ireland in March 2009. Together, the three of them were able to call for a combined response on the part of the community to the latest outrage—the shootings at Massereene Barracks in Antrim.

This catalogue of 'successes' should not, however, blind one to the difficulties still to be overcome. Whilst it is very important to recruit under-represented groups, it is equally important to retain them. In written exchanges with the Northern Ireland Office, CAJ learned that, 'of the 99 officers appointed in the last five years since 4 November 2001, and who had since left, 26 were Protestant, 72 were Catholic, and 1 was not determined'.[50] Moreover, subsequent equality impact assessment work has shown that Catholics do disproportionately less well than their Protestant counterparts at each stage of the recruitment process. Women, too, are being attracted to the police service in larger numbers, but equality impact assessment studies have shown that the testing is disproportionately failing them.[51] If these kinds of problems are not adequately addressed, many of the gains of the past ten years in terms of the transformation of policing can be easily lost.

Patten also made some far-seeing recommendations about community policing, but it is not clear whether these have been adequately embraced and integrated into routine policing. Anecdotal evidence would suggest that there is still some considerable way to go. Any transformation of policing is only as successful as its efforts to ensure good policing on the ground: it is yet to be seen whether Northern Ireland has developed the necessary tools to assess changes in that regard. The continuation of dissident activity is an obviously destabilising factor that *Patten* might of course have hoped to have ended ten years on. However, this sort of threat in local neighbourhoods from current and former paramilitaries, on the loyalist and republican sides, makes policing with the community even more, not less, important than the Commission argued at the time.

LESSONS FOR OTHERS?

Elsewhere in this publication, there are a number of reflections on the lessons that Northern Ireland has to share with others. Here, however, it is perhaps worth considering the learning that may be of particular relevance to human-rights NGOs working elsewhere on policing change.

First, the importance of politicians and political movement in facilitating radical policing change can often blind people to the importance of other actors in bringing about that change. Many of Northern Ireland's politicians (like much of Northern Ireland society) were totally committed to political negotiations that would either 'disband' or 'defend/reform' the RUC. CAJ challenged this dichotomy by concluding in *Human rights on duty* that it was both sterile and unhelpful, since 'societies have introduced radical change sometimes by disbanding, and sometimes by reforming, their current policing structures'.[52] Human-rights NGOs like CAJ instead argued that it was important to develop principles of good policing, and to measure all proposals for change against their capacity to ensure human-rights compliant policing. This had the added advantage of allowing people and politicians to focus on what united rather than what divided them.

Moreover, the fact that groups like CAJ had commented extensively and knowledgeably about failures in human-rights compliant policing in the past placed it in a unique position to advise others as to what would/would not work in human rights terms in the future. Politicians alone could not have developed a comprehensive agenda for policing change; nor could the police. CAJ and other human-rights NGOs brought an expertise to the table that was invaluable, and Patten Commission members Maurice Hayes and Peter Smith were kind enough to acknowledge that publicly.[53] So, one lesson for other human-rights NGOs is that they have an important and often unique role to play in bringing about policing change. After all, effective problem-solving in this domain requires an in-depth knowledge both of the policing problems to be addressed and of the concrete and specific human-rights measures that have proved useful elsewhere.

Second, the importance of the role to be performed by human-rights NGOs should not obscure the fact that policing is often a highly politicised debate, and that transformative policing change requires political will above all else. Whilst fundamental policing change of the kind undertaken in Northern Ireland cannot be undertaken solely by politicians, neither can it be undertaken without political leadership. By making bad policing increasingly difficult to justify, and by steadily building up a reputation for expertise and credibility, human-rights NGOs should position themselves so as to encourage and exploit any political window of opportunity that may suddenly arise. Human-rights NGOs can also play an important role in engendering the necessary political will and leadership needed for changing policing practice by working with all parties, and addressing competing political concerns. To be effective, human-rights NGOs must be both non-partisan and highly politically astute. CAJ argued that human rights created a non-negotiable framework within which to have political negotiations, but it also recognised that some political disputes have no 'right' or 'wrong' human-rights answer, and should be left to politicians and wider society to resolve.[54]

A third lesson is the value of relying upon international parallels and turning to external advisers and sources to help exert pressure and provide momentum to domestic processes of transition. Other jurisdictions may be more hesitant when turning to external expertise and there are, of course, limits to international involvement. It is difficult to imagine how an international human-rights group could, for example, have performed the role of groups on the ground in Northern Ireland like CAJ.

At the same time, there is no doubt that the assistance of international human-rights NGOs like Amnesty International, Human Rights First and Human Rights Watch, together with the scrutiny provided by inter-governmental bodies and other outsiders, played a vital role in securing change in Northern Ireland. The Patten Commission was able to draw on numerous in-depth and independent studies of past policing problems in Northern Ireland, and was also able to draw on extensive external goodwill. It was no accident that two of the eight Commission members were from the US. Nor was it an accident that the Commission came to the conclusion that: 'There should be no conflict between human rights and policing. Policing means protecting human rights'.[55] This assertion was not one that was commonplace in Northern Ireland; it was, however, common currency in international human-rights circles. The Commission was given sufficient international comparators to know the value of this starting premise for its work, and much of its report is therefore suffused with human-rights thinking.

Last but not least, any transformative process must be carefully monitored. Those in authority are rarely eager to engage in fundamental change. In CAJ's experience, the resistance of government and of the police to change was not experienced merely in the years leading up to the Agreement, but just as much so afterwards. Therefore, in the dark days of active resistance to change, human-rights NGOs need to be both insistent and persistent, but the same groups need to remain alert once the long-argued-for policy or legislative change is secured. CAJ's experience was that there is a grave risk in any complacency and that power tends simply to re-group rather than genuinely embrace or adapt to the new dispensation. A lesson for others is that human-rights NGOs can never afford to lose momentum and take their eyes off the prize—they need to strategise and organise, and re-strategise and re-organise constantly. If the legislation or the policy change does not happen immediately (and it rarely does), the pressure must be maintained. Human rights are not 'given'; they need to be claimed.

In summary, the Patten Commission provided Northern Ireland with an excellent template for transformative policing change; but no-one should think that the work is yet complete.[56]

NOTES

[1] Independent Commission on Policing for Northern Ireland, *A new beginning: policing in Northern Ireland* Report of the Independent Commission on Policing for Northern Ireland (Belfast: HMSO Northern Ireland Office, 1999), (hereafter cited as the *Patten Report*).

[2] This commission was chaired by the Honourable Lord Cameron, D.S.C., and its report, *Disturbances in Northern Ireland; Report of the Commission appointed by the Governor of Northern Ireland*, was presented to parliament by Command of His Excellency the Governor of Northern Ireland, September 1969, Cmd. 532; (Belfast: HMSO, 1969), hereafter cited as *Cameron Commission/Report*.

[3] *Cameron Report*, paragraph 145.

[4] *Cameron Report*, paragraph 179. Elsewhere in the report, the policing of the demonstration was said to have been 'in certain material respects ill co-ordinated and inept'; there was 'use of unnecessary and ill controlled force in the dispersal of the demonstrators'; the police 'did not provide adequate protection to marchers at Burntollet Bridge'; there were 'instances of police indiscipline and violence towards persons unassociated with rioting or disorder' and these 'provoked serious hostility to the police, particularly among the Catholic population of Londonderry, and an increasing disbelief in their impartiality towards non-Unionists'. (paragraph 229).

[5] *Cameron Report*, paragraph 230. In 1977 a Police Complaints Authority was instituted; this was subsequently replaced by an Independent Commission for Police Complaints; and only in October 1999 was the first Police Ombudsman for Northern Ireland appointed, with wide-ranging and fully independent powers of investigation into allegations of police misconduct (see http://www.policeombusdman.org). This trend from an internal police complaints system to one that has an external element is common to many jurisdictions; few if any, however, have moved further to institute a mechanism as completely external as the Northern Ireland model. In our view, this independent model bears replication elsewhere as a way of (re)building community confidence in policing.

[6] Subsequent investigations into allegations of police involvement in the death of Samuel Devenney encountered a 'wall of silence'; Mrs Devenney, his widow, is reported as saying in an interview in 1993 with the *Irish Times* that 'if a case had been brought against RUC officers back in 1969 there may not have been so much antagonism against the RUC and so many police officers killed', cited in David McKittrick, Seamus Kelters, Brian Feeney and Chris Thornton, *Lost lives: the stories of the men, women and children who died as a result of the Northern Ireland Troubles* (Edinburgh and London: Mainstream Publishing, 1999), 32.

[7] See *War on Terror: lessons from Northern Ireland*, (CAJ, 2008) which sets out (chapter 2) the historic human-rights context and provides a detailed bibliography to original sources.

[8] The total of 3,633 deaths consisted of: 1,232 Catholic and 698 Protestant civilians; 1,036 security force members; and 392 republican and 144 loyalist paramilitaries (*Lost lives*, tables 5 and 6, p. 1477).

[9] 'Bloody Sunday' occurred on 30 January 1972 in the Bogside area of Derry. Twenty-seven civil rights protesters were shot by the British Army Parachute Regiment during a Northern Ireland Civil Rights Association march. Thirteen people, seven of whom were teenagers, died immediately, while the death of another person four-and-a-half months later has been attributed to the injuries he received on the day. Many witnesses, including bystanders and journalists, testify that all those shot were unarmed. The Widgery Tribunal, held in the immediate aftermath of the event, largely cleared the soldiers and British authorities of any blame, but that tribunal was widely discredited and a new inquiry was established under Lord Saville in 1998. This latter inquiry is due to report in June 2010. See Don Mullan, *Eyewitness Bloody Sunday: the truth* (Dublin: Wolfhound, 1997) and see also the material on http://www.cain.ulst.ac.uk; Bloody Sunday occurred in January 1972—that calendar year was by far the worst of all the years of the Troubles in terms of fatalities, with 496 dead (*Lost lives*, 1473).

[10] For more discussion on NICRA, see Bob Purdie, *Politics in the streets: the origins of the civil rights movement in Northern Ireland* (Belfast: Blackstaff Press, 1990).

[11] As one of the safeguards intended to ensure that it could attract members from all political traditions, the CAJ took (and takes) no stand on the constitutional status of Northern Ireland.

[12] See the CAJ reports on police complaints systems in 1982, 1983, 1990, 1991 and 1993 (available at: http://www.caj.org.uk).

[13] See the CAJ reports on public order policing from 1988, 1990, 1994 and 1995 (available at: http://www.caj.org.uk).

[14] See the CAJ reports in 1985, 1990, 1995, 1996, 1997 and 1998. See, in particular, *The misrule of law: a report on the policing of events during the summer of 1996 in Northern Ireland*, (Belfast: CAJ, 1996). For almost uncanny resemblances to the finding of the *Cameron Report* cited earlier, note the following extracts from *The misrule of law*: 'people seeking to remove themselves from the area were batoned and on at least one occasion deliberately pushed back into the melee', 14; 'the police were seen behaving in what can only be described as a provocative and reckless way', 15; and note also that the CAJ report called for an investigation into 'why it was considered necessary to discharge 662 plastic bullets in the period between 7 and 11 July (the period of unionist protests), and more than eight times as many (5,340) between 11 and 14 July (the period of nationalist protests)', 29.

[15] See *Just News*, Special 21st anniversary edition, 'CAJ and its critics', October 2002, 2.

[16] The UN treaty bodies are committees of independent experts that monitor implementation of the core international human-rights treaties.

[17] For a discussion of some of the work carried out at the UN, see Martin O'Brien, 'Northern Ireland at the United Nations 1969—1996', unpublished LLM dissertation, QUB Law Faculty, 1996; see also CAJ submissions to various UN mechanisms between 1991 and 2007: S1, S2, S4, S5, S6, S10, S18, S22, S23, S24, S26, S30, S32, S35, S36, S 37, S46, S49, S52, S56, S64, S71, S74, S84, S85, S90, S100, S108, S112, S128, S154 and S182 (available at: http://www.caj.org.uk).

[18] CAJ made written submissions to President Clinton in 1993 and 1994, and made oral and written submissions to US Congressional Hearings on Northern Ireland in 1997, 1998, 1999 (April and September), 2000 (March and September), 2001, 2004, 2005 and 2006.

[19] See Shanaghan vs The United Kingdom (Appl. 37715/97); Kelly & Others vs The United Kingdom (Appl. 30054/96). The above cases can be found at: http://cmiskp.echr.coe.int/tkp197/portal.asp?sessionId=38260060&skin=hudoc-en&action=request.

[20] Concerns expressed by the UN Committee Against Torture about interrogations at Castlereagh were followed immediately by a marked decrease in the number of allegations of ill-treatment; and shortly after the UN Committee for the Elimination of Racial Discrimination expressed serious concern about the lack of anti-race discrimination legislation in Northern Ireland, the UK government introduced such legislation (twenty years later than it had been introduced for Britain).

[21] For example, the Ardoyne Association in a largely republican area in Belfast held a conference and issued a report in 1994: 'A Neighbourhood Police Service—Ardoyne'.

[22] Ronnie Flanagan, *Fundamental review of policing.* (Belfast: Royal Ulster Constabulary, 1996). See the text of the full report at: http://www.psni.police.uk/fundamental_review_policing_1996.pdf.

[23] See, *The agenda for change—human rights, the Northern Ireland conflict and the peace process* (Belfast: CAJ, 1995). This report includes the proceedings of a cross-community conference held in March 1995, and draws on earlier human-rights NGO statements and expert private seminars with civil servants and policing experts.

[24] Mary O'Rawe and Linda Moore, *Human rights on duty: principles for better policing—international lessons for Northern Ireland* (Belfast: CAJ, November 1997).

[25] O'Rawe and Moore, *Human rights on duty*, summary of recommendations, 1.

[26] The Belfast/Good Friday Agreement was signed in 1998; the text of the Agreement is available at: http://foreignaffairs.gov.ie/uploads/documents/Anglo-Irish/agreement.pdf (hereafter cited as Agreement).

[27] For a fuller account of the influence of human-rights groups on Agreement negotiations, see Paul Mageean and Martin O'Brien, 'From the margins to the mainstream—human rights and the *Good Friday Agreement*', Fordham International Law Journal (22) (1999), 1499–1538.

[28] Even a cursory glance at CAJ's *Human rights on duty* and the *Patten Report*, published two years later, shows that the two publications address the same issues, and propose many of the same solutions; this is hardly surprising in that they both drew extensively on good policing practice elsewhere.

[29] *Patten Report*, paragraphs 8.13 and 8.14, citing John McGarry and Brendan O'Leary in, *Policing Northern Ireland: proposals for a new start* (Belfast: Blackstaff Press, 1999).

[30] *Cameron Commission*, paragraphs 144 and 229.

[31] *Patten* reported: 'Whatever the outcome of these investigations, we are in no doubt that the RUC has had several officers within its ranks over the years who have abused their position. Many supporters of the RUC and both serving and retired officers have spoken to us about "bad apples". It is not satisfactory to suggest, as some people have, that one should somehow accept that every organisation has such "bad apples". They should be dealt with', paragraph 5.19.

[32] CAJ, 'The Patten Commission: the way forward for policing in Northern Ireland?', Proceedings of a conference on the findings of the Patten Commission held in October 1999.

[33] At a meeting in November 2000 with the CAJ, involving the two authors, the then Secretary of State, Peter Mandelson, initially claimed that the Patten Commission had not wanted the Police Ombudsman to inquire into policies and practices more generally. The CAJ delegation immediately drew Secretary of State Mandelson's attention to an unambiguous *Patten* recommendation on the question—i.e. 'The Ombudsman should exercise the right to investigate and comment on police policies and practices, where these are perceived to give rise to difficulties' (paragraph 6.42). Having lost the argument on the grounds of '*Patten* said XYZ', the Secretary of State retreated to the (more accurate) stance that the government did not agree with the *Patten* recommendation on this particular question.

[34] Speaking at the CAJ 'Policing with the Community' conference, cited in *Just News*, Policing Special, December 2009.

[35] For an account of those disputes at the time, see CAJ's *Just News*: 'Police Act' (15) (11), 2000.

[36] *Hansard*, House of Commons Debates, 20 October 1999, vol. 336, cc 424–8.

[37] *Patten Report*, recommendation 2; see also paragraph 4.2.

[38] One of the authors, in subsequent informal discussions with senior police officers about opposition to the oath, was told that this recommendation had been seen widely among the police as just 'a step too far'.

[39] This weakness has now largely been resolved, given the subsequent passage of a disciplinary code that applies to all serving officers, and incorporates reference to the oath.

[40] *Patten Report*, paragraph 6.40.

[41] See note 31 above. Neither legislation in 1998 to establish the Office of the Police Ombudsman for Northern Ireland, nor the Police Act of 2000 (legislating many of the *Patten* reforms) contained this provision; it did eventually appear, with some restrictions, in the Police (Northern Ireland) Act (2003).

[42] *Patten* explains the background: 'The most controversial aspect of public order policing in Northern Ireland has been the weaponry used by the police, in particular plastic baton rounds. These were introduced into service in the 1970s, replacing the earlier rubber bullets. Since 1981, a total of 41,657 have been discharged by the police, and 14,572 by the army. 11 deaths have been attributed to PBRs since 1981 (and 5 before that), and 615 injuries', paragraph 9.12.

[43] *Patten Report*, paragraph 9.14.

[44] For legislative debates on the creation, and subsequent activities, of the Policing Board, see 'Commentary on the Northern Ireland Policing Board', CAJ, November 2003; and http://www.nipolicingboard.org.uk.

[45] This proposal (see *Patten Report*, reccommendations 172–5) may have arisen as a result of submissions; certainly CAJ noted that excellent inquiries into and reports on policing in the past had not been adequately implemented, and urged the Commission to ensure that its recommendations did not suffer the same fate.

[46] A specific example of the 'tickbox exercise' approach can be seen in the fact that the Oversight Commissioner closed down consideration of *Patten*'s recommendation that the police appoint a lawyer with specific expertise in human rights to advise on operational matters (*Patten Report*, paragraph 4.11) once the appointment was made.

No attempt was made thereafter to ascertain if the post had the necessary seniority, and/or was having the direct operational impact that *Patten* had presumably intended.
[47] Current statistics as provided in a ministerial press statement, 31 March 2009 (available at: http://www.nio.gov.uk).
[48] Between 2001 and 2008, the proportion of female police officers increased from 12% to 24% (see http://www.nipolicingboard.org.uk).
[49] See the information available at: http://www.policeombudsman.org; http://www.nipolicingboard.org.uk; http://www.psni.police.uk; http://www.caj.org.uk.
[50] Correspondence cited in CAJ's Annual Report (2006/2007).
[51] See, Roundtable report, 27 March 2009, 'Positive action in theory and practice: experiences from the UK and Europe', available at: http://www.runnymedetrust.org/uploads/projects/europe/UK%20Positive%20Action%20Roundtable%20Report.pdf.
[52] O'Rawe and Moore, *Human rights on duty*, 10–11.
[53] At a conference organised by CAJ in the immediate aftermath of the publication of the Patten Commission's report, intended to encourage cross-community debate of the findings, Commission member Maurice Hayes said 'The main reason I'm here today is both on behalf of the Commission and personally, to express thanks to CAJ, and to the voluntary organisations associated with it, who were extremely helpful to us throughout the consultation…I had a practice of about once a month or thereabouts of meeting with representatives of the CAJ and the other NGOs and voluntary organisations, that were active on these issues. That was extremely helpful to us as well, and so too were the submissions that they all made…'. Commission member Peter Smith followed on: 'May I start my brief remarks by echoing what he (Maurice) has already said about the invaluable role of CAJ in our work', see 'The Patten commission: the way forward for policing in Northern Ireland', report of conference proceedings, 8 October 1999, CAJ, Ref. 44, November 1999, 11 and 14.
[54] For discussions of how this worked in practice and of the validity of applying a human-rights paradigm to deeply contested issues of policing change, see Maggie Beirne and Angela Hegarty, 'A view from the coal face: Northern Ireland, human rights activism and the War on Terror', in *Judges, transition and human rights*, by John Morison, Kieran McEvoy and Gordon Anthony (eds), (Oxford: Oxford University Press, 2007), 377–400; and Maggie Beirne, 'Progress or placebo? The *Patten Report* and the future of policing in Northern Ireland', *Policing and Society* (11) (2001), 297–319.
[55] *Patten Report*, paragraph 4.1.
[56] For a current statement on outstanding policing (and other human rights) issues, see the annual Stephen Livingstone lecture, delivered at Queen's University Belfast in October 2009 by Martin O'Brien, entitled 'A stock-take: human rights and the Agreement—how far have we come?', available at: http://atlanticphilanthropies.org/news/news/remarks_at_the_annual_stephen_livingstone_memorial_lecture_queen_s_university_belfast.

Part III

The wider lessons from the Northern Ireland case

CHAPTER 12

THE POLITICS OF THE
TRANSFORMATION OF POLICING

John Doyle

INTRODUCTION

T he issue of policing in Northern Ireland was both highly contested and of the foremost political salience for all the
political parties involved in the peace process, and also for their communities. The contributions in the first two sections of this book
demonstrate not only the centrality of this issue for all the actors involved but also the enormous difficulties that had to be overcome,
both to find and then to implement a workable agreement. Prior to
the peace process, on no other matter was there such a complete and
apparently unbridgeable divide between the two communities as there
was on policing. Based on this reality and the subsequent proposals to
'remake' policing in Northern Ireland, commentators from across the
political spectrum have portrayed the peace process as being built
upon the basic premise that nationalists agreed to local power-sharing
in the context of a constitutionally reformed UK, while in return they
were given reforms in the areas of civil and human rights, including
policing.[1] This perspective has the effect of reducing the transformation of policing in Northern Ireland to the status of a concession to
nationalists that was forcefully resisted by unionists, but finally agreed
once all sides believed that they had secured their constitutional pref-
erences. Contrary to the view of policing as a lower-order concession,
this chapter argues that the negotiations on policing were not at one
step removed from the core disputes on sovereignty and state power;
rather, the transformation of policing, as much as the new institutions
of government, reflected the consociational character of the 1998
Belfast/Good Friday Agreement and its institutionalised linkages
between Northern Ireland and Ireland.[2]

The attitudes of both communities to policing during the years of conflict in Northern Ireland demonstrate that this issue was inseparable from the wider constitutional question and from conflicting definitions of citizenship. Initially, in the late 1960s, the demands of the civil-rights movement focused on voting rights, equality of access to employment, housing and policing—specifically seeking the abolition of the police reserve unit referred to as the 'B-Specials'.[3] For unionists, on the other hand, the police, including the B-Specials, were defenders of the state against what they saw as an attempt at radical insurrection. The aggressive response of the police to the civil-rights protests from autumn 1968 onwards, radicalised and entrenched Irish nationalist hostility to the police and marked the beginning of international concerns with the RUC's human-rights record. The initial shock at the high level of inter-communal violence in Northern Ireland led to the deployment of British troops there in 1969. The escalating crisis saw the British government take full control of security, including policing, in 1972, leading to 'direct rule' from London and the end of the devolved Unionist government and parliament in Northern Ireland. Unionists opposed the loss of local control over policing, but in all other respects continued to support the RUC as 'their' police force. In this, as in other respects, the overall political divisions between unionists and nationalists were reflected in the debates on policing.

This chapter analyses the critiques of policing in Northern Ireland made by nationalists during the conflict, as represented by Sinn Féin and the Social Democratic and Labour Party (SDLP), who between them secure the votes of almost 100% of the nationalist community.[4] It frames their position under three headings:

• counter-insurgency and the demand for politically impartial policing;
• human rights issues; and
• the unrepresentative make-up of the RUC.

The chapter then analyses the arguments made by unionists in defence of the RUC—primarily examining the attitudes of the major unionist political parties, the Ulster Unionist Party (UUP)[5] and Democratic Unionist Party (DUP). This is done in some detail, as while nationalist critiques have been well documented and follow a familiar international pattern in divided societies experiencing conflict, less attention has been paid to the nuances of the nature of unionist defences of the RUC. Both of these diametrically opposed sets of views, in their different ways, centre on the constitutional issue and demonstrate how the divisions on policing are bound up with divisions on the nature of the state in Northern Ireland and on the meaning of citizenship. The chapter then deals with the public debates on the Report of the Independent Commission on Policing for Northern Ireland,[6] the subsequent legislation and the Agreements that saw both nationalist parties endorse the new policing arrangements. The nature of these public debates and Agreements highlighted the extent to which the transformation of policing in Northern Ireland is fully bound up with progress in the wider peace process, and the arrangements on recruitment, control and oversight of policing reflect the underlying principles of the 1998 Belfast/Good Friday Agreement.

NATIONALIST PERSPECTIVES ON POLICING DURING THE CONFLICT

Nationalist critiques of the RUC during the conflict in Northern Ireland can be conceptualised into three key areas. First, the RUC was seen as a counter-insurgency force, committed to upholding not only the Union with Britain but the dominant position of unionists in Northern Ireland society. This view was true for moderate nationalists as well as republicans, and in the case of moderate nationalists —who strongly opposed the use of political violence—was based on the perception that policing practice went beyond what was necessary, or functional, for counter-insurgency and was designed to uphold unionist privilege. The second key area of criticism, stemming from this, was of the RUC's human-rights record, with concerns centring on what were considered to be heavy handed and indiscriminate counter-insurgency practices. Third, nationalists opposed the RUC based on the unrepresentative nature of its membership, which during this period had less than 8% of officers from a Catholic background, and even fewer from the nationalist community in Northern Ireland.[7] This inequality was seen to reinforce, and reflect, the unionist ethos of the RUC and to contribute to making the force inherently incapable of policing the nationalist community. These criticisms are a consistent and key component of the public positions of the two major nationalist political parties in Northern Ireland—Sinn Féin and the SDLP.

*Counter-insurgency and the demand for politically
impartial policing*

Sinn Féin's core perspective on policing during the conflict centred
on its opposition, and indeed condemnation, of the RUC as an instrument of repression and counter-insurgency, whose primary aim was to
uphold British sovereignty over Northern Ireland. For Sinn Féin, this
view of the RUC was reflected in its title, both the use of the word
'Royal' linking it to the British Crown and the use of the geographical
descriptor Ulster (favoured by unionists) rather than the more neutral
Northern Ireland. The terminology used in Sinn Féin statements and
publications in the 1970s and 1980s reflected this perception of the
force, with the police usually referred to as 'Crown Forces'.[8] While
this view of the RUC as a force with a counter-insurgency mission
was logical and consistent from the perspective of Sinn Féin—
supporters of the insurgency—this form of critique of the RUC was
widespread in the nationalist community. Leading moderate nationalists also frequently criticised the force for the political bias of its
operational decisions and the behaviour of individual officers on the
ground.[9] Having no confidence in the willingness of either a unionist
or a British government to change the RUC's approach to policing,
the SDLP, shortly after its foundation, highlighted the need for
fundamental police reform. Institutionalised input from the Irish
government was a key demand of nationalists, and they also pursued
this position at the inter-party and inter-governmental talks at
Sunningdale in 1973.[10]

The RUC was fundamentally criticised by moderate nationalists for
going beyond what was required for effective counter-insurgency and
upholding the constitutional order (which was its legal duty) by effectively distorting its policing mission with an anti-nationalist bias. In a
1976 pamphlet, Fr Denis Faul, a leading critic of Sinn Féin, went so far
as to call the RUC 'an anti-Catholic paramilitary force'.[11] One of the
most frequently cited examples of biased practices was of the very
different ways that public protests were policed in nationalist and unionist areas. For example, during the Ulster Workers Council strike of 1974
organised by loyalist paramilitaries, which effectively led to the collapse
of the then power-sharing government, the security forces made no
credible attempts to remove road blocks or to arrest hooded paramilitaries on 'picket lines', who were clearly seeking to intimidate those who
supported power-sharing into not going to work.[12] In contrast, the

wide-scale protests and rioting in nationalist areas during the IRA hunger-strike of 1981 saw 29,657 plastic bullets being fired by police—leading to 7 deaths.[13] Protests, riots and road blockages organised by unionists opposed to the 1985 Anglo-Irish Agreement and against the re-routing of Orange Order marches saw a much more measured response. Even when major public institutions such as the port of Larne were closed by protests, the police did not attempt to move the protesters.[14] Similar protests around Orange Order parades in 1995 and 1996 were again policed very differently in the two communities.[15]

Repeated examples of this type of differentiated policing of nationalist and unionist public protest reinforced nationalist opinion that the RUC was not simply keeping the law, but was upholding in a partial manner unionists' relative power over nationalists. John Hume, when challenged at the time of the ceasefire as to whether the SDLP attitude to the RUC over the years of conflict had been a mistake, countered:

> The basis of order in any society is agreement on how
> you govern. When that is absent...the police are going
> to be seen as being on one side or the other—which is
> what happens in Northern Ireland...Until such time as
> the political problem was resolved our position was that
> we fully and unequivocally supported the police in up-
> holding the rule of law. Our only qualification was that
> they should do so impartially.[16]

The crucial point for Hume is that the RUC did not police impartially and therefore did not meet the basic criteria for SDLP endorsement.

For nationalists, the dominance of the counter-insurgency imperative within the RUC meant that all other forms of policing were subordinated to this primary aim. This was especially true of the Special Branch—described as a 'force within a force' in the Policing Commission's report[17]—however, it impacted on all aspects of policing. For example, petty criminals and youths involved in anti-social behaviour were frequently recruited to provide low-level intelligence in nationalist areas.[18] Their criminal activities were not interrupted provided they could fulfil this intelligence-gathering function. More generally, the gulf between the nationalist communities and the RUC was so wide that the RUC had little capacity to engage in low-level policing in nationalist areas, and the communities in those areas had little reason to see the RUC as a force capable of playing this role.

The SDLP repeatedly argued that the RUC's heavy handed counter-insurgency approach was counter-productive as well as indefensible and that it was the primary reason for the party's refusal to endorse the force. In the aftermath of the shoot-to-kill controversies in the 1980s, SDLP Deputy Leader Seamus Mallon asked

> can the Irish Government assume maximum trust when dealing with the chief constable, a deputy chief constable and an assistant chief constable all of whom a senior police officer…felt obliged to interview under criminal caution.[19]

He answered his own question with a 'resounding' no and called for an end to co-operation between the Garda Síochána[20] and the RUC until there were significant changes at RUC senior management level. He went on to say that progress on policing could be measured only by whether the RUC could gain sufficient confidence in mainstream nationalist communities to allow people to join and live as integrated members of the community with the community's support, and that this was a long way from being achieved

The hostile attitude of the broad nationalist community was highlighted by Seamus Mallon shortly after the ceasefires when he referred to

> the inability—the refusal, as it were, of a broad nationalist community in the north of Ireland to give its support and allegiance to a system of policing in Northern Ireland.[21]

His analysis cut to the heart of the problem when he argued that

> Such an inability or refusal has existed since the very foundation of the state. It cannot be solved by simplifying the issue, by getting Catholics into the police service. It is much broader, deeper and more fundamental than that. It is about nationalist identification with the process of policing and allegiance, not just to the police as one part of the instrument of administration but to the administration that is partly responsible for administering policing.[22]

Here, Mallon was encapsulating the nationalist critique of policing as bound up by the contested nature of the state in Northern Ireland,

and nationalists' refusal to give their support to the political and constitutional status quo. As long as nationalists were excluded from the effective governance of Northern Ireland, and as long as British policy refused to acknowledge the contested nature of the state and relied on a security-led approach to trying to manage the conflict, then no broad nationalist support for policing was possible.

Human-rights issues

Throughout the conflict both the SDLP and Sinn Féin made repeated and vocal criticisms of the RUC's human-rights record. The issues consistently raised by nationalists over the years were allegations of ill treatment and even torture during interrogation, summary executions, the reckless use of plastic bullets and police collusion with illegal loyalist paramilitary groups. The position the nationalist parties took was reinforced by the actions of external actors; for example, in the early 1970s the Irish state brought the UK to the European Court of Human Rights over the treatment of people in police custody, while the Carter administration in the USA banned the sale of firearms to the RUC, citing human-rights concerns.[23]

Local critiques of the RUC often drew on material from international human-rights organisations, such as Amnesty International and Human Rights Watch. These reports assisted the nationalist community in effectively calling for inquiries into human-rights abuses, which the British government found more difficult to ignore than purely local protests.[24] For example, in the early 1980s when the RUC was accused of a targeted assassination policy, which resulted in the deaths of six people including one civilian, international pressure led the British government to set up an investigation under John Stalker (deputy chief constable of the Greater Manchester Police in England).[25] Nationalists had sought an international investigation as they did not trust any senior British police officer to act independently; however, it is widely agreed that John Stalker attempted a rigorous inquiry, only to have his actions blocked by senior RUC management and officers. He was removed from the inquiry by the British government shortly after submitting his interim report, and after allegations of corruption were made against him (these were later proved to be groundless). The investigation was taken over by another senior British police officer (Colin Sampson, chief constable of the West Yorkshire Police), who ultimately reported on the matter in 1987.

Following the inquiry, the report of which was never made public, Attorney General Patrick Mayhew stated in 1988 that there would be no further prosecutions of any police or MI5 officers, as to prosecute would not be in the interests of 'national security'.[26] Consequently, only relatively junior officers were reprimanded for issues related to obstructing the original Stalker Inquiry. For nationalists the inadequacy of this response[27] was reinforced by new allegations of collusion between the RUC and illegal loyalist paramilitary groups that surfaced shortly after the Sampson report was completed, forcing the British government to bring in a third senior police officer (John Stevens, the deputy chief constable of Cambridgeshire Police) for yet another external investigation. Nationalist dissatisfaction with this third investigation, which had included an investigation into the killing of leading nationalist civil-rights lawyer Patrick Finucane, led to a lengthy and ultimately unsuccessful campaign for an international public inquiry into his death.[28]

Human-rights abuses were extensively documented and analysed,[29] and local protests by nationalists received strong international endorsement, all of which in turn impacted on nationalist critiques of the RUC and reaffirmed their belief that the RUC could not merely be reformed but had to be reconstituted. While nationalist campaigns on human-rights issues, bolstered by international pressure, resulted in investigations into these issues and in some minimal reforms, none of these measures were successful in persuading members of the wider nationalist community that the RUC was a legitimate police service deserving of their support. Indeed, the conduct of these investigations into human-rights abuses, and the limited and partial response to their findings, tended to re-inforce nationalist alienation from the police rather than mitigate it—the events around the Stalker Inquiry being an example of the pattern of interaction between the pressure for action on human-rights abuse and the desire on the part of the British state (and the unionist community) to defend its counter-insurgency policy.

An unrepresentative force

The small proportion of nationalists from Northern Ireland who were members of the RUC was also a target of criticism from the SDLP and Sinn Féin. They regarded the under-representation of nationalists both as a result of what they saw as the anti-nationalist ethos of the RUC, and also as a way in which that ethos was maintained. In 1998, when the Good Friday Agreement was signed, nationalists made up between 44% and 48% of the working-age population in Northern Ireland, but only 7.5% of RUC officers were 'Catholic', and as noted above, fewer still were likely to be Irish nationalists.[30] Nationalists argued that a police service that so under-represented its community could, by its very nature, never deliver policing in a manner acceptable to that community; although as Mallon argued, above, the issue was not one of numbers *per se*, but rather that nationalists' refusal to join or support the police was a clear indication of the need for change.

Nationalist critiques also linked the make-up of the RUC to what they regarded as its unionist ethos. The RUC reflected a unionist culture and identity; police stations displayed photographs of the British monarch and flew the Union Jack, and police officers were embedded in and had strong links with unionist communities. Nationalist communities were politically, culturally and geographically perceived as the 'other', re-enforcing the gulf between the police and the nationalist community.

Community distrust, the repeated release of credible reports of human-rights abuses related to the counter-insurgency imperative and the low representation of their community within the RUC ensured that nationalist rejection of it as a legitimate police organisation was strong throughout the period of the conflict in Northern Ireland, and this remained the position of both major nationalist parties in the aftermath of the ceasefires.[31] Nationalists therefore entered the period of the peace process with a strong sense that policing was a key issue of concern in post-ceasefire negotiations. Ulster unionists, however, drew on a very different narrative of support for the RUC and a rejection of nationalist critiques. An understanding of this alternative discourse on policing is crucial to recognising why the issue was so difficult to negotiate following the publication of the Patten Commission's *Report*.

UNIONIST PERSPECTIVES: A CITIZEN'S DUTY TO SUPPORT THE POLICING OF THE STATE

Unionists, like Irish nationalists, saw issues of policing and security as absolutely central to their political agenda. Unionist political parties were, and are, unanimous in their broad support for the police and in their rejection of nationalist critiques. A number of key themes are common to unionist interventions on policing throughout the conflict and into the early period of the peace process. Unionist parties rejected nationalist complaints about the pro-British ethos of the RUC. They insisted, rather, that the ethos of the RUC should reflect British sovereignty, and further argued that it was the duty of every citizen (and every party) to support the RUC and to encourage people to join. There was no acceptance of human-rights critiques and unionists regularly called for more 'hard line' security tactics, such as capital punishment, assassination of IRA members and internment without trial. All of this took place in a context in which over 3,500 people lost their lives in the conflict between 1969 and 1998, and the police and British Army suffered considerable casualties: over 300 police officers and over 700 British soldiers were killed.[32] This inevitably heightened tension and polarised political opinion. The low percentage of nationalist and Roman Catholic recruits to the RUC was dismissed as being caused by the nationalist community's support for terrorism or by IRA intimidation. Finally, most unionists sought to restore control of the police—which had been transferred to London in 1972—as they feared that international pressure, or a desire by Britain to reach a political agreement with the Irish government, would shape RUC strategy in a way that weakened its capacity, in their view, to defend the Union.

A duty of citizenship

Unionist politicians perceived Sinn Féin to be directly involved in an armed insurgency, and so they had no expectation that Sinn Féin or the party's support base would back the RUC. Criticisms of nationalist views on policing therefore focused on the more moderate SDLP, which was the largest nationalist party until 2001. Criticism of the SDLP for its failure to support the RUC unambiguously, or to encourage nationalist recruitment, spans the entire unionist political spectrum and the entire time period of the conflict.

Unionist politicians repeatedly argued that they would not take part in governmental power-sharing with the SDLP without the party's full support for the RUC. This was usually linked to an insistence that supporting the police was a requirement of accepting British sovereignty over Northern Ireland. David Trimble, exemplifying this insistence, said in 1976 that 'no one has the right to be in a government unless they can give full allegiance to the Province and publicly support the security forces'.[33] As the British and Irish governments sought to open talks on the governance of Northern Ireland in the late 1980s, the then DUP Deputy Leader Peter Robinson insisted that 'any party sharing responsibility for government should offer their full support to the security forces in Northern Ireland and encourage followers to support and even join them'.[34] Even the most moderate 'pro-Union' party—the Alliance Party—ruled out power-sharing with the SDLP unless it fully supported the RUC.[35] The then party leader John Cushnahan, in a letter to Prime Minister Margaret Thatcher in 1987, threatened to review Alliance support for the 1985 Anglo-Irish Agreement unless the SDLP called on Catholics to join the RUC.[36]

In a conference speech later that year, Cushnahan 'deplored' the SDLP refusal to 'wholeheartedly support the police' and said this was a major block to political progress.[37] Again, after the 1994 ceasefire, leading UUP MP William Ross argued that unless the SDLP members took their seats on the Police Authority and sought to persuade nationalists to support the RUC, it could not play a 'responsible part' in Northern Ireland.[38] The unanimity of unionist discourse on this issue is striking. Nationalists were not being offered power-sharing 'in return' for supporting the police. Nationalists had, in unionist eyes, an absolute duty to support the police. If nationalists refused to offer that support then they had, in the unionists' view, excluded themselves from any right to hold public office. It is also an indication of the scale of nationalist alienation from the RUC that the SDLP could not endorse the service, despite the party's strong desire to agree on power-sharing with unionists.

The extent to which SDLP critiques of policing were seen as a breach of the party's duty of citizenship is further illustrated by the degree to which unionists held SDLP members responsible for the deaths of security force members—despite the party's strong and consistent opposition to the IRA campaign. John Carson (UUP) stated in the House of Commons in 1976 that 'political maggots, namely Canavan, Mallon and Cooper are responsible for the deaths of UDR men'.[39] UUP leader Jim Molyneaux, said 'vindictive accusations against the security forces are treated as an incitement to murder Army, UDR and RUC personnel...those who engage in such vile propaganda are every bit as guilty as those who pull the trigger'.[40] SDLP deputy leader Seamus Mallon was attacked by the DUP's Willie McCrea as

> the man who has contributed more to the murder of innocent members of the security forces than practically any other person in the SDLP community...by his words [he] is stained with the blood of innocent people.[41]

Indeed, responsibility for the murder of members of the security forces was shared '*equally* by those who pulled the trigger and by those politicians and church leaders who by their constant vilification have endangered the lives of every member...', according to Frank Millar.[42] Unionists who directed such attacks at the SDLP were not simply arguing that the party was *morally* responsible for RUC deaths; they were insisting that it was the duty of all citizens to support the police. This was the embodiment of Northern Ireland's constitutional status as part of the United Kingdom. In unionist eyes, if the SDLP rejected this duty it was engaged in a constitutional insurgency against the state and was therefore lending support to the IRA's armed campaign.

Unionist perspectives on the role of the police in upholding the political status quo extended to the operational level. UUP Deputy Leader Harold McCusker, MP, in what represented a typical example of this perspective, attacked the deployment of the RUC against unionist protestors' attempts to break through police lines where the police had re-routed Orange Order marches away from nationalist districts:

> hundreds of policemen have been deployed, not against republican thugs but against Protestant bands and their supporters. How is that for getting your priorities wrong?...The real choice confronting any police force should be between the law abiding and the law breakers, between those who uphold the constitution and those who would subvert it, between the terrorists and their agents and the rest of us.[43]

Unionists in the protests described by McCusker were clearly breaking the law by attacking police lines once the police had made a decision on public order grounds to re-route the march. However, in McCusker's eyes the protestors were not 'law breakers'—as they, unlike nationalists, were 'upholding the constitution'. Thus, in unionists' perspectives, it was attitudes to the constitutional status quo and not the manner of protesting that divided 'law breakers' from the 'law-abiding'.

'Hard-line' security rather than a human-rights focus

During the conflict, the widespread human-rights-based criticisms of the RUC from groups and individuals who were not supporters of an Irish nationalist agenda did not open up any space within the major unionist parties for 'non-political' critiques of policing, based on legal values or even arguments that such abuses strengthened the IRA. The unionist parties attacked human-rights groups as being engaged in a campaign, deliberately or through naïveté, to undermine the state. UUP leader James Molyneaux sharply criticised human-rights groups 'who come to the rescue' whenever the security forces would get the upper hand on the IRA.[44] The Catholic Bishops Commission for Justice and Peace was called 'the Irish Roman Catholic Commission for Republican Victory in Northern Ireland' by Unionist MP Jim Kilfedder.[45] Robert Bradford, a UUP MP, argued that whenever the security forces came up with a strategy that was successful in 'hindering the IRA…the opposition [of human-rights groups and lawyers] magically emerges'.[46] UUP leader David Trimble queried the motives of human-rights groups, claiming that they had only emerged to oppose 'supergrass' evidence[47] when such evidence was used against republican organisations, and so this led him to 'wonder about their motives'.[48] After the ceasefire, UUP spokesperson on security Ken Maginnis, MP, continued to assert that even some of those involved in the law supported the gun and the bomb.[49]

The unionist suspicions of the motivations of human-rights groups were accompanied by a rejection of the substantive criticisms made of the RUC. There was cross-party unionist opposition to any disciplinary action over the 'shoot-to-kill' operations investigated by John Stalker.[50] Jim Wells argued that 'you can never kill an IRA terrorist and be in the wrong…let the police force…go out in the clear confidence that they can eradicate these gunmen and not have to face the courts'.[51] With this level of support even for the controversial operational decisions of the RUC and British Army, there is no evidence of any willingness on the part of unionist political elites to compromise on the issue of policing. In their view, the duty to defend the state is fundamental and prior to the right to protection from the state.

Not only was there was widespread unionist support for those RUC tactics that were criticised by human-rights groups, but politicians from the two main unionist parties also called, throughout the conflict, for what might be termed 'hard-line' security policies. There was near unanimous support, for example, for capital punishment and the use of ambush tactics against the IRA. Robert Bradford said 'when capital punishment is applied…at least one terrorist has been deterred'.[52] Bradford later suggested that the Cromwellian period was one of the few 'peaceful' periods in Irish history.[53] The DUP called the shooting of two IRA members in Derry in 1984 'an early Christmas present'[54] and also called for capital punishment and the placing of minefields along the Border.[55] William Ross supported a 'shoot-to-kill' strategy, saying: 'who the devil ever shot to miss?...I regret that the job is not done often enough'.[56] There is very little recognition that such security policies reinforce support for militant republicanism and support for the IRA. When this issue was put to Ernest Baird in the context of the gospel passages on peacemakers, he responded with a full defence of aggressive security, saying, 'if you also read the Old Testament there are some terrible things that God told his people to do, things even the SAS might not contemplate in South Armagh'.[57] UUP security spokesperson Ken Maginnis, MP, was absolute in his support for aggressive security strategies on the ground, and uncompromising in his defence of the security forces in the aftermath of controversial shoot-to-kill operations. He referred to such operations as a 'success'[58] and has supported in principle the idea of ambushing armed IRA members rather than trying to arrest them.[59]

The political wisdom of such security force activity is one of the few issues on which there is a minority view openly expressed by any significant section of unionist politicians. Independent MP Robert McCartney, though later an opponent of the peace process, questioned the tactical wisdom of aggressive and illegal security-force actions. While supporting strict security policies he argued that an overly aggressive military strategy which did not distinguish between IRA activists and 'ordinary' nationalists would only increase support for the IRA.[60] The Alliance Party also argued that no military solution could be found in Northern Ireland unless there was political agreement first, in order, in that party's view, to isolate the IRA from the community that supported it,[61] and Alliance was often critical of calls for hard-line security policies.[62] However, when the British Army shot eight IRA members and a passing civilian in an ambush in Loughgall, even Alliance was unambivalent in its support for the security forces, with party leader John Cushnahan calling it a 'successful security operation'.[63]

The extent of unionist rejections of human-rights-based critiques of the RUC meant that human-rights discourse did not provide a 'neutral' or non-political language for discussing police reform. Human-rights critiques were seen purely as instrumental attacks on the police by the two main unionist parties, and debates on these issues were always based on the core political divisions in Northern Ireland.

Rejection of the unrepresentative argument

As can be seen from the above discussion, there was no recognition that nationalists were alienated from the RUC due to its ethos or actions. Low levels of Catholic recruitment were explained, by unionists, as being due to IRA intimidation[64] or due to the subversive nature of the nationalist community.[65] These two explanations are at least potentially contradictory, and unionists were often not clear as to which was the dominant explanation.

Occasionally, unionist politicians argued that there was a 'silent' pro-British, Catholic minority and that the lack of Catholics in the police could mainly be explained by IRA intimidation. UUP leader James Molyneaux spoke in the 1970s and 1980s of the 'many' Roman Catholics who are not nationalists yet who support the RUC and/or reject the IRA.[66] His successor as UUP leader, David Trimble, argued in 1996 that 25 to 40% of Roman Catholics wanted to remain part of the United Kingdom.[67] This line of argument was re-inforced by the use of survey data from the police authority or other sources, which appeared to show that a significant proportion of Roman Catholics were satisfied with the RUC. However, such surveys need to be read cautiously. The late John Whyte repeatedly warned researchers in Northern Ireland (or those of any zone of conflict) of the dangers of using survey data, as he argued respondents tend to give a more moderate or pro-officialdom answer rather than offering their real views.[68] Graham Ellison highlights the fact that one of the most quoted surveys (the 1992 NI Social Attitudes Survey) records Sinn Féin support at 2.8%, at a time when the party's electoral support was between 16% and 17%.[69] It is difficult to assess whether researchers conducting the 1992 Social Attitudes Survey did not operate in the communities where Sinn Féin was strong, or if, in general, people surveyed about their views during times of conflict are more reluctant to express strong opinions. With such under-representation of the Sinn Féin support base it is difficult to give such surveys any credence. For this reason alone, the decision of the policing commission to hold so many public meetings across Northern Ireland, where members could directly hear the perspectives of large numbers of the public, was a wise one.[70]

The occasional public statement from unionist politicians over the years, claiming that there existed a silent 'loyal' Catholic grouping, is overwhelmed by the much larger number of unionist statements that are clear-cut in extending the definition of subversive to the entire nationalist community (or even to the Catholic community). In 1985 Ken Maginnis said:

> you believe in...[Roman Catholics'] decency, you want to get on well with them. But they come from the same community the IRA comes from, and from which it recruits. Therefore it is dangerous to get too close to them.[71]

The following year he focused on the relatively high rates of vote transfers, under the PRSTV system,[72] between the SDLP and Sinn Féin, to argue that 85% of nationalists were lending support to the IRA campaign.[73] In the House of Commons in 1991, David Trimble quoted as a form of precedent the practice of treating all 'enemy aliens' as suspects during wartime.[74] The possibility that some 'aliens' might actually sympathise with their host country was outweighed by the strategic and security imperative, and so all 'enemy aliens' were to be treated as suspect. The implication was that all nationalists were 'enemy aliens' and similarly were to be seen as a threat. Ian Paisley, speaking just prior to the ceasefires in 1994, said he could not 'trust the future of Ulster to any Roman Catholic and I say that unashamedly'.[75]

This depiction of the entire nationalist community in Northern Ireland as being subversive would suggest that nationalist views were a more important explanation than IRA intimidation for the low numbers of nationalists in the RUC. This perspective also strengthened unionist resistance to any suggestion that police reform was essential to meet nationalist concerns, as, to use a phrase from the UUP's William Ross, a lack of nationalist support for the RUC was not in itself an argument for reform of the police, as it would be 'unreasonable' to expect the RUC to get the support of 'law-breakers'.[76]

Despite these attacks on the nationalist community for refusing to support the RUC, individual Catholics who broke with their community and joined the RUC, or became members of the Police Authority, were frequently treated with suspicion. While unionists attacked the SDLP for not allowing its members to take seats on the Police Authority, John McCrea of the Orange Order attacked proposals to have individual nationalists appointed, saying they would be a security risk.[77] Following controversy over the re-routing of Orange Order parades attempting to march through nationalist areas of Cookstown in 1985, Alan Kane (DUP) attacked one of the most senior Catholic RUC officers, Chief Supt. Leo Dolan, saying that Dolan, as 'a Roman Catholic, a former neighbour of Owen Carron's family…is no friend of the Protestant people'.[78] Willie McCrea said Dolan was

> an ardent Roman Catholic who has shown his hatred of Protestant parades in the past. His removal should be forthcoming in order to ensure proper relations exist between the RUC and the people of Cookstown.[79]

Following a similar incident associated with a parade in Portadown in August 1995, the Portadown branch of the UUP issued a formal statement attacking another senior Catholic officer, Bill McCreesh.[80] In 1996 Peter Robinson called on Chief Constable Hugh Annesley to weed out 'Catholic moles' in the RUC who Robinson accused of making 'nationalist' comments to the media following newspaper coverage of sectarian harassment within the RUC.[81] This type of attack on individual Catholic officers again points to a strong tendency in unionism to treat the entire Catholic community as politically suspect and incapable of being trusted police officers. It reinforces the sense that the role of the police is to uphold a unionist vision of the constitutional order and not simply to uphold the law.

'Ulsterisation' of security

The majority of unionist politicians argued throughout the conflict that control of security should be returned to a unionist-controlled parliament,[82] and in the absence of such local authority saw the effective primacy of locally recruited security forces commanded by local officers as a good second best. UUP leader David Trimble, for example, said

> the IRA will only be defeated when they see that their ultimate goal is unattainable. That day will only come when the IRA see the control of security in the hands of Ulstermen, because the Provos know Ulstermen cannot afford to run away from the situation.[83]

This type of 'asymmetric' conflict, where one side sees it as an 'all-or-nothing' conflict while the other side may have options, has international parallels.[84] The US could pull out of Vietnam with very little threat to its domestic position. The South Vietnamese government had no such luxury. If it lost, its position was terminal. Unionists consciously analysed their position within an asymmetric model. For example, the Orange Order, comparing Northern Ireland to Israel, said: 'Having been betrayed before they [the Ulster people] are very alert now, for as Louis Gardner wrote, "Ulster, like Israel, can only lose once"'.[85] In a very similar vein, Clifford Smyth quotes Admiral Hugo Hendrik Bierman of the then South African Navy: 'in the nature of this protracted war our enemies have the opportunity to attack time and again and to lose, whereas we shall have but one opportunity to lose'.[86]

Raymond Ferguson (UUP) argued that ordinary unionists would not feel secure until control of security was returned to Ulster hands.[87] In the late 1970s and early 1980s his colleague, Robert Bradford, emphasised the hegemonic importance of the 'Ulsterisation' of security:

> with one stroke the House [of Commons] could remove the objective [of Irish unity] from the IRA—or at least its hopes of attaining the objective. The House could return to the people of Northern Ireland a devolved government,[88]

and again 'the will to win will emerge only when Ulster politicians have the right and the possibility of taking security decisions in their own parliament'.[89] Ian Paisley said in 1982 that 'only those who are fighting for their homes can really fight for their country'.[90] Two years later he returned to this theme, arguing that:

> we did beat terrorism for almost 50 years...because we had a government that was determined to beat terrorism and because the people fighting terrorism had a stake in this land. When you are fighting for your home, when you are fighting for your heritage and when you are fighting for your family, by the grace of God you will fight.[91]

During the conflict there was no likelihood of control over security being devolved from London to unionist hands. The debate on 'Ulsterisation' of control did allow unionists to blame the British government for the failure to defeat the IRA and to argue that a unionist-controlled police force could succeed. The support for devolution of control of policing also reflected a strong and deep-rooted support within Unionism for devolved government and local control of security. Later in the peace process this tension between mutually incompatible choices—seeking to exclude nationalists while also wresting control back from London to Northern Ireland—was finally resolved in favour of devolution, but at the cost of sharing power with nationalists and in the context of fundamentally reconstituted political institutions. More generally, the above discussion of unionist views during the conflict is repeated not to draw up old disputes or to demonise those involved, but rather to highlight the very significant shift in positions that was required to reach the agreement on the transformation of policing.

THE PEACE PROCESS AND THE TRANSFORMATION OF POLICING

The nationalist community saw police reform as one of the most important issues in the peace process. It did not believe any peace deal could be enduring if it did not deal with policing, because nationalists believed that policing was at the heart of the conflict.[92] The highly politicised nature of policing, the legacy of human-rights concerns in Northern Ireland and the highly unrepresentative make-up of the RUC ensured that no nationalist party could endorse the police and retain political support. It was also impossible for the RUC to provide policing in nationalist areas without community support. The centrality of policing to the wider peace process was reflected in public debates that began in the immediate aftermath of the ceasefires. The importance of this issue was also clear (as can be seen in the chapters by Policing Commission members in this volume) in the public meetings held by the Commission and in those published submissions made by a wide range of nationalist organisations.[93] The two nationalist political parties highlighted the issue of policing in regular statements. The SDLP made it very clear that it would not endorse a tokenistic reform programme. A survey of party members indicated that over 94% of them sought 'radical reform' of the RUC after the ceasefires.[94] Sinn Féin ran a high-profile, public campaign under the slogan 'Disband the RUC', and its members supported this approach.[95]

Initially, mainstream Unionism's position on policing led it to dismiss any requirement to even consider RUC reform as part of the process of a political settlement for Northern Ireland. In 1991 Ian Paisley listed as one of the key 'unacceptable' elements of the earlier Brooke talks-process the idea that the RUC was part of the problem.[96] After the IRA ceasefire, unionists were very vocal in rejecting any public debate on the reform of the RUC.[97] Even symbolic changes in the name and uniform were rejected by all unionist parties other than Alliance.[98] The UUP, DUP and UKUP all opposed even the minor administrative changes contained in the 1997 Police Bill.[99] Ken Maginnis went so far as to say that the very limited legislation 'smacks of thinking and planning that falls not short of treachery'.[100]

Rejecting any changes in the symbols used by the RUC, Unionist MP Robert McCartney argued

> that if a person lives in a part of the United Kingdom where his or her place within it is absolutely certain, such as Cornwall or Devon, symbols are not, perhaps, so important, but if a person lives in a part of the United Kingdom that is constantly under threat, along with one's identity, symbols take on a significance that they would not otherwise bear.[101]

UUP security spokesperson Ken Maginnis, in the same debate, said:

> the RUC is criticised because it holds on to its traditional symbols: the badge, the royal prefix, the allegiance to the Crown, the flying of the Union flag on pre-ordained days on public buildings such as police stations, but all of these are what makes the RUC a British police service, not the French gendarmerie, the German polizie or the Spanish civil guard. It is what gives a disciplined force its esprit de corps, its sense of identity and comradeship which has enabled it to endure and survive...I do not believe that the official trappings of the RUC give offence to anyone other than those who seek to be offended. Their campaign is not to create a neutral working environment but a neutered RUC, bereft of identity and effectiveness from a lack of self-confidence.[102]

There was no recognition, at this stage, that nationalists could not accept this *esprit de corps,* which was defined in exclusively unionist terms; indeed, by defining the nationalist community as the 'other' against which the *corps* was pitted, its very essence was the exclusion of Irish nationalism.

Likewise, changes in the oath of allegiance (to the British monarch) were rejected as symbolising a shift away from absolute support for the constitutional status-quo. Maginnis again said,

we are told that because it is an oath to the Queen it is un-
acceptable to some members of one tradition in Northern
Ireland. I think we all recognise that the oath to the
Queen shows loyalty to the state; the constitution.[103]

In a similar vein, Peter Weir said that the British government was
'only concerned...with increasing the nationalist community's confidence in the police service, and that is a recipe for disaster'.[104] Hugh
Smyth argued that politically motivated RUC reform would 'wreck
the confidence of the unionist community'.[105] Ian Paisley said the
police force should not be reformed, as 'the RUC has stood between
us and those who would destroy us'.[106] Even the Alliance Party supported only very limited calls for reform, with a policy statement in
1995 rejecting the idea of major structural changes in the RUC and
focusing instead on changes at the governmental level and in dealing
with individual complaints.[107] The Alliance Party Election Manifesto
in 1997[108] talks of RUC reform in very minimalist language, with no
discussion on the overall ethos and ideology of the Northern Ireland
police, and likewise Alliance's submission to the Patten Commission
made no serious criticism of the RUC and restricted its suggestions to
symbolic changes in name and uniform.[109]

Given the strength of these opposing perspectives, it was not surprising that all parties agreed, during the negotiations leading up to
the 1998 Agreement, that a solution to policing could not be negotiated at that time and that an independent commission should be
established to make recommendations on policing, which would be
'broadly representative' and have 'expert and international representation'.[110] As part of a trade-off to get the British government to accept
such an independent commission, a related 'review' of the criminal
justice system was to be carried out by a mechanism set up by the
British government itself—though with an 'independent element'.
This requirement was added at nationalist insistence and later on had
a significant impact in producing a much more far-reaching review
than had been anticipated by many observers.

There was no agreement during the 1998 talks on the specifics of
policing policy, but the terms of reference for an independent commission to be established were set out in the Good Friday Agreement,
which stated:

Its proposals on policing should be designed to ensure
that policing arrangements, including composition,

recruitment, training, culture, ethos and symbols, are
such that in a new approach Northern Ireland has a
police service that can enjoy widespread support from,
and is seen as an integral part of, the community as a
whole.[111]

The SDLP, Sinn Féin and the Irish government had put considerable resources into achieving the strongest possible terms of
reference for a commission on policing. Surprisingly, the UUP negotiators did not seem as focused on this issue. Nationalist
negotiators were prepared for a last minute backlash from the UUP
to reverse the text of the terms of reference for a policing commission, but it did not materialise. The UUP was hugely focused on
limiting the North–South institutional linkages. Its negotiators were
very influenced by an analysis of the collapse of the 1974 power-
sharing institutions, which (over) emphasised the importance of the
all-island Council of Ireland in explaining unionist opposition to
that agreement. On policing, the UUP seemed to assume that a
British-government-appointed commission would largely favour the
status quo. The terms of reference were, however, fundamental to
the direction given to the Independent Commission on Policing for
Northern Ireland as finally established. Indeed Sinn Féin, despite a
cautious response to the later *Report*, did not press for any last
minute strengthening of the terms of reference in the final days of
negotiations.

The other difficulty for unionists was that RUC reform was an
area that could have been imposed by the British government
without their consent. Trimble acknowledged this in the aftermath of
the Agreement, saying 'even had agreement not been reached in the
Talks a much more draconian series of reforms were planned for the
RUC'.[112] However, if unionist leaders realised that change was inevitable, they made few serious attempts to deal with the political
problems that change would cause. The Sinn Féin leadership devoted
a lot of time and energy to regular meetings with its membership and
wider support base, to prepare them first of all for a ceasefire announcement and then for the various concessions made in talks. Yet
there was no similar process of engagement by the UUP leadership
with its own supporters to convince them of the need for compromise, in advance of either the Good Friday Agreement itself, or the
publication of the Commission's *Report*.[113]

RESPONSES TO THE COMMISSION'S REPORT
AND THE LEGISLATION

In the immediate aftermath of the publication of the *Patten Report*, public debate was dominated by unionist rejection of its proposals. The DUP was, at that point, still in opposition to the 1998 Agreement and predictably opposed the *Report*, but UUP leader and First Minister David Trimble also attacked it in very trenchant terms, calling it the 'most shoddy piece of work I have seen in my entire life' and referring to the name change for the RUC as a 'gratuitous insult'. Trimble said his party would study the report carefully before making any judgement, but then said that the only fundamental change needed to the RUC was the recruitment of many more Catholic officers, while the only thing necessary to achieve that was 'to put an end to the intimidation and social exclusion of Catholics who join the police force'. He also expressed opposition to the proposed integration of the controversial RUC Special Branch into the mainstream of the new police service. Referring to this as the 'emasculation of Special Branch', he said it was 'above everything else, what the republican movement wants'.[114]

Nationalist parties, possibly because of the hostile unionist reaction, were very subdued in their responses to the *Report*. Nonetheless, both nationalist parties were relatively positive in their initial statements. While this might have been expected from the SDLP, Sinn Féin's Martin McGuinness also hinted that a positive response could come in time. Responding to media queries as to whether the *Report* met their 'definition' of disbanding the RUC, he said: 'If we create a new policing service, we will have effectively disbanded the RUC'.[115] As for the SDLP, Seamus Mallon said the party wanted an immediate ban on plastic bullets and a much shorter time-scale for the achievement of religious balance in the force, but he also said that the *Report*,

> taken in totality and implemented faithfully and speed-
> ily, contains the basis for the objectives of the Good
> Friday Agreement to be attained in terms of achieving a
> police service which can attract and sustain the whole
> community's support.[116]

Ulster Unionist Party opposition to the *Report* over the following months focused on a number of key themes. The most high-profile of these were opposition to the name change and to the dropping of the 'Royal' prefix; however, the UUP also opposed the proposals on 50:50

recruitment of Catholics and others, on neutral symbols and flags, on control of the Special Branch, on the International Oversight Commissioner and Sinn Féin members sitting on police boards.[117] Other unionist parties, organisations and high-profile individuals also joined in the debate in opposition to the *Report*, including the Orange Order and former RUC chief constable Jack Hermon.[118] The Police Authority, abandoning political neutrality, also publicly and strongly attacked the proposals for 50:50 recruitment and the name change.[119]

In the wake of these responses, the British government announced a three month period of debate on the *Report*, to finish on 30 November 1999. By the end of that period the SDLP had endorsed the *Report*, calling for the full implementation of its 175 Recommendations. That party did, however, repeat its disappointment that plastic bullets were not to be banned and said the 10-year deadline to reach a target of 30% Catholics in the new police service was 'hardly a radical target'.[120] Sinn Féin, while continuing to send positive signals, did not endorse the *Report*. In an initial response, party leader Gerry Adams said that he 'might...encourage young republicans to join the proposed force', saying 'if we do come to a conclusion that the *Patten Report* does contain the ingredients of a new policing service and that the RUC will have gone, of course Sinn Féin will come out in a very positive way'. He said it was

> not merely a question of whether Catholics should join a new policing service...It is a question of whether republicans and nationalists, and particularly working class republicans and nationalists, would join such a policing service and have peer approval for doing so. Ultimately, this will be the acid test by which the Patten Commission and its Recommendations will be judged.[121]

Later, in a formal response, the party said that it could not 'at present' urge nationalists and republicans to join a police service on the basis of the *Patten Report*.

> Sinn Féin is not convinced at present that the *Patten Report* goes far enough, and we are therefore unable at present to take up the call to encourage people from nationalist and republican communities to join any emerging police service...We recognise there are many good things in the *Report*.[122]

On the specifics of the *Report*, Sinn Féin welcomed the proposals for accountability but said that they could have gone further. It also welcomed the proposed closure of interrogation centres, but said that the *Report*'s target of achieving 30% Catholic members in ten years was inadequate, and that the *Report* should have proposed an end to emergency laws and the use of plastic bullets. In a further positive signal, however, a motion by one *cumann* (local branch) at the party's *Ard Fheis* (annual conference), which would have tied the party to seeking to exclude every RUC officer from membership of the PSNI, was rejected by the party delegates.[123]

The main point emphasised by Sinn Féin in this period was that it needed to know what the British government would do, and therefore it would reserve final judgement on whether it would urge people to join any new police service until it saw the appropriate legislation on implementing the *Report*'s recommendations. This point was the key issue of contention with the SDLP, whom Sinn Féin accused of acting prematurely.[124] Sinn Féin did not trust the British government to implement the *Report* and so it was wary that endorsing it might turn it into a nationalist 'wish list', rather than an Independent Commission Report, which did not, by any measure, represent all of Sinn Féin's positions. In fact, when the new Police Bill was published in May 2000, the British government had abandoned key recommendations in the Commission's *Report* and did indeed seek to present the legislation as a 'compromise' between a nationalist-supported Commission report and unionist opposition to change.

THE BRITISH GOVERNMENT'S LEGISLATIVE RESPONSE

The British government's implementing legislation (the Police Bill) and a parallel 'implementation plan', purporting to show how it would implement the Commission's *Report*,[125] was roundly criticised not only by the two nationalist parties in Northern Ireland but by most significant human-rights groups, nationalist commentators and civil society organisations.[126] The Irish government too signalled its displeasure that so many of the Commission's 175 recommendations had been rejected by the British government.[127] John Hume called the Police Bill 'defective',[128] while Gerry Adams stated

> there is no way at this time that I, or Sinn Féin, could recommend to nationalists or republicans that they

should consider joining or supporting a police force as described in that legislation.[129]

The Deputy First Minister and SDLP MP Seamus Mallon reacted to British Secretary of State for Northern Ireland Peter Mandelson's depictions of his legislation as a compromise between nationalist support for the *Patten Report* and unionist opposition, saying that '*Patten* is itself a compromise. It is policing not in the image of unionism or nationalism'.[130] Both the SDLP and Sinn Féin issued lengthy critiques of the Bill.[131] Nationalist critiques focused on the insertion of the phrase 'incorporating the RUC' in the formal title of the new PSNI; the potential continuation of the practice of flying the Union Jack on police stations; the weakening of oversight, human rights and accountability mechanisms; the potential weakening of the commitment to 50:50 recruitment; provisions allowing the British government or Chief Constable to veto investigations into allegations of police malpractice; and the limitation of a new oath of office to new recruits only (rather than having it apply to all existing officers as recommended by the Commission). Statements reflected all of the traditional nationalist critiques of the RUC—the counter-insurgency priority, human-rights issues and community representation and ethos issues.

The unionist public response was relatively muted; while still opposing much of the Bill, unionists clearly preferred it to the Commission's *Report*. They focused on the symbols of the service—the RUC title, the retention of British symbols in the police insignia, the flying of the Union Jack and displays of portraits of the British monarch in police stations.[132] The May 2000 Police Bill was seen as a victory for unionist lobbying in regard to these issues. The Police Bill also included a significant weakening of the oversight, human rights and accountability proposals made in the Commission's *Report*. While Ulster Unionists did not oppose the British government's overturning of the Commission's recommendations in these areas, there is little evidence of a vigorous unionist campaign—the motivation for rejecting the Commission's recommendations on oversight and human rights seemed to come from the British government itself and the police and security agencies. While the outgoing police authority had criticised the Commission's *Report*—in particular on the core unionist issues of name, symbols and ex-IRA prisoners being on police boards—during this phase of the debate members of the authority criticised the British government for weakening the powers of the proposed new policing board.[133]

Following an extensive campaign of pressure from the nationalist parties, some British Labour backbenchers, senior US politicians and human-rights groups,[134] and a series of inter-party talks in Weston Park in England in 2001, the British government introduced a number of significant amendments to its own proposed legislation, in order to bring it closer to the recommendations of the Commission's *Report*. It also promised a revised implementation plan,[135] which would further deal with some of the remaining Commission recommendations. Finally, the British government promised to have an international judge examine possible RUC involvement in the murder of Pat Finucane and to hold a public inquiry on the murder if that judge recommended it.[136]

This was sufficient for the Irish government and the SDLP to support the new arrangements, and in August 2001 the SDLP agreed to join the new policing board.[137] The SDLP claimed it had secured sufficient amendments from the British government to allow its members to do so. Seamus Mallon, referring to the previous British Secretary of State, Peter Mandelson, said the legislation had been 'de-Mandelised'. He highlighted in particular: the strengthening of the powers of inquiry of the Policing Board—now gaining powers formerly resting with the Chief Constable and the Secretary of State; new powers for the Police Ombudsman to access documents and investigate police policies and practices; commitment to the secondment of Gardaí (members of the Irish police service, An Garda Síochána) to the new police service; strengthened commitment to human rights; greater focus on community policing and the phasing out of the full-time RUC reserve.[138]

Sinn Féin refused to join the Policing Board or support the PSNI at this time, arguing that the proposed legislation and the British government's 'implementation plan' for police reform were still far weaker than the Commission's recommendations. Although Sinn Féin had not given unqualified support to the Commission's *Report* when published, from this time Sinn Féin explicitly used the Commission's *Report* as a benchmark against which to measure the transformation of policing.[139] Another very positive development for Sinn Féin was the quality and detail of the reports of the first Oversight Commissioner, Tom Constantine. His very detailed performance indicators, judging action on policing as compared to the Commission's recommendations, ensured that the British government did not have a monopoly of authoritative information.[140] The role of the Oversight Commission was, in hindsight, one of the most significant and innovative of the Commission's recommendations and greatly assisted in both clarifying Sinn Féin's remaining concerns and as an independent mechanism to judge progress on those concerns. Sinn Féin, from this point, focused on the remaining gaps between the Commission's recommendations and British government decisions—especially on accountability, human rights and oversight; on retention of some key powers in London; on control of the Special Branch and covert policing operations; on the need to avoid officers being deployed long-term into Special Branch, as had occurred in the RUC; and on the lack of certainty about the RUC name and badge. These Sinn Féin critiques, though fewer in number than their formal responses to the May legislation, continue to raise issues in each of the three areas that have dominated nationalist responses to policing in Northern Ireland: a concern that counter-insurgency policing dominates the entire policing system; a demand for stronger oversight on human-rights issues; and an insistence on politically impartial policing, free from symbolic attachment to the British state.[141]

Unionist parties, notwithstanding their opposition to elements of the reform agenda, also agreed to join the Policing Board. Both the DUP and UUP highlighted two continuing priorities in announcing their decision to join the Board. The first was to ensure that the police service's symbols would 'recognise Northern Ireland's constitutional position in the UK', indicating how important the police were to unionist definitions of the nature of the state. The second priority was the unionists' ongoing campaign to minimise the reduction in the size of the force and in particular the full-time RUC reserve.[142]

The Police Board unanimously agreed on a new PSNI symbol in December 2001.[143] While not strictly following the Commission's recommendation of having a badge that was 'entirely free from any association with either the British or Irish states', the new badge was widely judged to be acceptable. The badge's largest element is the 'cross of St Patrick', acceptable to both nationalists and unionists. It also incorporates the crown—as a symbol of Britishness—and the Irish symbols of the harp and shamrock, neither standing in a hierarchical relationship to the other, along with traditional symbols of justice—the laurel leaf, torch and scales of justice.

This achievement was swamped, however, by the wider crisis in the peace process that led to the suspension of the power-sharing executive and Assembly in October 2002, as the UUP refused to continue sharing power with Sinn Féin without the handover or destruction of IRA weapons. New elections in November 2003 saw the DUP emerge as the largest unionist party and Sinn Féin as the largest nationalist party—entitling the leaders of these parties to hold the offices of First Minister and Deputy First Minister, respectively.[144] No agreement on power-sharing was possible and the Assembly was immediately suspended. The key issues in dispute were unionists' refusal to share power with Sinn Féin without the IRA destroying its weapons, and the IRA refusal to do so while the peace process was stalled and while the newly agreed institutions of government within Northern Ireland and between North and South were not operational. Nationalists also demanded 'demilitarisation' by the British Army[145] and further moves on policing.

The IRA agreed to put its weapons 'beyond use' in a process overseen and observed by an International Commission on Decommissioning, led by Canadian General John de Chastelain, and completed in September 2005.[146] This was the key defining moment for Sinn Féin. The destruction of IRA weapons was a major political decision. The initial IRA ceasefire could be interpreted (or sold) as an experiment. An IRA campaign could have been restarted, and indeed was resumed (at a low level) between February 1996 and July 1997. However, symbolically, the destruction of weapons was a clear signal that the IRA was not intending to restart its campaign and that Sinn Féin would pursue republican goals by exclusively peaceful means. The next logical step was support for policing. However, no wider agreement on power-sharing with unionists or Sinn Féin support for the police was reached at this time.

Agreement seemed to have finally been reached in talks in St Andrews in Scotland in October 2006.[147] The St Andrews Agreement was officially between the Irish and British governments, but they expected (on the basis of the talks) that it would be endorsed by the parties in Northern Ireland after consultation with their membership. St Andrews provided for a deal whereby the suspended Northern Ireland Executive and Assembly would be re-constituted, with new provisions and commitments made by the parties to avoid the institutions collapsing again when the members were in dispute. New elections would be held as a means of gaining community endorsement of the power-sharing deal. New legislation on policing, human rights and the Irish language was promised—that on policing would be passed by the end of 2006; and the British government guaranteed that there would be no 'executive role' for the British secret service

(MI5) in Northern Ireland—even on 'national security' issues—when control of policing was devolved to Northern Ireland. Sinn Féin was expected to endorse the police service, and while there was no firm date to devolve control of policing from London to the Northern Ireland Executive, the two governments stated that it was their

> view that implementation of the Agreement published today should be sufficient to build the community confidence necessary for the Assembly to request the devolution of criminal justice and policing from the British Government by May 2008.[148]

Sinn Féin held up to 60 meetings with the party support base right across Ireland to gauge opinion on the question of supporting the PSNI.[149] A special party *Ard Fheis* was called with delegates from every local branch of the party, and the leadership needed to be certain that it would secure an overwhelming majority to avoid the danger of a split in the party. Difficulties began to emerge, however, when senior DUP MP (and later deputy leader) Nigel Dodds said publicly that devolution of control over policing from London (a key Sinn Féin demand) would not happen in a 'political lifetime'.[150] Sinn Féin also raised concerns that the proposed new role for MI5 in countering international terrorism would be extended to include Northern Ireland and would lead to institutionalised links with the new PSNI, creating, Sinn Féin feared, a new 'force within a force'—to use the phrase which had also been used to describe the old RUC Special Branch by the Commission in its *Report*.[151] British Prime Minister Tony Blair personally responded on this issue in a public statement, saying

> No police officers will be seconded to or under the control of the security service. The small number of police officers who act in a liaison capacity with the security service will be PSNI headquarters staff acting in that role for fixed time-limited periods to the extent that the Chief Constable deems necessary for them to perform their duties…Policing is the responsibility solely of the PSNI. The security service will have no role whatsoever in civic policing.[152]

This statement was welcomed by Sinn Féin and seemed to resolve tensions on the role of MI5.[153]

The debate within Sinn Féin was intense and relatively public—unusually so for a party whose internal discipline is legendary in Irish politics. Over 1,000 people attended a meeting, which the press were permitted to observe, in Gerry Adams's own constituency.[154] Letters for and against endorsing the PSNI were carried in the Sinn Féin newspaper *An Phoblacht*.[155] The newspaper also carried very prominent messages of support for the leadership position from former African National Congress chief negotiator Cyril Ramaphosa and the Palestinian ambassador to Ireland, Hikmat Ajjuri. The *Ard Fheis* itself was attended by 3,000 delegates, and the motion committing the party to 'fully' support the PSNI and the criminal justice system, and to take up places on the Policing Board and the local District Policing Partnership Boards was carried, with an estimated 90 percent 'yes' vote.[156] Gerry Adams, in proposing the motion, said party negotiators were now satisfied with the legislation on oversight of policing and on the model of a Justice Department to be established in the Northern Ireland Assembly. The motion was linked to the re-establishment of the power-sharing Executive in Northern Ireland and to the agreement on devolution of policing and justice powers. Or, in the absence of such agreement, to a new governance model for Northern Ireland based on stronger British–Irish 'partnership arrangements'. This was read by all to mean a formalised model of co-operation between the governments over the heads of the local parties.[157]

Despite linking the issue of policing to the restoration of power-sharing, party leader Gerry Adams, following a meeting of the party's *Ard Chomhairle* (national executive) held immediately after the conference, expressed Sinn Féin's support for the PSNI and for nationalists who wished to join it.[158] Sinn Féin now believed that there was sufficient progress for the party to offer support for the police service and to join the Policing Board. The three key criticisms of the RUC set out at the beginning of this chapter—its prioritisation of counter-insurgency, its human rights record and its unionist ethos and make-up—were no longer significant issues of concern for Sinn Féin. There were some continuing concerns on the role of MI5, on the future of the Special Branch and on the need for investigations into historical abuses by the RUC. However, the party believed all of these issues could be resolved through new accountability structures.

Following the Sinn Féin decision, elections to the Northern Ireland Assembly (the next step in the agreed process) were called for March 2007. Unionists were relatively subdued in their responses to the Sinn Féin change of policy, adopting a 'wait and see' attitude. The March 2007 elections saw further significant gains for both Sinn Féin and the DUP, meaning, under the power-sharing rules, that they would take the positions of First Minister and Deputy First Minister from a position of strength. Dissident republican candidates, standing on a platform of opposition to Sinn Féin's decision on policing, received only tiny levels of support.[159] The DUP agreed to form a power-sharing executive, with its party leader Ian Paisley as First Minister and Sinn Féin's Martin McGuinness as Deputy First Minister, and the Assembly was restored in May 2007.[160] Sinn Féin then joined the Policing Board, and even the nomination by the party of a former high-profile IRA prisoner (Martina Anderson) as one of its three nominees did not generate any significant unionist comment, with the DUP's Gregory Campbell saying 'we have to move on'.[161] However, senior DUP figures did continually cast doubt over whether they would support the May 2008 deadline for devolution of policing and justice powers from London, as had been set out in the St Andrews Agreement. They insisted they would not do so until the unionist community had 'confidence' in Sinn Féin having influence over such a ministry.[162] The progress made in transforming nationalists' relations with the police was highlighted when PSNI Chief Constable Hugh Orde attended a meeting in July 2007 at the invitation of Gerry Adams to discuss anti-social crime in the Sinn Féin heartland of West Belfast—the first ever such meeting to be attended by a Chief Constable.[163]

However, as the deadline for agreement on the devolution of control of policing approached, unionist parties raised new objections: calling for the IRA leadership structures to be publicly disbanded,[164] demanding a veto over the ministerial nominee (to ensure it would not be a Sinn Féin minister),[165] seeking further financial guarantees on public funding for policing from the British government[166] and linking the issue to the ongoing disputes over parades by the Orange Order through nationalist areas.[167] Despite some significant pressure from the two governments, unionists continued to refuse to agree to the devolution of control of policing. The DUP's public position was that greater unionist 'confidence' was required. In reality, the party seemed uncertain how such a decision would be received by its supporters.

As Sinn Féin had linked its earlier decision to support the PSNI to the devolution of control, this was a key issue for them. By mid-June 2008 the party was refusing to allow meetings of the Northern

Ireland Executive to take place (it had the power to do this as the office of 'Deputy' First Minister is in de-facto terms that of Joint First Minister, and both must agree to all decisions, including the agenda for Executive meetings). Sinn Féin's position was that the failure to devolve policing was a test case of the DUP's wider commitment to power-sharing and the peace process. If this could not be agreed, then perhaps the logic of the entire peace process was being questioned and Sinn Féin needed to look for another political strategy. In the short-term, this strategy was likely to involve walking out of the Northern Ireland Executive, triggering fresh elections and the party seeking a new mandate.

The decision was on a knife edge. The DUP clearly wanted to maintain devolution but was uneasy with sharing power with former enemies. The DUP leadership, with the party now headed by Peter Robinson following Ian Paisley's retirement at the end of May 2008, were also uncertain as to whether they could bring their own support base with them if they took a decision to devolve policing and thereby link their political fortunes clearly to sharing power with Sinn Féin and working the Belfast/Good Friday and St Andrews Agreements.

In September 2008 a report by the Independent Monitoring Commission[168] confirmed that the IRA 'Army Council' was not functional or operational and posed no threat to the peace process. After a five-month stand-off during which no Executive meetings took place, a breakthrough was achieved in November 2008 when the DUP and Sinn Féin agreed on a 37-point road plan towards devolution of policing and justice. The two parties also agreed that neither would seek to hold the Justice ministerial portfolio during its first Assembly term.

In March 2009, British Army soldiers Cengiz Azimkar and Mark Quinsey and PSNI Constable Stephen Carroll were killed in separate attacks in Antrim and Craigavon. Responsibility for these attacks was claimed by members of small 'dissident' splinter groups from the IRA who opposed the peace process. The Good Friday Agreement institutions survived this potential test of their durability, and a significant display of political unity and determination to uphold the Northern Ireland Executive and Assembly resulted instead. Work proceeded on the basis of the 37-point plan throughout the remainder of 2009, primarily at Assembly Executive Review Committee (AERC) level within the Assembly and also through the passage of necessary enabling legislation at Westminster. In the latter half of the year, the Irish and

British governments were involved in intensive efforts to assist and encourage the Northern Ireland parties to complete the devolution of policing and justice and to address other outstanding aspects of the St Andrews Agreement that still required implementation. In October, prospects for completion of the devolution project were further assisted by provision of a supportive financial package by the British government.

Towards the end of January 2010, it became clear that the Northern Ireland parties themselves were unable to agree on how to move ahead. Earlier that month, a totally unrelated crisis within the DUP and the forced resignation from the Assembly of the First Minister's wife (a prominent unionist politician in her own right) brought matters to a head for the party leadership. Continuing stalemate at that stage could perhaps see Peter Robinson's position as DUP leader and First Minister weakened. If he wanted to take the party in the direction of sharing power he had to make that decision quickly or he might lose the initiative. The pressure to reach a final decision seemed to create some flexibility and the opportunity for a new round of intense negotiations. The Taoiseach and the British Prime Minister met in London on 25 January and decided to travel directly to Hillsborough where they convened all party talks.

Following ten days of intensive negotiations, the DUP and Sinn Féin finalised a comprehensive agreement on 5 February 2010, which set up a process aimed at devolving policing powers to Northern Ireland by April 2010 and restoring the functioning of the Executive. This was endorsed by the Northern Ireland Assembly on 9 March 2010 and political control over policing was devolved to Northern Ireland on 12 April 2010, with Alliance Party leader David Ford appointed as Justice Minister by cross-community vote. Even if there are some further obstacles to a sustained agreement it is now clear that the main unionist and nationalist parties are willing to share power over policing—thus completing the last piece of the political/institutional framework of the transformation of policing.

CONCLUSION

Unionists and nationalists have not resolved or reconciled their different views on how policing was conducted during the conflict in Northern Ireland, but they have negotiated a series of agreements that puts in place an institutional framework that transcends their former deeply oppositional stances. Nationalist political discourse no longer characterises policing in counter-insurgency terms, and there is even support for the police in the face of the lingering threat of small and marginal IRA splinter groups who oppose the peace process. There are some continuing issues around human rights, in particular on the use of plastic bullets and control of intelligence agencies, but there is a degree of confidence that the new structures of accountability can progress on those issues. Finally, there is support amongst nationalists for recruitment to the PSNI and this, along with 50:50 recruitment, has seen the service's demography transformed. There is still some debate on whether 50:50 recruitment should continue into the future, until a higher target—perhaps of 40% of members from a nationalist background—is reached, and there is pressure to extend that policy to civilian posts in policing, which remain very unrepresentative of the nationalist community.[169]

Unionist political parties have been uncomfortable with some aspects of the process of transformation, but they have also achieved some of their key aims. The two major nationalist parties, representing nearly 100% of nationalist voters, now support the police and police recruitment. Control of policing is now in local hands, even if it must be shared with nationalists, and unionists have avoided the symbolic difficulty of having a Sinn Féin Minister for Justice. They remain uneasy with 50:50 recruitment, with the loss of British flags and symbolism in police stations and with some of the retrospective inquiries into allegations of human-rights abuses. Ultimately, unionists did not have the political power to veto those decisions, which could have been introduced directly by the British government. Where they did have a veto—on devolving power and sharing it with nationalists—they have accepted this political reality as part of the cost of getting and maintaining a local political authority and securing nationalist support for the police. The unionist community in particular has been fragmented by these changes, and a significant minority within that community continues to oppose the underlying logic of the peace process, including the new policing arrangements. This is demonstrated by the formation of a new political party—the Traditional Unionist Voice (TUV)—from among former DUP representatives.[170] It represents a minority view within unionism, but unlike IRA dissidents, has a significant level of public support and will continue to pressurise unionists who participate in the power-sharing institutions with Sinn Féin. In elections to the UK parliament in May 2010, however, the TUV got fewer votes than anticipated—polling only 3.9% of the vote, compared to 25% for the DUP and 15% for the UUP-British Conservative alliance.

The politics of policing transformation in Northern Ireland, the nature and timing of the Agreements that created the atmosphere for such transformation, and the difficulty in reaching them, are clear evidence that policing powers and structures are an integral part of the constitutional framework of contested societies and not a lower-order matter that can be more easily divided up as 'spoils of peace'. Each step in the process of change, from the 1998 Agreement, to the debate on the International Commission's *Report*, to the various inter-party talks and agreements, linked discussion on policing to other issues in the peace process, such as governmental power-sharing, North–South co-operative institutions, demilitarisation by the British Army, arms decommissioning by the IRA and other equality issues such as language rights. Both nationalists and unionists strongly linked police reform to the wider peace process, and progress on policing would have been impossible without agreement on an open-ended constitutional framework that required neither political community to abandon its longer-term political goals. Nationalists did not and would not have abandoned their political campaign for a united Ireland in return for policing reform. Unionists would not have accepted the transformation of policing without a balanced constitutional and political agreement and without the IRA ending its armed campaign.

Without a transformation of Northern Ireland itself there would have been no transformation of policing. The transformation was explicitly linked to the consociational power-sharing model at the heart of the new political structures in Northern Ireland, and the interlinked institutions between the Northern Ireland Executive and the Government of the Ireland. These institutions saw political power shared between the political communities at executive level, and on the policing board, and re-inforced the importance of equality—measured in particular, but not exclusively, as between the two national communities. They also saw a constitutional and institutional reflection of Irish nationalists' political identity and ambitions, while guaranteeing unionists that a united Ireland would not be enforced without majority support within Northern Ireland itself.

Policing transformation has its own particular agenda, as discussed throughout this book—issues such as accountability structures, human rights, training, management and police culture. These debates need to draw on international best practice and be adapted to local conditions. The Northern Ireland case can add to the debate on the nature of best practice in a number of these domains. However, most crucially, as a case study the Northern Ireland experience demonstrates that while you can have a 'police force' without consent or agreement, you can only have 'community policing' and a 'police service' in post-conflict societies if policing is embedded in a wider political agreement that deals with the political and social roots of the conflict, and if the structures, symbols and ethos of policing and the composition of the police service all reflect the ethos and spirit of that wider peace agreement.

NOTES

[1] See, for example, Ed Moloney, *The secret history of the IRA* (London: Penguin, Allen Lane, 2002), xv; and Paul Bew, *Irish Times*, 15 May 1998.

[2] See John Doyle, 'Governance and citizenship in contested states: the Northern Ireland peace agreement as internationalised governance', *Irish Studies in International Affairs* 10 (1999), 201–19; John Doyle '"Towards a lasting peace"?: The Northern Ireland multi-party agreement, referendum and assembly elections of 1998', *Scottish Affairs* 25 (1998), 1–20. The text of the Agreement is available at: http://foreignaf-fairs.gov.ie/uploads/documents/Anglo-Irish/agreement.pdf (hereafter cited as *Agreement*).

[3] Sabine Wichert, *Northern Ireland since 1945* (London: Longman, 1999), 106.

[4] See http://www.sinnfein.ie and http://www.sdlp.ie.

[5] See http://www.uup.org/ and http://www.dup.org.uk.

[6] Independent Commission on Policing for Northern Ireland, *A new beginning: policing in Northern Ireland*. Report of the Independent Commission on Policing for Northern Ireland (Belfast: HMSO Northern Ireland Office, 1999) (hereafter cited as *Patten Report* or *Report*).

[7] The proportion of Catholics published as being members of the RUC included Roman Catholics from outside Northern Ireland, who were unlikely to be Irish nationalists. Nationalists make up somewhere between 44% and 48% of the working age population of Northern Ireland (see http://www.equalityni.org/archive/pdf/ResearchUpdate_MonitoringReportNo19_FINAL_101209.pdf). Most nationalists are 'culturally' Roman Catholic (even if not personally religious), and likewise most Unionists are 'culturally' Protestant. The proportion of each community who support the dominant political ideology of the other, i.e. Roman Catholic unionists and Protestant Irish nationalists, is difficult to estimate, but voting trends and problematic attitude surveys suggest it is in low single figures and similar for each community. At a macro-statistical level, therefore, figures for employment equality (which are collected as 'Catholic' and 'others/Protestant') are a close approximation for nationalist versus unionist, even if at an individual level the terms are not inter-changeable. However, while unionist Roman Catholics were likely to support and join the police,

Protestants who supported nationalist parties were ideologically less likely to do so. Therefore, the percentage of nationalists (of even the mildest form) in the RUC was likely to be significantly lower than 7.5%.

[8] See almost every issue of the Sinn Féin newspaper *An Phoblacht*, right through the 1970s and 1980s.

[9] For example, Seamus Mallon, *Irish Times*, 6 January 1987; 28 January 1985; 5 October 1984; 29 July 1977.

[10] SDLP, *Towards a new Ireland* (Belfast: SDLP, 1976), 5; for the Sunningdale proposals see Garret FitzGerald, *All in a life: an autobiography* (Dublin: Gill and Macmillan, 1991), 240–1; Graham Ellison and Jim Smyth, *The crowned harp: policing Northern Ireland* (London: Pluto Press, 2000), 88.

[11] Denis Faul and Raymond Murray, *The RUC: the black and the blue book* (Dungannon: D. Faul and R. Murray, 1975), 1; available at: http://cain.ulst.ac.uk/issues/police/docs/faul.htm.

[12] See, for example, Robert Fisk, *The point of no return: the strike which broke the British in Ulster* (London: André Deutsch, 1975).

[13] Brendan O' Brien, *The long war: the IRA and Sinn Féin* (New York: Syracuse University Press, 1995), 44.

[14] *The Times* (London) 4 March 1986. The plan to close the port was leaked, see *The Times* (London) 22 February 1986, but little action was taken. There were clashes between the RUC and loyalist protestors on other occasions and the first and only death of a Protestant civilian from a plastic bullet occurred at this time, but the extent of police action was still very different from the policing of nationalist protests and riots in 1981.

[15] See 'In The Line of Fire'—a report on events in Derry, 10–14 July 1996 following from the 'Drumcree Standoff'; and 'One Day in August'—a report on alleged human rights abuses by the RUC during and after the Apprentice Boys march in Derry on 12 August 1995. Both reports are from the Pat Finucane Centre, Derry, and are available at: http://www.serve.com/pfc/.

[16] Cited in George Drower, *John Hume: peacemaker* (London: Victor Gollancz, 1995), 74.

[17] *Patten Report*, Paragraphs 12.10 and 12.11.

[18] See Malachi O'Doherty, 'Fear and loathing on the falls road', *Fortnight* no. 304, (March 1992), 23–24; Rachel Monaghan '"An imperfect peace": paramilitary "punishments" in Northern Ireland', *Terrorism and Political Violence* 16 (3) (2004), 439–61, 449; and *An Phoblacht* as late as 16 January 1997.

[19] Seamus Mallon, 'Time to grasp the nettle of policing', *Fortnight* no. 160, (March 1988), 11.

[20] The Irish police service.

[21] Hansard, House of Commons, col. 55 (15 December 1997).

[22] Hansard, House of Commons, col. 55 (15 December 1997).

[23] For a good overview of these issues, see Ellison and Smyth, *Crowned harp*.

[24] For example, Amnesty International, *Report of an Amnesty International mission to Northern Ireland* (28 November–6 December 1977) (London: Amnesty International, International Secretariat, 1978); Amnesty International. United Kingdom, *Killings by security forces in Northern Ireland* (New York: Amnesty International, National Office, 1986); Human Rights Watch, *Human rights in Northern Ireland : a Helsinki Watch report* (New York: Human Rights Watch, 1991).

[25] John Stalker, *Stalker* (London, Penguin, 1989).

[26] On 9 November 1988 and 5 May 1994, the Secretary of State for Northern Ireland issued public interest immunity certificates prohibiting the disclosure of sensitive security materials including the Stalker and Sampson reports. See http://news.bbc.co.uk/2/hi/uk_news/1312378.stm

[27] See Seamus Mallon, *Fortnight* no. 160 (March 1988), 11.

[28] See the website of the Pat Finucane Centre, http://www.serve.com/pfc/.

[29] For example, Human Rights Watch, *Human rights in Northern Ireland: a Helsinki Watch report*; Christine Bell, *Peace agreements and human rights* (Oxford: Oxford University Press, 2003); Brice Dickson, 'Counter-insurgency and human rights in Northern Ireland', *Journal of Strategic Studies* 32 (3) (2009), 475–93; Kadar Asmal, *Shoot to kill* (Cork: Mercier Press, 1985).

[30] See note 4 above.

[31] John Hume, 'Supporting the police in a divided society', *Fortnight* no. 239 (19 May–1 June 1986), 7–8; SDLP, *Policing in Northern Ireland* (Belfast: SDLP, 1995); Sinn Féin, *A policing service for a new future: Sinn Féin's submission to the Commission on Policing* (September 1998).

[32] For the most authoritative account of conflict related deaths, including statistical analyses, see David McKittrick, Seamus Kelters, Brian Feeney and Chris Thornton, *Lost Lives: The stories of the men, women and children who died as a result of the Northern Ireland troubles.* (Edinburgh: Mainstream Publishing, 1999).

[33] David Trimble, quoted in *Co. Down Spectator*, 30 January 1976. Trimble was then a leading opponent of power-sharing; he has since become leader of the UUP. Similar views can be found in the following newspaper reports: 'UUP position on attempts to re-build the collapsed 1973 power-sharing executive' , *Irish Press*, 30 August 1973; David Trimble, *Co. Down Spectator*, 18 September 1976 and 20 November 1976.; Glen Barr (leader of paramilitary UDA), *Londonderry Sentinel*, 8 December 1976.

[34] Peter Robinson, quoted in *Irish News*, 21 March 1989.

[35] Oliver Napier (leader of the centrist, pro-Union Alliance Party), *Alliance News*, December 1974. See also Napier's submission to the Atkins talks (a series of ultimately unsuccessful inter-party discussions led by Secretary of State for Northern Ireland Humphrey Atkins between January and March 1980); and *Alliance News*, February 1980; Oliver Napier, conference speech, *Alliance News*, May 1982. In addition, see John Cushnahan (Alliance Party leader), NI Assembly, vol. 16, p.1024 (29 June 1983); and John Cushnahan, conference speeches, *Alliance News*, May 1986 and May 1987.

[36] *Alliance News*, January 1987.

[37] *Alliance News*, May 1987.

[38] Hansard, House of Commons, vol. 248, col. 1051, 27 October 1994.

[39] Hansard, House of Commons, vol. 921, col. 1137, 2 December 1976. The three named were all leading SDLP politicians and all on the record as strongly opposing the IRA armed campaign. The Ulster Defence Regiment (UDR) was a locally recruited (and only locally deployed) British Army regiment.

[40] Hansard, House of Commons, vol. 978, col. 718, 7 February 1980.

[41] NI Assembly, vol. 14, p. 113–4, 4 March 1985. Similar views were expressed by: Ian Paisley, NI Assembly, vol. 8, p. 479, 7 February 1984; Ian Paisley, NI Assembly, vol. 9, p. 810, 10 April 1984.

[42] *Irish Press*, 2 February 1985, my emphasis. Frank Millar was UUP General Secretary 1983–7; he left the UUP in 1987 for a career in journalism and is now London Editor of the *Irish Times*. Similar views were expressed by: Peter Robinson, NI Assembly, vol. 13, p. 389, 13 February 1985.

[43] *Orange Standard*, August 1985.

[44] Hansard, House of Commons, vol. 939, col. 1736, 24 November 1977. Similar views from Thomas Passmore (UUP), NI Assembly, vol. 14, p.374, 13 March 1985.

[45] Hansard, House of Commons, vol. 8, col. 1374, 16 July 1981.

[46] Hansard, House of Commons, vol. 975, col. 1178, 11 December 1979.

[47] The term 'supergrass' was used to describe former IRA members turned RUC informants who gave evidence in large-scale trials against multiple defendants. The practice of using such informants collapsed when public pressure and judicial unease about the poor quality of 'evidence' led to cases being rejected—often after defendants had spent years in prison awaiting trial.

[48] Hansard, House of Commons, Standing Committee B, col. 43, 13 December 1990.

[49] Hansard, House of Commons, Report of Standing Committee B (NI Emergency Provisions Bill), col. 104, 23 January 1996.

[50] For example, Jim Wells (DUP), NI Assembly, vol. 7, pp. 911–2, 15 November 1983. Wells was DUP assembly member 1982–6 and 1998 to date. See also, statements from Paisley, Maginnis and Kilfedder, House of Commons, vol. 128, cols 427–8, 25 February 1988.

[51] NI Assembly, vol. 10, p. 484, 6 June 1984.

[52] Hansard, House of Commons, vol. 902, col. 709, 11 December 1975. For similar views, see: William Craig, House of Commons, vol. 959, col. 1515, 6 December 1978; Peter Robinson, NI Assembly, vol. 4, p.31, 22 November 1982; and Ian Paisley, House of Commons, vol. 193, col. 566, 20 June 1991.

[53] Oliver Cromwell's armies are infamous in Irish nationalist discourse for the brutality of their suppression of Irish opposition to the consolidation of British rule in 1649–50, in particular the massacre of almost the entire population of towns of Drogheda and Wexford. Bradford was speaking in the House of Commons, see Hansard, vol. 922, col. 2028, 17 December 1976.

[54] NI Assembly, vol. 12, p. 621, 12 December 1984.

[55] Peter Robinson, NI Assembly, vol. 4, p.31, 22 November 1982.

[56] Hansard, House of Commons, vol. 146, col. 925, 8 March 1989. Similar views had been expressed by: Harold McCusker, House of Commons, vol. 969, col. 49, 5 July 1979. For further examples of the general support for shoot-to-kill operations, see: Ian Paisley, Jim Kilfedder and Ken Maginnis, House of Commons, vol. 128, cols 427–8, 25 February 1988.

[57] *Belfast Telegraph*, 3 February 1976. Baird was leader of the United Ulster Unionist Party 1977–84. The UUUP was founded in 1975 as a hard-line splinter group from Vanguard, itself an anti-power-sharing splinter group from the UUP. Mid-Ulster MP John Dunlop, who had won as a Vanguard candidate in the 1974 elections, held the seat as a UUUP member in 1979, thanks to a Unionist pact. The party was wiped out in the 1982 Assembly election and Dunlop did not stand again. South Armagh was an area of strong IRA support and activity.

[58] Hansard, House of Commons, vol. 204, col. 1099, 27 February 1992. He also commends the British Army's restraint in only shooting four out of twelve IRA members allegedly present.

59 *Irish News*, 7 March 1989. Also, David Trimble, *Irish News*, 14 January 1993.

60 Robert McCartney, NI Assembly, vol. 4, p. 340, 7 December 1982.

61 For example, John Alderdice (party leader 1987–98), conference speech, *Alliance News*, April 1989.

62 *Alliance News*, September 1984.

63 *Sunday Tribune*, 10 May 1987. Similar sentiments had earlier been expressed by Oliver Napier, NI Assembly, vol. 14, p.400, 13 March 1985.

64 For example, Jim Kilfedder, Hansard, House of Commons, vol. 849, col. 1497, 31 January 1973; Robert Bradford, House of Commons, vol. 959, col. 1564, 6 December 1978; William Ross, House of Commons, vol. 70, col. 655, 20 December 1984; Jim Molyneaux, House of Commons, vol. 203, col. 1156, 13 February 1992; Hugh Smyth (PUP), NI Forum, vol. 58, col. 39, 23 January 1998.

65 Robert Bradford, Hansard, House of Commons, vol. 899, col. 283, 4 November 1975; Jim Molyneaux, House of Commons, vol. 922, col. 1961, 17 December 1976; William Ross, House of Commons, vol. 876, col. 1233, 9 July 1974; Ken Maginnis (UUP security spokesperson), House of Commons, col 64, 15 December 1997.

66 For example, House of Commons, vol. 882, col. 858, 28 November 1974; vol. 988, col. 622, 9 July 1980.

67 *Ulster Review*, Autumn 1996. In the same issue, Patricia Campbell (UUP) claimed that 'less that 40% of Ulster's Roman Catholics want anything to do with a United Ireland'.

68 Personal conversations with the late John Whyte. See also John Whyte, *Interpreting Northern Ireland* (Oxford: Clarendon press, 1990).

69 Graham Ellison. 'Reflecting all shades of opinion', *British Journal of Criminology* 40 (1) 2000, 88–111.

70 See *Patten Report* and Ellison and Smyth, *Crowned harp*, 150–76, and John McGarry and Brendan O' Leary, *Policing Northern Ireland: proposals for a new start.* (Belfast: The Blackstaff Press, 1999), 6–24.

71 *Newsletter*, 11 December 1985.

72 The voting system used in Northern Ireland's local, EU and assembly elections. Voters rank all candidates (or as many as they wish) in order and can therefore cross party boundaries. For a recent analysis, see Michael O'Kelly, John Doyle and Philip Boland, 'How many ways can you look at a proportion? Cross-community vote transfers in Northern Ireland before and after the Belfast Agreement', *Journal of the Royal Statistical Society, Series A*, 173 (1) (2010), 215–35.

73 *Orange Standard*, July 1986.

74 Hansard, House of Commons, Standing Committee B, col. 177, 22 January 1991.

75 *Irish Times*, 19 February 1994.

76 Hansard, House of Commons, vol. 876, col. 1233, 9 July 1974. Ross was an MP and leading member of the UUP until the late 1990s.

77 John McCrea, County Grand Master Belfast, Orange Order, *Orange Standard*, March 1986.

78 NI Assembly, vol. 15, p. 397, 28 May 1985. Kane is a former general-secretary of the DUP and Assembly member 1982–6. Owen Carron was at the time a prominent member of the Sinn Féin leadership. He had been elected as a Westminster MP for Fermanagh-South Tyrone in the by-election caused by the death of IRA hunger-striker and MP, Bobby Sands, on a non-party ticket in support of the hunger-striking republican prisoners.

[79] NI Assembly, vol. 15, p. 398, 28 May 1985.

[80] *Irish News*, 1 August 1995.

[81] *Newsletter*, 13 August 1996.

[82] For example, Robert Bradford, House of Commons, vol. 964, col. 1612, 21 March 1979. Also, Unionist Task Force Report, *Irish Times*, 3 July 1987.

[83] *Newsletter*, 17 August 1987. Similar references were made by: Ian Paisley, Hansard, House of Commons, vol. 833, col. 1131, 20 March 1972; Brian Faulkner, *Irish News*, 29 May 1973; Peter Robinson, *Newsletter*, 26 November 1974; David Calvert (DUP), NI Assembly, vol. 4, p.73, 22 November 1982.

[84] Andrew Mack, 'Why big nations lose small wars: the politics of asymmetric conflict', *World Politics* 27 (2) (1975), 175–200.

[85] Martin Smyth, Introduction to Orange Order, pamphlet, *The Twelfth*, 1982.

[86] *Protestant Telegraph*, 15 June 1974. Smyth was DUP Assembly Member 1973–4 and Convention Member 1975–6. He was secretary of the UUUC in the Northern Ireland Convention (1975–6). He joined the UUP 1977.

[87] *Sunday Tribune*, 7 September 1986.

[88] Hansard, House of Commons, vol. 964, col. 1612, 21 March 1979.

[89] Hansard, House of Commons, vol. 988, col. 647, 9 July 1980.

[90] NI Assembly, vol. 4, p. 342, 7 December 1982.

[91] NI Assembly, vol. 11, p.357, 17 October 1984.

[92] For example, '82 percent of Catholics believe that the RUC must be reformed, replaced or disbanded', *Irish Times*, 6 December 1996. See also, Seamus Mallon, House of Commons, vol. 303, col. 64, 15 December 1997; Cllr. Martin Morgan (SDLP), *Belfast Telegraph*, 26 January 1995; and Sinn Féin, *A policing service for a new future: Sinn Féin's submission to the Commission on Policing*, September 1998.

[93] For example, Falls Community Council, 'A new beginning: a new Police Service. A submission to the Independent Commission on Policing', 15 September 1998.

[94] Gerard Murray and Jonathan Tonge, *Sinn Féin and the SDLP: from alienation to participation* (Dublin: O'Brien Press, 2005), 206.

[95] See Seamus Mallon (SDLP Deputy Leader), *Irish Times* 7, 9 and 21 November 1994, for early SDLP responses to the IRA ceasefire, which was announced on 31 August 1994. For the Sinn Féin campaign, see regular articles in *An Phoblacht* in late 1994 and early 1995.

[96] Hansard, House of Commons, vol. 193, col. 568, 20 June 1991. The 'Brook Talks' were a series of inter-party talks convened by British Secretary of State for Northern Ireland Peter Brook (and his successor Patrick Mayhew) and held in 1991–92. The talks excluded Sinn Féin and failed to make any significant progress. Their failure prompted SDLP leader John Hume to engage in a series of secret discussions with Sinn Féin.

[97] For example, Ken Maginnis, *Belfast Telegraph* and *Irish News*, 3 January 1995; *Newsletter*, 4 January 1995; *Irish News*, 14 November 1995; David Trimble, House of Commons, col. 96, 15 December 1997 and *Irish Times*, 10 January 1995; Jim Molyneaux, Speech to UUC AGM, 18 March 1995; Ian Paisley Jnr, *Newsletter*, 2 February 1996, *Irish News*, 3 January 1995.

[98] Ken Maginnis, *Newsletter*, 5 November 1996; Ian Paisley, *Irish Times*, 5 May 1997; Jim Rodgers (UUP), *Belfast Telegraph*, 28 February 1995; Ian Paisley Jnr, *Belfast Telegraph*, 28 February 1995; John Taylor and Ian Paisley Jnr, *Irish News*, 3 February 1996; David Trimble, House of Commons, vol. 303, col. 96, 15 December 1997;

Progressive Unionist Party, Submission to the Policing Commission, 18 November 1998.

[99] *Irish News*, 17 December 1997.

[100] Hansard, House of Commons, vol. 303, col. 61, 15 December 1997.

[101] Hansard, House of Commons, vol. 303, col. 63, 15 December 1997.

[102] Hansard, House of Commons, vol. 303, cols. 63–4, 15 December 1997.

[103] Hansard, House of Commons, vol. 303, col. 69, 15 December 1997.

[104] NI Forum, vol. 58, p. 44, 23 January 1998. Weir was a high-profile, middle-ranking UUP member, who was expelled for failing to vote for party leader David Trimble to become First Minister of Northern Ireland in 2001, due to differences over political strategy on the peace process. Weir joined the DUP in 2002.

[105] NI Forum, vol. 58, p. 39, 23 January 1998. Hugh Smyth was a leading member of the Progressive Unionist Party—a small party linked to the illegal loyalist para-military Ulster Volunteer Force (UVF).

[106] NI Forum, vol. 58, p. 25, 23 January 1998. They received 3.5 percent support in the 1996 Forum elections, but this has declined to just over half of one per cent in 2007.

[107] Party leader, John Alderdice, *Irish Times*, 10 January 1995.

[108] Alliance Party of Northern Ireland, *Election Manifesto*, (Belfast: APNI, 1997).

[109] Alliance Party, *Continuity and change: an Alliance Party submission to the Commission on Policing*, published 15 October 1998.

[110] *Agreement*, p.27.

[111] *Agreement*, Annex A.

[112] *Newsletter*, 18 April 1998. This analysis is confirmed by Professor Conor Gearty of Kings College London, *Irish Times*, 6 May 1998. It is also supported by Professor Paul Bew, Queen's University Belfast, *Irish Times*, 15 April 1998.

[113] *Patten Report*

[114] All from *Irish Times* coverage, 10 September 1999.

[115] *Irish Times*, 10 September 1999.

[116] *Irish Times*, 10 September 1999.

[117] See *Irish Times*, 14 September, 6 November, 2 December; Debate in NI Assembly, 24 January 2000; Hansard, House of Commons Debates vol. 345, 6 April 2000.

[118] See *Irish Times*, 2 December 1999; 20 December 1999.

[119] *Irish Times*, 28 September 1999.

[120] *Irish Times*, 7 December 1999.

[121] *Irish Times*, 11 September 1999.

[122] *Irish Times*, 1 December 1999; from Sinn Fein Response to the Patten Commission, 1999.

[123] *Irish Times*, 10 April 2000

[124] See, for example, *Irish Times*, 28 January 2000; debate in Northern Ireland Assembly 24 January 2000.

[125] Implementation Plan, available at: http://cain.ulst.ac.uk/issues/police/patten/nio190102.pdf, and the Bill itself, available at: http://www.parliament.the-stationery-office.co.uk/pa/cm199900/cmbills/125/2000125.htm

[126] *Irish Times*, 18 May 2000; 22 May 2000; 6 June 2000.

[127] See for example *Irish Times*, 18 May 2000; 31 May 2000; 1 June 2000.

[128] *Irish Times*, 3 June 2000.

[129] *Irish Times,* 22 May 2000.

[130] *Irish Times,* 18 May 2000.

[131] *Irish Times,* 13 June 2000.

[132] *Irish Times,* 18 May 2000; 11 July 2000.

[133] *Irish Times,* 21 September 2000.

[134] See, in addition to nationalist comments in above notes, Labour MP Kevin McNamara, *Irish Times,* 31 May 2000; Amnesty International and the Committee on the Administration of Justice, *Irish Times,* 6 June 2000; Senator Edward Kennedy, *Irish Times,* 11 October 2000; Professor Paddy Hillyard, *Irish Times,* 2 August 2000; Professor Brendan O Leary, *Irish Times,* 28 July 2000; Paddy Hillyard and Mike Tomlinson, 'Patterns of Policing and Policing Patten', *Journal of Law and Society* 27 (3) (2000), 394–415.

[135] Ultimately delivered on 17 August 2001, available at: http://cain.ulst.ac.uk/issues/ police/patten/patten2001.pdf.

[136] The British government later reneged on that agreement when Judge Cory unexpectedly (from the government's perspective) did call for an inquiry. This led to a very rare case whereby the Irish parliament passed a formal resolution stating it 'deeply regrets the British Government's failure to honour its commitment to implement Judge Cory's recommendation', *Dáil Debates,* vol. 616 (2), 8 March 2006.

[137] See the SDLP response to the proposals for the new police service, as outlined on 20 August 2001—in effect setting out the improvements in the legislation that allowed the party to appoint members to the policing board. The response is available at: http://cain.ulst.ac.uk/issues/police/docs/sdlp200801.htm.

[138] Seamus Mallon, *Irish Times,* 21 August 2000.

[139] *Irish Times,* 25 August 2001; 27 November 2001.

[140] See the published summary reports, available at: http://cain.ulst.ac.uk/issues/ police/police.htm.

[141] *Irish Times,* 25 August 2001

[142] *Irish Times,* 22 September 2001.

[143] See http://news.bbc.co.uk/2/hi/uk_news/northern_ireland/1707059.stm.

[144] In fact, Sinn Féin became the largest nationalist party for the first time at the June 2001 British general (Westminster) election, when it polled 21.7 percent to the SDLP's 21.0 percent of the vote. The gap widened over the following years, and in the 2003 NI Assembly election, SF polled 23.5 percent to the SDLP's 17 percent. Elections results are available at: http://www.ark.ac.uk/elections.

[145] Meaning, in practice, the reduction in troop numbers, an end to army patrolling, the return of land taken over by the British Army and the dismantling of the highly visible and highly symbolic series of tall watchtowers in an area along the Irish border.

[146] See http://news.bbc.co.uk/2/hi/uk_news/northern_ireland/4283740.stm. For the reports on decommissioning, see: http://cain.ulst.ac.uk/events/peace/decommission/ iicdreports.htm.

[147] The full text of this agreement is available at: http://www.dfa.ie/uploads/documents/st_andrews_agreement.pdf (hereafter cited as *St Andrews Agreement*).

[148] *St Andrews Agreement,* paragraph 7.

[149] *Irish Times,* 3 November 2006.

[150] *Irish Times,* 14 November 2006.

[151] *Patten Report,* Paragraphs 12.10 and 12.11.

[152] *Irish Times*, 11 January 2007.

[153] *An Phoblacht*, 11 January 2007. Available at: http://www.anphoblacht.com/.

[154] *Irish Times*, 25 January 2007.

[155] For example, *An Phoblacht*, 11, 18 and 27 January 2007.

[156] *An Phoblacht*, 1 February 2007.

[157] *Irish Times*, 30 January 2007.

[158] *Irish Times*, 30 January 2007.

[159] See, for example, *Irish Times* 10 March 2007.

[160] *Irish Times*, 27 March 2007.

[161] *Irish Times*, 24 April 2007.

[162] For example, Ian Paisley jnr *Irish Times*, 5 June 2007; Nigel Dodds 1 October 2007.

[163] *Irish Times*, 4 July 2007.

[164] *Irish Times*, 3 March 2008 and 4 September 2008.

[165] *Irish Times*, 1 July 2008, 27 October 2008.

[166] *Irish Times*, 3 November 2008. The NI Executive has no tax-raising powers and the DUP wanted agreement on a multi-annual police budget from the British government.

[167] *Irish Times*, 4 September 2008.

[168] The Independent Monitoring Commission was set up by the British and Irish governments on 7 January 2004 to help promote the establishment of stable and inclusive devolved government in a peaceful Northern Ireland by reporting to the governments on such issues as activity by paramilitary groups and the normalisation of security measures. The four Commissioners are entirely independent of both governments. See http://www.independentmonitoringcommission.org/.

[169] As of February 2010, only 17.5 percent of civilian police staff were from a Catholic background. See http://www.psni.police.uk/index/updates/updates_statistics/updates_workforce_composition_figures.htm.

[170] See http://www.tuv.org.uk/.

Chapter 13

THE IMPORTANCE OF GENDER
IN THE TRANSFORMATION
OF POLICING

Mary O'Rawe[*]

INTRODUCTION

A chapter on gender[1] as part of a broader examination of polic-ing reform is never going to make *the* definitive statement on how gender and security do, do not or should intertwine.[2] In itself, leaving such discussion to a separate chapter might be considered to-kenistic, indicative of a general approach in policing reform circles, which sees gender as something to be considered separately from the main debate. Too often, in practice, engendered[3] understandings are viewed as an 'add on', a footnote or codicil to what really needs to be done—if they are considered at all. According to the 2009 edition of the OECD DAC *Handbook on Security System Reform*, 'gender issues are often relegated to the bottom of the list when it comes to priori-tising programming and funding'.[4]

At base, this speaks to what could be termed a foundational flaw in the general design and planning of security reform endeavours. A failure to recognise or properly accommodate gender as a key organ-ising principle and potential catalyst for change perpetuates a situation whereby masculinised and highly essentialised notions of security are accorded primacy. This allows finite resources to be pumped into meeting (sometimes overblown or unnecessarily exacerbated) security threats,[5] often connected to narrowly framed notions of national security and the protection of dominant elites. At the same time, terror perpetrated on a daily and nightly basis, for example by high levels of domestic and sexual violence or poverty is, relatively speaking, neglected.[6] This is clearly problematic in a context where domestic violence and rape are deemed to be a leading cause of death and disability for women on a world-wide scale,[7] and where poverty impacts disproportionately on women and children across the globe.[8]

Part 1 of this chapter will chart the development of an international legal imperative to mainstream gender and achieve gender balance in all matters pertaining to peace and security. Part 2 will consider the extent to which the policing reform project in Northern Ireland over the past decade has met that imperative. Part 3 will explore why, in practice, it has proved so difficult for even the most robust security reform endeavours to engage dynamically, fully and creatively with gender as a core organising principle for change. The chapter will conclude by emphasising the potential of gender as a transformative agent in policing change so as to change policing.

RECENT INTERNATIONAL TRENDS—THE THEORY

Internationally, a legal imperative has developed for states to ensure the equal participation of women in public life, with attention over the past decade focusing in a very particular way on matters pertaining to peace and security.[9] The benefits to society of mainstreaming[10] gendered concerns in policing and security reform processes have been specifically highlighted, though all too often transformative methodologies have failed to follow.[11]

In the aftermath of World War II, women were deemed to be included in human-rights declarations and conventions, without the need for this to be spelled out. The necessity for international provision to move from this position, to concede and specifically address the particular and pernicious nature of rights abuses against women and the absence of women from key decision-making processes, did not gain official credence until the late 1970s. The shift came about as a result of extensive research, monitoring and lobbying by women's groups, human-rights NGOs and others pointing to the clear and undeniable reality that, around the world, women are much more likely than men to be marginalised and excluded, socially, politically and economically. They are also statistically more likely to be victims of certain crime,[12] with the types of crime disproportionately suffered by women remaining unrecognised, under-acknowledged or otherwise poorly handled by mainstream criminal-justice and human-rights provision.[13]

Research had also begun to indicate that women, particularly poor women, tend to bear the brunt of wider societal conflict in visible and not so visible ways. As with other forms of violence, conflict related violence, while very public and openly devastating, equally has a private and sometimes a multiple dynamic both within and underneath the conflict itself.[14] This impacts,[15] and continues to impact post-conflict, in a highly gendered way. Gender-based suffering is compounded by its very invisibility and the failure of peace and security initiatives either to recognise its existence or, much less, insist that it be addressed. This byzantine reality is further impacted by frequently under-acknowledged or overly compartmentalised issues such as race, religion, class and urban/rural divide.[16]

From a hard law perspective, the UN Convention on the Elimination of all Forms of Discrimination against Women (CEDAW, 1979) remains the key international treaty aimed at gender equity.[17] Its focus is on the need to ensure appropriate legislative protection for women in terms of guaranteeing equal rights and freedom from discrimination, eliminating prejudices and gender stereotyped roles and providing equal opportunities, job security and remuneration for women in the workplace. The Declaration on the Elimination of Violence Against Women (DEVAW, 1993), though not having the binding effect of a convention, provides a strong statement of principle, recognising the pervasive and insidious nature of violence against women and defining violence to include sexual harassment and intimidation in the workplace and other arenas.[18] The Declaration calls for the thorough investigation and prevention of violence against women through a comprehensive programme of action, including training for law enforcement officials and the collection of statistics on the incidence of such violence. These documents were further supplemented by the Beijing Declaration and Platform for Action in 1995, which committed governments, among other things, to gender-sensitive human-rights education and training for security-sector and immigration personnel; the adoption of laws to investigate and punish state agents who use their position to engage in acts of violence against women; and the establishment of gender balance in government bodies and public administrative entities, including the judiciary.[19] As part of a strategy to give practical effect to this work, the UN Office of Special Adviser on Gender Issues and the Advancement of Women (UN OSAGI) was established in 1997.

More recently international statements of import have turned their attention to the specific nexus between gender and security. The explicit linkages between gender, exclusion, continued impunity for gender-based violence and the insufficiency of security-reform initiatives are beginning to be recognised on the global stage as being in need of focused and concerted attention. As well as violence against women causing prolonged physical and psychological suffering to women, it is also being progressively recognised as having significant knock-on effects in respect of the well-being and security of their families and communities. Increasingly, in theory, connections are being drawn between 'violence against women as a human rights issue, as a public health crisis'[20] and as fundamentally tied up with the need for radically different interpretations and orientations in security-reform agendas.

UN Security Council resolution 1820 on 'Women, Peace and Security: Sexual Violence in Armed Conflict' (passed in 2008) for the first time clearly sets out as part of the development of an international normative framework that sexual violence is an issue of international peace and security.[21] The resolution emphasises the need for UN-assisted justice, Security System Reform (SSR) and Disarmament, Demobilisation and Reintegration (DDR) initiatives to consult with women and women-led organisations so as to develop effective mechanisms for providing protection from violence. The resolution specifically states that violence includes sexual violence and that there is a clear necessity to end impunity in this sphere and ensure equal protection of the law for victims of such violence. In the aftermath of scandals whereby peacekeeping troops in conflict zones have themselves been perpetrators of sexual violence, the resolution emphasises the need for pre-deployment and in-theatre training for those undertaking such missions and the benefits of using a higher percentage of women as peacekeepers and police.[22] Two other related Security Council resolutions have recently been adopted, indicating a very belated recognition of the centrality of sexual violence to questions of peace and security. By virtue of their very existence, these resolutions amount to an admission that not addressing sexual violence has curbed the potential of many women to contribute to and influence peace processes and the development of security reform endeavours across the globe and vice versa. Resolution 1888 adopted in September 2009 notes:

> with concern the underrepresentation of women in formal peace processes, [and] urges the Secretary General, Member States and the heads of regional organizations to take measures to increase the representation of women in mediation processes and

decision-making processes with regard to conflict resolution and peacebuilding.[23]

Resolution 1889, adopted in October 2009, also addresses the specific issue of sexual violence during armed conflict and the need to end impunity in this regard.[24]

These resolutions all build on the ground laid by landmark UN Security Council resolution 1325 on Women, Peace and Security (passed in 2000), which stresses the importance of women's equal participation and full involvement in all efforts toward maintaining and promoting peace and security.[25] In theory, through this resolution, the Security Council 'fundamentally changed the image of women in conflict situations from that of exclusively victims of war to that of active participants as peacemakers, peace-builders and negotiators'.[26] Architects of peace agreements are charged to ensure an equal place and voice for women in negotiating and decision-making around security. The particular need is emphasised to include measures to ensure protection of and respect for the human rights of women and girls, particularly as they relate to the constitution, the electoral system, the police and the judiciary. The resolution further encourages all those involved in DDR initiatives to take account of the differing needs of female and male ex-combatants and their dependants.

UNSCR 1325 underscores the particular need to ensure equal participation of women and to mainstream gender in all security endeavours. The aim is to ensure the development of a holistic and inclusive vision and understanding of security, more attuned to the full spectrum of harms and risks requiring societal attention. This links to a broader discourse on human security that has developed over the past decade, and to a recognition that, particularly in post-conflict and transitional societies, the opportunity is there to do some radical rethinking and restructuring. In theory, this will be informed by an international legal regime that recognises what can be added to the process by full gender awareness. In practice, even in terms of the UN's own endeavours in this regard,[27] restructuring of security apparatus often happens without gender really entering fully into the thinking, except in superficial or stereotypical ways.

GENDER AND THE NORTHERN IRELAND EXPERIENCE

So, how did the policing reform process begun in the late 1990s in Northern Ireland respond to the gender challenge? The Patten

Commission was clearly a creature of its time,[28] and it is arguably unfair to judge it against international Security Council resolutions that were not in existence at the time of its deliberations. However, no effort has been made to give effect to UNSCR 1325 in the ten years of implementation of the *Patten Report* recommendations, and, even in 1998, the importance of gender to the Patten Commission's deliberations was not exactly unascertainable as it set about its work. CEDAW, DEVAW and the Beijing Platform were all in place as important international benchmarks to be drawn upon. As well as this, a wealth of academic literature existed, speaking to the inherent sexism of police organisational culture and the difficulties in impacting meaningfully to change this without strong, proactive strategies in place.[29] Furthermore, submissions to the Patten Commission from groups such as the Equal Opportunities Commission and the Women's Coalition made the importance of gender very clear.[30]

Gender-based violence was (and still is) an issue crying out to be addressed in Northern Irish society, with high levels of domestic violence and low levels of prosecution and conviction for crimes such as rape. Such crime had not been a priority during the period of 'the Troubles', with research indicating that it was not really on the security agenda. Policing focus, in terms of budget and other resources, was instead geared fixedly on masculinised notions of how to meet the 'terrorist threat'.[31] More than this, because of the complexities of political/community relations with the police, women in republican communities in particular could not turn to the police for assistance. Nor did the police have any strategy in place to ensure a degree of protection was offered in these areas.

In 1998 when the Patten Commission was established, 12.6% of RUC officers were women (a third of these in the Part Time Reserve).[32] Women numbered 88 of 709 elite special branch officers, of whom only 4 were Catholic women.[33] Promotion to middle, let alone senior, ranks was problematic. Meanwhile, women comprised 66% of clerical staff attached to the police. Despite all of this, gender did not form a key unit of analysis for the policing reform project. In part this might be traced back to the fact that Northern Irish society itself is, in many ways, highly conservative. The Commission's terms of reference, stemming from the Good Friday Peace Agreement of 1998, although widely drawn, made no specific reference to gender. This said, the Agreement did indicate the need for new policing arrangements to attract and sustain 'the support of the community as a whole' and to be based on 'the protection and vindication of the human rights of all' with 'partnership, equality and mutual respect the basis of relationships.'[34]

In terms of make-up, two of the eight Patten Commissioners were women; neither of them local—one from a US police agency background, the other from the UK business sector. Neither had any stated interest or expertise in addressing security deficits in respect of gender. Neither were any of the males on the Commission appointed for their gender expertise. Of the named members of the Secretariat to the Commission, only one was a woman; of the unnamed administrative and clerical staff, it is highly likely the majority, if not all, were.[35] These points are worth noting as they highlight the stereotypical situation of an under-representation of women in respect to major deliberations and any final decision-making, while women are likely to be found disproportionately in a servicing role.

The Patten experience, which could, in the climate at the time, be praised for having any women commissioners, highlights the fact that '[b]eing a woman does not automatically make someone "gender expert", and increasing the number of women in the room does not necessarily guarantee gender-responsive policy and programming'.[36] In fact, any expectation that women per se should be the ones to fulfil this role is also problematic. Women clearly can have reasons to be at the table other than for 'windowdressing' purposes or to speak 'for' their gender. They should not be deemed to have to represent 'all women' by virtue of the fact of being female themselves. Any essentialisation of who women are and what they (should) contribute because of that fact speaks to an insufficiently sophisticated approach to gender, which runs the risk of viewing gender issues as 'women's issues' only. To construe gender in such terms permits the assumption that issues such as childcare, flexible working arrangements, equal participation and an end to gender-based violence are *merely* about making things better for women—a conception that itself is part of the problem and colludes in the peripheralisation of gender concerns as marginal rather than central to the whole process of change. An unnuanced view of gender as 'all women' also fails to recognise the structural inequalities among women while at the same time ignoring masculinity and differentially positioned males as a feature to be more fully interrogated, and bypassing altogether the intersectional realities of, for example, race, sect and class.[37]

A truly engendered process is not about pointing to the fact of a couple of women on a panel of experts or an increase in the number of women in a police organisation as evidence that gender has been duly considered. It is about seeking answers to questions commonly left unposed—such as whose security are we seeking to protect, why and what are the different priorities for men and women?[38] These questions must be carefully considered in the context of other inequalities and differential treatment in society that might multiply impact some women (for example because of their race, economic or social standing) or straddle gender lines, leaving some working-class men more oppressed than some middle- or upper-class women. These realities in turn create further questions around the harnessing, use and abuse of power and the need for institutional transformation. Following these conversations through, will, of necessity, surface contradictions and dilemmas in the broader policing reform project, and so can be invaluable in the unpacking and setting of priorities aimed at benefiting not only women, but hitherto marginalised men, women and children. An engendered approach can assist in reimagining, reconstituting and challenging policing initiatives to deliver in more holistic and inclusive ways,[39] thus contributing to the security and well-being of society as a whole.

Where such a critical approach is not adopted, the likelihood is that, even following extensive reform initiatives, policing will remain, if not synonymous with, then at least inherently incapable of addressing deep levels of insecurity, particularly those experienced by women, notably poor women and other marginalised groups within society.

GENDER AND THE *PATTEN* REPORT

Having set up these parameters, the main focus of this analysis will be the Commission report itself, its recommendations and, just as tellingly, its implementation to date.

The following discussion will analyse the extent to which the Patten Commission engaged with gender in its attempt to craft new and acceptable post-conflict policing arrangements in Northern Ireland. The purpose of such interrogation is twofold. While accepting that the Patten blueprint for change has much to commend it as a policing reform initiative, it is by no means an unqualified success. An engendered analysis can help explore the extent to which Patten arguably 'missed the boat' in terms of a transformative rather than a merely reformist agenda. Furthermore, the ease with which the more radical participatory elements of the *Patten Report* were 'gutted' by the government charged with its implementation might be explained, at least in part, by Patten's own foundational deficit where gender is concerned.

The discussion of the report will be divided into two parts given that the Commission's recommendations, while largely top-down and organisational in orientation, also had a more radical edge designed to pluralise the policing function and further democratise its governance. Each strand of this endeavour will now be considered in turn.

Patten—*the top-down endeavour*

According to Sally Baden, '[t]ypically, gender perspectives in mainstream governance literature [and practice] are limited to an examination of the need for more women in formal political life and strategies to achieve this, without consideration of the need for transformation of the institutions of power'.[40] The organisational, managerial aspects of *Patten*, in many respects, conform to this mainstream view. Although being unusual in the extent to which a programme was put in place for the fairly dramatic restructuring of policing institutions,[41] the opportunity to engender the process was not taken and gendered power relations in Northern Ireland remained disappointingly unaddressed.

While recommending that an 'independent recruitment agency should advertise imaginatively and persistently, particularly in places likely to reach groups who are under-represented in the police',[42] *Patten's* treatment of gender overall was neither imaginative nor persistent. The 133-page report made a grand total of 6 references to gender, with women meriting mention in only 13 paragraphs. Of 175 recommendations, only a handful addressed gender in any shape or form, and these were essentially geared to facilitating the employment of women with caring responsibilities—an important category, but by no means the only issue.[43] Viewing the main problem as one of retention rather than recruitment,[44] the Commission's main response to the dearth of women police officers revolved around 'providing opportunities for job sharing, flexible working arrangements and career breaks'. Given the 'particular attractiveness of part time work' to a range of women, the Commission recommended the part-time reserve force be retained and developed, while calling, in vague terms, for 'determined effort [to] be made to attract women into full time police work, not only in Northern Ireland but in policing worldwide'.[45]

The framing and content of such recommendations conformed with mainstream notions that issues such as childcare are not equally men's issues and that gendered concerns could largely be addressed by ensuring more recruitment, retention and advancement of women within the force (become service). Numerous public meetings held by Patten in the course of its deliberations indicated that having more women in the police organisation was an area of mutual identification and agreement across communities with very different political ideologies.[46] However, this potentially useful avenue for further consensus building was left unexplored. Rather than being used creatively to the Commission's advantage to lever in and build consensus around a broader-based equality framework, interfacing with other core areas of discrimination such as class and race, the Commission went down the 'traditional route' of over-valorising narrowly framed conflict related identities for proactive engagement.

While prepared to advocate and stand over time limited 50:50 recruitment of Catholics and Protestants, the Commissioners, on the basis of legal advice, concluded that European legislation ruled out such a proposal 'in respect of recruitment of women'. European legislation, even on this reading, did not rule out targets and timetables to enhance gender representation within the organisation, yet Patten did not follow this path either. Instead the Commission's recommendations in respect of gender were pedestrian at best. While 'convinced that a much higher proportion of female officers would enhance the effectiveness of policing and [keen] to see Northern Ireland leading the way in this area', the Commission made no recommendation in relation to achieving an equal number of men and women within the public police itself.[47]

In fact, in a somewhat comedic display of circular argumentation, the report justified the Commission's decision not to 'set specific target percentages for the proportion of women officers because, on the one hand, the experience elsewhere cautions against setting them too high and, on the other hand, since women are half the population it is hard to justify setting them much lower than that'.[48] The Commission, therefore, dodged the gender challenge on the basis that '[t]he under-representation of women is a problem for police services everywhere',[49] and contented itself with recommending that the staff composition of organisations and bodies responsible for policing should be 'representative in terms of gender'.[50]

Hillyard et al. deem it 'significant' that gender (either as an area of expertise or as a particular category of representation) was not specifically recommended in terms of the composition of the new Policing Board—the body recommended by Patten to oversee policing in

Northern Ireland. The recommendation in terms of the staffing of the Policing Board did contain a specific reference to gender representation as part of a longer list of considerations. However, in terms of its own membership, the Board itself was only required to be 'representative of the community as a whole'.[51] Whether or not this was an oversight, the failure to attach any particular significance to gender representation is further borne out in that it is not mentioned at all in the recommendations on the establishment of District Policing Partnership Boards. This insufficiency of concern perhaps contributed to a situation whereby only two women were appointed to the first nineteen-member Policing Board in November 2001, with women members reaching a high water mark of six in 2004 and falling back again to four in 2007 with the advent of Sinn Féin participation in the ranks of policing governance. Ironically, there was a much higher level of recruitment of women to District Policing Partnerships (as they became)[52]—but it must be borne in mind that these bodies were given much less power and influence than intended by *Patten* and have, in many ways, been hamstrung by Policing Board control and narrow interpretation of their role.

While it might be possible at some level to praise *Patten* for not getting caught up in the distraction of the numbers game as a significant indicator of real change, this is diminished by the extent to which the report equally failed to engage creatively with issues of organisational police culture as stifling and abusive of women, and was insufficiently attentive to tackling gender-based violence. Empirical evidence both locally and internationally attests to endemic sexism, homophobia and other discriminatory characteristics within police organisational cultures and subcultures.[53] The 'canteen culture'[54] within the RUC clearly mitigated against the equal treatment and advancement of women being achieved within Northern Ireland's police service without some proactive and imaginative engagement designed to impact radically and effectively on its negative sexist, sectarian and other discriminatory aspects. Despite this, only seven recommendations were made in the *Patten Report* on 'culture, symbols and ethos', and none of these engaged gender dynamics or pernicious subcultures as requiring particular attention.

The Policing Commission did advocate that 'the maintenance of a neutral working environment should become an assessed management responsibility at all levels of management'.[55] The creation of a 'neutral working environment,' has since been recommended by

OSCE guidelines on policing in multi-ethnic societies. While this can undoubtedly have its up-sides, it is not unproblematic as it operates very much on the surface level of appearances. While attempting to deal with a very real issue of chill factor caused by intimidating and oppressive atmospheres and practices in the workplace, it can also strip out some of the positive aspects of workplace diversity. Where positive and harmonious expressions of identity are treated as morally equivalent to obnoxious ones, diversity in uniformed organisations suffers. For example, if recruits are disembedded too firmly from their roots by the organisational shaping and training processes, the valuable link into particular communities and constituencies might be somewhat diluted to the detriment of the 'finished' police organisation being deemed to be reflective in reality of the whole society.

Equally, there can be a backlash against what might be seen by some as too much 'political correctness'—which can also manifest in terms of negative response to lateral entry and fast-tracking processes for under-represented groups. 'Old school' officers may well group together at an informal level to continue sectarian, racist, homophobic or sexist behaviours. This, in itself, can send bullying and harassment underground, to a deeper level, where it is much harder to identify and address and is, in itself, another reason to recommend the vetting of police officers[56] in terms of previous wrongdoing or capacity for human-rights abuse, specifically considering potential for and attitudes towards gender-based violence. *Patten* made no recommendation in terms of vetting, purging or lustration processes.

The final issue for consideration in this section is *Patten*'s exhortation that '[m]erit must remain a critical criteria for selection for the police service'.[57] The difficulty is not in the merit principle itself, but in how merit is conceived, in what precisely are deigned to be core policing competencies and in how that designation takes place. If merit is constructed in the absence of a full societal conversation about what policing is expected to deliver and what values, attitudes, skills and experience are key to that delivery, the lack of a specifically engendered input will frustrate the merit and the validity of the merit principle itself. In terms of implementation of gender relevant recommendations, the Police (NI) Act (2000)[58] tasked the Chief Constable of the newly named Police Service of Northern Ireland to prepare and submit a plan to the newly established Policing Board to monitor the number of women in the service and to focus on the recruitment, retention and progression of females within the organisation.

In the period following, female representation within the organisation rose to an all-time high of around 22% of the service by 2008. The PSNI has continued to raise awareness of issues facing women in the police service through its gender steering group. Among its counted successes to date are the publication of an appropriate language guide, the redrafting of a new, flexible working policy and the hosting of a number of workshops highlighting promotional opportunities. Human-rights and equality 'proofing' of internal policies has also taken place. Despite this, female police staff continue to be over-represented at the lower grades of the organisation, a position that has remained largely unchanged since 2004.[59] This situation, coupled with evidence that female officers were disproportionately not putting themselves forward for promotion to higher ranks led to the PSNI conducting an equality impact assessment resulting from its legislative duty under S.75 Police (Northern Ireland) Act (1998) to have due regard to the promotion of equality of opportunity.[60] Unfortunately, while identifying a small number of positive actions, such as individual personal interviews with those women eligible to apply for promotion to the higher ranks of the organisation, the impact exercise itself could be criticised for a failure to engage at a sufficiently deep level with how and why gender clearly impacts on this state of affairs in the context of the broader organisational culture.

Traditionally, in terms of delineating the success of top-down reform strategies, statistics are notoriously over-valued, and the much vaunted percentage increase of women in the PSNI must be viewed with caution as a key indicator that things have changed. Measurements more likely to be of value lie in deeper qualitative analysis of what it feels like and why to be a woman at various points within the policing organisation; how the organisation might need to change to take fuller and better account of this reality; and whether, in fact, a bureaucratic organisation of this nature is, actually, the most appropriate locus to make use of different skills, set gender aware priorities and deliver in accordance with diverse engendered needs. As the OECD handbook points out, 'it is important to note that the inclusion of women alone does not guarantee that gender equality issues will be addressed'.[61] Under-the-radar indicators such as an arbitary reduction in time given in recruit training to issues such as rape, at a time when conviction levels are pitiful, help paint a fuller and perhaps more disappointing picture of the extent to which gendered concerns have been fully mainstreamed within the PSNI.

Hillyard and Maguire critique the 'feminisation' approach, which seeks to recruit more women into policing structures, in part because it continues

> to identify the state as solely responsible for the provision of security through policing, rather than recognising the need for broader social, community and political involvement in policy approaches to women's [or others'] marginalisation from policing.[62]

Patten *and plurality—the bottom-up endeavour*

It is to these aspects of *Patten* that discussion now turns. Although, essentially a managerial document, elements of the *Patten Report* did attempt to address less visible but no less tenacious concerns around creating equitable and reflective policing for all. Highly influential in this regard was Clifford Shearing's conception of nodal governance, further articulated in the Loader and Walker[63] notion of an 'anchored pluralist' approach to security provision. This approach is found in the elements of *Patten* that attempted to facilitate community provision to work in tandem with and inform local and national policing policy, while ensuring women and others were not marginalised in the process.

Paradoxically, therefore, as well as shoring up many aspects of the traditional gender and policing order, Meyer McAleese argues that many of the Patten Commission's recommendations at the same time challenged this order 'by recommending a "softer" police force—a police service that is community-based, accessible, friendly, and helpful'.[64] The desire to move from force to service was certainly a palpable element of the Patten strategy. Meyer McAleese demonstrates how the Patten Commission can be presented as a kind of 'New Man'[65] model for policing, with the added authority that its softened approach to policing represented the distillation of global 'best practices'.[66] Recommendations geared towards the creation of a 'softer' form of policing range from making police stations and armoured vehicles less forbidding and more user-friendly, to integrating community awareness as a core element of training,[67] to facilitating the resourcing and utilising of different community-based policing and security endeavours. These kind of recommendations stem from *Patten*'s insistence that policing is actually about the protection and vindication of the human rights of all. As part and parcel of this approach, *Patten* considered that '[p]olicing with the community should be the core function of the police service and the core function of every police station'.[68] To this end, a number of further recommendations dealt with broadening and diversifying the policing base from both a service delivery and oversight point of view.

Governance wise, it was recommended that policing be overseen by a civilian board comprising a range of experiences and skills. The Policing Board was to function not just as legislative overseer of the effectiveness and efficiency of the police as an organisation, but to perform a meta-auspice role, rowing and steering policing as a much broader function within Northern Ireland. The vision was that this would include any number of other service providers as well as the public police. This has not come to fruition in practice.[69] On the plus side, a Community Engagement strategy has recently been established, with a women's reference group comprised of women NGOs, acting in an advisory capacity to support Policing Board scrutiny of police strategy. However, this group is not resourced and 'participation is straining the resources of the women's groups taking part'.[70] Another important recommendation in terms of the pluralising of power and the redistribution of resources was that District Councils were to be given the power to raise a specific tax 'towards the improved policing of the district, which could enable the DPPB to purchase additional services from the police or other statutory agencies, or from the private sector'.[71] This proposal was never implemented.

At a police level, attempts were to be made to demonstrate the benefits of community involvement to police officers. Where possible, it was recommended that training and education should be outsourced and that police should take courses with and from civilians.[72] A state-of-the-art police college was to be built to provide training not just for police, but for members of the community involved in DPPs and other aspects of the policing function. This facility has not yet been built and its planned site raises a number of issues around access. Space precludes a fuller discussion, but the fact remains that most of the more participatory aspects of *Patten* were lost in translation, and potentially more gender-aware, emancipatory and participative policing lost out as a result. UNSRC 1325 was never integrated into the implementation package, to the point where the CEDAW examining committee in 2008 had to call for the 'full implementation' of the resolution in Northern Ireland.[73]

Paddy Hillyard and Mike Tomlinson[74] argue that the Commission's radical model of policing—a network of regulating mechanisms in which policing becomes everyone's business—failed, because it gave insufficient attention, like much modern writing on policing, to the role of the state and the vested interests within policing. A further reason might be the project's lack of understanding of the need to embed gender and a gendered way of seeing and doing deep into the process to guard against its eventual unpicking and repackaging in state-centric terms. The overall outcome is that the Patten Commission has been effectively policed, and Northern Ireland has been left with a traditional, largely undemocratic and unaccountable model of policing with most of the control resting with the Secretary of State and the Chief Constable. This is unlikely to change significantly with the devolution of policing and justice powers to the Northern Ireland Assembly and the appointment of a Northern Ireland Justice Minister.

Clearly, given the expense involved in maintaining and resourcing public police, a key post-conflict issue should be whether such organisations require to be strengthened, or the extent to which necessarily finite resources might be directed towards other policing models and development processes that could be supported and monitored to more fully, fairly and safely fulfil security goals. For example, as the public police have been demonstrated not to deal effectively with a range of antisocial behaviours and resultant harms, community restorative justice and informal processes exist or can be developed in a range of transitional societies.[75] In this respect, Northern Ireland has important examples to offer in terms of, for example, the development of effective community restorative justice mechanisms. Civil-society-based endeavours draw on community, family and other processes to engage more holistically with causes of and restorative approaches to harm. As such, they contain the seeds of much that is useful. None of this is to say that situating more responsibility for security outside of traditional police organisations or state offices—something that an engendered analysis might advocate—does not have its own attendant difficulties. Even if the state were to 'play ball' in facilitating such a process, shifting the locus of power to civil society is not a panacea and also needs to be carefully monitored for gender awareness and equitable process. Community based processes can also prove problematic where, for example, they are too fixedly culturally based in their application or insufficiently accountable or educated in human-rights requirements.

For example, while local ownership and participation are key strategies in terms of inclusiveness, there are clearly dangers in cultural specificity being reified in contexts where the dominant culture condones domestic violence or prohibits women from working within the security system. Adelman, Erez and Shalboud-Kevorkian caution that making justice dependent on multicultural understandings framed as cultural sensitivity 'can become a convenient and institutionally acceptable and perhaps even encouraged mechanism of culturalising violence against minority women'.[76] Linking into or giving pre-eminence to indigenous or other non-state approaches needs to be carefully thought through, regulated and evaluated in terms of the delivery of justice to all.

Trying to ensure local ownership while not simply cutting a slice of power to patriarchal and dominant groupings within civil society is a significant challenge to gender-responsive SSR processes. Though it is essential to adapt initiatives to local cultural realities and present them in a culturally sensitive way, it is also important to keep in mind that cultures change, that they are not monolithic and that overvalorising discriminatory custom and practice at a time of transition can sow seeds for the creation of new outgroups or perpetuate historic discrimination through the facilitated entrenchment of attitudes and behaviours that might otherwise evolve more quickly.

WHY IS GENDER MAINSTREAMING AND EQUAL PARTICIPATION OF WOMEN SO DIFFICULT IN PRACTICE?

And so we come full circle in terms of the discussion. If gender mainstreaming and the equal participation of women are such important aims, relatively easily agreed in theory and a key element of the international legal landscape, why has it been so difficult to date to embed engendered security praxis?

First, security is an area dominated by men and masculinised understandings of what security is and how it can be achieved. Where this degree of maleness is seen as acceptable or not registered as potentially problematic, security needs and expectations will be narrowly framed. 'Whose security?' is a question that either does not arise or is insufficiently explored and problematised. Instead, it can appear as simply 'common sense' that more men than women will be involved as architects for change and that gendered concerns are simply not a priority when it comes to bringing violent conflict to an end. When many gendered issues and problems remain under the radar, connections are not made as to how the 'maleness' of security might actually exacerbate or perpetuate (gender-based) insecurities and harms, and how addressing these is actually fundamentally linked to the achievement of sustainable peace and security at a global level.

It is, after all, men who have the experience and organisational knowledge. It is men who are physically stronger and more likely to be respected and obeyed.[77] It is men who are the traditional protectors and who understand security requirements. Where such gendered assumptions are in the ascendancy, it can be difficult to dislodge 'common sense' notions despite the fact that research shows women have much of value to bring to policing, even in respect of the 'traditional' police officer role.

Studies around the world have demonstrated that

> women officers rely on a style of policing that uses less physical force, are better at defusing and de-escalating potentially violent confrontations with citizens, and are less likely to become involved in problems with use of excessive force. Additionally, women officers often possess better communication skills than their male counterparts and are better able to facilitate the cooperation and trust required to implement a community policing model.[78]

Clearly, 'not all women are able to handle all police jobs—but neither are all men'. What empirical research has shown is that 'in some respects, at least, women are better suited for police work than men'.[79] As ever, this needs to be interpreted to take account of and explicate counter-findings. For example an internal organisational 'culture of disrespect and harassment' can result in a situation whereby some female police officers

> act tougher on female victims of crime and employ increased use of force with citizens in an attempt to gain acceptance into the dominant group. The reform process needs to address the challenges associated with organisational culture, and work towards a police service that respects colleagues and the population served.[80]

Unfortunately, this is rarely done.

Security relations are power relations and security reform changes power relations.[81] This is another reason why transformative change might be balked at. While they may be prepared to countenance technocratic, managerial or minimalist solutions, paradigm shifts are likely to be strongly resisted by the powerful, including those who may have managed security/policing in the past. It can be difficult to get on the inside track necessary to both spot and overcome such resistances. Gender strategies must confront a tendency, either through lack of sufficiently sophisticated understanding or a desire to do the minimum and tick the box, to conflate gender mainstreaming and equal participation of women when they are in fact two distinct imperatives. Gender mainstreaming is facilitated where women participate on equal terms, but, as has been illustrated above, the fact of female participation alone will be insufficient to achieve gender equity, particularly where gender issues are seen as women's issues in already masculinised contexts. Where one woman is viewed as capable of representing any other, the inclusion of women, any women, becomes the goal and it is more difficult to cross the necessary rubicon to really transform institutional thinking and systemic practice.

A further tendency to guard against is where women are added into the picture in a way that results in their apparently unidimensional portrayal as victims. If this is done, their agency variously as survivors, militants,[82] conflict resolvers, transmitters of values and empowerers of themselves and their communities is totally overlooked and unharnessed.[83] The role of many women as peacemakers, carers and providers of security, within their families and communities, are particular realities that tend to be either unarticulated and rendered invisible or otherwise overly essentialised and poorly understood in security reform processes.[84]

The OECD *Handbook* has recently emphasised the need for security reform projects to recognise, register and work to effectively and appropriately accommodate the differing needs, experiences and expectations of security that may be significantly impacted on by the simple fact of being a man, woman, girl or boy in any given society. The Organisation for Security and Co-operation in Europe (OSCE), the Geneva Centre for Democratic Control of the Armed Forces (DCAF) and the United Nations International Research and Training Institute for the Advancement of Women (UNINSTRAW) have jointly developed a toolkit on gender and security to help move this thinking forward in practical ways[85]—but this is not a quick fix, nor a matter of adding 'gender bits' to an already conceived programme of reform. Such an *à la carte* approach[86] is inherently problematic as it permits the notion that technocratic one-off solutions can achieve gender mainstreaming, rather than the reality that gender main-streaming processes 'must necessarily be sustained as long as policymaking endures'.[87]

Where gender is not sufficiently seen as a significant or useful lens through which to view the totality of the project under consideration, it can quickly become just another box to be ticked. Superficial strate-gies such as simply increasing female recruitment to police/military organisations, possibly looking at issues of retention, promotion and/or training, and developing civilian oversight processes then become ends in themselves rather than steps on the way to fuller goals. Failure to fully grapple with how policing can impinge for good and ill on the lived reality of the marginalised and less powerful in the spe-cific cultural context under consideration can significantly undermine the potential import of security reform initiatives in practice. The danger then is that an essentially failed model of security provision will be largely replicated rather than transformed within any suppos-edly new dispensation.[88]

Policing reform must grapple with these issues to be truly effective. This requires a whole of governance, engendered approach where 'the transformation of institutions becomes the agenda, rather than the continuing attempt to improve women's access and performance within organizations and their hierarchies'.[89] This, of necessity, in-volves the development and context-appropriate utilisation of participatory methodologies, for example conducting meaningful and inclusive needs assessments, linking in constitutional, legislative, policy and training issues across the justice and development spec-trum. It also means evaluating the usefulness of reform endeavours not in terms of increased representation in one or more organisations or the development of civilian oversight per se, but at the levels of meaningful participation, effectiveness and impact.[90] In turn, these indicators link directly into issues around political will, resource allo-cation, equal decision-making, respectful, accessible and inclusive processes and felt changes in lived reality for women and other mar-ginalised groups within society. If policing is too big for one organisation, policing reform is certainly too big for one gender, a reality that is slowly being recognised, but remains to be fully acted on anywhere in the world.[91]

CONCLUSION

International law and experience point to the need for gender to form a cornerstone of analysis where security and policing reform is being developed and undertaken. This is not about a nod to feminism, 'political correctness', or to get the 'harpies' off our backs. Nor need it be driven by a paternalistic sense of women as victims, the gentler sex requiring special protection. Instead, the incorporation of an engendered approach has validity from both a welfare and an agency perspective in the development of sustainable peace and security.

As women and girls make up more than half the world's population and suffer disproportionately from insecurity, conflict and bad policing, addressing the security/gender interface is important at a very basic level and implies the need for a whole of governance approach.[92] Policing does not take place in a vacuum—contextualising the policing reform endeavour to take account of local gendered experience, conditions and connectedness requires looking outside organisational reform of 'the police' to how security is constructed and might be constructed more effectively on a legal, political, social, economic and cultural level.

Adopting an engendered approach to security reform opens up and enables different ways of seeing and doing that can both affect process design and facilitate results to be more transformative of untenable situations. Appropriate and systemic attention to gender as a nuanced and intersecting concept surfaces all kinds of other exclusions, prejudices and stereotypical practices that hurt people and damage security for different reasons and require to be addressed in different ways.

Women, if appropriately resourced and facilitated, are core potential contributors in respect of crafting strategic alliances and priorities to imbue diversity, representation and change efforts with real meaning. The understanding that a critical mass of women can bring to the table in terms of factoring gendered realities and experiences more fully into the picture cannot be underestimated. This is not just important for women but is imperative, in order to provide trusted (and therefore more likely to be) effective services to women, to marginalised communities, as well as to society as a whole.[93]

Ultimately, the conclusion must be that gender can be, but rarely is, transformative of the way we look at policing reform. It is not a question of 'add women and stir'. Instead, if a gendered way of doing and seeing can be fully integrated into reform processes, the whole basis on which security and insecurity have been built to date will be irreversibly shaken to reveal potentially new landscapes of protection, empathy and caring,[94] which might prove firmer foundations for a global world order.

NOTES

*The author would like to thank Aisling Swaine and Eilish Rooney for helpful comments on an earlier draft of this chapter.

[1] For conceptual clarity and internal consistency, this chapter adopts the definition of gender set out by Tara Denham in 'Police reform and gender', in Megan Bastick and Kristin Valasek (eds), *Gender and security sector reform toolkit*, Toolkit 2, Geneva: DCAF, OSCE/ODIHR, UN-INSTRAW, (2008), 3, whereby 'Gender refers to the particular roles and relationships, personality traits, attitudes, behaviours and values that society ascribes to men and women'. 'Gender' therefore refers to *learned* differences between men and women, while 'sex' refers to the *biological* differences between males and females. Gender roles vary widely within and across cultures, and can change over time. Gender refers not simply to women or men, but to the relationship between them. Note also the definition of gender set out at page 1 of the *OECD DAC Handbook on security system reform section 9: integrating gender awareness and equality* (Organisation for Economic Co-operation and Development: Paris, 2009 edition) (hereafter cited as *OECD Handbook*), whereby gender 'refers to the economic, social, political and cultural attributes and opportunities associated with being male and female. In most societies, men and women differ in the activities they undertake, in the control of resources, and in participation in decision making. In most societies, women as a group have less access in these domains than men. Such inequalities are a constraint to development because they limit the ability of women to develop and exercise their full capabilities, for their own benefit and for that of society as a whole'. The text of this handbook is available at: http://www.oecd.org/dataoecd/4/52/42168607.pdf. The problematic nature of gender stereotyped assumptions and ascriptions is particularly marked in the field of security provision, regulation and reform.

[2] 'Human security in its broadest sense, embraces far more than the absence of violent conflict. It encompasses human rights, good governance, access to education and health care and ensuring that each individual has opportunities and choices to fulfil his or her own potential. Every step in this direction is also a step towards reducing poverty, achieving economic growth and preventing conflict. Freedom from want, freedom from fear and the freedom of future generations to inherit a healthy natural environment—these are the interrelated building blocks of human—and therefore national security'. See former UN secretary-general Kofi Annan's 2000 millennium report, *We the peoples—the role of the United Nations in the 21st century* (New York: United Nations Department of Public Information, 2000), available at: http://www.un.org/millennium/sg/report/.

[3] This term is employed throughout the chapter to indicate that security discourse is already 'gendered', in a way that is highly masculinised and patriarchal. Engendering

denotes a more inclusive and participatory approach, which is sensitive to the common as well as differing needs of women, men, girls and boys.

[4] *OECD Handbook*, 15; this is borne out in experience of UN peacekeeping, Security System Reform (SSR) and Demobilisation, Disarmament and Reintegration (DDR) initiatives.

[5] 'In a post 11 September context, peace and security dominate much of the global agenda. In the West, what counts as insecurity has largely been reduced to the fear of terrorism. Whether the threat is real, imagined, or perceived, often gets lost in the construction of fear'; see Elisabeth Porter, 'Connecting human security, gender justice and peacebuilding' (2010; forthcoming).

[6] See *OECD Handbook*, 15.

[7] For example, Lori L. Heise, Jacqueline Pitanguy and Adrienne Germain, *Violence against women: the hidden health burden* World Bank Discussion Paper 255 (New York: World Bank, 1994), using data from a 1993 World Bank modelling exercise, found that, of ten selected causes and risk factors for disability and death among women between the age of 15 and 44, rape and domestic violence rated higher than cancer, traffic accidents, war and malaria. NB: A high level of under-reporting must be factored into the onward interpretation of this statistic. The explanatory memorandum to the Council of Europe Parliamentary Assembly (2004) Doc 10273, 16 September 2004, further notes that domestic violence is on the increase. The text of this memorandum is available at: http://assembly.coe.int/Documents/WorkingDocs/doc04/EDOC10273.htm.

[8] Although poverty data is not reported by sex in most countries, it is clear that women make up the majority of the world's poor—owing to unequal access to resources and opportunities, discriminatory land and inheritance laws and unequal distribution of household resources. According to UNICEF, *Gender equality—the big picture* (Paris/New York: United Nations, 2007), women perform 66 percent of the world's work, produce 50 percent of the food, but earn 10 percent of the income and own 1 percent of the property. In Northern Ireland, according to Eilish Rooney, 'Recently reported indices of deprivation…indicate that…[b]etween 2001 and 2005, 12 of the 17 [most deprived] West Belfast wards…increased their rank of deprivation', 'Women's equality in Northern Ireland's transition: intersectionality in theory and place', *Feminist Legal Studies* (14) (2006), 353–75: 365. See also Eilish Rooney, 'Intersectionality in transition: Lessons from Northern Ireland', *Web Journal of Current Legal Issues* (2007), 5, available at: http://webjcli.ncl.ac.uk/2007/issue5/rooney5.htm. The Committee on the Administration of Justice has further concluded that 'Northern Ireland is one of the most unequal societies in the developed world, and the inequality is increasing', see CAJ, *Briefing on religious and political inequalities in Northern Ireland* (Belfast: CAJ, 2006), 6.

[9] As Margaret Ward states, 'There has been increasing international recognition that a "gender-blind" approach to conflict resolution and reconstruction has been a critical element in the global failure to achieve a sustainable peace', see 'Gender, citizenship and the future of the Northern Ireland peace process', *Éire-Ireland* 40 (3) and (4) (Fall/Winter 2005), 1–22, available at: http://cain.ulst.ac.uk/issues/women/docs/ward05peaceprocess.pdf.

[10] Although gender mainstreaming lacks one agreed definition, it broadly speaking involves the process of assessing the implications for women and men of any planned action, including legislation, policies or programmes, and acting in a way that takes full

account of these implications in terms of providing equity as between different men and women.

[11] On this point see, for example, Joan Eveline, Carol Bacchi and Jennifer Binns, 'Gender mainstreaming versus diversity mainstreaming: methodology as emancipatory politics', *Gender, Work and Organization* 16 (2) (March 2009), 198–216.

[12] For example, globally, one in every three women has experienced some form of gender-based violence. See *OECD Handbook*, 15; also see *Northern Ireland Crime Survey* (2008), available at: http://www.nio.gov.uk/08_northern_ireland_crime_survey.pdf. It should be noted that men and children also experience such violence, and serious underreporting is the norm.

[13] For example, raped women and girls are, in some cultures, murdered by family members in so called 'honour killings' for bringing shame to their families. See, for example, Anuradha M. Chenoy, 'Women in the South Asian conflict zones', *South Asian Survey* (2004) 11, 35; *The Northern Ireland crime survey* (2008) evidenced that the police do not become aware of 75 percent of the worst incidents of domestic violence; the results of that survey are available at: http://www.nio.gov.uk/08_northern_ireland_crime_survey.pdf.

[14] For instance, as Bastick *et al.* point out, 'conflict-related sexual violence occurs in homes, fields, places of detention, military sites, and camps for refugees and displaced persons…at the height of armed conflict, during population displacement, and continues after conflict'; see Megan Bastick, Karin Grimm and Rahel Kunz, *Sexual violence in armed conflict. Global overview and implications for the security sector* (Geneva: Centre for the Democratic Control of Armed Forces, 2007), 9.

[15] Sixty percent of the women interviewed for research by Monica McWilliams and Joan McKiernan during the conflict in Northern Ireland had experienced violence during pregnancy and thirteen percent had lost their babies as a result, yet domestic violence was not seen as a police priority where there was a 'terrorist threat' to counter. This marginalisation of women's experiences and needs is reflected in many other conflicted societies. See McWilliams and McKiernan, *Bringing it out in the open: domestic violence in Northern Ireland* (Belfast: DHSS, 1993).

[16] For ground-breaking work on the importance of adopting an intersectional approach to the achievement of gender equity, see Kimberle Crenshaw, 'Demarginalizing the intersection of race and sex: a black feminist critique of antidiscrimination doctrine, feminist theory and anti-racist politics', *University of Chicago Legal Forum* (1989) 139–67; also Kimberle Crenshaw, 'Mapping the margins: intersectionality, identity politics and violence', *Stanford Law Review* 43 (6) (1991), 1241–99.

[17] The Convention on the Elimination of All Forms of Discrimination against Women (CEDAW) was adopted by the UN General Assembly in 1979. It is often described as an international bill of rights for women. The full text of the convention is available at: http://www.un.org/womenwatch/daw/cedaw/cedaw.htm.

[18] The Declaration on the Elimination of Violence against Women was adopted by the UN General Assembly in 1993. The full text of this declaration is available at: http://www.un.org/documents/ga/res/48/a48r104.htm.

[19] This declaration and platform for action emerged from the Fourth World Conference on Women, which took place in Beijing, China, in September 1995. See http://www.un.org/womenwatch/daw/beijing/pdf/BDPfA%20E.pdf for the text of the of this document.

[20] See Amnesty International, 2006 Report, available at: http://web.amnesty.org/report2006/key_issue-4-eng.

[21] Further information on this Security Council resolution can be found at: http://www.securitycouncilreport.org/atf/cf/%7B65BFCF9B-6D27-4E9C-8CD3-CF6E4FF96FF9%7D/WPS%20SRES1820.pdf.

[22] In this regard, see the experience in Liberia of deploying an all-female peacekeeping contingent at the insistence of the first female African president. Initial indications are that this has had a huge positive impact on women's involvement in policing, the behaviour of peacekeepers and on addressing huge issues around sexual violence and impunity.

[23] United Nations, Security Council resolution 1888, adopted on 30 September 2009; the text of the resolution is available at: http://www.peacewomen.org/un/sc/SCR1888.pdf.

[24] United Nations, Security Council resolution 1889, adopted on 5 October 2009; the text is available at: http://www.peacewomen.org/un/sc/SCR1889.pdf.

[25] United Nations, Security Council resolution 1325, adopted on 31 October 2000; the text is available at: http://www.peacewomen.org/un/sc/res1325.pdf. Hereafter cited as UNSCR 1325.

[26] UNOSAGI speech at the international conference 'Women negotiating peace—experience, obstacles, opportunities: United Nations security resolution 1325 (2000) on women, peace and security', which took place at the University of Iceland, 19–20 June 2009; see also Amartya Sen, *Development as freedom* (New York: Alfred A. Knopf, 1999); and Sen's entitlements and capabilities framework, 'Development as capability expansion', in Keith Griffin and J. Knight (eds), *Human development and the international development strategy for the 1990s* (London: Macmillan, 1990).

[27] The experience of the UN peace-building commission is instructive in this regard.

[28] The Independent Commission on Policing for Northern Ireland, chaired by Chris Patten and generally referred to as the 'Patten Commission'.

[29] See, for example, Jerome H. Skolnick, *Justice without trial* (New York: Wiley, 1966); P.K. Manning *Police work* (Cambridge, MA: MIT Press, 1971); Robert Reiner, *Politics of the police* (3rd edn, Oxford: Oxford University Press, 2000); Janet B.L. Chan, *Changing police culture: policing in a multicultural society* (Cambridge: Cambridge University Press, 1997).

[30] Northern Ireland has a very vibrant civil society, and women's groups have worked extremely hard to put gender on the agenda. Some political headway was made with the development of an all-woman political party, the Women's Coalition, in 1996, which managed to have an impact on the wording of the 1998 peace agreement, through the involvement of the party's two elected representatives in the negotiations. However, it has not been possible to sustain this party and the momentum to ensure attention to gendered concerns as the peace process developed was lost.

[31] McWilliams and McKiernan, *Bringing it out in the open*. It might be assumed that once the 'high' conflict is over, there would be more space for gendered issues to be considered. However, experience has shown that in the immediate transitional/post-conflict phase, the focus is on accommodating 'conflict-related' identities and issues, with gender-based issues once again being squeezed out of the picture, making it even more difficult to try to insert these centre stage as time goes by.

[32] Independent Commission on Policing for Northern Ireland, *A new beginning: policing*

in Northern Ireland, Report of the Independent Commission on Policing for Northern Ireland (Belfast: HMSO, 1998), 81, (hereafter cited as *Patten Report*), available at: http://www.nio.gov.uk/a_new_beginning_in_policing_in_northern_ireland.pdf.

[33] This was an answer to a parliamentary question, see House of Commons, Hansard written answers for 24 January 2000, part 2, available at: http://www.publications.parliament.uk/pa/cm199900/cmhansrd/vo000124/text/00124w02.htm. This statistic emphasises the need for a gender strategy to equally embrace cross-cutting issues such as sect, race, age, sexual orientation, etc., which result in multiple layers of discrimination and exclusion.

[34] Good Friday/Belfast Agreement (1998). The agreement was signed in Belfast on 10 April 1998; the full text of the document (hereafter cited as *Agreement*), is available at: http://foreignaffairs.gov.ie/uploads/documents/Anglo-Irish/agreement.pdf. cmnd 53.

[35] *Patten Report*, 2 (2), 10.

[36] Inter-Agency Standing Committee (IASC), 'Gender and security toolkit 1', from *Women, girls, boys and men, different needs—equal opportunities:IASC gender handbook in humanitarian action* (IASC, 2006), 4–5; this document is available at http://www.humanitarianinfo.org/iasc/gender. The reference continues: 'However, a balance of women and men at all levels of institutions creates greater possibilities for identifying and addressing the different impacts of policy and programming on women and men'.

[37] For further discussion see, for example, Eilish Rooney, 'Engendering transitional justice: questions of absence and silence', *International Journal of Law in Context* 3 (2) (2007), 93–107.

[38] For example, in Timor Leste, two years after the exit of Indonesia and the end of the occupation, 51 percent of women said they felt 'unsafe' in their homes. Their notion of security was very different from that being used by the UN and bi-lateral donors to inform the development of policing structures post-conflict.

[39] As an example of the benefits to be gained from adopting an engendered and systemic approach, see, for example, Brandon Hamber, Paddy Hillyard, Amy Maguire, Monica McWilliams, Gillian Robinson, David Russell and Margaret Ward, 'Discourses in transition: re-imagining women's security', *International Relations* 20 (4) (2006), 487–502; William O'Neill, *Gender sensitive police reform in post-conflict societies*, Policy briefing paper for United Nations Development Program (UNDP) (New York: UNDP, 2007), available at: http://www.undp.org/cpr/documents/gender/Gender_Sensitive_Police_Reform_Policy_Brief_2007.pdf.

[41] Sally Baden, 'Gender, governance and the feminization of poverty', in *Women and political participation: 21st century challenges* (New York: UNDP, 2000), available at: http://www.undp.org/governance/docs/Gender-Pub-21stcentury.pdf.

[41] Ranging from, for example, the flattening of rank structures to the amalgamation of Special Branch and Criminal Investigation under one command, to changing the names and symbols associated with policing, to developing an interconnected and complex oversight framework to insisting human rights should be at the heart of policing.

[42] *Patten Report*, Recommendation 118 (paragraph 15.8).

[43] The main recommendations in this regard were: Recommendation 122: Priority should be given to creating opportunities for part-time working and job-sharing, both for police officers and police service civilians, and career breaks should be

introduced (paragraph 15.11), and Recommendation 123: Child care facilities should be introduced where practicable, or child care vouchers and flexible shift arrangements offered (paragraph 15.11); see *Patten Report*, 118.

[44] *Patten Report*, 88.

[45] *Patten Report*, 14.5, 82.

[46] *Patten Report*, 17.

[47] This, despite the Equal Opportunities Commission advocating a quota system to achieve a critical mass of women within the police. Although quotas clearly bring their own attendant controversies and were deemed by the legal advice obtained by the Commission to breach European legislation, neither were the less radical alternatives of targets and timetables advocated in respect of enhancing the position of women within the police organisation.

[48] *Patten Report*, 14.5, 82.

[49] *Patten Report*, 81–2.

[50] Recommendation 112 stated: 'Every effort should be made to ensure that the composition of the staff of the Policing Board, and the NIO Police Division (or any successor body) and the Office of the Police Ombudsman should be broadly reflective of the population of NI as a whole, particularly in terms of political /religious tradition and gender'.

[51] Recommendation 17 stated: The nine independent members of the Board should be selected from a range of different fields—including business, trade unions, voluntary organisations, community groups and the legal profession—with the aim of finding a group of individuals representative of the community as a whole, with the expertise both to set policing priorities and to probe and scrutinise different areas of police performance, from management of resources to the safeguarding of human rights. Paddy Hillyard, Monica McWilliams and Margaret Ward, *Re-imagining women's security: a comparative study of South Africa, Northern Ireland and Lebanon*, Northern Ireland Gender Audit (2006), available at: www.incore.ulst.ac.uk/research/project/rwsst/finalaudit.pdf.

[52] An independent recruitment process saw 127 women among the 207 first independent DPP members appointed; political party DPP members still tend to be mostly male.

[53] See, for example, Jennifer Brown, 'European policewomen: a comparative research perspective', *International Journal of the Sociology of Law* 25 (1) (March 1997), 1–19; Nigel Fielding 'Cop canteen culture', in Tim Newburn and Elizabeth A. (Betsy) Stanko (eds), *Just boys doing business: men, masculinity and crime* (London: Routledge, 1994); also Skolnick, Reiner, Manning, Chan, above.

[54] See, for example, John D. Brewer and Kathleen Magee, *Inside the RUC: routine policing in a divided society* (Oxford: Clarendon Press, 1991).

[55] *Patten Report*, Recommendation 156 (paragraph 17.9) at 121.

[56] On vetting, see Alexander Mayer-Rieckh and Pablo de Greiff, *Justice as prevention: vetting public employees in transitional societies* (New York: Social Science Research Council, 2007).

[57] *Patten Report*, 87; see also Recommendation 120.

[58] Police (NI) Act (2000), Section 48 part 2.

[59] PSNI Gender Action Plan (2008), 8.

[60] PSNI Equality Impact Assessment Report, Promotion: Police Officers March 2008, available at: http://www.psni.police.uk/index/updates/index/updates/consultation_zone/eqia_promotion_full_report.pdf.

[61] OECD DAC, *Handbook on security system reform*, § 9: integrating gender awareness and equality (Paris: OECD, 2009), 7.

[62] Paddy Hillyard and Amy Maguire, 'Gender, security and policing in post-conflict transition: some reflections on post-agreement developments in Northern Ireland', (2006, on file with author) draws on data gathered by a two year INCORE study, 'Re-imagining women's security and participation in post-conflict societies', which carried out focus groups, interviews, and gender audits in Lebanon, Northern Ireland and South Africa.

[63] Ian Walker and Neil Loader, 'Necessary virtues: the legitimate place of the state in the production of security', in Jennifer Wood and Benoit Dupont (eds), *Democracy, society and the governance of security* (Cambridge: Cambridge University Press, 2006); see also Lucia Zedner, 'Policing before and after the police: the historical antecedents of contemporary crime control', *British Journal of Criminology* 46 (2006), 78–96, available at: http://bjc.oxfordjournals.org/cgi/content/full/46/1/78.

[64] Mary Meyer McAleese, 'Gendering police, policing gender: community policing and police reform in Northern Ireland', unpublished paper presented at the annual meeting of the International Studies Association 48th Annual Convention, Hilton Chicago, Chicago, IL, (28 February 2007), 25, available at: http://www.allacademic.com/meta/p180918_index.html.

[65] Charlotte Hooper, *Manly states: masculinities, international relations, and gender politics* (New York: Columbia University Press, 2001).

[66] Meyer McAleese, 'Gendering police, policing gender', 36.

[67] Community awareness was 'not [to] be seen as a stand-alone element of recruit training; it should be integrated into all aspects of training', *Patten Report*, Recommendation 139, paragraph 16.17. Also, Recommendation 146 stated that standard training for [unfortunately only] neighbourhood officers should include modules on such community problems as domestic violence, child abuse, rape, drugs and youth issues and this training should be updated as necessary; see paragraph 16.24, 120.

[68] *Patten Report*, Recommendation 44, paragraph 7.9, 11.

[69] For further discussion of the extent to which this has succeeded in practice, see Graham Ellison and Mary O'Rawe, 'Security governance in transition: the compart-mentalising, crowding out and coralling of policing and security in Northern Ireland', *Theoretical Criminology* (2010, forthcoming).

[70] See, for example, Women's Research and Development Agency, 'Structures for pro-moting participation in peace building, democracy and governance: a case study of Northern Ireland', available at: http://www.wrda.net/wrdanews/data/upimages/salzburg_paper.pdf.

[71] *Patten Report*, Recommendation 32, paragraph 6.33.

[72] For example, Recommendation 143 states 'All police managers should have manage-ment training, as appropriate, and every manager should at some stage of his/her career do a management course in a non-police environment, such as a business school or university'. However, less inspiringly, the recommendation continues, 'Use should be made of management workshops, so that managers can discuss and develop *with each other* how best to reshape the police organization', paragraph 16.22 (emphasis added).

[73] Committee on the Elimination of Discrimination against Women, 41st Session, UK and Northern Ireland, 5th and 6th Report, 10 July 2008, Concluding remarks,

paragraph 285, available at: http://www2.ohchr.org/english/bodies/cedaw/docs/CEDAW.C.GBR.CO.6.pdf.

[74] Paddy Hillyard and Mike Tomlinson, 'Patterns of policing and policing Patten', *Journal of Law and Society* 27 (3) (2002), 394–415.

[75] Community-based endeavours in Northern Ireland have been shown to have some very positive results in recent years.

[76] Madelaine Adelman, Edna Erez and Nader Shalboud-Kevorkian, 'Policing violence against minority women in multicultural societies: "community" and the politics of exclusion', *Police and Society* 7 (2003), 105–33: 125.

[77] See, for example, Fielding, 'Cop canteen culture'.

[78] Kim Lonsway, Margaret Moore, Penny Harrington, Eleanor Smeal and Katherine Spillar, *Hiring and retaining more women: the advantages to law enforcement agencies* [US] (National Center for Women and Policing, A Division of the Feminist Majority Foundation, Los Angeles CA Spring 2003), 2; see other NCWP publications for further research evidence in this regard, available at: http://www.womenandpolicing.org/publications.asp.

[79] Joseph Balkin, cited in Lonsway *et al.*, *Hiring and retaining more women*, 4; For an albeit dated review of international research, see Joseph Balkin, 'Why policemen don't like policewomen', *Journal of Police Science and Administration* 16 (1) (1988), 29–38.

[80] See, for example, Denham, 'Police reform and gender', 5.

[81] Herbert Wulf, *Security sector reform in developing and transitional countries* (Berlin: Berghof Research Centre, 2004), available at: http://www.berghofhandbook.net/uploads/download/dialogue2_wulf.pdf, 48.

[82] See, for example, Miranda Alison, 'Women as agents of political violence: gendering security', *Security Dialogue* 35 (4) (2004), 447–63.

[83] See, for example, A. Chenoy (above) for an interesting analysis and typology in this regard; see also Rooney (above) for discussion of invisibility and conceptions of women during and post conflict.

[84] For example, women's groups in Bougainville, Papua New Guinea, Northern Ireland, Liberia; see for example, Elisabeth Porter *Peacebuilding: women in international perspective* (London and New York: Routledge, 2008); also Karen Barnes and Peter Albrecht, 'Tool 9 civil society oversight of the security sector and gender', in *The gender and security sector reform toolkit*, 16.

[85] *The gender and security sector reform toolkit* referenced throughout notes.

[86] Mary Daly uses this to denote the adoption of a particular toolkit or technique, often in the absence of an overall theoretical framework or if the research and analysis is needed for a full gender-based assessment; see Mary Daly, 'Gender mainstreaming in theory and practice', *Social Politics: International Studies in Gender, State and Society* 12 (3) (2005), 433–50: 436.

[87] Joan Eveline and Carol Bacchi, 'What are we mainstreaming when we mainstream gender?' *International Feminist Journal of Politics* 7 (4) (2005), 496–512: 503.

[88] *OECD Handbook*, 'In many countries SSR policies and programming currently fail to involve both women and men in decision-making processes and do not adequately acknowledge gender dynamics in attempting to understand issues—such as sexual violence or small arms violence. This failure frequently results in security system institutions not adequately providing security and justice, continuing to perpetrate human rights violations, and remaining strongholds of discrimination and harassment', 1.

89 T. Rees, *Mainstreaming equality in the European Union: education, training and labour market policies* (London: Routledge, 1998), 41.

90 For further detail, see, Sally Baden, 'Gender, governance and the feminization of poverty', in *Women and political participation: 21st century challenges* (New York: UNDP, 2000), 37, available at: http://www.undp.org/governance/docs/Gender-Pub-21stcentury.pdf.

91 Note, however, as mentioned above, the situation in Liberia of an all-female UN peacekeeping unit deployed in 2007 and the relative successes of that deployment to date in terms of tackling massive problems related to widespread sexual violence and faith in policing; see, for example, Carolyn Cohan, 'Women as peacekeepers in Liberia: the role of the Indian female police unit in operationalizing UN gender policy', paper presented at the annual meeting of the ISA's 49th Annual Convention, 'Bridging Multiple Divides', Hilton San Francisco, San Francisco, Ca., 26 March 2008, abstract available at: http://www.allacademic.com/meta/p251917_index.html.

92 For instance, in the words of Rachel Mayangja, the UN special adviser on gender issues and the advancement of women, 'to successfully transform the national legal framework for addressing violence against women, an enabling national environment is required. In this regard: Policies that promote and encourage the participation of men and boys in the elimination of violence against women must be adopted. Consideration must be given to rethinking the approach to education in order to transform educational curricula to eliminate stereotypical presentations and violence. Above all, consideration must be given to establishing a mechanism for holding actors accountable for the implementation of policies and enforcement of laws', Rachel Mayangja, speech at G8 International Conference on Violence against Women, Rome, 9 September 2009 *Sala delle conferenze internazionali*, available at: http://www.un.org//womenwatch/osagi/pdf/G8%20conference%20on%20VAW.sep09.pdf.

93 See, for example, the UN code of conduct for law enforcement officials, (1979).

94 See, for example, Elisabeth Porter on the 'politics of compassion', in *Peacebuilding: women in international perspective* (London and New York: Routledge, 2008) and 'Connecting human security, gender justice and peacebuilding' (2010, forthcoming).

CHAPTER 14

POLICE–COMMUNITY RELATIONS IN NORTHERN IRELAND IN THE POST-*PATTEN* ERA: TOWARDS AN ECOLOGICAL ANALYSIS

Graham Ellison

INTRODUCTION

I t has now been over ten years since the publication of the Report of the Independent Commission on Policing for Northern Ireland (henceforth ICP), which was established as a principal component of the Belfast Agreement (1998)[1] and which was tasked with '…bring[ing] forward proposals for future policing structures and arrangements, including means of encouraging widespread community support for those arrangements'.[2] After a somewhat shaky start, itself the result of political squabbling and legislative inertia, the majority of the proposals of the ICP have now been legislated for, albeit some in a rather more watered-down version from what the ICP intended. The sheer scale of the police reform process in Northern Ireland has attracted considerable attention, both internationally and nationally, with a succession of police chiefs, government ministers and other interested parties travelling to Belfast to witness first-hand the changes that have taken place in relation to policing structures and arrangements in the region. Indeed, at a recent 'Policing the Future' conference held at Belfast's prestigious Waterfront Hall, and attended by policing dignitaries from across the globe, the policing change process in Northern Ireland was heralded as a 'blueprint for democratic policing anywhere in the world', while the previous chairperson of the Northern Ireland Policing Board (NIPB), Professor Desmond Rea, has recently suggested that the Police Service of Northern Ireland (PSNI) 'represents what is best in modern day policing'.[3]

Certainly, much has changed in policing terms in Northern Ireland. Structures for the governance and oversight of the police have been established, such as the Policing Board, District Policing Partnership Boards and, perhaps most fundamentally of all, a fully independent police complaints machinery in the form of the Police Ombudsman for Northern Ireland. In addition, Catholic recruitment to the PSNI stands at almost 28% as of February 2010, compared to less than 8% for its predecessor the Royal Ulster Constabulary (RUC) pre-2001, and the force seems on track to meet its 30% target for Catholic recruitment by 2011.[4] There has also been an increase in female recruitment to the PSNI (currently 22%), and the service has recently announced the establishment of a Gay and Lesbian Police Officers Association—a development that would have been unthinkable just a few years ago.

While it is important to recognise that major advances in policing have been made in Northern Ireland and that the PSNI is arguably a more progressive and forward looking organisation than the RUC had been, it is, however, questionable whether the change process to date warrants some of the eulogies ascribed to it. In many ways the vigorous promotionalism regarding the 'success' of the transformation process has glossed over many fundamental difficulties, and it is not being churlish, but simply realistic, to suggest that there have been numerous setbacks and that many obstacles remain to be overcome. The reality is that the contours of police reform have followed developments in the broader political process in Northern Ireland, and both have depended on a degree of mutual dynamism to drive them forward. However, the stop-start nature of devolved government in Northern Ireland—the Assembly was suspended between October 2002 and May 2007—has undoubtedly impacted on policing developments. Indeed, it is probably more useful to take as the starting point for any assessment Sinn Féin's decision in May 2007 to take its seats on the Northern Ireland Policing Board—or 'day one for republicans' as Alex Maskey, Sinn Féin's Policing and Justice spokesperson put it.[5] The condition upon which this participation was based—devolving policing and criminal justice powers to the Northern Ireland Assembly—was only met in April 2010 after three years of political wrangling, and consequently it is too soon to assess properly the impact that this development is likely to have for local policing. Therefore, what we have currently in Northern Ireland is a situation in which at the institutional level, the mechanisms recommended by the ICP are up and running, but the position is rather less clear-cut at the level of cross-community *participation* in the working of the institutions and the degree to which the PSNI has been able to foster the trust of those communities traditionally most alienated from the police in the past. It is to this issue that I now turn.

This chapter is divided into three parts. In Part One, I outline the importance of community consent for policing in liberal democracies before sketching the nature of police–community relations in Northern Ireland during the decades of political conflict. I then consider whether the situation has changed in the aftermath of the ICP reforms, by examining recent survey data from the Northern Ireland Policing Board and the Northern Ireland Statistics and Research Agency. Part Two suggests that while official surveys are useful in highlighting trends in police–community relations over time, a more refined conceptual framework is required if we are to take stock of such relations in marginalised and alienated communities. It is in this context that we need to be clear that one of the main rationales for the ICP in the first place was to redress the severe legitimacy deficit between the police and working-class republican, and to a lesser extent, working-class loyalist communities historically in Northern Ireland. Drawing upon the ecological model of police–community relations proposed by scholars such as Sung[6] and Weitzer,[7] I suggest that any analysis needs to dig deeper and consider residential fragmentation, the spatial distribution of power, specific modalities of police–community relations across and between neighbourhoods and problematic assumptions about the nature of 'community' itself. In the context of Northern Ireland, it may well be the case that working-class loyalist and republican communities, as well as the young and the marginalised more generally, will have differing experiences of, and hence attitudes to, policing than those living in residential and suburban areas. In Part Three, I subject some elements of the ecological model of police–community relations to empirical scrutiny, by outlining the results of a recent research project assessing community attitudes to the PSNI, crime and victimisation in a staunchly republican area of North Belfast.

PART ONE: POLICE LEGITIMACY AND CONSENT

It is fair to say that Western governments and their public policing agencies devote a relatively large proportion of their time and energy to monitoring and assessing public attitudes to the police. Police managers for their part are generally fairly sensitive to charges that their organisation's standing in the community is low, or that they are under-performing in some aspect of their role, or to suggestions that they discriminate against some social groups rather than others. Certainly there is a particular sensitivity around the vexed issue of police/minority-ethnic relations in many jurisdictions, as illustrated by the furore surrounding the brutal beating of Rodney King in Los Angeles by the LAPD in 1991 and the botched investigation into the death of the black teenager Stephen Lawrence by the London Metropolitan Police in 1993. At one level this sensitivity to public attitudes—at least in the United Kingdom and North America—is the result of the managerialist turn in the public sector from the early 1980s, which in rhetorical terms saw the development of a 'customer' focus within the police organisation and a shift in emphasis from 'force' to 'service'. However, at a deeper structural level the focus on public attitudes has its roots in an assumed relationship between the citizenry and the police in liberal democracies, particularly those based on a common-law heritage.

Enshrined by Sir Robert Peel as a core foundational principle of the New Police of the Metropolis in 1829 (later to become the London Metropolitan Police), it is through the doctrine of public consent that the legitmacy of the police is said to be derived; this also implies that the police require the support of the public in order to do their job effec-tively. The official importance attached to public consent for policing is, as Mike Brogden has vociferously argued, 'not contrived' or some kind of 'ideological conspiracy'.[8] Rather, it represents 'a concrete ideology, a major and substantive view of the relation between civil society and the police'[9] that is pursued as the Holy Grail by a succession of chief police officers and strongly reiterated in organisational discourse.[10] The emer-gence of community-oriented policing (COP) as the dominant strategy in Western policing agencies from the 1980s was the consequence of a widening legitimacy deficit and an attempt to establish consent from within minority-ethnic communities in particular.[11] Community atti-tudes to the police assessed through opinion poll surveys and such like are seen as an important barometer of police legitimacy and are closely scrutinised by government ministers and police managers.

Considered historically it is difficult to argue that there existed widespread consent and legitimacy for policing in Northern Ireland, particularly from the Catholic/nationalist minority. Following the es-tablishment of the new northern state after partition under the Government of Ireland Act (1920), the organisational form of policing adopted in Northern Ireland was imported virtually wholesale from the Irish Colonial Model (ICM) associated with the Royal Irish Constabulary (RIC); this was, initially at least, to become the dominant organisational form for policing the length and breadth of the British Empire.[12] Space precludes a full discussion, but policing in Northern Ireland from the creation of the state was hardly 'normal' in a liberal-democratic sense, with officers in the predominantly Protestant Royal Ulster Constabulary (RUC) and its exclusively Protestant auxiliary, the Ulster Special Constabulary (USC), having as their 'key practice'[13] the control and management of nationalist dissent and protest.[14] This is not to deny that the RUC and USC performed ordinary or routine policing functions, nor is it to deny that in many areas across Northern Ireland policing operated in an atmosphere of relative calm; but it is to emphasise that in the final analysis, when push came to shove, the core function of the police became the historical one of managing (nationalist) dissent and protest.

Tensions between the unionist and nationalist communities were exacerbated during a phase of nationalist civil-rights mobilisation in the mid-1960s over what was perceived as discrimination by the Unionist government at Stormont.[15] By the end of the decade these tensions had spilled over into violent ethno-sectarian conflict and political unrest. The role of the RUC and USC in exacerbating the situation has been well documented,[16] and a similar point is made by Brendan O'Leary when he suggests:

> We must not, of course, ever forget that over 300 police officers were killed in the current conflict, but we must also not forget that the outbreak of armed conflict in 1969 was partly caused by an unreformed, half-legitimate police service, responsible for seven of the first eight deaths.[17]

By the end of the 1960s reform of the RUC had displaced *all* the other demands of the civil-rights campaigners—for instance in relation to employment and housing—to become *the* civil-rights issue.[18]

Following the slide into overt violence and confrontation from the 1970s onwards, and after a number of failed attempts by the British Army to deal with the deteriorating situation, a change in British security strategy (referred to as criminalisation and Ulsterisation) saw the RUC pushed to the forefront in the 'war' against the IRA, in particular. Escalating levels of violence and the threat posed by the IRA undoubtedly made policing a tremendously difficult and dangerous occupation in Northern Ireland. The dual role performed by the force—counter-terrorism and routine policing—meant that community policing, or anything resembling it, was well nigh impossible in many nationalist and republican areas. However, it was a number of practices stemming from the RUC's counter-terror mandate that had a deleterious impact on the support of the wider nationalist community for the police. Allegations of collusion with loyalist paramilitaries—which have been given credence in recent reports by Judge Cory[19] and the Police Ombudsman for Northern Ireland[20]—together with claims of a 'shoot-to-kill' policy against republican suspects; the indiscriminate use of plastic bullets; and the seeming inability or unwillingness of the police to take-on loyalist protestors—as evidenced with events at Drumcree[21] —all had a negative resonance with even middle-class nationalists.

A group-position perspective on police–community relations

In a systematic analysis of police–minority relations in the United States, Weitzer and Tuch[22] point to the variable levels of inter-group support for the police among members of white, Hispanic and African-American communities and attempt to explain why attitudes to the police are consistently more positive among whites of all social classes, slightly less so among Hispanics and considerably less so among African-Americans. They develop a 'group-position thesis' based on the sociological work of Herbert Blumer and which focuses the inter-play of power dynamics between various racial/ethnic groups. Expressed simply, this group-position thesis holds that dominant groups are mobilised by *perceived threats* to their way of life and their privileged position, while subordinate groups are mobilised by the *perceived advantages* of challenging the existing order.[23] If extended to an analysis of social institutions such as the criminal justice system and the police, the thesis holds that dominant groups will align themselves to those social institutions that are perceived as best serving their interests. Dominant groups see the police as 'allies',[24] and this goes some way to explaining the high levels of white support for the police in the United States, which as Weitzer and Tuch acknowledge, has 'traditionally been strong and widespread'.[25] There are also high levels of dominant group support in the US for tough law and order measures, providing these are directed towards the behaviour and activities of subordinate groups.

While Weitzer and Tuch's analysis is primarily concerned with explaining the ways in which police–community relations in the United States are fractured along racial lines, they note that their thesis is relevant, albeit in an exaggerated form, to an analysis of police–community relations in divided societies such as Northern Ireland.[26] Protestants and unionists of all persuasions have all traditionally viewed the RUC (even more so than the British Army) as the first line of defence for the protection of the Northern Irish state and have been strongly supportive of a tough law and order stance to deal with IRA violence. The RUC was organic—it was recruited mainly from within the Protestant/unionist community—and shared a genesis with the creation of the state itself. Indeed, in a series of heartfelt and emotional meetings that took place during the public consultation phase of the ICP reform process, the Commissioners noted that 'our focus group survey had examples of Protestants referring to "our" police, but none of Catholics doing so'.[27]

Protestant/unionist attachment to the RUC extended beyond the mundane, pragmatic or routine and into the realms of culture and emotion, and there was a very tangible sense in which members of this group saw their national identity refracted through the lens of the RUC, with the fear commonly held that the dismantling of the RUC was the first step towards the dismantling of the state.[28] Conversely, for many nationalists and republicans their relationship with the RUC veered from active hostility (virtually all republicans) to indifference (many nationalists). However, in a general sense there was quite simply a lack of trust, either in the state itself, or in its social institutions. Republicans may have borne the brunt of hard-edged policing tactics, but even middle-class nationalists in suburban or residential areas who were much less likely to have what is termed adversary contact with the police, were still much less likely than were their unionist counterparts to view the RUC positively. This bifurcation was explicitly recognised by the ICP in its report when it noted that 'in one political language they [the RUC] are the custodians of nationhood. In its rhetorical opposite they are the symbols of oppression'.[29]

If we examine survey data collected by the Northern Ireland Police Authority prior to the signing of the Belfast Agreement in 1998, it is clear that in both years under consideration—1996 and 1997—considerably fewer Catholic respondents rated the RUC's overall performance as 'very/fairly good' than did their Protestant counterparts (Table 1). The even more negative response in 1997 is probably accounted for by the serious crisis in RUC–Catholic relations as a consequence of the second Drumcree standoff in 1996.[30]

TABLE 1: PERFORMANCE OF RUC AS A WHOLE IN
NORTHERN IRELAND 1996–97

	% Protestant		% Catholic	
	1996	1997	1996	1997
Very/Fairly good	85	85	48	37
Neither good nor bad	8	5	16	20
Very/Fairly poor	6	6	33	39
Don't know/Refusal	1	1	3	3

Source: Police Authority for Northern Ireland, *Annual Report*, 1996–97

In terms of cross-community attitudes as to whether the RUC
needed to be reformed, an even starker picture emerges (Table 2).
When we aggregate the responses, an overwhelming majority of
Catholic respondents want to see some change to the RUC—although it is not immediately clear what the precise difference between
'replaced' and 'disbanded' might be—rising from 82% in 1996 to
86% in 1997. By contrast, Protestant respondents were almost universally in favour of allowing the RUC 'to carry on as now', with only a
small majority of respondents (4%) favouring 'replacement' and none
at all favouring 'disbandment'.

TABLE 2: THE FUTURE OF THE RUC

	% Protestant		% Catholic	
	1996	1997	1996	1997
Allowed to carry on as now	61	68	13	11
Reformed	32	26	46	52
Replaced	4	4	32	29
Disbanded	0	0	4	5
Don't know/Refusal	2	2	5	4

Source: Police Authority for Northern Ireland, *Annual Report*, 1996–97

Recent attitudinal survey evidence in relation to the PSNI

The data in Table 3 are based on attitudinal research commissioned by the Northern Ireland Policing Board in 2007, and show a fairly large upward swing in cross-community support for the PSNI in the aftermath of the ICP reforms. Two things are of note, however. First, the percentage of Catholic respondents expressing their general support for the PSNI is markedly higher than we noted in the discussions above in relation to its predecessor, and that fact alone is encouraging. Second, Catholic support for the PSNI increased from 69% to 75% following Sinn Féin's decision in May 2007 to lend its support to the PSNI and participate in the operation of the Policing Board and DPPs. This highlights the possibility that, for Catholics and nationalists, support for policing structures tends to ebb and flow with broader developments in the political sphere and that Sinn Féin's decision to lend its support for policing was crucial in this respect.

TABLE 3: CROSS-COMMUNITY SUPPORT FOR THE PSNI
PRE-/POST-SINN FÉIN DECISION, 2007

	% Protestant	% Catholic	% Overall
Pre-decision	84	69	78
Post-decision (May 2007)	83	75	80

Source: J. Byrne, *Policing loyalist and republican communities: understanding key issues for local communities and the PSNI*
(Institute for Conflict Research: Belfast, 2008), 31.

However, if we consider satisfaction with the practice of local policing, then things take on a slightly different complexion (Table 4). Data from four attitudinal surveys compiled by the Policing Board/Northern Ireland Statistics and Research Agency between October 2007 and April 2009 illustrate that when we disaggregate perceived *performance* from generalised *support*, then just over half of Catholics, and slightly under two-thirds of Protestants, rate the performance of their local police as 'fairly/very good'. However, the PSNI can perhaps take some cold comfort in the finding that similar proportions of Catholics and Protestants in each cohort rate the performance of their local PSNI as either 'very/fairly poor'—there is a cross-community consensus on this issue, at least!

Public views about the performance of local police are undoubtedly mediated by perceptions of crime and disorder in particular neighbourhoods and by the success or willingness of the police in responding to this. A number of factors influence perceptions of police performance at local level: the length of time taken to respond to a call; dealing with anti-social and nuisance behaviour; clear-up rates and the ability to implement successful community policing and crime-prevention initiatives. The PSNI, like many police organisations, faces difficulties in many of these areas and, in addition, has had to cope with budgetary cuts that have forced the closure of many smaller police stations. Perhaps the most important factor of all though, concerns the somewhat fragile nature of the political process in Northern Ireland, which, when coupled with the threat from dissident republicans, has meant that it is still extremely difficult for the PSNI to conduct routine patrols in some nationalist and republican areas. This makes it difficult for officers to respond immediately to calls for assistance, which serves to reinforce the view held among members of the public that the police are uninterested in tackling local crime.

TABLE 4: PERFORMANCE OF LOCAL POLICE 2007–09

Rating	Percentage of respondents											
	2007 OCT			2008 APR			2008 SEPT			2009 APR		
	C	P	ALL	C	P	ALL	C	P	ALL	C	P	ALL
Very/Fairly good	54	67	62	56	60	58	59	64	62	59	69	64
Neither good nor poor	21	16	19	21	21	21	20	16	18	24	14	18
Very/Fairly poor	23	16	19	20	18	19	19	18	18	16	15	16
Don't know/Refusal	1	0	1	3	2	2	2	2	2	1	1	1

Source: Northern Ireland Policing Board, *Annual Report*, 2008–09

PART TWO: TOWARDS AN ECOLOGICAL MODEL
OF POLICE–COMMUNITY RELATIONS

It should be stressed that the data presented above outline general trends in relation to police–community relations in Northern Ireland,

and taken at face value they suggest that there exists a broadly positive swathe of cross-community support for the PSNI, although this tails off somewhat when the performance of the police locally is factored in. However, while the survey data described above are useful in pointing to general trends, they are rather less useful in highlighting police–community relations in specific neighbourhoods and among specific social groups. There are two issues that arise here, a conceptual one and a methodological one. Both will be dealt with in turn in this part of the chapter.

In regard to the conceptual difficulties, a number of years ago I critiqued the use of official attitudinal survey data in assessing community attitudes to the police in Northern Ireland during the decades of conflict.[31] While it is not the intention to rehearse my arguments again here, some aspects of the earlier discussion are relevant to the current chapter. Drawing upon the work of Colin Sumner in relation to social censure,[32] I examined the role that official attitudinal surveys played in manufacturing consent for policing in Northern Ireland and argued that they could be seen as an instrument of 'censure' insofar as they consistently under-represented and negated those views and opinions critical of the RUC. Therefore, one of the most consistent problems with the use of conventional attitudinal surveys in relation to the police is that they invariably overstate positive opinion and understate negative opinion. There are many reasons for this, but the main flaw is that randomised sampling techniques simply do not accurately reflect the experiences of those neighbourhoods that are subject to denser and harsher policing tactics and those social groups who are likely to have adversary contact with and thus express negative attitudes to the police.

In methodological terms, researchers have traditionally found it difficult if not impossible to draw a representative sample population from within staunchly republican and loyalist communties in Northern Ireland. In such areas there is a deep-seated suspicion of outsiders, particularly when they are asking questions about such a sensitive issue as policing; in one particular case a census worker was murdered, while others have faced the risk of attack.[33] The implications that this can have for social surveys can be seen from the Northern Ireland Social Attitudes Survey (NISAS), which for several years in the mid-1990s included a sub-set of questions about policing and justice in Northern Ireland. Generally, the NISAS data suggested that there was a relatively high level of public support for the RUC, but the data itself was flawed in that it excluded extremes of political opinion. For instance, the sample included just over 2.5% declared republicans, even though Sinn Féin was polling upwards of 17% in elections during the period, and its supporters would have been highly unlikely to express positive attitudes about the RUC. Conversely, 'moderate' opinion represented by Alliance Party supporters was over-represented, even though this party rarely obtains even 10% of the total vote in Northern Ireland and its supporters would be unlikely to have had adversary contact with the police.[34] The general point that we can make here is that it is difficult to conduct attitudinal research in a conflicted context such as Northern Ireland. However, even when methodological defects are corrected for, all that traditional attitudinal research can alert us to are general trends in police–community relations; they tell us next to nothing about the particular relationship between the police and traditionally marginalised groups. In Northern Ireland this represents a serious anomaly, given that community dissatisfaction about policing in republican (and to a lesser extent loyalist) areas of Northern Ireland was a prime motivating factor for the ICP reforms in the first place.

Just as criminologists recognised nearly two decades ago that crime was not distributed uniformly across society, rather it was concentrated in particular locales and neighbourhoods—or 'hotspots' in the parlance of contemporary crime analysts—so too are policing scholars recognising that police–citizen interactions are also determined spatially by neighbourhood context. As Ron Weitzer puts it, '…in terms of police treatment of citizens, where one lives matters as much or more than individual characteristics', such as officer behaviour and so forth.[35]

Sung[36] has also attempted to navigate the spatial variability in police–citizen interactions by proposing an ecological model that goes some way towards shedding conceptual light on the differential standards of policing experienced by various social groups. Drawing upon the insights advanced by the Chicago School of Urban Ecology in the 1930s, which emphasised the role of space and place in the aetiology of crime, Sung's thesis is simply that the political-economy of neighbourhoods determines policing context, which in turn determines the nature of police–community interaction. Structural characteristics of neighbourhoods, levels of deprivation and wealth, the extent of social and other problems, population demographics, levels of crime and disorder all configure the behaviour and attitudes of citizens to the police, and of the police to citizens. Middle-class residential and suburban neighbourhoods are relatively crime-free, and calls to the police from such neighbourhoods, if they occur at all, usually involve requests for

assistance of one form or another. Conversely, inner-city neighbourhoods, particularly those that suffer from high levels of social and
economic deprivation, are significantly underprotected, with the police
unwilling or unable to respond to the many social problems, for
example around drugs, alcohol, nuisance and anti-social behaviour by
teenagers, that tend to blight them. Paradoxically, however, such areas
provide the staple of police business and are comprised of those social
groups that the police have traditionally viewed as 'their property'.[37]
What we typically find in urban working-class deprived areas then, are
parallel processes of underprotection and punitive law-enforcement.

As Ron Weitzer suggests:[38]

> A combination of *depolicing* and *harsh policing* is often
> characteristic of disorganised, poor neighbourhoods. On
> the one hand, the police approach to these neighbour-
> hoods tends to be marked by unresponsiveness to calls
> from residents, poor service when they arrive at a call, or
> general underenforcement of the law. On the other
> hand, residents of these communities are often the
> targets of overly aggressive police behaviour.

The starting point for any assessment of police–community interaction therefore needs to dig deeper at the neighbourhood level, and
Sung[39] constructs a typology to explain how such interactions manifest
themselves in terms of the police perception of: (a) the *moral respectabil-
ity/social power* of particular neighbourhoods and their inhabitants, and
(b) the perceived *marginality/centrality* of particular neighbourhoods
and their inhabitants to dominant group interests and political structures. Police–community interactions are of course, first and foremost,
founded on the individual officer's reading of the situation—'situation-
ally applied rules' in Manning's terminology[40]—but there is also a huge
repertoire of accumulated knowledge that comes into play based on
the assessment of particular neighbourhoods and social groups. This
has been accumulated and transmitted within the occupational culture
of the organisation over time, and may even be given an official impri-
matur in force policy and procedure.[41] As Sung suggests:

> [A person's] residence in a 'marked' neighbourhood is
> often used by the police as a general indicator for iden-
> tifying potential offenders. Varying social conditions—
> the presence of danger in the community, the political
> complexion of the community, the demographic dissim-

ilarity of the population—all contribute to the conception of the criminal held by the police. Based on this judgement they develop rules about what deviance should be handled, and how crime should be processed in accordance with the wealth, education, respectability and conventionality of local residents.[42]

Community and the ecology of police–community relations in Northern Ireland

Mulcahy has pointed to the problematic usage of 'community' in such concepts as 'community-oriented policing' on the basis that it homogenises the policing experiences of very divergent social groups.[43] Certainly, any assessment of policing in urban, working-class areas of Belfast and Derry/Londonderry—particularly republican and loyalist communities—would have to concede that the PSNI are not at this current moment in time making the much vaunted and hoped-for community impact. As we shall see in Part Three of this chapter, recent research conducted within a staunchly nationalist/republican district of Belfast suggests that much work remains to be done by the police service in establishing the trust and support of local residents.

At one level the policing problems affecting urban, working-class loyalist and republican communities are different and rooted in politics, history and culture; however, at another they are strikingly similar and are structural in origin. Both communities are afflicted by extremely high levels of socio-economic deprivation, and data from the Northern Ireland Index of Multiple Deprivation indicates that the top-twenty electoral wards with the highest deprivation scores are all majority loyalist and republican communities that have borne the brunt of the conflict. However, there are also specific issues at play. In republican areas the impasse in the political process, the refusal until 2007 by Sinn Féin either to lend its support to the PSNI or to participate in the structures for police governance and oversight, and the very real threat posed by dissident republicans have all in their own way contributed to a policing vacuum, and in the absence of any other form of community controls, crime—both serious and low-level—has flourished. For example, in Belfast the five electoral wards recording the highest rates of violent assaults in 2007–08 were all in designated nationalist/republican areas, and the assault rates in all five were considerably higher than the city average. However, as we shall discuss later, the PSNI response to the situation of crime and criminality in many working class areas—and it makes little difference here whether they are republican or loyalist—has been somewhat lacklustre.

In some respects, the PSNI is finding it difficult to respond to (often stratospheric) community expectations about what is achievable, but it is also fair to say that the force has not as yet developed a clear and coherent strategy for dealing with crime—particularly low-level crime in urban, working class areas. For Dawn Purvis—leader of the Progressive Unionist Party (PUP) and until recently a political representative on the Northern Ireland Policing Board—the PSNI's 'Policing with the Community' strategy has drifted aimlessly, and has suffered from a rather mechanical 'bolt on' approach rather than being something integrated into an entire policing philosophy.[44] Much of what has occurred thus far has been fairly unimaginative (such as Neighbourhood Watch and the use of CCTV), with a number of piecemeal and ad hoc initiatives substituting for any grand vision in relation to local crime. Several commentators have also pointed to the rather traditionalist mindset that permeates official discussions of crime and anti-social behaviour in Northern Ireland, with a failure to move beyond the police–crime binary and see Northern Ireland's diverse community infrastructure as an important resource for tackling low-level crime and disorder.[45] Of course, while we need to be realistic about what the police are capable of doing by themselves, the cumulative impact of all this is to reinforce to local residents—many of whom are unaccustomed to civil policing and who have memories of policing during the conflict—that the PSNI is either unwilling or unable to take crime in their neighbourhood seriously.

As noted earlier, the PSNI has made tremendous strides over the course of the past ten years in recruiting from the Catholic community. However, in terms of recruiting Catholics specifically from predominantly nationalist/republican working-class areas, the situation is less clear cut. Although Consensia (the private consortium that oversees recruitment to the PSNI) does not publicly release a detailed demographic breakdown of recruitment, there is little evidence that young people from such backgrounds are applying to join the PSNI in large numbers. This is not simply a pedantic point, but reflects the very different experiences and expectations of middle- and working-class Catholics in Northern Ireland and the degree to which they may feel threatened or ostracised for joining the PSNI.[46] A community development worker in the Falls area of Belfast commented in 2005 (admittedly before Sinn Féin signed up to policing) that 'Those people joining the police [PSNI] are middle-class Catholics, they don't represent the kids here. If you had young nationalists or republicans joining then that would be progress'.[47] He went on to note that he could see little evidence of this happening at that particular point in time. Certainly, this view seems to be supported by recent research by McAlister, Scraton and Haydon, which among other things assessed young people's attitudes to the police in predominantly loyalist and re-publican areas. As they note:

> ...young people's responses were similar to those of adults. While their attitudes were informed by adults, they also reflected personal experiences. Within some communities, historical resistance to the police, past ex-perience of discriminatory policing and heavy-handed tactics, had been passed down. None of the young people in Republican/Nationalist communities trusted the police'.[48]

This situation is mirrored to a large extent in traditional working-class loyalist districts. One of the most staunchly loyalist districts of Belfast—the Shankill—has the highest index of multiple deprivation anywhere in Northern Ireland[49] and is beset with social problems stemming from long-term structural unemployment and decades of political conflict. Loyalists, also for reasons to do with politics, history and culture, have had a somewhat more ambivalent relationship with the RUC in Northern Ireland: supporting the service when it was seen to be tackling republican violence but resenting it when it was re-routing Orange Order marches and so forth. However, as Dawn Purvis points out, 'the RUC never policed the Shankill [loyalist area of Belfast] "normally"…There was always a disconnect between the police and working-class loyalist communities'.[50] Certainly, the Progressive Unionist Party was alone among Northern Ireland's unionist parties in supporting the recommendations of the ICP on the basis that fair, effective and accountable policing applied to loy-alist communities too.

In relation to the current situation with policing in loyalist areas and community relations with the PSNI, Purvis describes it as 'a work in progress', noting that while loyalist communities want to see a fair and effective policing service, the PSNI's seeming inability to deal with low-level offending and anti-social behaviour is having a serious impact on confidence in the new policing structures. She also adds that during the past ten years not a single working-class loyalist from the Shankill area of Belfast has been recruited to the PSNI, a fact that was corroborated by the then chief constable, Sir Hugh Orde.[51] Purvis is philosophical about this point—blaming it in part on the educational system whereby Protestant working-class males in Northern Ireland have one of the highest rates of educational under-achievement in the United Kingdom; but she also argues that young people cannot have confidence or trust in a policing system if they do not see their friends, neighbours or family members recruited to it.

What I have suggested thus far is that the police reform process in Northern Ireland has been quite successful at the level of establishing the institutional structures for policing, but much less evidently so in establishing cross-community participation with the PSNI. Drawing upon the ecological model outlined earlier, it is clear that higher levels of support exist for the PSNI among those groups and in those areas where the practice of policing is largely service-orientated, and where the potential for adversary contact is minimised. Conversely, among the urban poor, and loyalist and republican working-class communities in particular, the picture is much more ambiguous and levels of trust and confidence in the PSNI remain low. In the following section I outline a research project conducted in the staunchly republican/nationalist area of New Lodge, Belfast, and suggest that in spite of the current failings in the delivery of policing there may be a glimmer of hope here.

PART THREE: THE NEW LODGE
COMMUNITY CRIME SURVEY

In August 2008 the author (along with Dr Peter Shirlow from Queen's University Belfast) was commissioned by the New Lodge Community Empowerment Partnership (CEP) to undertake research into crime and policing in the New Lodge area of North Belfast.[52] The research was the first of its kind to be conducted exclusively within a staunchly republican area of Northern Ireland, and the only research to focus specifically on policing and crime issues following Sinn Féin's May 2007 decision to join the Policing Board. In spite of Sinn Féin's endorsement, there still existed a high level of community nervousness and suspicion about proactively engaging with the PSNI, and for the New Lodge CEP the research would perform two functions. First, it could be taken as a local community referendum on whether or not to engage with the PSNI and on what basis this engagement should take place. Second, it would provide some unique empirical data about levels of crime and victimisation in the area, as well as about people's experiences of policing since the ICP reforms. Sinn Féin played no role whatsoever in commissioning the research, project design, data collection or the analysis and subsequent dissemination of the findings.

New Lodge: Background and demographics[53]

New Lodge is an inner-city district in Belfast that is highly segregated in religious terms (97.3% Catholic in the 2001 Census of Population)[54] and is bounded to its east and west by the Shankill and Duncairn electoral wards, which are predominantly unionist/loyalist communities. The boundary to the west with Duncairn is physically demarcated by a series of interface walls. This particular interface is the second highest recorded site for sectarian crime within the city.[55]

According to the 2001 Census of Population,[56] New Lodge is the fifth most deprived of all 582 electoral wards in Northern Ireland. The population in 2001 was 5,224, of which 40% are aged under 25 and 25% aged under 16. The population density, at 72.95 per hectare, is 3 times higher than the average for Belfast. High levels of social, health and other forms of deprivation are indicated in a range of community needs and difficulties. The Standardised Mortality Ratio in New Lodge (2001–05) was twice that of the city average. In addition, only 3.2% of New Lodge residents possess a third-level educational qualification, compared to the city average of 19.2%. The number of post-primary school pupils with Free School Meal entitlements runs at over 70%, while the economic activity rate is 26.8% below the average for the city. The share of residents who are economically inactive and who claim housing benefit are both twice as high as the city average, and home ownership is extremely low. Small Area Income Estimates presented for the period 2003–05, as measured by the proportion of households whose income is below the UK median household income, showed that just over half (52.5%) of all households in New Lodge were living just on or slightly above the poverty line.[57]

Crime and victimisation in New Lodge

There has long been a recognition of the disproportionate impact of crime on urban, working-class communities, which led a number of criminologists in the mid-1980s to propose conducting 'local victimisation studies' that sought—in line with the ecological model proposed above in Part Two of this chapter—to assess crime, victim-isation and experiences of policing in relation to 'place'.[58] Because of their more concentrated geographical focus, such surveys suggest far higher rates of crime and victimisation than are revealed in national level data, and they further reveal that those areas that rank highly on some indices of socio-economic deprivation also tend to have markedly higher levels of criminal victimisation.

Local surveys also emphasise the cumulative nature of much crim-inal victimisation: that it occurs not as a one-off, but multiple times over a longer period of time. There has been a tendency in national surveys to dismiss much victimisation as 'trivial', particularly that as-sociated with petty crime and anti-social behaviour. However, the New Lodge research suggests that, by contrast, significant numbers of respondents, particularly women and the elderly, regard such activ-ities as 'non-trivial' and that cumulative instances of vandalism or other anti-social activity over a period of time have a serious and dele-terious impact on an individual's quality of life. Finally, local victimisation surveys inform us about police performance in urban, working-class areas and alert us to a growing perceptual disparity between what the public want from the police (*i.e.* to deal with anti-social behaviour, public drunkenness, noisy neighbours, kids on the street, vandalism, etc.) and what the police think the public need (*i.e.* an organisation solving serious crime, and so forth). What local neigh-bourhood surveys have done, as Jock Young suggests, is 'shift the focus of crime away from what are traditionally police priorities to those which are the priorities of the wider public'.[59] This disparity, at least from the point of view of the residents in the New Lodge area, is borne out starkly in the results of the August 2008 research.

The 'Dark Figure' of crime in New Lodge

As part of the research undertaken in New Lodge, respondents were asked whether they had been the victim of crime during the recall period (Table 5). What is immediately obvious from the data is that levels of crime and victimisation in the New Lodge area are considerably higher than those depicted in both the Northern Ireland Crime Survey (NICS)[60] and the British Crime Survey (BCS).[61] This is the case for all offences recorded in the 2008 New

Lodge survey. Of course, we need to be careful about reading too much across from one survey to another, particularly where a different methodological approach may have been deployed and different catégories of offences listed. While the data in Table 5 are illustrative only, they are nevertheless comparable with prevalence rates recorded by other local victimisation surveys conducted in England that suggest higher rates than those recorded in national-level data.[62]

TABLE 5: RESPONDENTS' EXPERIENCE OF CRIME
COMPARED TO NICS/BCS

Type of crime	NLS % 2008	NICS %[1] 2007/08	BCS %[2] 2007/08
Vandalism to home/vehicle/other property	39.27	4.8	7.3
Burglary	15.38	1.2	2.4
Theft/attempted theft of vehicle	13.41	3.0	6.4
Physical assault	10.57	1.8	3.3
Theft from person	10.16	1.6	3.5
Any violent crime	6.91	2.6	2.8
Street robbery/Mugging/Snatch theft	3.66	0.1	0.7

Notes: [1] R. Freel, D. Quigley and S. Toner, *Experience of crime: findings from the 2007/08 Northern Ireland crime survey* Research Bulletin 1/2009 (Belfast: Northern Ireland Office, Statistics and Research Branch, 2009). [2] C. Kershaw, S. Nicholas and A. Walker, *Crime in England and Wales 2007–2008: findings from the British crime survey and police recorded crime* Home Office Statistical Bulletin 07/08 (London: Home Office, 2008).

Reporting crime to the PSNI

The issue of reporting such crime to the PSNI was also assessed. In sum, 413 incidences of crime were recalled by respondents during the recall period and of these 230 incidents (55.69%) had not been reported to the PSNI. This high level of non-reporting is close to the Islington Crime Survey average (49.9%) but higher than the Northern Ireland average (40%) and the GB average (42%). Criminologists are aware that there is a high level of non-reporting to police; a fact evidenced across any number of jurisdictions. In general terms people do not report crime to the police for a variety of reasons. For instance, they may feel that the police are unable to do anything about it; that the police will not believe them; that the police are too busy; that the matter is too embarrassing; that the victim is too scared; that the victim is afraid of reprisals; or that the incident is considered too trivial.[63]

However, the level of under-reporting tends to be more acute in those areas, such as New Lodge, where there have been historical problems around the nature and character of public policing, and a sense that the police are either unable or unwilling to do anything about crime levels in the area. It is often the case that people will report an incident to the police simply for insurance purposes, but in deprived communities such as New Lodge some households may not have house or home contents insurance, and a significant number may not have motor vehicle insurance either. This aside, such high levels of non-reportage are an important barometer of the nature of public confidence in the police, and as Trevor Jones and his colleagues emphasise in the Islington Crime Survey, '...one thing is eminently clear from the Islington Crime Survey data: there is an alarming lack of confidence in the local police's ability to deal with crime'.[64] They further suggest that it is precisely this lack of confidence about police effectiveness that serves to reinforce or justify even higher levels of non-reporting in the future.

Policing, crime and anti-social behaviour

Respondents were asked a series of questions regarding what the PSNI's policing priorities should be in the New Lodge area (Table 6). When participants were asked to select priorities for the PSNI in terms of targeting their resources and policing strategies, the following emerged (in order of most frequently cited). Illegal drug use, under-age drinking, physical assaults, sectarian violence, burglary and street robbery were all ranked by more than half of respondents as priority areas for the PSNI to tackle. Issues that had a nuisance/anti-social quality—people hanging around the street, noisy neighbours, family rows, and graffiti—were also flagged up by respondents; but the key issue that concerned respondents in anti-social terms and which was mentioned by over half of respondents in the sample was 'people hanging around the streets'.

The high level of importance attached to anti-social behaviour by respondents resonates with the signal-disorders[65] perspective developed by Martin Innes and which has informed the UK Home Office Reassurance Policing Programme.[66] Signal disorders—which may include behaviours such as drinking or 'hanging out' on the street—are those that impart a series of semiotic 'signals' (or messages) to local residents about the 'state' of a particular neighbourhood, and which influence perceptions of risk and security. Of course, it is by no means axiomatic that all residents will interpret such signals in the same way—young people and elderly residents are likely to be at variance for instance. Nevertheless, according to the signal-disorders perspective, when enough people interpret the signal in a particular way this can impact negatively on generalised feelings of ontological security, and in the absence of any meaningful social control mechanisms, can exert a disruptive effect on local neighbourhood order. Certainly, the public appears to be *as* concerned about the 'signals' emanating from anti-social behaviour as about the signals from serious crime, since the former is seen to signify a lack of respect, the invasion of public/private spaces and is often suggestive of a dismissive and contemptuous attitude on the part of the perpetrator(s). Compared to those acts or behaviours where there is a clear line between legality and illegality and where there is scope for definitive action, cumulative exposure to anti-social behaviour can result in heightened feelings of helplessness and powerlessness quite simply because of its irregularly patterned and elusive character.

Of course, we need to be realistic about what the police can be expected to do (by themselves) in relation to anti-social behaviour. A number of the issues identified above (for example noisy neighbours) are the responsibility of Belfast City Council's Environmental Health Department; while in regard to 'people hanging around streets', the legal justification for police intervention may be unclear, particularly if no obvious offence is being committed. Indeed, there is a fine line here between the police deciding to act by moving young people on, and the perception (very often held by young people) that they are being 'picked on' by the police. Nevertheless, what this suggests is that the public and the PSNI may have contrary views regarding what crimes/behaviours need to be targeted for priority attention, and a much more fluid information exchange between the community residents and the PSNI seems to be required.

TABLE 6: WHAT SHOULD THE PSNI
TARGET ITS RESOURCES ON IN THIS AREA?

Activity	%
Illegal drug use	81.2
Under-age drinking	77.9
Physical assaults	73.2
Car theft	71.1
Interface/sectarian violence	71.1
Burglary	68.2
Mugging/Street Robbery	64.6
People hanging around the streets	63.1
Noisy neighbours	20.9
Family rows	20.9
Graffiti	18.4

The PSNI's response to crime

What emerges strongly from the New Lodge survey data is that a majority of respondents simply do not have confidence in the PSNI's ability to deal with crime in the New Lodge area (Table 7). For instance, if we aggregate the responses, just over half of participants in the survey (51.5%) believed the PSNI's response to crime in the New Lodge area to be either 'very poor' or 'fairly poor', with only a minority of respondents (12.5%) stating that it was 'fairly good' or 'very good'. On the other hand, a large number of respondents (27.8%)—who either could not decide or did not want to say—stated that the PSNI's performance was 'neither good nor poor'. Again, there is a considerable divergence here from the Northern Ireland average, in which almost two-thirds (65.0%) of respondents to the Northern Ireland Crime Survey (NICS) felt that the PSNI was 'doing a good job'.[67]

TABLE 7: PERCEPTIONS OF THE PSNI'S RESPONSE TO CRIME
WITHIN THE GREATER NEW LODGE AREA

How do you rate the PSNI's response to crime within this area?	N	%
Very good	9	3.2
Fairly good	26	9.3
Neither good nor poor	77	27.8
Fairly poor	39	14.0
Very poor	104	37.5
Don't know/Not sure	22	7.9

In terms of how well the PSNI is perceived in regard to tackling anti-social behaviour, just over half of respondents in the New Lodge survey felt that that the PSNI was not effective (53.6%), compared to only 15.4% of respondents who felt that the police were effective in this role (Table 8). Again, we can draw parallels with the signal crimes perspective discussed above and the results of other local victimisation surveys, such as the Islington Crime Survey, which suggest very strongly that visible symbols of neighborhood decay (litter, broken-down cars, vandalism, graffiti) and manifestations of anti-social behavior (public drinking, kids hanging around on the street, noisy neighbours) are linked in the public's mind to a heightened sense of awareness, worry or anxiety about crime per se. What this means for public perceptions of the police is that in order for the police to be seen to be having a positive impact on crime, they *also* need to be seen to be having a positive impact on anti-social behavior, since both issues are linked in the public consciousness. Clearly, in the case of the data from the New Lodge area, this is not happening at this present point in time.

TABLE 8: PERCEPTIONS OF THE PSNI'S TACKLING ANTI-SOCIAL BEHAVIOUR

Is the PSNI tackling anti-social behavior in an effective way?	N	%
Yes	43	15.4
No	150	53.6
Don't know	56	20.0
Does not apply/no answer	27	9.6

Contacting the police

In terms of reporting a crime directly to the PSNI, just over half of the New Lodge respondents (51.99%) said that they would do this. However, the body most likely to be contacted if a crime needed to be reported was a community group (61.73%) such as the New Lodge CEP. The PSNI can perhaps take some encouragement from the fact that a majority of respondents—albeit an extremely slim one—would contact the police service directly to report crime, but what is perhaps more striking is that so many respondents would use a local community group or organisation as a surrogate to indirectly report a crime to the PSNI. Community organisations are clearly trusted within communities and are an important source of local capital. Their particular place within the community and the role that they can play in crime prevention and dealing with anti-social behaviour is an important resource that can and should be utilised by the PSNI. However, this needs to be done from a position of mutual trust and respect, and the situation whereby the police assume the position of dominant actor should be guarded against.

Perceptions of policing

Respondents were also asked about their perception of policing and whether they felt it had changed in respect of the ICP reforms of the past few years (Table 9). Just over one-third of respondents (35.14%) felt that 'positive change' had occurred within policing, with just under one-quarter of the sample disagreeing (24.28%). However, a similar proportion appeared to be undecided, stating that they 'didn't know' (25.36%), with a further 15.22% not answering the question.

When we cross-tabulate this question by the age of respondents there is little difference in the responses of people in the various age cohorts (Table 10). While there are minor differences these are not significant in statistical terms, and broadly similar numbers of respondents in each age cohort felt that the police 'have changed positively', 'have not changed' and 'did not/would not' answer the question. The only statistically significant response concerns the majority of respondents aged 65+, who felt that policing has changed positively (62.5%). If we cross-tabulate the results by gender (Table 11), slightly more males (40.1%) than females (32.0%) felt that policing had changed for the better. However, as was the case with the other questions relating to the issue of policing, a sizeable number of respondents refused to be drawn, stating that they 'didn't know' or refused to answer the question.

Overall, it is difficult to draw any definitive conclusions from the New Lodge data relating to respondents' perceptions of policing. A significant minority of respondents feel that policing has changed in a positive way, but this is offset by those respondents who do not know or who remain ambivalent and those who do not answer the question. What this may tell us is that people's overall impression of policing is structured by their perception of signal disorders, with the feeling that the PSNI is making little headway in relation to dealing with crime and anti-social activity. Equally, it may well be the case that perceptions of the police are still heavily interlaced with historical memories, while the fragility of the political process and the uncertainty over devolved policing arrangements during the time of the survey may have reflected a degree of ambivalence on the part of respondents. The survey data suggest that while respondents are somewhat circumspect about the PSNI's performance in dealing with crime and anti-social behaviour, there nevertheless is a strong sense that residents in New Lodge are keen for community organisations to work closely with the police to target crime and anti-social activity.

The role that community organisations can play as communicative conduits between residents and the police is a vitally important one. However, it is important that both the police and the 'community' be aware of what each other's limits are: the officers of the PSNI cannot and will not control anti-social behaviour by themselves; they depend on community support to perform this role and this is something that the community (public) needs to understand and accept. Conversely, the PSNI must be aware of community sentiment. Too

TABLE 9: IS POLICING CHANGING POSITIVELY %

Policing is changing in a positive way?	N	%
Yes	97	35.14
No	67	24.28
Don't know	70	25.36
Does not apply / no answer	42	15.22
Total	276	100

TABLE 10: IS POLICING CHANGING POSITIVELY % (BY AGE GROUP)

Age Group	Yes	No	Don't Know	Does Not Apply/No Answer	N
16–21	32.6	32.6	32.6	2.1	46
22–30	33.3	24.4	26.6	15.5	45
31–45	35.7	22.8	28.5	12.8	70
45–64	17.9	26.8	28.3	26.8	67
65+	62.5	14.5	8.3	14.5	48
Total					276

TABLE 11: IS POLICING CHANGING POSITIVELY % (BY GENDER)

Gender	Yes	No	Don't Know	No Answer	N
Male	40.1	24.5	19.6	15.5	122
Female	32.0	22.6	30.6	14.6	150
Total					272

often partnerships fail because the police become the main power-broker and agenda-setter in such relationships. This benefits neither the police nor the public and should be guarded against. The PSNI must recognise the salience of anti-social activities in people's lives since very often it is the small things that matter and minor problems have a tendency to escalate unless they are addressed.

Historically, while police managers have paid lip service to the ideals of neighbourhood and community policing, this has not been matched by resources or prioritised in any tangible way 'on the ground', since the 'successes' of such initiatives are sometimes difficult to discern and cannot easily be quantified in managerialist terms. Likewise, for many officers, status and prestige are seen to lie with re-active policing and high-profile detective work. However, there is an abundance of research evidence that suggests that while members of the public value the police's criminal investigation prowess, they also, and perhaps even more so, want quality-of-life issues addressed. A high-profile murder investigation in another part of the country might arouse a passing interest, but it is the group of teenagers drinking cider up an alleyway that the public wants dealt with as an immediate priority. This is perhaps a lesson that senior police managers have been rather slow in learning.

CONCLUSIONS

This chapter has provided an overview of the state of police–community relations since the ICP published its recommendations in September 1999. A central theme has been that the ICP reforms have been relatively successful at the institutional level—in establishing the institutions for police governance and oversight, for example—but arguably less so at the cross-community participative level. Similarly, we can point to a generalised level of cross-community support for the PSNI, but when we apply the ecological analysis to the situation in particular communities and neighbourhoods, such support tends to be considerably more variable. There are, and remain, particular difficulties in relation to the policing of local crime. Of course, in many respects the situation in Belfast is little different to that found in any large urban environment with pockets of socio-economic deprivation, whether it be Liverpool, Manchester or Dublin. Nevertheless, given the relative fragility of police-community relations in Northern Ireland it assumes a particular importance, since a failure of the police to deal with local crime and disorder may be interpreted teleologically as signifying the failure of the new policing structures generally, and perhaps by a further teleology to a perceived failure of the new political institutions and the peace process.[68] In relation to the latter, the perceived failure of the PSNI to deal with the resurgent threat from dissident republicans is interpreteted by many others—though particularly unionists—in much the same way.

However, three further issues may serve to impede whatever progress has been made in relation to policing. The first is organisational and relates to the change process itself. In August 2009 an internal confidential report compiled by the PSNI's Senior Command Team was leaked to the media. The document, entitled *Strategic review: making choices for the future*,[69] paints a rather gloomy assessment of the overall state of policing in Northern Ireland. It notes that progress has been made in a number of key areas, Catholic recruitment for example, but it nevertheless identifies an organisation that lacks any kind of strategic vision, suffers from retention problems and high levels of absenteeism, is wallowing under the weight of paperwork and bureaucracy, and appears to have lost the plot in relation to average clear-up rates, which by 2008 had fallen to 20%. Clearly, no change process is going to be without its difficulties; but that these issues have been identified ten years into the ICP implementation process suggests an organisation that is struggling to cope with the pressures of change and in adapting to the new policing dispensation.

The second problem is rooted in politics and the fragile nature of the political process. What the situation in relation to policing in Northern Ireland has demonstrated over the course of the past ten years is that police reform and political change tend to be two sides of the same coin, and that movement or inertia in one impacts either negatively or positively on the other. Certainly, the difficulties around devolved government and the suspension at various times of the Northern Ireland Assembly have tended to inhibit cross-community participation in policing and have contributed to the creation of a policing vacuum. In fact, since Sinn Féin only lent its support to the new policing structures in 2007, it is still too early to make any grand predictions about the relationship between the police service and nationalist and republican communities. While there was a desire on the part of respondents in the New Lodge survey to work with the PSNI to deal with a host of community problems around anti-social behaviour, this was a view not universally held, and there still remains a lack of trust between communities such as this and the police. Arguably, the situation is little better in loyalist areas. Nevertheless, that republicans are prepared to deal with the PSNI even minimally, should in Northern Ireland be taken as a sign of progress, however tentative it may seem at this point.

Police reform—along with prisoner releases—was one of the most difficult and sensitive areas of the entire Northern Ireland peace process, and during the negotiation stage it was put on the long finger by local politicians fearing it could derail the entire process.[70] However, the spectre of policing may yet come back to haunt Northern Ireland's power-sharing Assembly. While the devolution of policing and justice powers was returned to Stormont as of the 12 April 2010, how the new Justice Ministry will operate in practice remains something of an unknown quantity. It may well turn out to be a somewhat bumpy ride for the new Justice Minister, particularly if the—not quite hypothetical—situation arises where the minister is called upon by the PSNI to authorise electronic surveillance against local politicans or their close associates,[71] or is requested to re-open inquests into cold-case deaths arising from the conflict.[72] There is also the danger that the Justice Ministry will simply become a lightning rod for the mutual antagonisms of the larger political parties such as the DUP and Sinn Féin, particularly in relation to issues around policing and security policy. Both these parties have to 'manage' their core support base, and increasingly this has resulted in them taking positions that are less than conciliatory.

The third and final problem is represented by the rise of dissident republican activity by the Real IRA and Continuity IRA.[73] It is difficult to know with any degree of certainty what level of tacit support dissident republicans have within the broader republican community, but Sinn Féin has to ensure that republican waverers are not actively driven to sympathise with dissidents' aims by a botched anti-terrorist operation by the PSNI, or indeed by anti-terrorist operations more generally.[74] However, the growing threat from dissident groups makes such policing operations more, not less, likely. Parallels with the situation that emerged between the pro- and anti-Treaty factions prior to the Irish Civil War (1922–3) are probably a bit wide of the mark, but Sinn Féin is having to perform an increasingly delicate balancing act between lending its full support to the PSNI against claims by disaffected republicans that the party has sold out. Conversely, the DUP favours a tough security response to the dissident republican threat, evidenced by Ian Paisley Junior's controversial call for the PSNI to shoot dissident republican activists on sight.[75] Clearly this call is un- likely to be heeded, but increasingly unionists are becoming more vociferous in their demands for tougher law-and-order tactics against dissident groups, and it may be the case that some loyalist paramilitary organisations decide to take matters into their own hands.[76] These uncertainties do not bode particularly well for long-term policing de- velopments, and all that has been achieved thus far could well be unravelled by a deterioration in the political or security situation. This, perhaps, remains the biggest challenge facing Northern Ireland in the future.

NOTES

[1] The Belfast/Good Friday Agreement was signed in 1998; the text of the agreement is available at: http://foreignaffairs.gov.ie/uploads/documents/Anglo-Irish/agreement.pdf.
[2] Independent Commission on Policing for Northern Ireland, *A new beginning for policing in Northern Ireland* (Belfast: Northern Ireland Office, 1999), 123. (henceforth cited as *Patten Report*).
[3] Northern Ireland Policing Board, *Annual Report 2008–2009* (Belfast: Northern Ireland Policing Board, 2009), 7.
[4] Further details are available at: http://www.publications.parliament.uk/pa/cm200910/cmhansrd/cm100203/debtext/100203-0002.htm.
[5] Alex Maskey, quoted in *An Phoblacht*. The full text is available at: http://www.an-phoblacht.com/news/detail/19379.
[6] Hung-En Sung, *The fragmentation of policing in American cities* (Connecticut: Praeger, 2002).
[7] Ron Weitzer, 'Race and Policing in Different Ecological Contexts', in S. Rice and M.White (eds), *Race, Ethnicity and Policing* (New York: NYU Press, 2010), 118–39
[8] Mike Brogden, *The police: autonomy and consent* (Brighton: Harvester Press, 1982), 170.
[9] Brogden, *The police*, 170.
[10] Indeed, as recently as November 2009, Her Majesty's Inspectorate of Constabulary was warning that the British police were in danger of 'losing the battle for the public's consent'. See http://www.guardian.co.uk/commentisfree/libertycentral/2009/dec/16/photography-policing-consent-defiance.
[11] See David H. Bayley, *Police for the future* (Oxford: Oxford University Press, 1994); M. Brogden and P. Nijhar, *Community policing: national and international models and approaches* (Cullompton: Willan Publishing, 2005).
[12] See D.M. Anderson and D. Killingray (eds), *Policing and decolonization* (Manchester: Manchester University Press, 1992); J.D. Brewer, *Black and blue: polic- ing in South Africa* (Oxford: Clarendon Press, 1994); G. Ellison and C. O'Reilly, 'From empire to Iraq and the "war on terror": the transplantation and commodifica- tion of the (Northern) Irish policing experience', *Police Quarterly* 11 (4) (2008), 395–426.

[13] M. Cain, 'Trends in the sociology of policework', *International Journal of the Sociology of Law* 7 (1979), 143–67.

[14] For extended discussions on policing in Northern Ireland, see G. Ellison and J. Smyth, *The crowned harp: policing Northern Ireland* (London: Pluto, 2000); A. Mulcahy, *Policing Northern Ireland: conflict, legitimacy and reform* (Cullompton, Devon: Willan, 2006); John McGarry and Brendan O'Leary, *Policing Northern Ireland: proposals for a new start* (Belfast: Blackstaff Press, 2000).

[15] See Bob Purdie, *Politics in the streets: the origins of the civil rights movement in Northern Ireland* (Belfast: Blackstaff Press, 1990).

[16] See Niall Ó Dochartaigh, *From civil rights to armalites: Derry and the birth of the Irish Troubles* 2nd edn, (London: Palgrave Macmillan, 2005); G. Ellison and G. Martin, 'Policing, collective action and social movement theory: the case of the Northern Ireland civil rights campaign', *British Journal of Sociology* 51 (3) (2000), 681–99.

[17] Brendan O'Leary, *Protecting human rights and securing peace in Northern Ireland: the vital role of police reform* Hearing before the Commission on Security and Co-Operation in Europe (CSCE), 106th Congress, Second Session, 22 September (Washington: CSCE, 2000), 14.

[18] See O Dochartaigh, *From civil rights to armalites*.

[19] Cory Collusion Inquiry Report (Belfast: Northern Ireland Office, 2004), available at: http://www.nio.gov.uk/cory_collusion_inquiry_report_(with_appendices)_pat_finucane.pdf.

[20] Office of the Police Ombudsman for Northern Ireland (OPONI), *Statement by the Police Ombudsman for Northern Ireland on her investigation into the circumstances surrounding the death of Raymond McCord Junior and related matters* (Belfast: OPONI, 2007).

[21] The Drumcree issue relates to the routing of an Orange Order parade in Portadown, Co. Armagh, and to how objections by nationalist residents of the Garvaghy Road to the parade proceeding along that road were handled by the police. Between the years 1995 and 2000, the controversy surrounding the Drumcree parade was at its most fraught. For further information, see 'Parades and marches—developments at Drumcree 1995–2000', on the Conflict Archive on the Internet (CAIN) website, at: http://cain.ulst.ac.uk/issues/parade/develop.htm#1.

[22] Ronald John Weitzer and Stephen A. Tuch, 'Racially biased policing: determinants of citizen perceptions', *Social Forces* 83 (3) (March 2005), 1009–30; Weitzer and Tuch, *Race and policing in America: conflict and reform*, (New York: Cambridge University Press, 2006).

[23] Weitzer and Tuch, 'Racially biased policing', 1010.

[24] Weitzer and Tuch, 'Racially biased policing', 1010.

[25] Weitzer and Tuch, 'Racially biased policing', 1010.

[26] Weitzer and Tuch, 'Racially biased policing', 1010–12.

[27] *Patten Report*, 16.

[28] Ellison and Smyth, *The crowned harp*, see Chapter 10; for policing as a cultural category, see I. Loader and A. Mulcahy, *Policing and the condition of England: memory, politics and culture* (Oxford: Oxford University Press, 2003).

[29] *Patten Report*, 2.

[30] See note 17 above.

[31] G. Ellison, 'Reflecting all shades of opinion: Public attitudinal surveys and the

construction of police legitimacy in Northern Ireland', *British Journal of Criminology* 40 (1) (2000), 88–111.

[32] C. Sumner, 'The violence of censure and the censure of violence' in C. Sumner (ed.), *Violence, culture and censure* (Abingdon, Oxon: Taylor & Francis, 1997). 1–7.

[33] The risks to survey researchers could be severe. For instance, Joanna Mathers was shot and killed in Derry-Londonderry while she was collecting data for the 1981 government census. No organisation claimed responsibility, but the IRA had previously issued a warning that such workers would be regarded as legitimate targets.

[34] See Ellison, 'Reflecting all shades of opinion' for a more detailed elaboration of this issue.

[35] Weitzer, 'Race and policing in different ecological contexts', 120.

[36] Sung, *Fragmentation of policing in American cities*.

[37] J. Chan, 'Changing police culture', *British Journal of Criminology* 36 (1) (1996), 109–34.

[38] Weitzer, 'Race and policing in different ecological contexts', 120.

[39] Sung, *Fragmentation of policing in American cities*, xii.

[40] P.K. Manning, *Police work: the social organization of policing* (Cambridge, MA: MIT Press, 1977).

[41] For a discussion of the role played by senior police managers in the organisational context of police work, see R. Grimshaw and T. Jefferson, *Interpreting policework* (London: Allen and Unwin, 1987).

[42] Sung, *Fragmentation of policing in American cities*, 8.

[43] Aogán Mulcahy, 'Community policing in contested settings: the Patten Report and police reform in Northern Ireland', in T. Williamson (ed.), *The handbook of knowledge-based policing: current conceptions and future directions* (Chichester: Wiley, 2008), 117–38.

[44] Personal interview, 13 November 2009.

[45] See John R. Topping, 'Diversifying from within: Community policing and the governance of security in Northern Ireland', *British Journal of Criminology* 48 (6) (2008), 778–97. Graham Ellison and Mary O'Rawe, 'Security governance in transition: the compartmentalising, crowding out and corralling of policing and security in Northern Ireland' *Theoretical Criminology,* 14 (1) (2010), 31–57.

[46] The PSNI appears to have a problem with the retention of Catholic officers. In 2008, 91 Catholic officers left the police force, compared to 74 in 2007. See 'Worryingly high numbers of Catholics leaving the force', *Irish News*, 17 November 2008, available at: http://www.irishnews.com/appnews/540/5860/2008/11/17/603059_3636801564828216Wor.html.

[47] BBC News, 15 April 2005.

[48] S. McAlister, P. Scraton and D. Haydon, *Childhood in transition: experiencing marginalisation and conflict in Northern Ireland* (Belfast: Queens University Belfast, 2009), 74.

[49] Out of 582 local electoral areas in Northern Ireland.

[50] Personal interview, 13 November 2009.

[51] Sir Hugh Orde made his comments at a meeting in Dublin organised by the Public Relations Institute of Ireland in April 2008. See: http://www.4ni.co.uk/northern_ireland_news.asp?id=74244. Purvis had access to a demographic breakdown of recruits to the PSNI during her time on the Policing Board.

[52] Methodological note: The members of the CEP are mainly youth and community development workers. The data were recorded from a quantitative questionnaire dis-

tributed to respondents in the New Lodge which examined their attitudes in relation to policing, community relationships with the PSNI and experiences of crime and anti-social behaviour. The sample (n = 280) equates to 7.2% of the survey area's population aged 16 and over. The New Lodge survey was linked to the demographic profile of the study area, and only one respondent from each household visited by the researcher completed the survey. The survey was also stratified between households at, or near, the sectarian interface with Duncairn and those that were at least 100 metres from the interface. Note that the percentages in some tables below do not add to 100 since only valid cases were included in the analysis.

[53] Data from this section are taken from G. Ellison and P. Shirlow, *Community attitudes to crime, anti-social behaviour and policing in the Greater New Lodge* (Belfast: Queen's University School of Law, September 2008).

[54] Northern Ireland Census of Population (2001), available at: http://www.nisranew.nisra.gov.uk/census/Census2001Output/index.html.

[55] Police Service of Northern Ireland Crime Statistics (2009), available at http://www.nisranew.nisra.gov.uk/census/start.html.

[56] See http://www.nisranew.nisra.gov.uk/census/start.html.

[57] Northern Ireland Statistics and Research Agency (NISRA), *Northern Ireland neighbourhood information service*, available at: http://www.ninis.nisra.gov.uk/.

[58] See R. Kinsey, *First report of the Merseyside crime survey* (Liverpool: Merseyside County Council, 1984); T. Jones, B.D. Maclean and J. Young, *The Islington crime survey: crime: victimisation and policing in inner city London* (London: Gower, 1986).

[59] Young, 'Left realism and the priorities of crime control', 12.

[60] Northern Ireland Crime Survey, available at: http://www.csu.nisra.gov.uk/survey.asp8.htm.

[61] British Crime Survey, available at: http://www.homeoffice.gov.uk/rds/index.html.

[62] See Jones, Maclean and Young, *Islington crime survey*.

[63] See T. Newburn, *Criminology* (Cullompton:Willan, 2007), 57.

[64] Jones, Maclean and Young, *Islington crime survey*, 39.

[65] Innes makes a distinction between signal crimes and signal disorders. The emphasis in the current discussion is on signal disorders, since this best resonates with concerns about anti-social behaviour.

[66] M. Innes, 'What's your problem: signal crimes and citizen-focused problem-solving' (Reaction Essay), *Criminology and Public Policy* 4 (2) 2005, 187–200. M. Innes, 'Signal crimes and signal disorders: notes on deviance as communicative action', *British Journal of Sociology* 55 (3) (2004) 335–55.

[67] Northern Ireland Crime Survey, 2009.

[68] It is not the intention to exaggerate this point, but some of the qualitative comments made by older respondents in the New Lodge survey strongly intimated that things had become much worse under the peace process. Whether this conveys a more deep-seated sense of ontological insecurity about the pace of change, or whether it is an accurate assessment of of rising crime rates it is difficult to say.

[69] See *The Newsletter*, 27 August 2009, available at: http://www.newsletter.co.uk/news/PSNI-has-lost-touch-.5593318.jp.

[70] G. Ellison, 'A blueprint for democratic policing anywhere in the world? Police reform, political transition, and conflict resolution in Northern Ireland', *Police Quarterly* 10 (3) (2007), 243–69.

[71] The journalist Liam Clarke highlights a number of potential pitfalls for the Justice Minister in this regard, relating to recent allegations about the financial dealings of some politicans and their associates in Northern Ireland. See: 'Ford has hard call to make over bugs', *Belfast Telegraph* 18 March 2010, available at: http://www.belfast-telegraph.co.uk/opinion/ford-has-hard-call-to-make-over-bugs-14726326.html.

[72] Ed Moloney argues that the allegations made in the posthumously released memoirs of the senior IRA commander, Brendan Hughes, could have implications for the future Justice Ministry as well as the Sinn Féin leadership. See: 'Will we ever know the truth about Paddy Joe?', *Belfast Telegraph*, available at: http://www.belfasttele-graph.co.uk/opinion/will-we-ever-know-the-truth-about-paddy-joe-14748752.html.

[73] To date, dissident republican activity has been fairly sporadic but nevertheless has resulted in the deaths of two British soliders and a PSNI officer. Another police officer and captain of the PSNI's GAA team was severely maimed in a bomb explosion, while traffic in Belfast has been reduced to gridlock at several times over security alerts. The Real IRA has claimed responsibility for an explosion outside MI5 head-quarters in Belfast, which left a man injured on the eve of the devolution of policing and justice powers to the NI Assembly.

[74] While the overall responsibility for national security in Northern Ireland has been transferred to MI5, which has recently constructed new multi-million pound offices in Belfast, the PSNI is still responsible on a day-to-day basis for the operational polic-ing of terrorist incidents and threats.

[75] See http://news.bbc.co.uk/1/hi/northern_ireland/7571688.stm.

[76] There are already signs that this may happen. See 'Dissident attacks provide growing loyalist unrest', *Belfast Telegraph*, available at: http://www.belfasttelegraph.co.uk/news/local-national/dissident-attacks-provoke-growing-loyalist-unrest-14767623.html.

CHAPTER 15

BETWEEN SYMBOLISM AND SUBSTANCE: POLICE REFORM IN POST-CONFLICT CONTEXTS

Mark Downes[*]

INTRODUCTION

In his 2005 report *In larger freedom*, the former UN secretary-general Kofi Annan argued that there can be no security without development, and no development without security.[1] While his argument was somewhat controversial at the time, experience has shown that tackling the nexus between insecurity and underdevelopment is central to preventing conflict and building peace. The reform of security structures, most notably the police, has not only been central to the resolution of the conflict in Northern Ireland, but is increasingly becoming an essential component of conflict-prevention and peace-support operations abroad.

Northern Ireland, and the implementation of the *Patten Report*,[2] has provided both an example and a cause for reflection for international policing practitioners. Issues of representation and taking a service-delivery approach to community relations are as relevant in Belfast as they are in Bujumbura, while the need to ensure continually that increased effectiveness of the police service is balanced with adequate accountability and oversight is a lesson that transcends context.

This chapter is divided into four sections; the first involves a discussion on the changing nature of policing, the nation-state and particular challenges faced when reforming, rebuilding or creating policing structures in the aftermath of conflict. The second section places police reform within the emerging development agenda of 'security sector reform' (SSR), which has seen an increase in international support to police and security reform in post-conflict contexts. The third section of this chapter presents reflections on the applicability abroad of the experience of police reform in Northern Ireland from a number of policing practitioners from the island of Ireland, who are working on police and security reform in an international environment.[3] Section four will attempt to answer the question of whether police reform, and international assistance to such processes, is purely a symbolic part of post-conflict political settlements or whether it has also tackled the very real issues of how the police operate and their evolving role within a democratic context. This will be done through attempting to define the key facets of police reform, and by identifying some of the lessons and challenges that remain for the next generation of post-conflict policing missions. This chapter is not meant to provide an overview of the *Patten Report* or its implementation in Northern Ireland; other chapters in this publication will tackle those issues in a more comprehensive manner.

THE CHANGING NATURE OF POLICING AND SPECIFIC CHALLENGES IN POST-CONFLICT CONTEXTS

The modern era of organised policing, especially in the Anglophone world, has its origins in the political developments of the nineteenth century. A central catalyst for the establishment of, for example, the London Metropolitan Police was the concern at the time about the possibility of social unrest, or what Silver calls the need to prevent the 'dangerous classes' challenging the prevalent social order.[4] The dangerous/working classes were a direct bi-product of the trend towards urbanisation that swept through Western Europe following the industrial revolution. The formative years of the British police service were, as such, characterised by both political and social upheaval. Silver refers to the early police force as an organised means of maintaining public order against an 'internal enemy'.[5] This resulted in a police structure that was highly centralised, quasi-military and decidedly political; being viewed as an arm of an unrepresentative government and the means through which the ruling classes maintained the inequitable social order that prevailed at the time. A police service ill at ease with the community it is tasked with controlling continues to be an issue within countries emerging today from conflict, civil strife and political transition.

The model of policing established by the Metropolitan Police Force was exported abroad through the colonial endeavours of the British Crown. Finnane has characterised the development of colonial policing, and its role in political conquest in places such as Australia, as 'policing strangers by strangers'.[6] The evolution of colonial policing provides a clear example of the political role of the early police forces and their primary role in the maintenance of public order, a trend that is maintained in many emerging democracies and societies afflicted by internal conflict. It is worth considering also the lessons and experience that can be garnered from the challenges faced by establishing national police agencies as a consequence of de-colonisation. Page and McCullough drew parallels between the creation of An Garda Síochána in the aftermath of the establishment of the Irish Free State and the creation of the new police service in Timor Leste in the aftermath of the referendum in favour of independence from Indonesia in 1999.[7] Following the disbandment of the Royal Irish Constabulary (RIC) in 1921, An Garda Síochána [8] was dependent both on those who had served in the RIC as well as those who had previously been part of the armed struggle against British rule. Building a new police service required both those who had the requisite experience and technical skills when it came to policing and new recruits with little policing experience but who were seen as more representative of the new social order. Such experience has clear parallels with the (re)building of a police service in post-conflict contexts today.

While the trajectory of development of policing in different parts of the world may differ, the beginnings of organised police forces as a means through which the social order was to be maintained, through which regime security was ensured, can be viewed as a common thread throughout. The police force in many emerging democracies remained representative of the ruling elite for many years following its inception. The presence, for example, of ethnic and social minority police officers amongst the rank-and-file of the police in the US did not occur until well into the twentieth century. Profound changes have, however, occurred over the past two decades in the political and social structure of the nation-state, changes that have challenged the very concept of policing as we know it. A crisis of legitimacy has been augmented by significant political and social changes that have challenged police managers to rethink their role and approach. Politically, the nation-state has declined in importance, the unitary state and social structure that gave the national police much of its authority has been replaced by multilevels of legality, influence, power and identity.[9] The fragmentation of power and identity has had a profound effect on the ability of state institutions to ensure the necessary levels of legitimacy. The police service, often viewed as a symbol of national unity and social order, now faces the challenge of policing a pluralistic and culturally fragmented society. With such changing demographics there is a clear need for the police service to reflect, both in terms of principles and representation, the culturally diverse and pluralistic society that it serves. There has also been the challenge to adapt its approach and integrate new technologies to tackle the changing nature of crime and sources of insecurity.

Particular post-conflict challenges

States emerging from conflict or afflicted by fragile state institutions face significant challenges. The police service in such contexts inevitably lacks capacity, is centralised and quasi-paramilitary in structure, is weighed under the burden of unreformed bureaucracies, and lacks an approach in line with the challenges faced by the public. There is also the problem that police personnel are not homogeneous, thus they may have multiple, and in some cases competing, loyalties. Roles and responsibility of the police often overlap with those of the military, and the police service itself is often politicised. There is little delegation of operational authority, and an overwhelming need for greater standardisation of police practices, systems and procedures.

Whereas it is often viewed as a panacea for many of the challenges faced by post-conflict societies, police reform is just one part of a complex schematic of efforts required to tackle conflict triggers and the causes of insecurity. Efforts of the international community over the past decade have focused on tackling the nexus of insecurity, organised crime and under-development. The international community has learned hard but valuable lessons about the need to ensure a basic level of security provision so as to facilitate the emergence of an environment conducive for political, social and economic developments to take root. Police reform plays a significant role in this process. The emergence of what is known as the 'security sector reform' agenda has done much to place these issues on the international agenda, and has highlighted the role that police reform plays in international efforts to help prevent conflict and build peace.

POLICING AND THE EMERGING DEVELOPMENT AGENDA OF SECURITY SECTOR REFORM (SSR)

Recent work by the United Nations has effectively argued that security from violence and fear is fundamental for reducing poverty and, more broadly, for sustainable economic, social and political development.[10]

Where violent conflict breaks out, within or between countries, community development is arrested. Related problems—such as trans-national crime and corruption, terrorism, the emergence of 'war economies', arms and drug trafficking and the illicit proliferation of small arms and light weapons—pose increased threats to people, nations and international security. Security has thus emerged as a vital concern for development. This is most explicitly enunciated in the human security agenda[11] with its focus on building open and responsive states that ensure the livelihoods and safety of their people. How security and justice institutions function is fundamental to people's lives. At a most basic level, people want to feel safe and secure just as much as they need food to eat, clean water to drink and a job to give them an income. Without security there can be no development. Farmers cannot farm if they are afraid that their land, livestock or family will be attacked. Girls cannot be educated if they are scared of the journey to school. And businesses will not invest where there is armed violence, or where the rule of law is not upheld.

If 'states are to create the conditions in which they can escape from the downward spiral wherein insecurity, crime and underdevelopment are mutually reinforcing, socioeconomic, justice and security dimensions must be tackled simultaneously'.[12] Recognition of this has led, over the past decade, to the emergence of what is know as the security sector reform (SSR) agenda within the international development community. The reform of security and justice institutions has now become a central component of efforts to overcome fragility and conflict in a number of countries, from Afghanistan to Iraq, and from Sudan to the Solomon Islands. Democratically run, accountable and efficient security and justice institutions can help enhance the security of people and reduce the risk of violent conflict. At the heart of the SSR agenda is the realisation that enhancing the effectiveness of security actors, such as the police, without the requisite balanced increase in accountability can have unforeseen and dangerous consequences. This balance between effectiveness and accountability, between capacity and integrity is the main objective of SSR.[13] SSR goes well beyond the narrower focus of security assistance to the armed forces, intelligence and policing personnel. Within this new policy framework, the security system includes judicial and penal institutions; the elected and duly appointed civil authorities responsible for control and oversight (e.g., parliament, the executive, and government ministries); and civil society institutions, including the media.

The emergence of the SSR agenda can be linked to the evolution of our understanding of the concept of security, and its links to long-term development. Traditionally viewed purely in military terms, efforts to improve security have in the past focused primarily on regime or state security, with an overwhelming emphasis on the military or armed forces.[14] International efforts prior to the late 1980s focused largely on 'train and equip' type of support programmes. The experience of such transitions as those from military regimes in Latin America, to post-communist democratisation in Eastern Europe and the end of apartheid in South Africa, has highlighted the importance of democratic accountability, access to justice and the need to move beyond regime security to more human-security focused assistance.

These lessons led to two major developments in our understanding of security and security provision. The first is that the military is not the sole provider of security within a state. Other actors, most notably the police, play a crucial role in security provision; but by the same standard can equally be a negative influence or purveyor of insecurity. There is also a better understanding today of the interconnected nature of the security 'system' and the need to understand how the military, police, justice, prisons and democratic oversight institutions collectively impact on the perceived and real sense of (in)security in a given context. It is also worth noting that in most countries the state is no longer the sole provider of security and justice services. In countries emerging from conflict this is even more the case. The challenge in such contexts is how to enhance service provision, whether state or non-state, while at the same time ensuring that security and justice services are held accountable and have adequate democratic oversight. In this context, we have witnessed a steady increase in the support for, and engagement in, international efforts to support the reform, transformation and building of security, policing and justice institutions in conflict-affected and fragile states.[15]

Greater scrutiny of security and justice service provision has helped to highlight that security and access to justice are basic services; this has helped them to be viewed as public goods, and should be seen as such by governments and ordinary people alike. There is now indisputable evidence from surveys throughout the developing world that security and justice are valued as much as other development objectives such as health, clean drinking water and education.[16] It is therefore key that governments, the international community and those working within security and justice institutions adjust their approach to demystify and mainstream justice and security objectives as core public service delivery issues, and to subject them to the same scrutiny and debate to which we subject other development concerns.

Security and justice reform is not only a post-conflict or development issue, it is an issue at the core of how a state defines itself and its legitimacy. SSR is an urgent issue in fragile, post-conflict situations; however, it is also part of ongoing democratisation efforts in more stable countries. As such, human security and a balance between increased effectiveness and enhanced accountability should feature as an objective in any security sector initiative. In practice, this means complementing activities that focus on increasing the capacity of security providers such as the police or gendarmerie with measures to enhance internal (e.g., codes of conduct or disciplinary procedures), external (e.g., office of the ombudsman or policing boards or civil society) and parliamentary (e.g., security and defence committees) oversight. In addition, efforts to help citizens understand the role of their security sector and engage in discussions with security actors are integral to driving sustainable reforms within the security sector.

Serious questions still remain, however, about whether the international community has the right type of capacity or approach to support the reform of the security and justice system in a country emerging from conflict. While the number of SSR, and international policing, missions has increased in recent years, there is still no universally agreed approach to either. It is here, as will be outlined in the following section, that the experience from Northern Ireland could be invaluable. While each context presents different challenges, and while each institution has it own political and historical context, there are certain principles that transcend context. Likewise, the experience of Northern Ireland has highlighted how the reform of security and justice institutions, while being technical in nature, is also part of a political process. Experience beyond Northern Ireland has also reinforced this point, with countries like Burundi and Sierra Leone underlining how political security sector reform can be, given that SSR is, at its very core, about the re-distribution of power. In many ways it was the design of the process for police reform in Northern Ireland that helped ensure its sustainability and the likelihood of success. It is these three issues—the process, the principles and the politics—that are the main lessons that can be drawn from the *Patten Report* and the police reform process in Northern Ireland.

PROCESS, PRINCIPLES AND POLITICS—TRANSFERABLE
LESSONS FROM THE *PATTEN* REPORT

The Independent Commission on Policing for Northern Ireland, established as part of the Belfast Agreement, produced its report entitled *A new beginning: policing in Northern Ireland* in 1998. The report, which is popularly known as the *Patten Report*, contained 175 recommendations, some of which provided a blueprint for a new form of policing for Northern Ireland and some of which were symbolic in nature. Based on extensive consultation both within the police service, across the community, and with international policing agencies, the report is not only a reflection on how to police a divided society, but very much a review of how policing should be conducted in the face of today's expectations and challenges.

The *Patten Report* provided a comprehensive road map for the creation of the Police Service of Northern Ireland (PSNI). While some issues were specific to the situation in Northern Ireland, a number of key themes highlighted by the report resonate and are equally relevant for other police bodies emerging from conflict. Such issues include how to enhance police accountability, how to undertake policing with the community and in line with human rights, transiting from policing in a high-security context to a relatively peaceful one and the composition, culture and training required to police a divided society.

Learning from the Patten Process

Few policing organisations have been more scrutinised than the Royal Ulster Constabulary (RUC) and the PSNI, and few countries have had such an opportunity to undertake a fundamental review of policing than Northern Ireland in the aftermath of the Belfast Agreement. The key to the success and sustainability of any reform initiative is 'the process' that defines and frames it. And when looking for what is transferable to other contexts from the *Patten Report*, the process involved in the development of the report can be seen as one of its most transferable attributes and as an example for other reform processes to follow.

The first issue that should be noted is that the Independent Commission on Policing was not the first review of the police force in Northern Ireland. The *Patten Report* was preceded by an internal review of policing undertaken by the RUC in 1996. The 'Fundamental

Review of Policing', which was led by the then Assistant Chief Constable Ronnie Flanagan, highlighted many of the issues about how to establish the 'nature, level and style of police service which would be appropriate in an environment free from the threat of terrorism and sectarian strife'.[17] While the panel involved in the review received inputs from different community groups, it was fundamentally an internal review run by the RUC's leading officer, and someone with the credibility to bring the rank-and-file on board to engage in what was an ambitious reform agenda. What was also key is that each of the proposals presented by the report was reviewed by a senior panel of police officers, to ensure their operational applicability, thus ensuring that the reforms were not seen as 'weakening' the service. This facilitated the acceptance of the review's findings and sensitised the police service to the need for a change in the manner of policing, including the more fundamental changes that would be proposed by the subsequent report of the Independent Commission on Policing.

The Independent Commission itself was made up of eight members, including three external experts on policing from the US, Canada and South Africa. It also included political and policing representatives from the United Kingdom, a representative from the Irish Senate, as well as a leading member of the business community. Chaired by Chris Patten, the commission included the right mix of political levity and policing expertise. The approach adopted by the commissioners was a very public and comprehensive consultation process, accepting submissions from the public, political parties, church groups and non-governmental organisations, as well as from those involved in the broader debate on policing worldwide. What was key was the clear presence of political will to make police reform a central component of the post-Belfast peace dividend.

Two other factors were critical to the success of the *Patten Report*. The first was the availability of adequate funding to put into action the recommendations of the *Patten Report* and the second was the creation of a mechanism to oversee their implementation. The availability of adequate funding cannot be underestimated. In any reform process there will be those who are not able to adapt to the new approach to policing; likewise, in order to fulfil the requirement to ensure a demographic balance of police officers, a large scale demobilisation/ retirement scheme may need to be put in place. The availability of funding in order to provide generous benefits for those who were eligible for early retirement ensured that those who left the force in

Northern Ireland did so with a sense that their previous service was being honoured, and so prevented them turning into potential spoilers towards the reform process. In many post-conflict environments the lack of funding can be pin-pointed as one of the main causes for limiting the scope and breadth of reform initiatives.[18]

Very often, reform processes aim to reduce the running costs of an organisation through increasing effectiveness and downsizing of personnel. However, it should be understood that a reform process itself generates a cost. The police service will have to continue to provide its services while at the same time getting in place the new procedures, skill sets, etc. This will inevitably generate a certain additional cost in the short term. Below is a figure developed as part of the police restructuring programme in Bosnia and Herzegovina, on the cost implications of a reform process in the short to medium term.

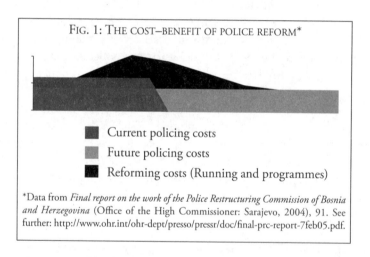

FIG. 1: THE COST–BENEFIT OF POLICE REFORM*

■ Current policing costs
■ Future policing costs
■ Reforming costs (Running and programmes)

*Data from *Final report on the work of the Police Restructuring Commission of Bosnia and Herzegovina* (Office of the High Commissioner: Sarajevo, 2004), 91. See further: http://www.ohr.int/ohr-dept/presso/pressr/doc/final-prc-report-7feb05.pdf.

The second issue affecting the success of the *Patten Report* was equally critical, that being the establishment of an oversight mechanism to periodically review and report on the implementation of the recommendations from the *Report*. The 'Office of the Oversight Commissioner' was established and tasked with monitoring the implementation process, to assess progress and provide public assurance that the implementation process was moving forward. Through having the power to undertake periodic reviews, call review meetings and provide explanations for any delays, the Oversight Commissioner ensured that political pressure was maintained throughout the implementation process. By appointing the Oversight Commissioner, 'the Patten Commission not only directed the police of Northern Ireland to change in fundamental ways, but also required it to demonstrate compliance publicly and repeatedly at short intervals'.[19] The transparent nature of the Commissioners' deliberations and the political independence of their role meant that the reports of the Oversight Commissioner were viewed as credible by all stakeholders, and as such helped to build public confidence in the reform process.

While much international effort often goes into the assessment of policing needs in post-conflict environments, the big gap remains the lack of oversight regarding implementation. Given the significant input from international actors, such as the UN and EU, to international police reform efforts, such oversight needs to include some level of mutual accountability regarding both inputs and outputs.

Reform as a political process

Few in Northern Ireland would argue that the reform of the police service was not a political endeavour. However, many within the international policing community still perceive police reform in post-conflict contexts in purely technical terms. As discussed earlier in this chapter, how security is provided within a state, how the role and responsibilities of internal security are divided between different actors and how those actors are held accountable, is central to defining the nature of the state, how it engages its citizens and the balance of power within the state. What made Northern Ireland unique in many ways was that police reform was part of the political settlement of the conflict; there was strong political pressure and support for the reforms, but, relatively speaking, little political interference.

Reform processes inevitably create winners and losers as they challenge the vested interests and existing power relationships.[20] Resistance to change can result from a political, institutional or individual perspective, and needs to be addressed from such perspectives. The police reform process in Northern Ireland was able to deal with potential resistance at each of these levels. The process created incentives and overcame potential resistance to reform at a political level through greater engagement in policing oversight; at an institutional level through symbolic gestures such as the awarding of the George Cross to the RUC;[21] and at an individual level through ensuring greater public input into the development of policing policy and its oversight.

By failing to recognise the political nature of SSR and police reform, the international community often limits its engagement to the technical aspects of reform, and fails to recognise important linkages to other, broader political processes. The local context will inevitably shape and inform the objectives, challenges and outcomes of any police reform process.

Learning from the Patten Principles

While each context differs, and as a result certain reform issues require more attention depending on the context, there are key principles for police reform that transcend context. These principles can be seen as the central components of the *Patten Report* and include issues such as the mainstreaming of human rights; the need for enhanced accountability of the police service; policing with the community; representation within the police service; and the modernisation of police culture and training. While the *Patten Report* dealt with many other issues, the above represent the major pillars around which the *Patten Report*, and most major police reform processes, are built. These principles can be further explained as follows:

• Human rights, or, to be more exact, how to operationalise adherence to human rights in the every day functions of the police, was a central component of *Patten*. The report recommended the mainstreaming of human rights into training, into the oaths of officers and into how operations were conducted, and argued for making human rights central to staff evaluations for both future and all current staff. The implementation of human rights into police policy and practice was such a high priority for the Patten Commission that it recommended that an independent audit of human-rights compliance be conducted annually, and the results published.

• The *Patten Report* recommended the implementation of multiple levels of accountability. The first focused on the relationship between the Chief Constable and the Policing Board, with both having joint responsibility for the development and approval of the 3–5 year objectives for the organisation, and for agreeing an Annual Policing Plan. The Board is also responsible for monitoring police performance, is independent from the police and the political executive. It is composed of nineteen members, ten selected proportionally from members of the legislative assembly and nine non-political individuals, with the necessary experience and credentials, appointed by the government.

The second level of accountability focused on the municipal level, with the District Commander accountable to the District Policing Partnership Board (DPPB); while the final level of accountability focused on strengthening external oversight through the Office of the Police Ombudsman and the establishment of a complaints-tribunal of senior members of the legal profession. These multiple levels of accountability helped to signal an increase in the transparency of police action and did much to rebuild public confidence in the police service.

- The emphasis on 'policing with the community' signalled both a change of approach to policing within a peaceful society and a political decision to decentralise decision-making and authority. It marked a fundamental and cultural shift in the approach to policing in Northern Ireland away from force protection, which is what it effectively was during 'the Troubles', towards more mainstream policing functions of crime prevention and investigation. With time, this change of approach has done much to build public confidence in the police; and through greater use of techniques such as crime pattern and complaint pattern analysis, the police have been able to improve their role as a security provider for all of the community.

- Representation within the police service is a key issue in most countries and was a central pillar of the *Patten Report*. The efforts to ensure that the Northern Ireland police was representative of the society it aims to serve included outreach to the Catholic community but also to other minority groups.[22] This policy also aimed to integrate parallel police structures under the authority, control and oversight of Northern Ireland police.

- Probably one of the central political pillars of the *Patten Report* was the need to make a symbolic change, to underline a break with the past and a new beginning for the police for a new era for Northern Ireland. The name change from the RUC to the PSNI, together with the change in symbols, while difficult to accept for some, did much to underline the neutrality of the police in what was still a divided society.

But are these lessons transferable?

Bayley makes a strong argument for why the *Patten Report* is not necessarily easily transferable to other post-conflict contexts.[23] He argues that in the first instance, meaningful police reform requires a clear political settlement, something that not all post-conflict contexts have.

Second, Northern Ireland already had a strong democratic culture, and appreciation of the rule of law. Third, it had well developed governance structures, it did not require any external assistance to develop legislation, monitor budgets or manage government departments. Bayley underlines that in Northern Ireland, it was about the reform of a pre-existing, well managed and professional police service, not about building a capacity where there was previously none. Finally, he highlights that Northern Ireland had a high level of social capital, both within civil society and amongst the general population. It is these factors that Bayley credits with creating the conducive environment within which the reform process could succeed; without such conditions, he argues that the prospects for police reform in post-conflict contexts is limited at best.

While Bayley's analysis is largely correct, and the capacity of the police service in post-conflict contexts, such as the Democratic Republic of the Congo, cannot reasonably be compared to that of the RUC, the actual capacity of the RUC in terms of a policing organisation equipped to police a peaceful society should not be overstated. The management and operations of the RUC were so dominated by intelligence, Special Branch and counter-insurgency that other aspects of 'normal' policing remained largely undeveloped and always took place in a counter-insurgency context. The level of reform and re-skilling that was required, together with the fundamental overhaul of policing procedures, provides some strong transferable lessons, not least in the area of how to manage organisational change.

In the next section, we will see that the experience of the international community is not altogether positive when it comes to supporting police reform in post-conflict contexts. Inevitably, our aspirations need to be tailored to the context; few would argue that the success of the PSNI can easily be replicated in other contexts. However, given the right political environment, the presence of political will and clear principles on which to build policing practice, progress can be made and policing service delivery can be enhanced; but this takes time and the right type of support from the international community. While the PSNI is rightly heralded today for its openness and accountability, that was not always the case. Accountability issues were a real challenge for the RUC and the PSNI; the move from a situation of allegations of collusion and cover-up to where accountability functions at multiple levels represents major progress.

FROM SECURING THE PEACE TO ENSURING STABILITY—INTERNATIONAL EFFORTS TO SUPPORT POLICE REFORM IN POST-CONFLICT CONTEXTS

The international community's engagement in civil crisis management has expanded significantly in the past decade.[24] With the nature of conflict shifting from inter-state to intra-state, the inability of the military alone to cope with the demands of peacekeeping operations has resulted in an increase in the deployment of international police missions in post-conflict situations.

There are effectively three approaches to police support taken by the international community in post-conflict contexts: in the most severe of circumstances international police can take on an executive mandate; in most cases, however, international support is provided through police assistance missions, whereby officers from an international mission provide advice and guidance on both the technical aspects and process of police reform. The third approach is a hybrid of the first two; for example, there are UN missions that combine Pre-Formed Units (PFUs), with responsibility for riot control, with a police assistance programme with the objective of reforming or building policing bodies.

Both the UN and the EU provided executive and police assistance programmes in Bosnia and Herzegovina in the 1990s, while other UN efforts to build new police service's *ex-nihilo* include efforts in Kosovo in1999, Timor Leste in 1999 or Haiti in 1995. The police are often the security institution that most impacts on people's daily lives, they are the gatekeepers of the criminal justice system and, as mentioned previously, they provide a litmus-test for the state's legitimacy in the eyes of the public. A professional police service that has the trust and confidence of the public it is meant to serve can play a crucial and positive role. In many post-conflict countries, however, the lack of a culture of accountability, and a history of abuse, defines relations with the public and limits the constructive role that the police might play.

Recent efforts to reform policing in post-conflict contexts such as the Balkans, and to re-align the role of the police in line with democratic values and human-rights standards, have all provided invaluable input into the international discourse on the role of the police in post-conflict rehabilitation. That said, the results of such efforts have been variable. Efforts to reform the police and improve their service delivery face daunting political, financial, logistical and historical obstacles. The very complexity of reform can be intimidating, touching issues of management, leadership, political will and attitudes, established behaviours and negative public perception.[25]

It is important to recognise that the reform of the police service in Northern Ireland, or the transformation of the policing institutions that resulted from the transition in Eastern Europe and the Balkans, differs greatly from the building of policing institutions in countries such as the Democratic Republic of the Congo, Somalia or Afghanistan. This is not said to discount the challenges faced by the process in Northern Ireland or countries such as the Republic of Serbia, but the very fact that there is a police service of sorts in place, a legal (if somewhat outdated) framework and a history of policing, provides some basis on which to work. For many fragile or post-conflict contexts, the challenges faced mean that many of the lessons from Northern Ireland are not directly applicable, or at least not directly applicable in the immediate aftermath of the conflict, where the focus is on 'securing the peace'.

In such cases, police reform and the support provided by the inter-national community should be viewed as a two-phased process. The first phase in the immediate aftermath of a conflict should be seen as a process of securing the peace; this may entail having a policing mission, with international officers on the streets. This may involve joint patrols and then clear confidence-building measures between the national policing authority and the public, monitored by the international com-munity. For transition countries that have not suffered from conflict, an international policing mission can be utilised as a conflict-prevention measure, and here again should focus on confidence-building measures, monitoring of police–public relations, supporting dialogue on security needs, etc.

The second phase of an international policing mission should focus on the development of a viable police reform process, a process that provides for the evolution of the mission from 'securing the peace' to 'ensuring stability'. It is in this phase that the lessons from Northern Ireland are most applicable. During this phase the policing mission should focus on the reform of the national police service. Co-ordination of the international community is key at this stage, as is the political will to remain until the reform process has reached a point of self-sustainability. The main area of focus or the main guiding prin-ciples of the police reform process in this phase are not unlike those identified in the *Patten Report*, although the emphasis and needs will vary depending on the context.

There are a number of ways of conceptualising a police reform process. One such method, the 'Capacity and Integrity Framework (CIF)'[26] was first utilised as part of the 'OHR [Office of the High Representative] Report on a Police Follow-On Mission to UNMBIH and the UN International Police Task Force',[27] which has subsequently been used in other missions such as the OSCE Mission in Serbia[28] and the UN assessment mission in Timor Leste.[29] The OHR report proposed the matrix below, which highlights the need to develop both the integrity and the capacity/approach of the police service, something which resonates well with the *Patten Report*, as well as the new SSR agenda and its focus on the need to balance capacity and accountability.

FIG. 2: THE CAPACITY AND INTEGRITY MATRIX*

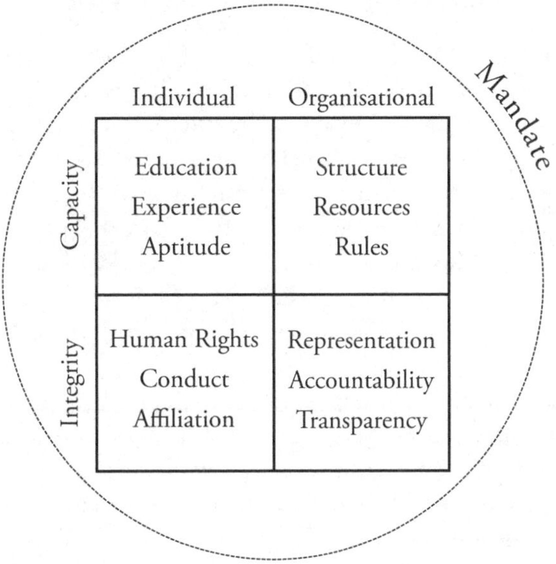

*The 'Capacity and Integrity Framework' was developed by the Human Rights Office within the UN Mission in Bosnia and Herzegovina (UNMIBH) in 2000, by Alexander Mayer-Rieckh and Serge Rumin, and was utilised as part of the UNMIBH mandate implementation plan for the reform of the BiH police service.

The above matrix can be used to define the scope and depth of the need for reform, and it can assist when defining milestones or indicators of success for the reform process. In this context individual capacity could include the provision of technical training in areas such as crime mapping, or community policing, while individual integrity would be developed through the provision of training on subjects such as police ethics and human rights. Organisational integrity would refer to the development of internal affairs procedures, equitable and fair human resource guidelines, internal regulations and the legal framework within which the police service operates. Organisational capacity relates to infrastructure development, that is, the resources and technical equipment required for the police service to carry out the task of crime prevention and investigation.

In many ways the above matrix provides a simple visual through which to map the normative approach to police reform, as also articulated in the *Patten Report*.

Challenges that remain for international policing and support to reform in post-conflict contexts

Even though there has been a significant increase in international support for police reform, substantial challenges remain. The first relates to the question of whether the international community has the right type of capacity available to support police-reform processes. In many cases, the international community is sending police officers into situations for which they were never trained. They may be the best crime scene investigators or community police officers in Belfast or Dublin, but we are now sending them to post-conflict situations with the task of building up a system of policing where there previously was none. While technical knowledge of policing is essential in such cases, equally relevant is an understanding of management, human resources, financial management, as well as the level of political aptitude for what is inevitably a very fluid situation. Rarely, however, is a full complement of such skills utilised as part of a police assistance mission, and as a result we focus on the individual aspects of capacity and integrity, as outlined in Fig. 2 above, without the requisite focus on organisational capacity and integrity. This results in assistance programmes that have a limited level of sustainability and impact. One of the key challenges going forward is to ensure that police assistance missions, be they within the UN, EU or bilateral contexts, have the multi-disciplinary skills required to support the reform of the police and to support the change management process required to see the reforms implemented.

A second key challenge is the lack of policing standards against which to assess reform needs and reform progress. The lack of such standards or principles of police capacity and accountability means that there is little to measure progress against. One option would be to support the development of regional standards, codes of conduct and principles of security-sector management. Once established, such principles, codes and standards would provide a means by which to measure reform priorities and progress. Such principles are not about creating a blueprint for policing, but about creating a general framework that can then be tailored to a local context. Linked to this there is a general lack of lessons identified and experience shared of previous police reform processes, including the process in Northern Ireland; without such lesson learning the international community will continue to re-create the wheel when it comes to supporting reforms.

Finally, there needs to be mutual accountability when it comes to the support being provided by the international community. There now exists a body of experience from multilateral and bilateral efforts to support police reform processes. The UN mission in Timor Leste has been present on the ground providing police support for most of the last decade, what needs to be asked is whether that support has been effective, and if not, why not. The lack of mutual accountability (both of national authorities and international assistance) means that the international community cannot effectively argue for greater national accountability of the police services if its own input into the reform process is not held accountable. Establishing a system not only to monitor the implementation of the reform process from the national perspective, as was the case in Northern Ireland, but also to monitor the input from the international community would do much to raise standards and mean that the international community could lead by example.

CONCLUDING REFLECTIONS

While every context is different and the development of policing in each country has its own trajectory of change, there are some fundamental lessons that can be taken from the experience of the implementation of the *Patten Report* in Northern Ireland. The first is that the process to articulate reform goals is central to whether the reforms will be sustainable in the long term. The second is that the availability of the necessary funding facilitated the implementation process, and curtailed potential blockages to change. The principles upon which the *Patten Report* was built are equally transferable, once tailored to the national context.

What was surprising during the research for this chapter was the discovery that the experience of de-colonisation and the emergence of An Garda Síochána as the police force in Ireland could equally provide lessons for those countries whose previous policing system was based on a colonial policing structure, or where there was no indigenous police force to begin with.

The need to balance increased capacity with robust governance and accountability structures resonates well with the current thinking within the international community and the emerging SSR agenda. But what of the balance between symbols and substance? What is clear is that one of the conclusions that can be drawn from the implementation of the *Patten Report* was the importance that symbols play in rebuilding the legitimacy of policing institutions and overcoming a deficit of trust within segments of the population. Mayer-Rieckh and Duthie argue that targeted measures can both verbally and symbolically reaffirm a commitment to overcome the legacy of the past, and signal a new beginning.[30] Such symbolic measures can include apologies from representatives of security institutions (both formal and informal) that were involved in serious abuses; memorials or commemorative days; the changing of coats of arms, insignia, uniforms; or institution-based truth-seeking efforts. While viewed as painful for some, the changing of insignia and uniforms provided a significant step forward in Northern Ireland in terms of building confidence and legitimacy with the nationalist community; likewise the lifting of the ban on members of security forces joining the Gaelic Athletic Association opened the way for members of the nationalist community to sign up to the new PSNI. These actions sent strong messages to both communities that ground was been given and that through such symbolic gestures a clear break with the past was possible.

On the applicability abroad of the experience of the police reform process in Northern Ireland, it is clear that there are lessons to be drawn; but equally there are contextual issues specific to Northern Ireland that helped to make the reform process there a success. From the experience of international policing assistance programmes, a number of remaining challenges have been highlighted. The need for the international community to develop standards for policing, gather lessons from previous and on-going missions and to implement these lessons in the future design and deployment of police assistance missions is critical. The need to ensure that the right type of capacity is deployed in support of reform and to be open to the review of UN and EU police support operations is fundamental if international support to reforms are to be more substantive than symbolic.

NOTES

* The views expressed in this chapter do not necessarily represent the view of Centre for the Democratic Control of Armed Forces or it member states. The author would like to thank Serge Rumin and Dr Rory Keane for their comments on an earlier draft of this chapter.

[1] See Kofi Annan, *In larger freedom: towards development, security and human rights for all* (United Nations: New York, 2005), available at: at http://www.un.org/largerfreedom/contents.htm. This development was preceded in 2000 by the *Report of the Panel on United Nations Peace Operations* (United Nations: New York, 2000), commonly known as the Brahimi report (available at: http://www.un.org/peace/reports/peace_operations/), which emphasised the role that the rule of law and, within that, police reform plays in helping to prevent conflict and build peace.

[2] Independent Commission on Policing for Northern Ireland, *A new beginning: policing in Northern Ireland* Report of the Independent Commission on Policing for Northern Ireland (HMSO/Northern Ireland Office: Belfast, 1999), generally referred to as the *Patten Report*.

[3] The author would like to thank Chief Superintendent (retd) Maggie Hunter; Chief Superintendent (retd) Dr Cecil Craig; Murray McCullough; Michael Page; Dr Gordon Peake and Dr Rory Keane for taking the time to discuss the *Patten Report*, share views on its implementation in Northern Ireland and share their experiences of supporting police reform processes in countries such as Albania, the Democratic Republic of Congo, Poland, the former Yugoslavia, Serbia, Turkey and Timor Leste.

[4] A. Silver, 'The demand for order in civil society', in T. Newburn (ed.), *Policing key readings* (Willan Publishing, Devon 2004), 7–20.

[5] Silver, 'Demand for order in civil society'.

[6] M. Finnane, *Police and government* (Oxford University Press: Oxford, 1994), 13.

[7] Interview with Murray McCullough and Michael Page, members of the United Nations Mission (Security Sector Support Unit) in Timor Leste, October 2009.

[8] Following the Civil War and the truce of July 1921 the RIC was disbanded and a new police force, 'The Civic Guard' (renamed *Garda Síochána na hÉireann* on 8 August 1923), was established by the Irish government. For more on the history of the force, see http://www.garda.ie.

[9] For an excellent depiction of the effect of changing socio-political structures on police practices, see R. Reiner, 'Policing a postmodern society', *Modern Law Review* 55 (6) (1992), 761–81.

[10] See further Annan, *In Larger Freedom*, as well as *A more secure world: our shared responsibility*, the report from the UN High Level Panel on Threats, Challenges and

Change (United Nations: New York, December 2004), available at: http://www.un.org/
secureworld/ (3 December 2009).

[11] The final Report from the Commission on Human Security (by Sadako Ogata and
Amartya Sen) to the United Nations Secretary-General on 1 May 2003 articulates the
relevance of human security to development.

[12] OECD DAC, *Handbook on security system reform* (OECD: Paris, 2007), 20.

[13] OECD DAC, *Guidelines: helping prevent violent conflict* (OECD: Paris, 2001),
policy statement, 15.

[14] For an in-depth discussion of the changing nature of the concept of security, see
Heiner Haënggi, 'Conceptualising security sector reform and reconstruction', in H.
Haënggi and A. Bryden (eds), *The reform and reconstruction of the security sector*
(Geneva Centre for the Democratic Control of Armed Forces: Geneva, 2004), 1-11.

[15] See the diagram on Official Development Assistance (ODA) spending on security
sector reform from 2004 to 2007, which highlights a four-fold increase in spending
on SSR activities, in M. Downes and R. Muggah, 'Buying time: how interim stabilisation can enhance security sector reform in post-war settings', in M. Sedra (ed),
The Future of SSR (CIGI: Waterloo, 2010).

[16] See the World Bank Report, 'Voice of the poor', (World Bank: New York, 2000),
where security is ranked one of the most important needs of poor people around the
world.

[17] From the 'Preface' to the 'Summary and key findings from the fundamental review
of policing' (RUC: Belfast, 1996), 1–16.

[18] Interviews conducted with international policing practitioners September–October
2009. See further, note 3 above.

[19] D.H. Bayley, 'Post-conflict police reform: Is Northern Ireland a model?', *Policing*
2 (2) (2008), 233–40: 237.

[20] OECD DAC, *Handbook on security system reform*, 28.

[21] The George Cross was awarded to the RUC in 1999 by the Queen on the advice
of the Labour government; it was awarded 'to honour the courage and dedication of
the officers of the Royal Ulster Constabulary and their families who have shared their
hardships'. See further http://www.gc-database.co.uk/collective.htm.

[22] The composition of the Police Service has changed dramatically in the ten years
since the publication of the *Patten Report*, when it was 92% Protestant and only 8%
Catholic; by 2010–11 it is expected that Catholic representation will be in the region
of 30%. Figures quoted are from the Police Board (2002–06), as presented in Bayley,
'Post-conflict police reform'.

[23] See further Bayley, 'Post-conflict police reform'.

[24] This is evidenced not only by the use of policing missions by the UN, but also by
the OSCE and, more recently, EU engagement in the Balkans, in the Democratic
Republic of the Congo and in Guinea Bissau under the European Security and
Defence Policy (ESDP).

[25] H. Groenewald and G. Peake, *Police reform through community-based policing: philosophy and guidelines for implementation* (International Peace Academy: New York, 2004).

[26] The 'Capacity and Integrity Framework' was developed by the Human Rights
Office within the UN Mission in Bosnia and Herzegovina (UNMIBH) in 2000, by
Alexander Mayer-Rieckh and Serge Rumin, and was utilised as part of the UNMIBH

mandate implementation plan for the reform for the BiH police service.

27 R. Monk, T.T. Holm and S. Rumin, *OHR report on a police follow-on mission to UNMBIH and the UN International Police Task Force* (Office of the High Representative: Sarajevo, November 2001).

28 See further, OSCE Mission to Serbia and Montenegro, *Police reform in Serbia, towards a modern and accountable police service* (OSCE: Belgrade, 2004), 15.

29 UN Joint Assessment Mission to Timor Leste, January 2003.

30 A. Mayer-Rieckh and R. Duthie, 'Justice sensitive security sector reform', in P. De Geiff and R. Duthie (eds) , *Traditional justice and development* (Social Science Research Council: New York, 2009), 214–52: 233.

BIBLIOGRAPHY

Abbreviations	
CAJ	Committee for the Administration of Justice
CDCAF	Centre for the Democratic Control of Armed Forces
CIGI	Centre for International Governance Innovation
CSCE	Commission on Security and Co-Operation in Europe
DAC	Development Assistance Committee
DHSS	Department of Health and Social Services
ECPR	European Consortium for Political Research
HMSO	Her Majesty's Stationery Office
IASC	Inter-Agency Standing Committee
IBEI	Institute Barcelona d'Estudis Internationals
ISA	International Studies Association
NIPB	Northern Ireland Policing Board
OPONI	Office of the Police Ombudsman of Northern Ireland
OSCE	Organization for Security and Co-operation in Europe
ODIHR	Office for Democratic Institutions and Human Rights
UNICEF	United Nations International Children's Fund
UN-INSTRAW	UN International Research and Training Institute for the Advancement of Women
UNMIBH	United Nations Mission in Bosnia and Herzegovina

Adelman, Madelaine, Erez, Edna and Shalboud-Kevorkian, Nader 2003 'Policing violence against minority women in multicultural societies: "community" and the politics of exclusion', *Police and Society* 7, 105–33.

Alison, Miranda 2004 'Women as agents of political violence: gendering security', *Security Dialogue* 35 (4), 447–63.

Amnesty International 1978 *Report of an Amnesty International mission to Northern Ireland*. London. AI International Secretariat.

Amnesty International 1986 *Killings by security forces in Northern Ireland*. New York. Amnesty International National Office.

Amnesty International 2007 *Above the law 12/005*. London. AI International Secretariat.

Anderson, D.M. and Killingray, D. (eds) 1992 *Policing and decolonisation*. Manchester. Manchester University Press.

Annan, Kofi 2000 *We the peoples—the role of the United Nations in the 21st century*, Millennium Report of the Secretary-General of the UN. New York. United Nations.

Annan, Kofi 2004 *A more secure world: our shared responsibility*, Report from the UN High Level Panel on Threats, Challenges and Change. New York. United Nations.

Annan, Kofi 2005 *In larger freedom: towards development, security and human rights for all.* New York. United Nations.

Asmal, Kadar 1985 *Shoot to kill.* Cork. Mercier Press.

Baker, Bruce 2004 *Post-conflict policing: lessons from Uganda 18 years on.* Coventry. African Studies Centre, Coventry University.

Baker, Bruce 2007 'Post-war policing by communities in Sierra Leone, Liberia, Rwanda', *Democracy and Security* 3 (2), 215–36.

Bakic, Branka and Novak, Gajic 2006 'Police reform in Serbia: five years later', *Balkan Series* 6 (21) London. Conflict Studies Research Centre.

Balkin, Joseph 1988 'Why policemen don't like policewomen', *Journal of Police Science and Administration* 16 (1), 29–38.

Barnes, Karen and Albrecht, Peter 2008 'Tool 9: civil society oversight of the security sector and gender', in Megan Bastick and Kristin Valasek (eds), *Gender and security sector reform toolkit.* Geneva. DCAF/OSCE/ UN-INSTRAW.

Bastick, Megan, Grimm, Karin and Kunz, Rahel 2007 *Sexual violence in armed conflict: global overview and implications for the security sector.* Geneva. Centre for the Democratic Control of Armed Forces.

Bayley, David H. 2006 *Changing the guard: developing democratic policing abroad.* Oxford. Oxford University Press.

Bayley, David H. 1994 *Police for the future.* Oxford. Oxford University Press.

Bayley, David H. 2008 'Post-conflict police reform: is Northern Ireland a model?', *Policing* 2 (2), 233–40.

Beirne, Maggie 2001 'Progress or placebo? The *Patten Report* and the future of policing in Northern Ireland', *Policing and Society* (11), 297–319.

Beirne, Maggie and Hegarty, Angela 2007 'A view from the coal face: Northern Ireland, human rights activism and the "War on Terror"', in John Morison, Kieran McEvoy and Gordon Anthony (eds), *Judges, transitions and human rights*, 377–400. Oxford. Oxford University Press.

Bell, Christine 2003 *Peace agreements and human rights.* Oxford. Oxford University Press.

Brewer, John D. 1994 *Black and blue: policing in South Africa.* Oxford. Clarendon Press.

Brewer, John D. with Magee, Kathleen 1991 *Inside the RUC: routine policing in a divided society*. Oxford. Clarendon Press.

Brewer, John D. 1991 'Policing in divided societies: theorizing a type of policing', *Policing and Society* 1, 179–91.

Brogden, Mike 1982 *The police: autonomy and consent*. Brighton. Harvester Press.

Brogden, Mike and Nijhar, Preeti 2005 *Community policing: national and international models and approaches*. Cullompton. Willan Publishing.

Brown, Jennifer 1997 'European policewomen: a comparative research perspective', *International Journal of the Sociology of Law* 25 (1), 1–19.

Byrne, J. 2008 *Policing loyalist and republican communities: understanding key issues for local communities and the PSNI*. Belfast. Institute for Conflict Research.

Cain, M. 1979 'Trends in the sociology of policework', *International Journal of the Sociology of Law* 7, 143–67.

CAJ 1995 *The agenda for change—human rights, the Northern Ireland conflict and the peace process*. Belfast. CAJ.

CAJ 1996 *The misrule of law: a report on the policing of events during the summer of 1996 in Northern Ireland*. Belfast. CAJ.

CAJ 1997 *Human rights on duty: principles for better policing—international lessons for Northern Ireland*. Belfast. CAJ.

CAJ 2006 *Briefing on religious and political inequalities in Northern Ireland*. Belfast. CAJ.

CAJ 2008 *War on Terror: lessons from Northern Ireland*. Belfast. CAJ.

Cameron, Honorable Lord 1969 *Disturbances in Northern Ireland: Report of the Commission appointed by the Governor of Northern Ireland*. Belfast. HMSO.

Celador Collantes, Gemma 2005 'Police reform: peacebuilding through "democratic policing?"', *International Peacekeeping* 12 (3), 364–76.

Celador Collantes, Gemma 2007 'The European Union police mission: the beginning for a new future for Bosnia and Herzegovina?' *IBEI Working Papers*, 9. Barcelona. IBEI.

Chan, J. 1996 'Changing police culture', *British Journal of Criminology* 36 (1), 109–34.

Chan, Janet B.L. 1997 *Changing police culture: policing in a multicultural society*. Cambridge. Cambridge University Press.

Chenoy, Anuradha M. 2004 'Women in the South Asian conflict zones', *South Asian Survey* 11, 35–47.

Crenshaw, Kimberlé 1989 'Demarginalizing the intersection of race and sex: a black feminist critique of antidiscrimination doctrine, feminist theory and anti-racist politics', *University of Chicago Legal Forum*, 139–67.

Crenshaw, Kimberlé 1991 'Mapping the margins: intersectionality, identity politics and violence', *Stanford Law Review* 43 (6), 1241–99.

Daly, Mary 2005 'Gender mainstreaming in theory and practice', *Social Politics: International Studies in Gender, State and Society* 12 (3), 433–50.

Denham, Tara 2008 'Police reform and gender', in Megan Bastick and Kristin Valasek (eds), *Gender and security sector reform toolkit*, Toolkit 2. Geneva. DCAF, OSCE/ODIHR, UN-INSTRAW.

Dickens Mushemeza, Elijah 2008 'Policing in post-conflict environment: implications for police reform in Uganda', *Journal of Security Sector Management*, 6 (3), 1–18.

Dickson, Brice 2009 'Counter-insurgency and human rights in Northern Ireland', *Journal of Strategic Studies* 32 (3), 475–93.

Dimbleby, Jonathan 1998 *The last governor: Chris Patten and the handover of Hong Kong*. London. Time Warner Books.

Doyle, John 1998 '"Towards a lasting peace?": The Northern Ireland multi-party Agreement, referendum and assembly elections of 1998', *Scottish Affairs* 25, 1–20.

Doyle, John 1999 'Governance and citizenship in contested states: the Northern Ireland Peace Agreement as internationalised governance', *Irish Studies in International Affairs* 10 (1999), 201–19.

Doyle, John 2007 'Re-examining the Northern Ireland conflict', in, Vassilis Fouskas (ed.), *The politics of conflict: a survey*, 132–46. London. Routledge.

Drower, George 1995 *John Hume: peacemaker*. London. Victor Gollancz.

Eck, J.E. and Rosenbaum, D.P. 1994 'The new police order: effectiveness, equity and efficiency in community policing', in D.P. Rosenbaum (ed.), *The challenge of community policing: testing the promise*, 3–23. Thousand Oaks, CA. Sage.

Ellison, Graham 2000 'Reflecting all shades of opinion: public attitudinal surveys and the construction of police legitimacy in Northern Ireland', *British Journal of Criminology* 40 (1), 88–111.

Ellison, Graham 2007 'A blueprint for democratic policing anywhere in the world? Police reform, political transition, and conflict resolution in Northern Ireland', *Police Quarterly*, 10 (3), 243–69.

Ellison, Graham and Martin, Greg 2000 'Policing, collective action and social movement theory: the case of the Northern Ireland civil rights campaign', *British Journal of Sociology* 51 (3), 681–99.

Ellison, Graham and Smyth, Jim 2000 *The crowned harp: policing Northern Ireland*. London. Pluto.

Ellison, Graham and O'Reilly, Conor 2008 'From empire to Iraq and the "War on Terror": the transplantation and commodification of the (Northern) Irish policing experience', *Police Quarterly* 11 (4), 395–426.

Ellison, Graham and Shirlow, Peter 2008 *Community attitudes to crime, anti-social behaviour and policing in the Greater New Lodge*. Belfast. Queen's University School of Law.

Ellison, Graham and O'Rawe, Mary 2010 'Security governance in transition: the compartmentalizing, crowding out and corralling of policing and security in Northern Ireland', *Theoretical Criminology* 14 (1), 31–57.

Eveline, Joan and Bacchi, Carol 2005 'What are we mainstreaming when we mainstream gender?', *International Feminist Journal of Politics* 7 (4), 496–512.

Eveline, Joan, Bacchi, Carol and Binns, Jennifer 2009 'Gender mainstreaming versus diversity mainstreaming: methodology as emancipatory politics', *Gender, Work and Organization* 16 (2), 198–216.

Faul, Denis and Murray, Raymond 1975 *The RUC: the black and the blue book*. Dungannon. D. Faul.

Fielding, Nigel 1994 'Cop canteen culture', in Tim Newburn and Elizabeth A. (Betsy) Stanko (eds), *Just boys doing business: men, masculinity and crime*, 46–63. London. Routledge.

Finnane, Mark 1994 *Police and government*. Oxford. Oxford University Press.

Fisk, Robert 1975 *The point of no return: the strike which broke the British in Ulster*. London. André Deutsch.

FitzGerald, Garret 1991 *All in a life: an autobiography*. Dublin. Gill and Macmillan.

Flanagan, Ronnie 1996 'Summary and key findings', *Fundamental review of policing*, 1–16. Belfast. RUC.

Freel, R., Quigley, D., and Toner, S., 2009 *Experience of crime: findings from the 2007/08 Northern Ireland Crime Survey* Research Bulletin 1/2009. Belfast. Northern Ireland Office, Statistics and Research Branch.

Godson, Dean 2004 *Himself alone—David Trimble and the ordeal of unionism*. London. HarperCollins.

Goldstein, Herman 1990 *Problem-oriented policing*. New York. McGraw-Hill.

Grimshaw, R. and Jefferson, T. 1987 *Interpreting policework*. London. Allen & Unwin.

Groenewald, H. and Peake, G. 2004 *Police reform through community-based policing: philosophy and guidelines for implementation*. New York. International Peace Academy.

Hayes, Maurice 1996 *A Police Ombudsman for Northern Ireland: a review of the police complaints system in Northern Ireland*. Belfast. Northern Ireland Office.

Haënggi, Heiner 2004 'Conceptualising security sector reform and reconstruction', in Heiner Haënggi and Alan Bryden (eds), *The reform and reconstruction of the security sector*. Geneva, Centre for the Democratic Control of Armed Forces. LIT verlag.

Hamber, Brandon, Hillyard, Paddy, Maguire, Amy, McWilliams, Monica, Robinson, Gillian, Russell, David and Ward, Margaret 2006 'Discourses in transition: re-imagining women's security', *International Relations* 20 (4), 487–502.

Heise, Lori L., Pitanguy, Jacqueline and Germain, Adrienne 1994 *Violence against women: the hidden health burden*. World Bank Discussion Paper 255. New York. World Bank.

Hills, Alice, 2008 'The dialectic of police reform in Nigeria', *Journal of Modern African Studies*, 46 (2), 215–34.

Hillyard, Paddy and Tomlinson, Mike 2002 'Patterns of policing and policing Patten', *Journal of Law and Society* 27 (3), 394–415.

Hillyard, Paddy, McWilliams, Monica and Ward, Margaret 2006 *Re-imagining women's security: a comparative study of South Africa, Northern Ireland and Lebanon*. Belfast. Northern Ireland Gender Audit.

Hooper, Charlotte 2001 *Manly states: masculinities, international relations, and gender politics*. New York. Columbia University Press.

Human Rights Watch 1991 *Human rights in Northern Ireland: a Helsinki Watch report*. New York. Human Rights Watch.

Hume, John 1986 'Supporting the police in a divided society', *Fortnight*, 239, 7–8.

Independent Commission on Policing for Northern Ireland 1999 *A new beginning: policing in Northern Ireland* Report of the Independent Commission for Policing in Northern Ireland. Belfast. HMSO Northern Ireland Office.

Inter-Agency Standing Committee (IASC) 2006 'Gender and Security Toolkit 1', in *Women, girls, boys and men, different needs—equal opportunities: gender handbook in humanitarian action*. Geneva. IASC.

Jones, T., Maclean, B.D. and Young, J. 1986 *The Islington crime survey: crime: victimisation and policing in inner city London*. London. Gower.

Kelling, George L. and Wilson, James Q. 1982 'Broken windows', *Atlantic Monthly* (March), 29–38. Washington. Atlantic Monthly Group.

Kelling, George L. and Wilson, James Q. 2002 'Making neighbourhoods safe', *Atlantic Monthly* (February), 46–52. Washington. Atlantic Monthly Group.

Kempa, Michael 2007 'Tracing the diffusion of policing governance models from the British Isles and back again: some directions for democratic reform in troubled times', *Police Practice and Research* 8 (2), 107–23.

Kershaw, C., Nicholas, S., and Walker, A. 2008 *Crime in England and Wales 2007-2008: findings from the British Crime Survey and police recorded crime*. Home Office Statistical Bulletin 07/08. London. Home Office.

Kinsey, R. 1984 *First report of the Merseyside crime survey*. Liverpool. Merseyside County Council.

Lijphart, Arend 1977 *Democracy in plural societies*. New Haven, CT. Yale University Press.

Loader, I. and Mulcahy, A. 2003 *Policing and the condition of England: memory, politics and culture*. Oxford. Oxford University Press.

Lonsway, Kim, Moore, Margaret, Harrington, Penny, Smeal, Eleanor and Spillar, Katherine 2003 *Hiring and retaining more women: the advantages to law enforcement agencies*. Los Angeles, CA. National Centre for Women and Policing.

Lynch, Gerald W. 1999 'Impact and importance of human dignity training for emerging democracies in the newly independent nations of Eastern and Central Europe', in Gerald W. Lynch (ed.), *Human dignity and the police: ethics and integrity in police work*, 98–103. Springfield, Illinois. Charles C. Thomas.

Marenin, Otwin 2005 *Restoring policing systems in conflict torn nations: process, problems, prospects*, Occasional Papers, 7. Geneva. CDCAF.

McAlister, Siobhán, Scraton, Phil and Haydon, Deena 2009 *Childhood in transition: experiencing marginalisation and conflict in Northern Ireland*. Belfast. Queen's University Belfast.

McGarry, John and O'Leary, Brendan 2000 *Policing Northern Ireland: proposals for a new start*. Belfast. Blackstaff Press.

McKittrick, David, Kelters, Seamus, Feeney, Brian and Thornton, Chris 1999 *Lost lives: the stories of the men, women and children who died as a result of the Northern Ireland Troubles*. Edinburgh and London. Mainstream Publishing.

McWilliams, Monica and McKiernan, Joan 1993 *Bringing it out in the open: domestic violence in Northern Ireland*. Belfast. DHSS, Northern Ireland.

Maalouf, Amin 2000 *On identity*. London. Harvill Panther.

Maalouf, Amin 2001 *In the name of identity: violence and the need to belong*. New York. Arcade Publishing.

Mack, Andrew 1975 'Why big nations lose small wars: the politics of asymmetric conflict', *World Politics* 27 (2) 175–200.

Mageean, Paul and O'Brien, Martin 1999 'From the margins to the mainstream—human rights and the Good Friday Agreement', *Fordham International Law Journal* (22), 1499–538.

Mallon, Seamus 1988 'Time to grasp the nettle of policing', *Fortnight* 160, 11.

Moloney, Ed 2002 *The secret history of the IRA*. London. Penguin, Allen Lane.

Manning, P.K. 1971 *Police work*. Cambridge, MA. MIT Press.

Manning, P.K. 1977 *Police work: the social organization of policing*. Cambridge, MA. MIT Press.

Mayer-Rieckh, Alexander and de Greiff, Pablo (eds) 2007 *Justice as prevention: vetting public employees in transitional societies*. New York. Social Science Research Council.

Mayer-Rieckh, Alexander and Duthie, Roger 2009 'Enhancing justice and development through justice-sensitive security sector reform', in

Pablo de Greiff and Roger Duthie (eds), *Transitional justice and development: making connections*, 214–49. New York. Social Science Research Council.

Millar, Frank 2004 *David Trimble: the price of peace*. Dublin. Liffey Press.

Monaghan, Rachel 2004 '"An imperfect peace": paramilitary "punishments" in Northern Ireland', *Terrorism and Political Violence* 16 (3), 439–61.

Monk, Richard, Holm, Tanke and Rumin, Serge 2001 *OHR report on a police follow-on mission to UNMBIH and the UN International Police Task Force*. Sarajevo. Office of the High Representative.

Mulcahy, Aogán 2006 *Policing Northern Ireland: conflict, legitimacy and reform*. Cullompton, Devon. Willan Publishing.

Mulcahy, Aogán 2008 'Community policing in contested settings: the Patten Report and police reform in Northern Ireland', in T. Williamson (ed.), *The handbook of knowledge-based policing: current conceptions and future directions*, 117–38. Chichester. Wiley.

Mulcahy, Aogán and Ellison, Graham 2001 'The language of policing and the struggle for legitimacy in Northern Ireland', *Policing and Society* 11 (3–4), 383–404.

Mullan, Don 1997 *Eyewitness Bloody Sunday: the truth*. Dublin. Wolfhound.

Murray, Gerard and Tonge, Jonathan 2005 *Sinn Féin and the SDLP: from alienation to participation*. Dublin. O'Brien Press.

Newburn, T. 2007 *Criminology*. Cullompton. Willan Publishing.

Northern Ireland Policing Board 2009 *Annual Report 2008–09*. Belfast. NIPB.

Northern Ireland Policing Board 2007 'Monitoring the compliance of the Police Service of Northern Ireland with the Human Rights Act 1998', Human Rights Annual Report. Belfast. NIPB.

O' Brien, Brendan 1995 *The long war: the IRA and Sinn Féin*. New York. Syracuse University Press.

O'Doherty Malachi 1992 'Fear and loathing on the falls road', *Fortnight* 304, 23–24.

Ó Dochartaigh, Niall 2005 *From civil rights to armalites: Derry and the birth of the Irish Troubles* (2nd edn). London. Palgrave Macmillan.

O' Kelly, Michael, Doyle, John and Boland, Philip 2010 'How many ways can you look at a proportion? Cross-community vote transfers in Northern Ireland before and after the Belfast Agreement'. *Journal of the Royal Statistical Society*, Series A, 173 (1), 215–35.

O'Leary, Brendan 2004 *The Northern Ireland conflict: consociational engagements*. Oxford. Oxford University Press.

O'Leary, Brendan 2000 *Protecting human rights and securing peace in Northern Ireland: the vital role of police reform* Hearing before the Commission on Security and Co-Operation in Europe, 106th Congress, Second Session, 22 September. Washington, DC. CSCE.

O'Rawe, Mary and Moore, Linda 1997 *Human rights on duty: principles for better policing—international lessons for Northern Ireland*. Belfast. CAJ.

O'Rawe, Mary 2007 'Human rights, transitional societies and police training: legitimating strategies and delegitimating legacies', *St. John's Journal of Legal Commentary* 22 (1), 199–259.

O'Rawe, Mary 2002–03 'Transitional policing arrangements in Northern Ireland: the can't and the won't of the change dialectic', *Fordham International Law Journal* 26, 1015–73.

OECD DAC 2007 *Handbook on security system reform*. Paris. OECD.

OECD DAC 2009 *Handbook on security system reform*. Section 9: Integrating gender awareness and equality. Paris. OECD.

OECD DAC 2001 *The DAC guidelines: helping prevent violent conflict*. Paris. OECD.

OSCE Mission to Serbia and Montenegro 2004 *Police reform in Serbia, towards a modern and accountable police service*. Belgrade. OSCE.

OSCE 2006 *Recommendations on policing in multi-ethnic societies*. The Hague. OSCE.

Office of the Oversight Commissioner 2007 *Final Report*. Belfast. Office of the Oversight Commissioner.

Office of the Oversight Commissioner 2000 *Overseeing the proposed revisions for the policing services of Northern Ireland—Report 1*. Belfast. Office of the Oversight Commissioner.

Office of the Oversight Commissioner 2001 *Overseeing the proposed revisions for the policing services of Northern Ireland—Report 2*. Belfast. Office of the Oversight Commissioner.

Office of the Police Ombudsman for Northern Ireland 2007 *Developments in police complaints—7 years on. Overview of trends and patterns in police complaints*. Belfast. OPONI.

Office of the Police Ombudsman for Northern Ireland 2007 *Statement by the Police Ombudsman for Northern Ireland on her investigation into the circumstances surrounding the death of Raymond McCord Junior and related matters*. Belfast. OPONI.

Patterson, Henry 2004 'The limits of new unionism: David Trimble and the Ulster Unionist Party', *Eire-Ireland* 39 (1 and 2), 163–88.

Pfetsch, Frank R. and Rohloff, Christopher 2000 *National and international conflicts, 1945–1995: new empirical and theoretical approaches.* London. Routledge, ECPR.

Porter, Elisabeth 2008 *Peacebuilding: women in international perspective.* London, New York. Routledge.

Porter, Elisabeth (forthcoming, 2010) 'Connecting human security, gender justice and peacebuilding'.

Powell, Jonathan 2008 *Great hatred, little room.* London. Bodley Head.

President's Commission on Law Enforcement and Administration of Justice 1967 *The challenge of crime in a free society.* Washington. Government Printing Office.

Purdie, Bob 1990 *Politics in the streets: the origins of the civil rights movement in Northern Ireland.* Belfast. Blackstaff Press.

Rees, T. 1998 *Mainstreaming equality in the European Union: education, training and labour market policies.* London. Routledge.

Reiner, Robert 1992 'Policing a postmodern society', *Modern Law Review* 55 (6), 761–81.

Reiner, Robert 2000 *Politics of the police* (3rd edn). Oxford. Oxford University Press.

Rooney, Eilish 2007 'Engendering transitional justice: questions of absence and silence', *International Journal of Law in Context* 3 (2), 93–107.

Savage, Stephen P. 2007 'Give and take: the bifurcation of police reform in Britain', *Australian and New Zealand Journal of Criminology* 40 (3), 313–34.

SDLP 1976 *Towards a new Ireland.* Belfast. SDLP.

Sebit Lokuji, Alfred, Abatneh Sewonet, Abraham and Wani, Kenyi 2009 'Police reform in Southern Sudan'. CPDS/NSI Working Paper. Ottawa, Ontario.

Sen, Amartya 1990 'Development as capability expansion', in Keith B. Griffin and John Knight (eds), *Human development and the International Development Strategy for the 1990s*, 41–58. New York. Macmillan/United Nations.

Sen, Amartya 1999 *Development as freedom.* New York. Alfred A. Knopf.

Sen, Amartya 2006 *Identity and violence: the illusion of destiny.* New York. W.W. Norton.

Silver, Allan 2005 'The demand for order in civil society', in Tim Newburn (ed.), *Policing key readings.* Cullompton. Willan Publishing. 7–20.

Stalker, John 1989 *Stalker.* London. Penguin.

Stenning, Philip 2009 'Governance and accountability in a plural policing environment—the story so far', *Policing* 3 (1), 22–33.

Skolnick, Jerome H. 1966 *Justice without trial.* New York. Wiley.

Stodiek, Throsten 2006 'The OSCE and the creation of multi-ethnic police forces in the western balkans', *Working Paper* 14. Hamburg. Zentrum fèr OSCE-Forschung.

Stodiek, Throsten and Zellner, Wolfgang 2007 *The creation of multi-ethnic police services in the Western Balkans: a record of mixed success.* Georgsmarienhütte. Deutsche Stiftung Friedensförderung.

Sullivan, Gordon R. 1997 *Hope is not a method: what business leaders can learn from America's Army.* New York. Broadway Books.

Sumner, Colin 1997 'The violence of censure and the censure of violence', in Colin Sumner (ed.), *Violence, culture and censure*, 1–7. Abingdon, Oxon. Taylor & Francis.

Sung, Hung-En 2002 *The fragmentation of policing in American cities.* Connecticut. Praeger.

Topping, John R. 2008 'Diversifying from within: community policing and the governance of security in Northern Ireland', *British Journal of Criminology* 48, 778–97.

UNICEF 2007 *Gender equality—the big picture.* Paris, New York. United Nations.

Walker, Ian and Loader, Neil 2006 'Necessary virtues: the legitimate place of the state in the production of security', in Jennifer Wood and Benoit Dupont (eds), *Democracy, society and the governance of security*, 165–95. Cambridge. Cambridge University Press.

Wallenstein, Peter 2007 *Understanding conflict resolution.* London. Sage.

Walsh, William F. and Vito, Gennaro F. 2004 'Meaning of Compstat: analysis and response', *Journal of Contemporary Criminal Justice* 20 (1), 51–69.

Ward, Margaret 2005 'Gender, citizenship and the future of the Northern Ireland peace process', *Éire–Ireland* 40 (3–4), 262–83.

Weber, Max 1971 *Economie et société* [*Economy and society*], vol. 1. Paris. Plon.

Weitzer, R. 1995 *Policing under fire: ethnic conflict and police community relations in Northern Ireland*. New York. State University of New York Press.

Weitzer, R. and Tuch, S.A. 2005 'Racially biased policing: determinants of citizen perceptions', *Social Forces* 83 (3), 1009–30.

Weitzer, R. and Tuch, S.A. 2006 *Race and policing in America: conflict and reform*. New York. Cambridge University Press.

Weitzer, Ron 2010 'Race and policing in different ecological contexts', in S. Rice and M. White (eds), *Race, ethnicity and policing*, 118–39. New York. NYU Press.

Wichert, Sabine 1999 *Northern Ireland since 1945*. London. Longman.

Wilson, James Q. 1983 'Thinking about crime', *Atlantic Monthly* (September), 72–88. Washington. Atlantic Monthly Group.

World Bank 2000 'Voice of the poor', World Bank Report. New York. World Bank.

Wulf, Herbert 2004 *Security sector reform in developing and transitional countries*. Berlin. Berghof Research Centre.

Young, J. 1991 'Left realism and the priorities of crime control', in K. Stenson and D. Cowell (eds), *The politics of crime control*, 146–60. London. Sage Publishing.

Zedner, Lucia 2006 'Policing before and after the police: the historical antecedents of contemporary crime control', *British Journal of Criminology* 46, 78–96.

CONFERENCE PAPERS, ELECTRONIC RESOURCES AND OTHER PUBLICATIONS

Anglo-Irish Agreement, available at: http://www.dfa.ie/uploads/documents/anglo-irish%20agreement%201985.pdf.

Baden, Sally 2000 'Gender, governance and the "feminization of poverty"', paper presented at the meeting on *Women and political participation: 21st century challenges*, held in New Delhi, India, 24–26 March 1999. New York. UNDP, available at: http://mirror.undp.org/magnet/events/gender/india/Badefeb2.htm.

Belfast/Good Friday Agreement, available at: http://foreignaffairs.gov.ie/uploads/documents/Anglo-Irish/agreement.pdf.

British Crime Survey, available at: http://www.homeoffice.gov.uk/rds/index.html.

Cohan, Carolyn 2008 'Women as peacekeepers in Liberia: the role of the Indian female police unit in operationalizing UN gender policy', paper presented at the ISA's 49th Annual Convention, entitled 'Bridging multiple divides', held in San Francisco, CA, 26 March 2008.

Committee on the Elimination of Discrimination against Women, 41st Session, UK and Northern Ireland, 5th and 6th Report, 10 July 2008, available at: http://www2.ohchr.org/english/bodies/cedaw/docs/CEDAW.C.GBR.CO.6.pdf.

Council of Europe, Committee on Equal Opportunities for Women and Men, 'Memorandum to the Council of Europe Parliamentary Assembly, 16 September 2004', available at: http://assembly.coe.int/Documents/WorkingDocs/doc04/EDOC10273.htm.

Council of Europe, 'Convention for the Protection of Human Rights and Fundamental Freedoms', available at: http://www.echr.coe.int/nr/rdonlyres/d5cc24a7-dc13-4318-b457-5c9014916d7a/0/englishanglais.pdf.

Downes, Mark and Muggah, Robert 2009 'Buying time: how interim stabilisation can enhance security sector reform in post-war settings', in M. Sedra (ed.), *The future of SSR*. CIGI Conference, Waterloo, Ontario, 2009.

Equality Commission for Northern Ireland, 'Fair employment monitoring report, no. 19', available at: http://www.equalityni.org/archive/pdf/ResearchUpdate_MonitoringReportNo19_FINAL_101209.pdf

Hillyard, Paddy and Maguire, Amy 2006 'Gender, security and policing in post-conflict transition: some reflections on post-Agreement developments in Northern Ireland'. Conference paper.

House of Commons, *Hansard*, written answers for 24 January 2000, part 2, available at: http://www.publications.parliament.uk/pa/cm199900/cmhansrd/vo000124/text/00124w02.htm.

International Commission on Decommissioning, reports available at: http://cain.ulst.ac.uk/events/peace/decommission/iicdreports.htm.

Mani, Rama 2003 'Policing in post-conflict situations'. London. Concept Paper for Whitehall Policy Seminar.

Mayangja, Rachel 'Speech at G8 International Conference on Violence against Women, Rome, 9 September 2009', available at: http://www.un.org//womenwatch/osagi/pdf/G8%20conference%20on%20VAW.sep09.pdf.

Meyer-McAleese, Mary 2007 'Gendering police, policing gender: community policing and police reform in Northern Ireland', unpublished paper presented at the International Studies Association 48th Annual Convention, Chicago, IL, 28 February 2007; available at: http://www.allacademic.com/meta/p180918_index.html.

Northern Ireland Census of Population (2001), available at: http://www.nisranew.nisra.gov.uk/census/Census2001Output/index.html.

Northern Ireland Office, May 2000 Implementation Plan; available at: http://cain.ulst.ac.uk/issues/police/patten/nio190102.pdf.

Northern Ireland Office, 'Cory Collusion Inquiry Report', available at: http://www.nio.gov.uk/cory_collusion_inquiry_report_(with_appendices)_pat_finucane.pdf.

Northern Ireland Office, *Northern Ireland Crime Survey (2008)*, available at: http://www.nio.gov.uk/08_northern_ireland_crime_survey.pdf.

Northern Ireland Policing Board, 'Monitoring the compliance of the Police Service of Northern Ireland with the Human Rights Act 1998', available at: http://www.nipolicingboard.org.uk/nipb_hr_ar-2.pdf.

Northern Ireland Statistics and Research Agency, *Northern Ireland neighbourhood information service*, available at: http://www.ninis.nisra.gov.uk/.

O'Brien, Martin, 'A stock-take: human rights and the Agreement—how far have we come?', the annual Stephen Livingstone lecture, delivered at Queen's University Belfast in October 2009; available at: http://atlanticphilanthropies.org/news/news/remarks_at_the_annual_stephen_livingstone_memorial_lecture_queen_s_university_belfast.

O'Neill, William 2007 *Gender sensitive police reform in post-conflict societies*. Policy Briefing Paper for UNDP. New York. UNDP; available at: http://www.undp.org/cpr/documents/gender/Gender_Sensitive_Police_Reform_Policy_Brief_2007.pdf.

OECD, *OECD DAC Handbook on security system reform*, available at: http://www.oecd.org/dataoecd/4/52/42168607.pdf.

Office of the Oversight Commissioner, 'Overseeing the proposed revisions for the policing services of Northern Ireland—Report 1 (16 October 2000)', available at: http://cain.ulst.ac.uk/issues/police/oversight/oversight-rep1-161000.pdf.

Office of the Oversight Commissioner, 'Overseeing the proposed revisions for the policing services of Northern Ireland—Report 2 (12 September 2001)', available at: http://www.oversightcommissioner.org/reports/pdfs/sept2001.pdf.

Office of the Oversight Commissioner, 'Final report—Report 19 (31 May 2007)', available at: http://cain.ulst.ac.uk/issues/police/oversight/oversight-rep19-310507.pdf.

Operation Banner; text available at: http://www.mod.uk/DefenceInternet/FactSheets/OperationBannerNotableDates.htm.

OPONI, 'Report on matters relating to the Omagh bombing on August 15 1998', available at: http://www.policeombudsman.org/publicationsuploads/omaghreport.pdf; see also the report on the CAIN website: http://cain.ulst.ac.uk/issues/police/ombudsman/po121201omagh1.pdf.

OPONI, 'Report into the circumstances of the death of Mr Neil McConville on 29 April 2003', available at: http://www.policeombudsman.org/Publicationsuploads/McCONVILLE.pdf.

OPONI, 'Report on the complaint by James and Michael McConville regarding the police investigation of the abduction and murder of their mother Mrs Jean McConville', available at: http://www.policeombudsman.org/Publicationsuploads/JEAN%20McCONVILLE%20Final%20report%20August%202006.doc.

OPONI, 'Statement by the Police Ombudsman on her investigation into the circumstances surrounding the death of Raymond McCord Junior and related matters', January 2007; available at: http://www.policeombudsman.org/Publicationsuploads/BALLAST%20PUBLIC%20STATEMENT%2022-01-07%20FINAL%20VERSION.pdf.

OPONI, 'Report into the circumstances of the death of Mr Samuel Devenny', available at: http://www.policeombudsman.org/Publicationsuploads/devenny.pdf_.

OPONI, 'Report on the investigation of the murder of Mr Sean Brown', available at: http://www.policeombudsman.org/Publicationsuploads/ Sean%20Brown%20report.pdf.

Orde, Hugh, Comments at a meeting organised by the Public Relations Institute of Ireland, Dublin, April 2008; available at: http://www.4ni.co.uk/northern_ireland_news.asp?id=74244.

Pat Finucane Centre, 'In The Line of Fire'—a report on events in Derry, 10–14 July 1996, and 'One Day in August'—a report on alleged human rights abuses by the RUC during and after the Apprentice Boys march in Derry on 12 August 1995; available at: http://www.serve.com/pfc/.

Police (Northern Ireland) Act (1998); text available at: http:// www.opsi.gov.uk/acts/acts1998/ukpga_19980032_en_1.

Police (Northern Ireland) Act (2000); text available at: http:// www.opsi.gov.uk/acts/acts2000/ukpga_20000032_en_1.

PSNI, Crime Statistics (2009), available at http://www.nisranew.nisra.gov.uk/ census/start.html.

PSNI, Equality Impact Assessment Report, Promotion: Police Officers (March 2008), available at: http://www.psni.police.uk/index/updates/ index/updates/consultation_zone/eqia_promotion_full_report.pdf.

PSNI, Workforce Statistics, available at: http://www.psni.police.uk/ index/updates/updates_statistics/updates_workforce_composition_fig ures.htm.

Queensland Police Service 2004 *Strategic directions for policing with ethnic communities*, available at http://www.police.qld.gov.au/Resources/ Internet/programs/community/documents/Ethnic_Strategic_ Directions.pdf

Regulation of Investigatory Powers Act (2000), available at: http://www.opsi.gov.uk/acts/acts2000/ukpga_20000023_en_1.

Rooney, Eilish 2007 'Intersectionality in transition: lessons from Northern Ireland', *Web Journal of Current Legal Issues* (5), available at: http://webjcli.ncl.ac.uk/2007/issue5/rooney5.html.

RUC, *Fundamental review of policing*, available at: http:// www.psni.police.uk/fundamental_review_policing_1996.pdf.

Runnymeade Trust, Roundtable report, 27 March 2009, 'Positive action in theory and practice: experiences from the UK and Europe', available at: http://www.runnymedetrust.org/uploads/projects/europe/UK% 20Positive%20Action%20Roundtable%20Report.pdf.

Shaw, George Bernard quoted in *Reader's Digest*. November 1942.

St Andrews Agreement, available at: http://www.nio.gov.uk/st_andrews_agreeement-2.pdf.

Stevens Enquiry: overview and recommendations, available at: http://cain.ulst.ac.uk/issues/collusion/stevens3/stevens3summary.htm; see also http://news.bbc.co.uk/1/shared/spl/hi/northern_ireland/03/stephens_inquiry/pdf/stephens_inquiry.pdf.

United Kingdom Election Results, available at: http://www.ark.ac.uk/elections.

UN Fourth World Conference on Women, 'Declaration and platform for action', available at: http://www.un.org/womenwatch/daw/beijing/pdf/BDPfA%20E.pdf.

UN General Assembly, 'Convention on the Elimination of All Forms of Discrimination against Women', available at: http://www.un.org/womenwatch/daw/cedaw/cedaw.htm.

UN General Assembly, 'Declaration on the Elimination of Violence against Women', available at: http://www.un.org/documents/ga/res/48/a48r104.htm.

UN Security Council, 'Resolution 1820', available at: http://www.securitycouncilreport.org/atf/cf/%7B65BFCF9B-6D27-4E9C-8CD3-CF6E4FF96FF9%7D/WPS%20SRES1820.pdf.

UN Security Council, 'Resolution 1888', available at: http://www.peacewomen.org/un/sc/SCR1888.pdf.

UN Security Council, 'Resolution 1889', available at: http://www.peacewomen.org/un/sc/SCR1889.pdf.

UN Security Council, 'Resolution 1325', available at: http://www.peacewomen.org/un/sc/res1325.pdf.

UN Universal Code of Ethics for Law Enforcement, available at: http://www.un.org/documents/ga/res/34/a34res169.pdf.

United Nations, *Report of the Panel on United Nations Peace Operations* (Brahimi report, 2000), available at: http://www.un.org/peace/reports/peace_operations/.

Women's Research and Development Agency, 'Structures for promoting participation in peace building, democracy and governance: a case study of Northern Ireland', available at: http://www.wrda.net/wrdanews/data/upimages/salzburg_paper.pdf.

ABOUT THE AUTHORS

MAGGIE BEIRNE

Maggie Beirne is currently working as a freelance consultant based in London. Between 1988 and 2004 she worked as a volunteer and then as Research and Policy Officer at the Committee on the Administration of Justice (CAJ) in Belfast, latterly succeeding Martin O'Brien as CAJ Director, for 2004–08. At the time the work of the Patten Commission was ongoing, Ms Beirne had special responsibility for policing issues and was closely involved in editing CAJ's international comparative policing report, entitled *Human Rights on Duty*.

Prior to moving to Northern Ireland, Ms Beirne worked for 17 years at the International Secretariat of Amnesty International in a range of posts, latterly as head of the Campaign and Membership Department. This post led to extensive travel, working and campaigning on human-rights issues with Amnesty's worldwide membership.

Ms Beirne has various language qualifications (French and Spanish), a BA (Hons) in Politics, Philosophy and Economics from Balliol, Oxford, and an MSSc in Irish Politics from Queen's University Belfast. She is currently a Visiting Fellow at the University of Bristol.

DENIS BRADLEY

Denis Bradley was educated at St Columb's College, Derry and later studied in Rome. He served as a priest in the Bogside and was a 26-year-old curate on Bloody Sunday, but left the priesthood later in the 1970s.

Mr Bradley lives in Derry and has been deeply involved in community affairs there for many years. In 1973 he was a founding member of Northlands alcohol and drugs residential counselling centre. He served as chairman at the charity for a number of years and he remains involved with the centre, working as a consultant. He is also a consultant to the North West Alcohol Forum in Co Donegal.

Through MI6, Denis Bradley was a pivotal link in passing messages between senior Provisional IRA figures and the British government—a move that eventually led to the IRA's 1994 ceasefire. A well known political commentator, he also writes a monthly column for the *Irish News*, and he received an Honorary Doctorate of Law from the University of Ulster (July

2005) for his contributions to the community and the peace process. He was vice chairman of the Northern Ireland Policing Board from its formation on 4 November 2001 until his resignation in 2006. In 2007 Denis Bradley was appointed as co-chairman, along with Rev. Robin Eames, of the Consultative Group on the Past in Northern Ireland.

THOMAS A. CONSTANTINE

Thomas A. Constantine was born in Buffalo, New York, on 23 December 1938. He began his law enforcement career in 1960 as a deputy with the Erie County Sheriff's Department, and joined the New York State Police (NYSP) in 1962. Governor Mario M. Cuomo appointed Thomas Constantine to be the tenth superintendent of the NYSP on 2 January 1987. The first superintendent in 30 years to rise through the ranks, he immediately undertook a division-wide review of all NYSP operations and procedures. The outcome of this review was the drafting of specific plans to improve agency performance in all targeted areas, including a phased-in requirement for all applicants to have at least two years of college education, a total revision of the NYSP post structure, revised promotional procedures and new hiring practices, including establishing a cadre of permanent recruiters.

Thomas Constantine's tenure as superintendent marked the emergence of the state police as a major force in combating drug trafficking. In 1994, President Clinton appointed Superintendent Constantine to be administrator of the United States Drug Enforcement Agency. In that capacity he created new programs to foster closer cooperation with state and local law enforcement agencies and to enhance their ability to fight violent drug crime. He also directed efforts to help foreign governments combat the world's most powerful drug trafficking organisations. He retired from the DEA in July 1999.

In the fall of 1999 Superintendent Constantine began a new career as a public service professor at the Rockefeller College of Public Affairs and Policy in Albany, NY. He also serves on the board of directors of the Partnership for a Drug-Free America. In May 2000 he tackled what he regards as the biggest challenge of his career when he accepted an appointment by the Secretary of State for Northern Ireland to serve as Oversight Commissioner of the Independent Commission on Policing for Northern Ireland. In September of 2007 Superintendent Constantine was appointed to a select Senior Advisory Group to the US Director of National Intelligence.

MARK DOWNES

Mark Downes is the head of the International Security Sector Advisory Team (ISSAT) at the Geneva Centre for the Democratic Control of Armed Forces (DCAF), see further www.dcaf.ch/issat. ISSAT is a standing capacity established to provide the international community, bilateral donors and multilateral organisations (including the EU and the UN) with comprehensive advice both on the technical and the process aspects of supporting security and justice reform. As head of ISSAT, Mr Downes is responsible for managing all of ISSAT's operational activity, relations with the ISSAT governing board and the smooth running of the ISSAT team, including the roster of security sector reform (SSR) experts. He previously worked for the OECD's Development Assistance Committee (DAC), where he was responsible for conceptualising and developing the *OECD DAC Handbook on SSR*. While at the OECD he also worked on a number of other security and conflict related issues, including eligibility for Official Development Assistance and armed violence reduction.

Prior to his work with the OECD, Mr Downes worked on a variety of issues, including parliamentary oversight of security forces, armed violence reduction and police reform; the latter as Head of the Strategic Development Unit within the Law Enforcement Department of the OSCE Mission to Serbia and Montenegro (2002–04). Mr Downes currently chairs the coordination committee of the Association for SSR Education and Training (ASSET), a global association of training organisations that promotes SSR education and training methodology. Mark has a PhD in political science and has published widely on security and police reform; he is a frequent trainer on SSR issues for the UN and a number of bilateral training institutions; and has provided support to security reform processes in a number of countries in Africa, Asia and South Eastern Europe.

JOHN DOYLE

John Doyle is Head of the School of Law and Government and a board member of the Centre for International Studies in Dublin City University, which offers Ireland's largest and most sought after programmes in international relations at BA, MA and PhD level (http://www.dcu.ie/~cis/). His research interests include comparative nationalist and ethnic conflict, Northern Ireland, conflict in South Asia and Irish foreign policy.

Dr Doyle has been a visiting professor in conflict resolution in India, at the Nelson Mandela Centre in Jamia Millia Islamia, New Delhi, and in Pakistan, in the School of Social Sciences in Lahore University of Management Sciences (LUMS). He has taken part in a number of studies of comparative peace processes, including two EU-funded projects with colleagues in South Asia, which brought academics from India, Pakistan, Sri Lanka and Afghanistan together for a series of workshops. These took place in New Delhi, Brussels and at DCU and examined European examples of comparative peace processes, such as Northern Ireland and the Balkans, and South Asian cases including Kashmir, Sri Lanka, Nepal, the Indian North East and Afghanistan.

Dr Doyle's publications include: 'How many ways can you look at a proportion? Cross-community vote transfers in Northern Ireland before and after the Belfast agreement' (with Michael O'Kelly and Philip Boland), *Journal Of The Royal Statistical Society* (2010); 'Northern Ireland: The Belfast (Good Friday) Agreement' (with Adrian Guelke), in Radha Kumar (ed.) *Negotiating peace in deeply divided societies* (Sage: New Delhi, 2009); 'Irish nationalism and the Israel–Palestinian conflict', in Rory Miller (ed.), *Ireland and the Middle East: trade, society and peace* (Irish Academic Press: Dublin, 2007); 'Re-examining the Northern Ireland conflict', in Vassilis Fouskas (ed.), *The politics of conflict: a survey* (Routledge: London, 2007); 'The place of the United Nations in contemporary Irish foreign policy' (with Eileen Connolly), in Michael Kennedy and Deirdre MacMahon (eds), *Obligations and responsibilities: Ireland and the United Nations 1955–2005* (IPA: Dublin, 2005); and 'Irish diplomacy on the UN Security Council 2001–02: Foreign policy-making in the light of day', *Irish Studies in International Affairs* (vol. 15) (2004), 73–102.

GRAHAM ELLISON

Graham Ellison is a senior lecturer in Criminology at Queen's University Belfast. His research interests include policing in divided societies, crime prevention, 'bottom up' security governance and, more recently, donor assistance to overseas policing missions and the transnational movement of 'policing knowledges' globally. He has recently worked with the United Nations Development Programme (UNDP) in Ankara to make recommendations for the civilian oversight of the internal security sector, in respect of Turkey's reform commitments under EU accession criteria. His research has also looked critically and problematically at aspects of Northern Ireland's police reform process and its increasing status as a model for overseas emulation.

Dr Ellison has published in the *British Journal of Criminology*, the *British Journal of Sociology*, *Police Quarterly*, the *Journal of Crime, Law and Social Change* and *Policing and Society*; he is the co-author (with Jim Smyth) of *The crowned harp: policing Northern Ireland* (Pluto/University of Michigan Press, 2000). He is currently working on a book for Palgrave Macmillan (with Nathan Pino) entitled *Police reform, globalization and development* (forthcoming, December 2010), which examines the impacts of official development assistance to police reform efforts in a number of post-conflict and transitional states.

BARRY GILLIGAN

Barry Gilligan lives in Belfast where he runs his own property, investment and development company. He has a degree in Economics and is a Fellow of the Institute of Chartered Accountants in Ireland. He was appointed as a member of the Northern Ireland Policing Board in 2001 and was elected Board chairman in May 2009, having held the position of vice-chairman since April 2006.

Mr Gilligan served as chairman of the Colin Glen Trust for ten years and also undertook the role of chairman for Groundwork NI. He has also been a board member of Investment Belfast, Belfast City Centre Management and Common Purpose.

MAURICE HAYES

A native of County Down, Maurice Hayes is a graduate in Literature and in Law of Queen's University Belfast. He has spent most of his life working in the public service in Northern Ireland, variously as Town Clerk, as Head of Human Resources, Northern Ireland Civil Service, as Permanent Secretary, Department of Health and Social Services, and as Northern Ireland Ombudsman. He was the first chairman of the Northern Ireland Community Relations Commission and a member of the Human Rights Commission. He has acted as Electoral Boundary Commissioner, as senior advisor to the chair of the Constitutional Convention and as chair of a body to review acute hospital services. He is a Member of the Royal Irish Academy; served for ten years as a member of Seanad Éireann; and chaired the National Forum on Europe.

Dr Hayes was a member of Lord Patten's Independent Commission on Policing for Northern Ireland and also authored the report that led to the establishment of the Office of Police Ombudsman. He has also advised and produced reports on management issues in An Garda Síochána. He

has published three books of memoirs: *Sweet Killough let go your anchor,*
Black Puddings with slim and *Minority verdict, experiences of a Catholic*
public servant, as well as numerous articles and papers on conflict resolution and other aspects of social policy. He is a regular political columnist
and book reviewer in the *Irish Independent* and the *Belfast Telegraph.*

GERALD W. LYNCH

Gerald W. Lynch is President Emeritus of the John Jay College of Criminal
Justice of the City University of New York and University Professor of
Psychology and Criminal Justice. He served as the President of John Jay
College for 28 years, from 1976 to 2004. John Jay College is the only insti-
tution of higher education in the United States dedicated exclusively to the
study of criminal justice, law enforcement, police science and public service.

During Lynch's presidency, John Jay College developed from a small
police science college to an internationally recognised centre of research,
education and training in criminal justice and public safety. In the earlier
years of his term as president, he initiated exchange programs with
Bramshill (the British Police College), the Royal Ulster Constabulary and
An Garda Síochána (the Irish Police College).

'Human Dignity and the Police', an innovative course to improve relations between police and public, was developed at John Jay College
under Lynch's supervision. An internationally known expert and advocate
of criminal justice education, Lynch has lectured throughout the United
States, the Caribbean, Europe, the former Soviet Union, the Middle East
and Australia. He teaches, chairs panels, writes, and speaks on issues
regarding police corruption and ethical behaviour, and many other topics
related to criminal justice and policing. He holds a PhD in Clinical
Psychology from New York University and resides in New York.

MARTIN O'BRIEN

Martin O'Brien works for Atlantic Philanthropies, directing its global
Reconciliation and Human Rights Programme. He also acts as country
representative for Atlantic in Northern Ireland. Prior to joining Atlantic,
Mr O'Brien spent 17 years co-ordinating the work of the Committee on
the Administration of Justice (CAJ), an organisation dedicated to securing the highest standards in the administration of justice in Northern
Ireland. It was in 1998, during Mr O'Brien's tenure, that CAJ received
the prestigious Council of Europe Human Rights Prize in recognition of
its contribution to the peace process in Northern Ireland.

Mr O'Brien has written, spoken and publicly campaigned on a wide range of civil-liberty issues and was particularly active in securing strong human-rights protections in the historic Good Friday Agreement. He is the co-founder of several organisations, including Youth for Peace, the Irish Network for Nonviolent Action Training and Education (INNATE) and Kilcranny House, a rural education centre committed to healing the divisions that exist in Northern Ireland. He is the recipient of numerous international awards, including the the Reebok Human Rights Prize

Mr O'Brien received his degree in sociology and social administration in 1987 and a Master's degree in human rights law in 1996, both from Queen's University Belfast. In May 1999 Notre Dame College awarded him an Honorary Doctorate in recognition of his work to promote justice and peace.

NUALA O'LOAN

Nuala O'Loan was born in Hertfordshire, England, and studied law at King's College London. She was appointed lecturer in law at the then Ulster Polytechnic, now part of the University of Ulster, in 1974, and was appointed to the Jean Monnet Chair in European Law at the University in 1992. Among her many public appointments, she served as a member of the old Northern Ireland Police Authority; as a special commissioner for the Commission for Racial Equality's Formal Investigation into Racism in Policing in England and Wales; as Vice-Chair of the Police Authority's Community Relations Committee; as a member of the Northern Health and Social Services Board; and as Legal Expert Member of the European Commission's Consumers' Consultative Council.

Ms O'Loan was appointed as the Police Ombudsman-designate for Northern Ireland in October 1999—a reform which pre-dated the establishment of the Patten Commission. She held office by Royal Warrant from November 2000 for a non-renewable term of seven years, charged to provide a system of independent, impartial investigation of the police in Northern Ireland. In February 2008 she was appointed by the Irish government as special envoy in Timor Leste (East Timor), and later that year was awarded honorary degrees of Doctor of Laws (LLD) by the University of Ulster, the National University of Ireland, Maynooth, and the Higher Education Technical Awards Council, Ireland, in recognition of her work as Police Ombudsman and for her contribution to the social development of Northern Ireland. In July 2009 it was announced that she was to be appointed to the British House of Lords. Consequently, in September 2009 she was raised to the peerage as Baroness O'Loan, of Kirkinriola in the County of Antrim, and sits as an independent member in the House.

MARY O'RAWE

Mary O'Rawe is a barrister, mother of six and senior law lecturer in the School of Law, University of Ulster. Her main research interests lie in the field of policing and human rights, with a particular emphasis on policing in transition and expanding notions of human security. She has acted as human-rights advisor to An Garda Síochana, particularly in relation to policy formulation, organisational learning and the inculcation of a culture of human rights. She has also been involved in the design, development, delivery and evaluation of a range of policing and human-rights initiatives in Ireland, North and South, and across all five continents.

Mary O'Rawe's publications include the co-authored book, *Human rights on duty: principles for better policing—international lessons for Northern Ireland* (CAJ, 1997), and a number of journal articles on policing and police change related issues. She has also been a frequent contributor to edited collections dealing with questions of police reform and policing transformation. In 2007–08 she acted as legal advisor to the Northern Ireland Bill of Rights Forum Working Group on Criminal Justice and Victims. She is currently a member of the Northern Ireland Coroner's Panel of Counsel.

KATHLEEN M. O'TOOLE

Kathleen M. O'Toole was appointed Chief Inspector of the Garda Síochána Inspectorate in May 2006. She was appointed to the Boston Police in 1979 and rose through the ranks of policing in Massachusetts. She served in field, investigative and administrative roles; as Chief of the Metropolitan District Commission Police, as Lieutenant Colonel in the Massachusetts State Police and as Massachusetts Secretary of Public Safety; and was the first female Police Commissioner of Boston, Massachusetts. She was also a member of the Independent Commission on Policing for Northern Ireland (the Patten Commission), which developed a new framework for policing and security in Northern Ireland. Kathleen O'Toole is a graduate of Boston College and New England School of Law and was admitted to the Massachusetts Bar in 1982. She is now enrolled in a PhD program at the Business School of Trinity College Dublin.

HUGH ORDE

Sir Hugh Orde joined the Metropolitan Police Service in 1977. In October 1999, having served in a number of specialist roles, he was promoted to Deputy Assistant Commissioner and was given day-to-day responsibility for the Commissioner's Enquiry (Stevens III) into collusion and the murder of Belfast solicitor Pat Finucane in Northern Ireland. In September 2002 Sir Hugh was appointed Chief Constable of the Police Service of Northern Ireland (PSNI), a position he held for seven years. During his time in Northern Ireland he oversaw the implementation of the *Patten Report*.

Sir Hugh was appointed vice-president of the Association of Chief Police Officers in 2006, and in 2009 he became its president, entrusted by his chief officer colleagues to steer policing in England, Wales and Northern Ireland into the twenty-first century. He was awarded an OBE in 2001 for services to policing, and in 2005 was knighted for his work. In 2008 he was awarded the annual Leadership Award from the Police Executive Research Forum, recognising his work in changing policing in Northern Ireland following the Good Friday Agreement in 1998. In 2010 he was awarded a Queen's Police Medal for services to policing. Sir Hugh is a graduate of the FBI National Executive Institute. He holds a degree in public administration, an honorary doctorate in Civil Law from the University of Kent and an honorary doctorate in Law from the University of Ulster, where he is a visiting professor.

CHRIS PATTEN

Lord Chris Patten was born in 1944 and educated at St Benedict's School, Ealing, and Balliol College, Oxford. He joined the Conservative Research Department in 1966, was seconded to the Cabinet Office in 1970 and was personal assistant and political secretary to Lord Carrington and Lord Whitelaw when they were Chairmen of the Conservative Party from 1972–74. In 1974 he was appointed as the youngest ever director of the Conservative Research Department, a post he held until 1979.

Lord Patten was elected as a Member of Parliament for Bath in May 1979, a seat he held until April 1992. He was appointed Parliamentary Under Secretary of State, Northern Ireland Office, and in September 1985 Minister of State at the Department of Education and Science. In September 1986 he became Minister for Overseas Development at the Foreign and Commonwealth Office. In July 1989 he became Secretary of State for the Environment and in 1990 he was appointed Chairman of the Conservative Party.

About the authors

Lord Patten was appointed Governor of Hong Kong in April 1992, a position he held until 1997, overseeing the return of Hong Kong to China. From 1999 to 2004 he was European Commissioner for External Relations, and in January 2005 he took his seat in the House of Lords. In 2003 he was elected Chancellor of the University of Oxford. In 2006 he was appointed co-chair of the UK–India Round Table. His publications include *What next? Surviving the 21st century* (2008); *Not quite the diplomat: Home truths about world affairs* (2005) and *East and West* (1998), about Asia and its relations with the rest of the world.

DESMOND REA

Professor Sir Desmond Rea lives in Belfast and is an independent member of the Northern Ireland Policing Board. He served as Chairman of the Board from 2001 to 2009. He was educated at Queen's University Belfast (QUB) and the University of California, Berkeley (UCB). He is an Emeritus Professor of Human Resource Management at the University of Ulster (UU) and was formerly Senior Lecturer in Business Studies and Assistant Dean, Faculty of Economics and Social Sciences QUB.

Desmond Rea is editor of First Trust Bank's quarterly *Economic Outlook and Business Review*. He is also a non-executive director and chairman of the Ulster Orchestra Society. He is a former chairman of the Northern Ireland Labour Relations Agency, Northern Ireland Council for the Curriculum, Examinations and Assessment and Northern Ireland Local Government Staff Commission. On 31 July 2004 he completed his term as a non-executive director of AIB (UK) plc.

CLIFFORD SHEARING

Clifford Shearing is chair of Criminology at the University of Cape Town, where he directs the University's Centre of Criminology. He also holds the South African Research Chair of Safety and Justice. He holds appointments at the Universities of Bergen, Griffiths, Montreal and Oxford, as well as at the Australian National University. His most recent books are *Imagining security* (with J. Wood; Willan Publishing, 2007), and *Lengthening the arm of the law* (with J. Ayling and P.N. Grabosky; CUP, 2008). His current research and writing focuses on physical and environment security.

PETER SMITH

Peter Smith was born in Belfast in 1942. He was educated at Belfast Royal Academy and Queen's University Belfast, graduating in law in 1966.

Thereafter he taught law in Leeds for two years and then at Queen's for one year before being called to the Northern Ireland Bar in 1969. In 1978 he was appointed one of Her Majesty's Counsel (QC) and retired from practice in 2001. In the mid-1980s Mr Smith was active in the Ulster Unionist Party, becoming chairman of his local branch and of South Belfast Constituency Association, as well as an honorary secretary of the Ulster Unionist Council.

In 1998 Mr Smith was appointed to the Independent Commission on Policing for Northern Ireland. Between 1996 and 2009 he served as a judge of the Courts of Appeal of Jersey and Guernsey, and between 2002 and 2009 as a deputy judge of the High Court of Justice in Northern Ireland. In 2001 he was appointed chairman of the Life Sentence Review Commissioners, and on the LSRC being renamed the Parole Commissioners for Northern Ireland in 2008 he became—and remains—Chief Commissioner. In 2008 also, he was appointed CBE for his services to criminal justice in Northern Ireland.

INDEX

Index